All About Language

All About Language

Barry J. Blake

OXFORD
UNIVERSITY PRESS

OXFORD

UNIVERSITY PRESS

Great Clarendon Street, Oxford OX2 6DP

Oxford University Press is a department of the University of Oxford.
It furthers the University's objective of excellence in research, scholarship,
and education by publishing worldwide in

Oxford New York

Auckland Cape Town Dar es Salaam Hong Kong Karachi
Kuala Lumpur Madrid Melbourne Mexico City Nairobi
New Delhi Shanghai Taipei Toronto

With offices in

Argentina Austria Brazil Chile Czech Republic France Greece
Guatemala Hungary Italy Japan Poland Portugal Singapore
South Korea Switzerland Thailand Turkey Ukraine Vietnam

Oxford is a registered trade mark of Oxford University Press
in the UK and in certain other countries

Published in the United States
by Oxford University Press Inc., New York

British Library Cataloguing in Publication Data

Data available

Library of Congress Cataloging in Publication Data

Data available

Typeset by SPI Publisher Services, Pondicherry, India
Printed in Great Britain by
Ashford Colour Press Ltd, Gosport, Hants.

ISBN 978–0–19–923839–2 (Hbk.)
978–0–19–923840–8 (Pbk.)

5 7 9 10 8 6 4

Preface

We use language most of the time every day. When we are not talking or listening or reading, we are thinking in language or constructing interior monologues and dialogues. We do this even when we are asleep and dreaming. However, few people can describe how language works. In fact many people would be better able to describe the digestive system or the solar system than the workings of language.

In the preceding paragraph the term 'language' is used, not 'languages'. Behind this usage is the belief that English, French, Hindi, Chinese, Japanese, and the other 5,000-odd languages of the world are all examples of the same phenomenon. These languages have their own words and their own rules for putting words together in phrases and sentences, but in essence they are the same. They are all communication systems that humans use to express their thoughts.

This book sets out to explain how language works. The first part of the text deals with words: types of word, how words are made up, and the meaning of words. We then proceed to the second part comprising three chapters on the way words are put together in phrases and sentences, and how sentences are used in discourse. The third part of the book covers the sounds of language and the ways they can be represented in writing. There are chapters on phonetics, phonology, and writing. Some readers might like to deal with phonetics and phonology first. A feature of the book is that the chapters on phonetics and phonology are independent of the preceding chapters and can be read first.

The fourth part comprises two chapters dealing with variation. The first of these, chapter eleven, deals with the fact that people from different areas speak different dialects, people from different social levels use different varieties, and men and women speak differently, as do the young and the old. On top of this pattern of different usage we are all able to choose to be formal or informal, aggressive or conciliatory, communicative or secretive. The variety of language we use, whether our regular dialect or a special style we adopt in certain situations, is important as a badge of identity.

Chapter twelve describes the ways languages change. Every other day we notice a new word, now and again we notice a new pronunciation or a new expression. Over a long period a language can change so much that speakers transported a thousand years back in time would have difficulty understanding their own language.

The final part of the book deals with language and the brain. One of the remarkable things about language is that children learn without any conscious effort whatever language or languages they are exposed to. Chapter thirteen describes the stages a child goes through in acquiring language. Chapter fourteen follows this up with some information on where language faculties are located in the brain, and some of the ways language can be analysed and manipulated with computers. Chapter fifteen looks back at the subjects covered in earlier chapters to throw light on the most difficult question of all, 'How did language begin?'.

Language is unique to humans. It enables us to survive, it enables us to think and solve problems, it plays an important role in consciousness, and it allows us to study the universe and ponder the very mysteries of our existence. But language itself is part of the mystery. Anyone who reads this book should come away with a general understanding of the nature of language, and be in a position to probe more deeply. The study of language is fascinating. Language is full of neat systems on the one hand and odd quirks on the other. It is full of variety and is forever changing. To be made aware of the way language works can be enriching. I hope readers will begin to notice all sorts of interesting features of language in everyday experience, features that probably went unnoticed in the past.

The book is aimed at the general reader and at students of languages and linguistics (the subject that deals with language as a whole), plus anyone taking communication studies, communication disorders, media studies, or English. The book assumes no prior knowledge of language other than the ability to read English. All technical terms are explained.

Chapters two to fourteen contain 'problems'. These are mostly short exercises designed to give the reader more familiarity with the subject matter or they are invitations to explore further. Answers to these problems are available on the OUP website at www.oup.com/uk/companion/blake.

Barry Blake
Melbourne 2007

Acknowledgements

A number of people helped with the preparation of this book by reading drafts or supplying data. Thanks to Gavan Breen, Randy LaPolla, Les Oates, Erma Vassiliou, and several anonymous readers. Thanks too to John Davey at OUP, whose advice during the writing of the manuscript proved invaluable.

Contents

Part II *Syntax and Discourse*

Part III *Speech and Writing*

Figures

Tables

Maps

Abbreviations and conventions

Examples in single quotes are from movies or literary works, or they are ones I have collected from the media or from everyday conversation. Examples not in quotes are made up for the purposes of illustration, though single quotes are also used for translations from other languages.

From chapter two onwards all important technical terms are introduced in bold. These terms also appear in the glossary.

Small capitals are used to represent *lexemes* and *predicates*.

AAVE	African American Vernacular English
abl	ablative
acc	accusative
act	active
adj	adjective
ASL	American Sign Language (Ameslan)
ben	benefactive
BSL	British Sign Language
caus	causative
CHILDES	The Child Language Data Exchange System
dat	dative
erg	ergative
fem	feminine
gen	genitive
GEVS	Great English Vowel Shift
IPA	International Phonetic Alphabet
masc	masculine
MRI	Magnetic Resonance Imaging
NP	noun phrase
OED	Oxford English Dictionary
perf	perfect
phr	phrase
pl(ur)	plural
prep	preposition
pres	present tense
RP	Received Pronunciation

sg	singular
TOT	Tip of the tongue
UG	Universal Grammar
VP	verb phrase
1	first person (I, we)
2	second person (you)
3	third person (he, she, it, they)
[ ]	phonetic transcription is enclosed in square brackets
/ /	phonemic transcription is enclosed in slashes (obliques)

*   The asterisk is used to mark examples that do not occur, e.g. the asterisk on */bsan/ in a discussion of possible words in English would mark this form as outside the range of possibilities. The asterisk on a phrase or sentence indicates it is ungrammatical as with *I is mad. In historical linguistics the asterisk marks a reconstructed form.

The following diacritics are illustrated with letter 'a':

ā	1. long vowel	2. high level tone in Chinese
á	1. primary stress	2. high tone, rising tone in Chinese
ã	nasalized vowel as in French	
ă	1. short vowel	2. rising tone, fall-rise tone in Chinese
à	1. secondary stress	2. low tone, falling tone in Chinese
â	falling tone	

1. Introduction

Language is the means of getting an idea from my brain into yours without surgery.

Mark Amidon

What is language?

It is easier to think about particular languages than about language in general, so let's start with one language, English. English consists essentially of a lot of words, tens of thousands of words in fact, some rules for making up new words, and some rules for putting words together into phrases and sentences. Each language is like English in these essentials. When we talk about 'language', we mean what is common to all the languages of the world.

Language enables us to describe a situation, including one that happened somewhere else at a previous time. It enables us to ask questions. It enables us to direct people to do things. In the world of large mammals humans are among the weakest and slowest. It is through mental capacity that we have managed to survive and flourish, a capacity manifest in our ability to use language. Language enables humans to convey complex information about a variety of topics from kinship to astronomy and to pass on such information to the next generation, a cumulative process that results in all the wonders of modern science and technology. However, language is not just a practical tool, it also serves important social functions. It is the principal means of maintaining social relations and the main medium of entertainment. Moreover, the variety of language we use is an important marker of identity.

A language is like a computer program plus a set of computer files where words and meanings are stored, but the program and the files are located in our brains. Communication with the computer consists of input via the keyboard and output via the screen. Communication between brains must be via the senses. Obviously the senses of smell and taste are not much use in communication, and touching, although a possibility, would be limited to close contact. This leaves seeing and hearing. We can make signs with our hands, and we can make facial expressions. These can be seen, but only in the light, and only with line of sight. We can make sounds with our vocal apparatus and these can be heard by night and day, and it is this mouth-to-ear channel that has been the basis for almost all language communication for thousands of years. However, sign language, that is language using signs made with the hands, does exist, and may be older than speech. It is used in some societies as a secondary means of communication in circumstances such as hunting where quiet is essential, and it is used in deaf communities as the primary means of communication.

Writing and signing

Humans have been speaking and signing for tens of thousands of years, perhaps hundreds of thousands of years, but writing is a comparatively recent invention. It was first developed by the Sumerians in Mesopotamia (the area between the Tigris and Euphrates in modern Iraq) and by the ancient Egyptians in the fourth millennium BC. The first attempts at writing were pictographic representations, but not everything can be represented pictographically. However, eventually some symbols came to be used for their phonetic value and this allowed any word to be written. The Sumerian word *lugal* for 'king', for instance, came to be represented by a symbol for *lu-* and one for *gal*. Writing was developed independently by the Chinese in the second millennium BC and by the Zapotec and others in Mexico some time in the first millennium BC (see chapter ten). At the beginning of the Modern Era only a few dozen languages were written, and the situation did not change much until comparatively recently. Even today only a few hundred of the 5,000-odd languages of the world are regularly committed to writing. These tend to be the 'big' languages, mostly national languages, the ones with millions of speakers. This gives the impression that writing and speaking are alternative ways of communicating in language, and so they are, but it is important to recognize that speech is basic, natural, and universal, while writing is derivative. Writing is based on speech. Children learn to speak by exposure to speech. All children learn to speak effortlessly whatever languages they are exposed to when they are young. Writing on the other hand is a conscious process that requires specific teaching and not everyone becomes proficient.

While writing is derivative and represents an attempt at making a record of spoken language, sign language is a primary, natural mode of communication. It is commonly thought that sign language is a means of encoding spoken language, and spoken language can in fact be represented by signs, but sign languages, and there are more than 100 such, are languages in their own right. The evidence for this lies in the fact that where deaf children have been placed in regular contact they have developed sign language. Interestingly where deaf children are exposed to sign language, they learn it without specific instruction just as hearing children pick up spoken language.

The remainder of this book will mainly deal with language in its spoken form, the form familiar to almost everyone, but it needs to be remembered that practically every feature of spoken language mentioned in this book has its parallel in sign language.

Speech sounds

Any language needs thousands of words, but humans cannot make thousands of separate sounds. What we do is we represent each word by a sequence of sounds. The English word *man* has three sounds, represented in writing by *m*, *a*, and *n*; the word *list* has four sounds, and the word *frost* has five. English has over forty speech sounds; the exact number depends on which variety of English we are talking about and on some points of interpretation. In chapter eight mainstream British English is described as having forty-two speech sounds.

It might come as a surprise to find there are over forty speech sounds in English since there are only twenty-six letters in the alphabet, but many sounds are represented by digraphs (pairs of letters). For instance, *sh* in *shut* represents a single sound as does *ng* in *sing*.

Humans can make well over 100 different speech sounds. Each language has its own selection, usually between a dozen and three score. Most languages have sounds such as the *m*-sound and *n*-sound and all languages have a vowel sound like the one in words like *cut* or the longer one in *calm*. Some languages have relatively unusual sounds. English, for instance, has the *th*-sound in *thistle*, *theology*, etc. It is also found in Greek and Castilian Spanish, but not many languages have that particular sound.

Each language has rules about which speech sounds can go where. Most people can recognize the 'look' of Italian words as opposed to German words, or Japanese words as opposed to Chinese words on the basis of their characteristic word shape. A visitor to New Zealand quickly recognizes place names of Maori origin such as *Rotorua*, *Wanganui*, and *Timaru*. And as the evidence piles up the visitor might reasonably conclude that Maori words have a number of syllables, lack consonant clusters, and end in a vowel. The visitor is likely to come across personal names such as *Ngaire* and *Ngaio*, as in *Ngaio Marsh*, the name of a New Zealand novelist, and realise that Maori has the *ng*-sound at the beginning of words.

English is unusual in having lots of consonant clusters, including long sequences such as the one as in *sixths*. These present a difficulty for second-language learners, and even for some native speakers!

Words and meanings

Since words are represented by sequences of sounds, it follows that there is no connection between the form of words and their meaning. This can be seen in the well-known fact that for the most part different languages have different words for the same thing. What we call a bird is *tori* in Japanese, *manumanu* in Fijian, and *Vogel* in German. (In German all nouns are spelt with an initial capital, not just proper names as in English.) There are a few exceptions. Some words are onomatopoeic, that is, the sound echoes the sense. English *gong* is an example as is Thai *meeu* 'cat' or Mandarin Chinese *māo* 'cat', but note that neither *gong* nor *meeu* and *māo* are found in a great range of languages. In some languages there seems to be an association between certain sequences of sounds and particular meanings. In English the sequence -*ump* recurs in words to do with a rounded or thick-ended protuberance as in *hump*, *lump*, *rump*, and *stump*. This is called sound symbolism. It is a fascinating aspect of language and is discussed on pages 53 and 54.

Variation

When we speak, we inevitably reveal something about ourselves. Suppose you hear someone on the phone, you can normally tell whether you are listening to a young child, older child, young adult, mature adult, or old person. Except with young children, you can normally pick out the sex of the speaker. People from different areas speak differently, as do people from different levels of society. Suppose you are at Heathrow Airport and you overhear someone behind you say, in a deep voice, *Oi never done nuffingk!* Without looking around you will be able to conclude from the words, the voice quality, and the accent something about the speaker, perhaps that the speaker is a young, uneducated male from the London area expressing indignation at what he sees as a baseless accusation.

People can vary the way they speak. Children soon learn that there's one way to speak among their friends and another to talk to parents and teachers.

A primary school child might ask a companion for a look at something by saying *Give [u]s a geek* (or a *squiz* or a *dekko* or whatever slang term happens to be current), but they know to say something like *Give me a look (please)*, when talking to a parent or teacher. Most people have a repertoire or range of styles, in particular they can choose a formal style or an informal one. They can talk baby-talk or doggy-talk, they can use rousing rhetoric or indulge in playful banter. They can choose language so as to avoid offence and be conciliatory, or they can choose language that is blunt, coarse, aggressive, or abusive.

All of this means that when someone speaks there is not just a message, a question, or a request in the words, but there is information about the speaker and the speaker's attitude in the voice and the style.

How many languages are there?

Reference books indicate there are about 5,000 languages in the world. That's a ball-park figure. It is hard to come to a definite figure since that involves the awkward question of how different the speech of two communities must be before we would say they speak separate languages. Where a language is spoken over an area large enough for all the speakers not to be in regular contact (the normal situation) different changes occur in different places so that over time local varieties or dialects develop and these may become so different from one another that they are not mutually intelligible and we would have to recognize separate languages. This happened with Latin, the language of the Roman Empire. Eventually the speech of various areas in Portugal, Spain, France, Italy, and Romania developed into different dialects and eventually into separate languages such as Spanish, French, and Italian. Such a development is gradual, and as we look at the languages of the world there will be borderline cases where it is hard to decide if we have different dialects or different languages. Anyway, 5,000 is a reasonable estimate. But whatever the figure is, we can be certain that it was greater in the past and is falling rapidly. If we could go back 10,000 years we would find more than 5,000 languages, mostly spoken by small populations. Where empires have sprung up, numerous languages have been lost, partly because of the slaughter of the defeated, and partly because there is pressure on the conquered to learn the language of the conquerors. The most recent example of this kind of thing was the colonial expansion of European powers from the fifteenth to the twentieth century. This resulted in the loss of scores of languages, with scores more reduced to very small numbers of speakers and not likely to survive much longer.

While the growth of large-scale societies or civilizations results in the loss of languages, it means that some languages come to acquire vast numbers of speakers. Chinese has over a billion speakers. The term 'Chinese' covers a range of different languages such as Cantonese, Hokkien, and Hakka, but most Chinese have some familiarity with Mandarin or Putonghua ('common speech'), the standard form of the language based on the Beijing dialect, and can read the distinctive Chinese writing system in which the symbols or characters represent words rather than component sounds. (Though in many instances there is also an indication of the pronunciation. See chapter ten.) Some of these characters retain something of their pictographic origins as with 門 representing *mén* 'gate'.

Over 350 million people have English as their first language, another 500 million have it as one of their languages, and another 500 million or so have at least a smattering or an ability to read a little English. English is currently the dominant language in business, science, and entertainment, and numerous people around the world find that they have to learn it to gain access to knowledge and employment. There is one other language with a vast number of speakers and that is Hindi-Urdu, which has over 300 million first-language speakers and about 300 million second-language speakers. Hindi is the national language of India and is written in a form of Indian (Devanagari) script; Urdu is the national language of Pakistan and is written in a form of Arabic script adopted from Persia, but the two are essentially different dialects of the same language, to which the term 'Hindustani' was often applied before the partition of India into India and Pakistan. Other languages with large numbers of speakers include Spanish and Bengali (Bangla), both of which have over 200 million speakers, and Arabic, French, Japanese, Indonesian, Portuguese, and German, which have over 100 million.

All languages are created equal

Some years ago students taking my first-year linguistics class had to fill in some administrative form or other, so I took the opportunity to ask them to write on the back of their forms what they would expect to find if they studied one of the native languages of Australia. Some said the sounds would be as the sounds of nature, some said there would be no grammar, and a large number said there would be very few words. These views reflect a widespread notion that some languages are 'primitive', in particular the languages of people living a traditional lifestyle. While it is true that such people have not been caught up in the growth of civilization and have not acquired a host of inventions ranging from telephones to television, it is not true that their languages are less sophisticated than languages like English and Japanese. All these languages have a set of speech sounds and they all have rules for making up words, and rules for putting words together in phrases and sentences. All these languages have words for whatever they want to talk about in their experience. Naturally they don't have words for radios, television, and mobile (cell) phones, but when they are introduced to new artefacts and ideas, they immediately acquire appropriate words. The Hmong of southern China made up a word *tsheb tuam* for 'bicycle' by combining *tsheb*, a word for vehicle, with *tuam*, which means to push with the foot. Some languages have extended words for 'bird' or 'eagle' to cover aeroplanes, and a number have borrowed words such as *motor car* and *town* from English.

A recent newspaper article about the Sentinelese from one of the Andaman Islands in the Bay of Bengal noted that they are hunter-gatherers and have no word for numbers higher than two. The facts are correct, but the article was unfortunate in that it suggested having no numbers higher than two is a sign of inadequacy. The fact is that many hunter-gatherer societies do not feel the need to count. When speakers of these languages are introduced to main-stream civilization, they have no trouble with numbers. They sometimes make up number-words in their own languages. For instance, a word for 'hand' will be used for 'five', so 'six' will be 'hand plus one', 'seven' will be 'hand plus two', and so on. This results in number words that are too big to use quickly, but they also learn numbers from English, Spanish, or whatever language they come into contact with and they have no trouble learning to handle money and play cards, and their children show the same mastery of numbers as children from societies with numbers.

PART I

Words

2. Word classes

They've a temper, some of them—particularly verbs: they're the proudest—adjectives you can do anything with, but not verbs.

Humpty Dumpty in *Alice through the Looking Glass*

Parts of speech

Nouns and verbs

As mentioned in chapter one, all languages contain thousands of words, but these words are not all of the same type. They fall into different classes or **parts of speech**, as they were traditionally called. All languages will have two major classes of word called **nouns** and **verbs**. Nouns include words for types of human (*woman, mother, baby*), various creatures (*fish, frogs, ants*), and various inanimate entities (*water, thunder, cloud, stone*). In English, nouns are distinguished by the fact that they when they refer to anything that can be counted, they can usually take a suffix spelt *-s* or *-es* to mark **plural**, i.e. more than one (*boys, churches*). A majority of verbs refer to actions and processes and in English the class includes *to yawn, to cough, to urinate, to bite, to spit, to scratch, to chase, to burn,* and *to melt*. Verbs are distinguished by the fact that they can be marked to indicate past time, or, to use the grammatical term, past **tense**. With most verbs past tense is shown by the addition of a suffix spelt *-ed* or *-d* (*yawned, melted, chased*) though with some common verbs, there is a change of vowel (*bite/bit, spit/spat*).

We use language to make statements, ask questions, and direct people to do things. Let's confine ourselves to making statements for the moment. A typical statement involves taking at least one noun and one verb:

Birds fly.
Flowers die.
Jane coughed.
Rome burned.
Blackbirds eat worms.
Serena defeated Maria.

These sentences can be described in terms of a **subject** (the first noun in each of these sentences) and a **predicate**. The subject represents what is being talked about (think of the use of 'subject' in expressions such as 'the subject of their talks') and the predicate expresses what is predicated or stated about the subject. The notion of subject will be described more precisely in chapter five, but for the moment we just need to note that the subject precedes the predicate. We also need to note that in these sentences the verbs *to eat* and *to defeat* are followed by nouns. Verbs like these are called **transitive verbs** since the action is thought of as transferring from the subject to the **object** (the noun following the verb). The word **transitive** is derived from the Latin verb *transire* 'to go over' and this Latin verb is also reflected in the words *transit* and *transition*. Verbs like *to fly, to swim,* and *to die* are **intransitive**.

The sentences given above illustrate two differences between nouns and verbs. One is that nouns can be marked for plural and verbs for past tense. This kind of marking is called **inflection**. The other is that nouns and verbs occupy different positions in sentences. These formal differences are import-ant in distinguishing nouns and verbs, for although it is true that in any language the words for *man, dog,* and *head* will be in the noun class, words can move from one class to another. We need to look at how a word functions in a particular context to see which **word class** it belongs to. The words *man, dog,* and *head* can be verbs in English as in *The women manned the lifeboats, The conviction for fraud dogged his career,* and *Maradona headed the ball past the keeper.* Similarly with words such as *like* and *hit.* We can expect them to be in the verb class in any language, but we need to allow for the possibility of them being used as nouns as in *Naomi has likes and dislikes,* and *Jake scored several hits.* I should add that English is unusual in allowing so much movement from one word class to another. Most languages allow much less shifting from one word class to another and when they do allow it, they mark the change of word class, usually by a suffix. English marks change of word class by using a suffix in some instances, as with a noun like *delivery* where the suffix *-y* marks the derivation of the noun from the verb *deliver.*

Determiners

In the example so far all the nouns have been in the plural or they have been **proper nouns** (**proper names**) such as *Rome, Serena,* and *Maria.* If we want to form a sentence using a **common noun** (a non-proper noun) in the singular, we need to use a word from the class of **determiners** in front of it, words such as *the, a(n), this, that, his,* and *their.*

> *Her sister wanted a girl.*
> *An agent bought this house.*

Within the general class of determiners *the* is known as the **definite article** and *a* or *an* as the **indefinite article**. Sequences such as *the woman* or *an agent* are noun phrases. A **phrase** is a group of words that forms a unit within a larger structure. A **noun phrase** has a noun as its **head** and there can be **modifiers** such as *the, this,* or *their.*

Adjectives

Words like *big, little, fast, slow, mighty, conclusive, temperamental,* and *invincible* are **adjectives**. They describe properties, qualities, or characteristics, so they often appear in the predicate.

> *Snails are slow.*
> *Cheetahs are fast.*
> *The baby became ill.*
> *The child grew strong.*

In English these **predicative adjectives** normally need to be used with a verb, either a form of the verb 'to be' such as *is, are, was,* or *were,* or a more specific verb such as *become* or *grow,* but in many languages the adjective on its own suffices to form a predicate. In Indonesian, for instance, one can say 'Ali is big' by simply using the adjective *besar: Ali besar* 'Ali is big'.

Adjectives can also be used **attributively**, that is, to modify nouns as in *her long speech, his short shorts,* and *conclusive evidence*. If one says *Her speech was long,* then one asserts that the speech was long, but if one says *Her long speech bored even her admirers,* one does not assert the length, it is taken as given.

In some cases a difference of order can distinguish an attributive adjective from a predicative one as in the following examples, though *The pies hot?* is colloquial. A more formal version would be *Are the pies hot?*

> A. *What are we having for lunch?*
> B. *The hot pies. (attributive)*
>
> A. *I think we are ready to eat.*
> B. *The pies hot? (predicative)*

Adjectives in English have **comparative** and **superlative** forms. The adjective *nice* has a comparative *nicer* (*Today is nicer than yesterday*) and a superlative *nicest* (*Sunday is the nicest day of the whole week*). This is the regular inflection. There are irregular forms such as *better* and *best* instead of **gooder* and **goodest* (the asterisk marks non-occurring forms), and longer adjectives form the equivalent of the comparative and superlative inflection by using *more* and *most*: *more beautiful, most beautiful*. On one occasion tennis player Anna Kournikova managed to illustrate all three possibilities in a single sentence addressed to Martina Hingis:

> *You're the <u>better</u> player, but I'm <u>prettier</u> and <u>more marketable</u>.*

Pronouns

Pronouns are words like *I, you, she,* and *they*. Traditionally they were described as words that could stand for nouns as in the following short passage where *she* refers to *Brenda,*

> *Brenda is growing up and soon she will be wearing make-up. Next thing you know, she will be changing her opinion about boys, and wanting to go out on dates.*

It was on the basis of this usage that words like *she* were called pronouns, that is, 'pro-nouns'. This example also illustrates just how useful pronouns are. It would be tiresome to have to keep repeating *Brenda*, even more tedious if the passage had begun with a noun phrase such as *that young girl*. The pronoun *I* stands for the speaker and *you* for the addressee, but not all pronouns can be said to stand for a noun, certainly not *nobody, no one,* and *nothing,* nor *it* in a sentence like *It is raining*. Pronouns occupy the same positions in phrases and sentences as nouns, but they do not take determiners as modifiers. You can't say **this me* or **that you* (there's that asterisk again, this time marking phrases that don't occur). Pronouns normally can't take adjectives as modifiers. You can't say **dull he* or **conclusive it*, though there are a few possibilities such as *Silly me!*

There are various types of pronoun:

personal pronouns: *I saw you with her.*
possessive pronouns: *I want <u>mine</u>. <u>Yours</u> is the best.*
reflexive pronouns: *I hit <u>myself</u> on the finger. Keep <u>yourself</u> nice!*
interrogative pronouns: *<u>Who</u> saw you? <u>What</u> kept you?*
indefinite pronouns: *<u>Somebody</u> loves me. <u>Everyone</u> likes him. I know <u>nothing</u>.*
demonstrative pronouns: *<u>This</u> annoys me. <u>That</u> irritates them.*

There are also relative pronouns. These are introduced in chapter six.
Note that *this* and *that* and their plural forms *these* and *those* are demonstrative pronouns in sentences such as *This puzzles me* and *These annoy me*, but they are determiners in sentences such as *This behaviour puzzles me* and *These flies annoy me*.

Preposition

Words such as *along, for, from, in, on, over, through, to*, and *under* as used in sentences like the following are **prepositions**:

> *We drove from downtown LA along Wiltshire Boulevard to Santa Monica in a convertible.*

Prepositions normally precede noun phrases and the sequence of preposition and noun phrase forms a **prepositional phrase**. You can show that these sequences are phrases by trying to move them to different positions in the sentence. The results will be grammatical, but not always felicitous. In the example above you could move *from downtown LA* to the front of the sentence or *in a convertible* to a position after the verb.

In some languages there are **postpositions** rather than prepositions. As the name implies, these follow noun phrases rather than precede. In Japanese 'in Tokyo' is *Tookyoo ni* and 'to America' is *Amerika e*.

Conjunctions

Conjunctions are joining words. The words *and, or*, and *but* are **co-ordinating conjunctions**. They co-ordinate or join constituents of equal status. They can join words as in *bread and butter, right or wrong*, and *naughty but nice*; they can join phrases as in *out of the frying pan and into the fire*; and they can join sentences to form compound sentences: *Jack Sprat could eat no fat and his wife could eat no lean*.

There are also **subordinating conjunctions** such as *since* in a sentence like *Since she learned how to skate, she spends hours on the ice every day*. Subordinating conjunctions are dealt with in chapter six.

Adverbs

In traditional descriptions of language a category of **adverb** was included. The term did not pick out a well-defined class, but was rather something of a ragbag into which almost every word was put that did not fit into the categories listed above. A more satisfactory classification would include a number of smaller classes of types of adverb, but we will accept 'adverb' for our present purpose. Adverbs modify verbs, adjectives, prepositions, or other adverbs. These possibilities are illustrated in turn in the following examples where the adverbs are underlined.

> *Elephants walk <u>slowly</u>.*
> *Pam drinks <u>awfully</u> weak tea.*
> *Susan walked <u>right</u> out the door.*
> *They walked <u>frightfully quickly</u>.*

Some adverbs such as *very* can modify adjectives (*very good*) and adverbs (*very quickly*), but not verbs. You can't say **He walked very.*

A very large class of **manner adverbs** are formed from adjectives by the addition of the suffix *-ly.* These include *swiftly, angrily, doubtfully,* and *frightfully.* They have comparative and superlative degrees formed with *more* and *most: more rapidly, most frightfully.* A few adjectives have the same form as adjectives and these have an inflectional comparative and superlative:

> *Brian worked harder last week.*
> *Bev works fastest under pressure.*

Interjections

There are a few words that do not play any part in the syntax. They stand outside the sentence. This class includes *ouch! gosh! yuk!* and the old-fashioned *alas!* as well as greeting words like *hello* and *hi,* and *yes* and *no.* These words may be used within a sentence as in *He said, 'yes',* but so can the sound of a blurt, a hiss (sssss) or a hush (shshsh).

Interjections and conjunctions aside, the word classes are illustrated in Table 2.1.

Table 2.1. Word classes in English

Determiner	Adjective	Noun	Verb	Adverb	Preposition	Determiner	Noun
The	*little*	*puppy*	*ran*	*quickly*	*towards*	*the*	*visitors*
		Pronoun					Pronoun
		It	*ran*	*quickly*	*towards*		*them.*

Open and closed classes

New words can be easily added to the classes of noun, adjective, verb, and adverb. These are **open classes**, open to new membership. The other word classes are **closed classes** in that they do not readily admit new members (like some snooty clubs!). New prepositions, for instance, are unusual but *re* as in *re that matter you mentioned the other day* meaning 'concerning' is a new preposition in English. It derives from the habit of putting the Latin word *re* 'in the matter of' at the head of formal business letters, particularly those from lawyers. Also *post* has gained some currency in English over the last generation, and it occurs in phrases such as *post the game* 'after the game'. Originally a Latin preposition it previously occurred in English in compounds such as *post-war* or *post-natal.*

Lexical words and function words

Besides words that have a clear meaning such as nouns like *lion* or *ticket* or verbs such as *push* or *shout*, there are words that can't really be said to have a meaning, rather they have a function. Consider the following sentence,

The queen *will* meet *a* leader *of the* delegation.

The nouns *queen, leader,* and *delegation* have a clear meaning, as does the verb *meet,* but the words shown in italics, namely *the, will, a,* and *of* do not have a clear meaning. You cannot pick out anything that they refer to, but they do play a part in how we interpret the sentence. We call these words **function words** as opposed to words like *queen* and *meet,* which are **lexical words** or **content words**. As noted above, *the* is called the definite article and *a* is the indefinite article. *Will* is an auxiliary verb (this is explained on p. 74). The word *of* belongs to the class of prepositions, but unlike prepositions such as *on, under, over, near,* and *through,* which have a clear lexical meaning, *of* is purely functional.

Some prepositions are lexical in some contexts, but purely functional in others. In a sentence like *Barbara stood by the bridge* the preposition *by* is lexical and means 'near', but it was used in contexts such as *She read by candlelight* and it came to be interpreted as not just 'near' but as 'by means of', and then came to be used to mark the demoted subject of the passive. In the following pair of sentences the first is the **active** construction with the **agent**, the doer of the action, as subject. The second is the **passive** in which the **patient** (the entity affected) of the active construction has been made the subject while the subject of the active construction has been demoted and marked by the preposition *by,* which is purely functional in this usage.

A sniper shot Smith.
Smith was shot by a sniper.

Beyond English

Some languages are claimed to have only three word classes, namely nouns, verbs, and **particles**, although one suspects interjections have probably been overlooked. Particles are words that do not fit into the noun and verb classes. They are typically words with a grammatical function. The term 'particle' is not used much in descriptions of English except to describe the second word in combinations such as *take up, take in, take off,* etc. These combinations function like one word in terms of meaning, but they are not compounds since a noun can come between the two words. We can say *Rob took out the* *rubbish* or *Rob took the rubbish out.* The second part of these combinations is referred to as the **verb particle**.

Readers might wonder how a language can get by without adjectives, determiners, prepositions, and adverbs. Adjective-type meanings can be expressed by words that behave like nouns or they can be expressed by words that behave like verbs. Consider the adjective *ill* in English. We can use *ill* as a noun as in *The ill have nowhere to go* and we have a verb 'to ail', which has pretty much the same meaning as 'be ill'. In some languages the function of the determiner is expressed within the noun. This happens to some extent in the Scandinavian languages. In Swedish, for instance, the definite article can be a suffix to the noun as in *hus-et* 'the house' and *flicka-n* 'the girl'. The function of prepositions and postpositions is expressed via inflection on nouns in many languages including Finnish where 'in Finland' is *Suome-ssa*. Adverbial functions can be expressed by inflection on nouns or verbs, or by particles.

Sources and further reading

In an effort to keep the presentation simple I have omitted numerous details such as what to do with number words such as *two* as in *these two books*. Interested readers can get a fuller account of word classes in English from numerous books such as Huddleston, *English Grammar: an Outline*, or chapter two of Bloor and Bloor, *The Functional Analysis of English: a Hallidayan Approach*. The latter uses the descriptive framework of Michael Halliday, as the subtitle indicates. This involves somewhat different terminology from other frameworks, but the presentation is very clear.

Problems

1 Which word class (or part-of-speech) do the underlined words in the following belong to?

We just google it.
The ranger spotted the deer. (So it was a spotted deer!)
For a pretty girl, your dress sense is pretty awful.
He said he had no say in the matter.
Natalie ran the last lap in 62 seconds, but she had left her run too late.
Tonya liked to swim in the lake, but that morning her swim was cut short.
Sharon was being good-nighted by her friends.
Wayne totalled his new car after just two weeks.
The parrot could parrot a few naughty phrases.
We overnighted in Mannheim, but Maria stayed overnight in Ludwigshafen.

2 English is unusual in allowing words to appear in more than one word class without any change in form. This switching from one class to another is most common between verbs and nouns. It happens too, purely by chance, that besides the -s/-es suffix that marks the plural of nouns, there is a suffix -s/-es on verbs as in *She runs, He watches TV.* All this means that there can be sentences where there are two interpretations according to whether one takes a word with an -s/-es suffix to be a noun or a verb. These ambiguities are common in headlines. See if you can find two interpretations for each of the following:

COMMITTEE PLANS WORK

STEEL SPRINGS UP

FEMALE RETURNS HIGH

GOVERNMENT FUNDS INCREASE

VICTIM REMAINS SAFE

3 The distinction between a predicative adjective and an adverb can be tricky. Consider the following example:

'"Early days," Kathy said, evasive.'   Barry Maitland, *The Chalon Heads*

At first glance this looks as if it should be *evasively* and that the author has omitted the -*ly*, as many speakers habitually do, but in fact *evasive* is a predicative adjective and the sentence could be paraphrased *'Early days', Kathy said, being evasive.* Consider the following and label the underlined words as either (predicative) adjective or adverb, and explain the difference in meaning between the members of each pair.

Michelle returned well.
Michelle appeared well.
Michelle drives well.

Lewis runs fast.
Lewis is fast.

Wendy played hard.
Wendy turned hard.

4 Some words can appear in several word classes. The word *round*, for instance, can be used as a noun, an adjective, a verb, a preposition, and an adverb. Make up a sentence to illustrate each possibility.

5 It was mentioned above that the words *more* and *most* are used with longer adjectives. This implies that the inflections -*er* and -*est* are confined to shorter adjectives. What counts as short and long? You need to think in terms of number of syllables. A **syllable** is the smallest unit one would break a word up into in giving very slow dictation. Words like *cake, rum,* and *push* are monosyllabic, words such as *sugar, pretty,* and *promise* have two syllables,

words such as *triplicate*, *sensible*, and *fantastic* have three syllables, and so on. But is it just a matter of number of syllables? What about the nature of the final syllable of the adjective? What part does it play in determining the choice between *-er/-est* and *more/most*? Are there words that can form their comparative or superlative in more than one way?

3. Forming new words

A: You're looking very dapper!
B: Yes, I'm certainly dapper today than I was yesterday.

In two words: im possible!   **Sam Goldwyn (the 'G' of MGM)**

Words are not the smallest meaningful elements in language. It is obvious that *careless* is made up of *care* and *-less*. It is also obvious that words like *books* and *tables* contain a suffix *-s*, which, as we saw in the previous chapter, indicates plural, that is, more than one. The study of how words can be broken down into meaningful constituents is called **morphology**, literally the study of form (Greek *morphē* 'shape', 'form'). The term was used in biology before it was applied to the study of words and probably counts as a learned word, but interestingly the root *morph* has now come into common use as a verb. It can refer to one image in a movie or television programme changing into another before our eyes ('The seed *morphed* into a flower'), it can refer to actors *morphing* into new roles, and in one airline advertisement we are told the business class seats *morph* into beds.

The word and its parts

New words can be formed by various processes, mainly by **compounding** (e.g. *tablecloth*) or by adding a prefix or suffix. The word *unhelpful* consists of a **root** *help* to which a suffix has been added to form *helpful*, and then a prefix to form *unhelpful*. *Unhelpful*, then, can be said to contain three meaningful parts: *un-*, *help*, and *-ful*. These parts are called **morphemes**. The form *help* can occur on its own as a word. It is a **free morpheme**. The forms *-ful* and *un-* cannot occur on their own. They are **bound morphemes**. More precisely *-ful* is a **suffix** since it is a bound form added at the end of a root or stem, while *un-* is a **prefix** since it is added at the front of a root or stem. The **stem** is whatever an affix is added to. With a word like *helpful*, the stem and the root coincide, but in *unhelpful* the prefix *un-* is not added to the root *help*. There is no word **unhelp*. It is added to the stem *helpful*.

Prefixes like *un-* (*unkind*), *super-* (*superhuman*), and *re-* (*recycle*) and suffixes like *-less* (*friendless*), *-ship* (*friendship*), and *-ise/-ize* (*modernise/ modernize*) are **derivational**. They are used to 'derive' or form new words. But the form of words can also be varied to indicate a grammatical notion such as the plural of nouns or the past tense of verbs. This variation is usually in the form of an outer layer of suffixation, as in English. For instance, as we saw in the previous chapter, we have the sibilant suffix, which is written *-s* or *-es*, to indicate the **plural** of nouns, as in *friendships* and *kindnesses*. We also have a suffix written *-d* or *-ed* to indicate past time with verbs as in *modernized* and *solidified*. These changes of form are called **inflection**. If you are uncertain whether a prefix or suffix is derivational or inflectional, ask yourself whether you would put words bearing the form in question as separate entries in the dictionary. It's pretty clear that it would be pointless to put *books* in the dictionary as a separate entry alongside *book*, and it would be equally pointless to put *criticized* in the dictionary as well as *criticize*. Inflectional suffixes are general in their distribution. For instance, the plural suffix can be used with any noun referring to something countable (*Jessica takes three sugars in her coffee*) and the meaning is always 'more than one'. The past tense inflection can be added to any verb and the meaning is always the same. Of course, the form may be irregular. For instance, we say *went* not **goed*, but the past tense notion still applies. Derivation on the other hand is more often than not irregular in its distribution and often inconsistent in terms of meaning. The derivational *-al* occurs in *arrival* and would appear to mean something like 'the act of', so that *arrival* is 'the act of arriving', but although *recital* can mean an act of reciting a poem or whatever, more often it refers to a musical performance. Moreover, *-al* cannot be added to just any verb. You can have an *arrival* but not a **departal*!

In some languages there are **infixes**, bound morphemes that are inserted into another morpheme rather like the colloquial use of swear words as in *abso-bloody-lutely*. In Cambodian (Khmer) there are a number of infixes. For example, there is a verb *sōm* 'to beg'. The noun 'beggar' is formed by infixing *m* after the initial consonant to form *smōm*.

The form or realization of a morpheme is called a **morph**. We need to make the distinction between the abstract morpheme and the concrete realization where there is more than one form or realization, and we call these variant realizations or shapes **allomorphs**. In English the plural is written with an -*s* as in *kids* or -*es* as in *churches*. In speech there are three allomorphs (apart from irregular forms like *teeth*). In the **International Phonetic Alphabet** (IPA) these would be represented as [s] in words like *cats* and *tops*, as [z] in words like *lads* and *rags* and as [əz] in words like *churches* and *judges*. The symbol [ə] ('upside-down e') is a symbol for the vowel you hear in the plural of these words. A full description of these allomorphs is given on page 156.

In words like *pushed* and *smacked* we can clearly recognize a root and the past tense morpheme, but what about words like *saw* and *took*? These contain a root and the notion of past tense, but there are no separate segments for the root and the tense, so we have to recognize that a word like *took* is a **portmanteau morph**. The word *portmanteau* refers to a travelling case or bag. The idea is that a portmanteau morph holds more than one morpheme. The word comes from Lewis Carroll's *Alice through the Looking Glass*. Humpty Dumpty explains that *slithy* means 'lithe' and 'slimy'. 'You see,' he says, 'it's like a portmanteau—there are two meanings packed into one.' In modern linguistics *slithy* would be called a **blend** (see below), and the term 'portmanteau' is usually reserved for forms like *took*, where one cannot find evidence of separate morphs.

It is not always easy to break words up into morphemes. English has a lot of words of Latin origin where one can see how a word breaks up on the basis of comparison with other words, but where one cannot easily assign a meaning to the parts. Here is an example. The word *demit* is in brackets because it is probably obsolete.

confer	defer			refer	infer
commit	(demit)	permit	admit	remit	
consist	desist	persist	assist	resist	insist

Obviously these words break up into *con-fer*, *re-fer*, *re-mit*, etc., but for practical purposes these words can be treated as if they consisted of only one morpheme.

The remainder of this chapter deals with the way words are formed in English and their inflection is treated in chapter five. Every language has ways of making up new words. The two most popular methods are compounding and using prefixes or suffixes.

Compounds

In English we have numerous compounds including nouns such as *bookcase, cloudburst,* and *raindrop,* adjectives such as *sky-high, oil-rich,* and *overactive,* and verbs such as *to whitewash* and *to dry-clean.* Sometimes the parts of the compound in English are written as one word *(crossword, windscreen/ windshield),* sometimes the parts are joined by a hyphen *(air-raid, drop-out, fast-track, good-looking, out-take),* and other times the words making up the compound are left as separate words *(role model, snail mail).* Some compounds can be written in more than one way, and hyphens are often introduced in some words only when the compound is used as a modifier, so one might write *fairy tale* with a space but use a hyphen in *fairy-tale romance.*

We should not take too much notice of conventions of writing, since we need to be able to distinguish compounds in any language, and, as we noted in chapter one, most languages are not written. In speech almost all compounds in English are distinguishable from a sequence of two words by the fact that a compound bears just one strong stress on the first word of the compound. Compare your pronunciation of the phrase *white house* (a house that is white) with your pronunciation of the compound *White House* (the residence of the US President), or your pronunciation of the phrase *green house* (a house that is green) with your pronunciation of the compound *greenhouse* (glasshouse). Compounds take a strong stress on the first word of the compound, whereas phrases take a strong stress on the final word.

Verbs composed of a preposition and a verb are exceptions to this general rule. Think how you pronounce *outrun, underestimate* and *overcook.* There are also idiosyncratic exceptions. While *applecake* clearly behaves like a compound in having a strong stress on the first syllable, *apple pie* is pronounced the same as a phrase (compare *greasy pie*). Some linguists would take *apple pie* to be a phrase rather than a compound since it is pronounced like a phrase, but if one demands a strong stress on the first word as a sign of a true compound, then *afternoon* fails the test. (Compare the rare word *forenoon* with stress on the first component.)

The verb *to dry-clean* has the main stress on *clean,* that is, it is pronounced like a phrase, but if we were to call it a phrase, we would find ourselves with a sequence that is not a recognizable phrase in English. It seems to me the borderline between compound and phrase is not absolutely clear. Readers are invited to think about the distinction in problem 1 at the end of the chapter.

With a compound like *bookshop*, the connection between the meaning of *book* and *shop* and the meaning of *bookshop* is transparent, but this is not always the case. A *bookmaker* does not make books! A *doghouse* looks as if it is another word for kennel, but usually only in the metaphorical sense of the 'sinbin' to which an errant husband is sent by an angry wife. While a *house cat* is indeed a cat that belongs to a house, a *cathouse* is a brothel.

Recently there has been a tendency in English to devise compounds self-consciously in an attempt to make up something cute, smart, or catchy. Examples include *granny bank* 'grandparents as loan source to finance a major purchase such as buying a house for their children or paying school fees for their grandchildren' and *granny dumping* 'sticking grandma or grandpa in the old folk's home'. In the colloquial language the constituents of compounds are often chosen so that there is a rhyme or alliteration. There is rhyme, for instance, in *fake bake* 'suntan achieved by lamp or bottle' and *gender bender* 'someone combining characteristics of both sexes', and there is alliteration in *bible basher* and *greedy guts*.

English has a number of compounds based on phrases such as *daughter-in-law* and *mother-of-pearl*. Many such compounds are used as adjectives. Examples include *dog-in-the-manger* (attitude), *once-in-a-lifetime* (opportunity), *never-to-be-forgotten* (experience), *couldn't-care-less* (attitude), and *take-it-or-leave-it* (attitude). This is not common across languages, but it is common in English and we even make up nonce (one-off) examples. For instance, you might hear someone say something like, 'He got that *if-I-feel-like-it* attitude,' or, to quote an example heard recently from a teenage girl, 'She's so *wouldn't-get-it*.' In the extreme case you find a whole sentence used as if it were a word. In an episode of the demanding TV drama *The West Wing* the character Josh (Bradley Whitford) says, 'It's one of those *Close-your-eyes-and-think-of-England* moments.'

Some words originate as compounds but subsequent reduction renders their compound origin opaque. *Daisy*, for instance, comes from **Old English** *dæges-eage* 'day's eye', while *lord* comes from Old English *hlaf-weard* 'loaf-ward', i.e. bread-guardian, and *lady* derives from *hlaf-dige* 'loaf-knead'. The pair makes an interesting comment on gender relations.

In fact compounds in general give an interesting insight into the way languages characterize and categorize. In Thai a wolf is *măa-pàa* (dog-forest) and large, wild members of the cat family are *mɛːw-pàa* (cat-forest). The use of transparent compounds like these relates domestic pets and their wild relatives, a relation that does not come out with the use of different roots such as *dog*, *wolf*, *cat*, and *tiger*.

Transparent compounds are often copied from one language to another. The clever English formation *skyscraper* is *gratte-ciel* in French and *grattacielo* in Italian where these languages use their own roots for 'scrape' and 'sky'. These formations are **loan translations** or **calques**.

Prefixes and suffixes

Almost all languages employ prefixes or suffixes or both, with suffixes being more popular than prefixes. The suffix *-ize* (*-ise*), for instance, has been used a lot in English over the last half century to yield new words such as *glamourize, tenderize* (meat), *personalize* (stationery), *moisturize* (the skin), *sanitize* (a hotel toilet or a news report), *pasteurize* (milk), and, recently, *novelize* (to turn a screenplay into a novel).

In English the suffix *-er* has served for centuries to mark the derivation of agent nouns like *cleaner, baker,* and *runner* from the verbs *clean, bake,* and *run.* There is also a suffix *-ee* (borrowed from French) as in *payee, evacuee, grantee* where *-ee* designates the patient of the verb (an *evacuee* is someone who has been evacuated) or a recipient (a *grantee* is someone to whom something has been granted). The suffixes *-ee* and *-er* can be used in nonce (one-off) formations. For example, in describing who the agent was and who the patient in a mugging, I could say *Jones was the mugger and Smith the muggee. Mugger* is a word of English, but *muggee* is not, but we can make up a word like *muggee* if it suits our purpose.

The *pre-* in the word *prefix* itself is historically a prefix and it occurs in words like *pregnant, prefer,* and *prepare,* but, as we pointed out earlier in this chapter, it is not much good breaking some of these words of Latin origin into component parts, since the meaning of some of the components is often hard to identify. However, the *pre-* in these words can be identified as meaning 'before' and it was resurrected during the last century and used in formations such as *pre-war, pre-school, pre-season, pre-set,* and *pre-owned.* Note that in the modern formations the prefix is always pronounced [pri:].

De- is another prefix that was introduced into English via words imported from Latin such as *demolish, deduce,* and *depend.* Like *pre-,* it has been given a new lease of life and is currently quite productive. Witness *defrost, dehumidify, delist, dehumanize,* and *decentralize.* In parallel with what we noted with *pre-* this prefix is always pronounced [di:] in modern formations.

One type of suffix that is common in some languages, particularly Latin and its daughter languages such as Spanish, Italian, and French, is a **diminutive** suffix. Diminutive suffixes basically mean 'small'. In Italian *libro* is 'book', but with the diminutive suffix *-etto* we have *libretto* 'booklet'. Words with diminutive suffixes tend to develop specialized meanings rather than just 'little so-and-so'. *Libretto* has acquired the meaning of the book of an opera, and it is used in English in this sense. The sister suffix *-ette* in French appears in *cigarette*. A cigarette might be like a small cigar, but is not in fact a small cigar. Words with diminutive suffixes often acquire overtones of endearment or affection on the one hand or scorn on the other. In English there is a productive diminutive found in words like *doggy* and *weepie*, where *doggy* is a term of endearment and *weepie*, a rather off-hand colloquialism for a sad movie, a 'tear-jerker'. The spelling of the suffix, incidentally, varies between *-y* and *-ie*. Diminutives are usually informal as in *undies* (female underwear) and the currently fashionable *hottie*, a sexually attractive person.

New prefixes and suffixes are rare, but here's an example of how one can arise. In 1972 supporters of President Nixon broke into the offices of the Democratic Party's National Committee at the Watergate Hotel in Washington DC. They were discovered and the name *Watergate* became synonymous with scandal. In 1980 President Carter's brother was found to be acting on behalf of the Gadhafi regime in Libya and this was dubbed *Billygate*. In 1986 the Reagan administration was found to have been selling arms to Iran and this became *Irangate*. They were found to be using the profits to supply the anti-Communist Contra guerrillas in Nicaragua. This was *Contragate*. Soon every scandal was some kind of *-gate*. We had *Dianagate* (Princess Di had a boyfriend), *Camillagate* (Prince Charles had a girlfriend), and Monica Lewinsky's involvement with President Clinton gave rise to *zippergate* and *fornigate*.

These *-gate* formations are interesting in relation to the distinction between compounds and words with affixes. Is the *-gate* part of these words a compounding element or a suffix? *Watergate* is a proper name, but obviously it is a compound of *water* and *gate* and this second element has been extracted for the new formations. One could argue that *-gate* is a suffix, since it is not really an independent word, but most of the formations seem like compounds, each one being some kind of 'gate' where *gate* means 'scandal'.

The question of what is an affix arises with numerous words made up from Greek or Latin elements. For instance, in words like *matricide, fratricide, suicide, regicide,* and *homicide* do we have prefixes *matri-, sui-,* etc., or do we have a suffix *-cide*? If we have both, we have no root and we will have to adjust our definition of prefix and suffix. The standard way of describing these formations is to admit there is no root and to call the constituents **combining forms**. Other examples include *telephone, telescope, telegraph, microphone, microscope,* and *micrograph*. However, a form like *micro-* is a prefix in *microsurgery* and *microclimate*, and *tele-* is a prefix in *telecommunications*.

Back formation

Consider the words *babysit* and *babysitter*. *Babysitter* appears to be made up from *babysit* plus the suffix *-er* and from the point of view of the language as we find it, that is true. Historically, however, *babysitter* was in use first and then the suffix was removed to yield *babysit*. Other words that result from this process of **back formation** are compounds such as *gate-crash*, *air-condition*, *lip-read*, and *stage-manage*, plus *to burgle*, *to edit*, *to enthuse*, *to hawk*, *to sculpt*, and *to reminisce*. There is an alternative to *burgle*, namely *burglarize*.

There is an adverb *gingerly* as in, 'After the fall, she got up *gingerly*,' but there is no corresponding adjective *ginger*. However, I now hear sports commentators using the missing adjective as in, 'He's got up [after that heavy fall], but he's looking pretty *ginger*,' so this could catch on. There is a word *uncouth*, but no word *couth*. However, over the last few years there have been a number of light-hearted attempts to use *couth* in the media, so this could also catch on.

Zero Derivation

Most languages have suffixes to mark the derivation of one part-of-speech from another. English sometimes uses a suffix to mark such derivation as with *-er* for agent nouns and *-ee* for patient/recipient nouns, but, as we noted in chapter two, it is unusual in allowing words to be shifted from one part-of-speech to another without any change of form, a process known as **zero derivation** or 'conversion'. Almost all the examples are of shifts between noun, verb, and adjective. In some instances the direction of the shift is clear. We have had the noun *text* for a long time, but it has come to be used as a verb only recently with reference to sending messages full of abbreviations via mobile/cell phone. In other instances we might hesitate to say which part-of-speech came first, as with *plot*, for instance. Was it a noun first or was it a verb first?

Derivation often involves an irregularity with meaning as we saw with *recite* and *recital*. This lack of predictability is also found with moving a word from one word class to another. A *ghost* is the disembodied spirit of a human, but to *ghost* is to write an examination paper or a literary work on behalf of another. The same form can also appear as a modifier in the compound *ghost writer*, which refers to the person who writes a literary work for someone else, usually the autobiography (sic) of a sports star or film star. A *paper* can be a newspaper, an academic text of chapter size, or a cigarette paper (for those who 'roll their own'), but *to paper* means 'to cover with wallpaper'.

Other examples of word forms that appear as more than one part-of-speech include the following. Many of these involve a shift of stress and/or vowel quality.

noun and verb: *arrest, estimate, finger, fish, import, play, torment*
noun and adjective: *comic, drunk, heavy, human, original, royal, sweet*
noun, verb and adjective: *average, square*
verb and adjective: *abstract, bare, clear, deliberate, frequent, perfect, separate*

Blends

The term **blending** refers to taking the first part of one word and last part of another to form a new word as with *smog* (smoke + fog) or *brunch* (breakfast + lunch). The use of the vague word 'part' in the description of blending is deliberate. It is not morphemes that are joined, nor syllables. Blending is not at all common in the world's languages, and it was not particularly common in English until the last fifty years. Then it caught on and it is common nowadays for people to try and come up with smart new blends such as *affluenza* (affluent + influenza) 'the disease of being too rich' and himbo (he or him + bimbo) 'male bimbo'.

Metrosexual is very much in vogue at the time of writing for a man who is up with the latest fashion in dress, cuisine, and lifestyle generally. It appears to be made up from the *metro-* of *metropolitan* and the *-sexual* of *homosexual*, not that it implies homosexuality, though it does reflect the fact that a metrosexual's lifestyle is likely to raise the question. A man who doesn't care about his appearance and lifestyle is a *retrosexual*, which combines *retro-* with *(homo)sexual*.

Forms of English spoken by second-language speakers are represented by blends. *Singlish* is English spoken by Singaporeans, and *Spanglish* is English spoken by native speakers of Spanish. The French have a blend *Franglais* (*français* + *anglais*, i.e. French + English) for English expressions used in French or for French that incorporates such expressions.

Shortening

Shortening refers to abbreviating a word as with *ad* (advertisement), *flu* (influenza), *mike* (microphone), *porn* from *pornography*, and *fan* from *fanatic*. *Mike* and *porn* don't really involve a change of meaning, but *fan* does not have the same meaning as *fanatic*. You can be a fan without being a fanatic. This is one of the reasons shortening is considered a way of making new words. Another reason is that the connection between the full form and the abbreviated form can easily be lost. Older speakers know that *pub* is an abbreviation of *public house*, but a recent survey I conducted showed that many young people don't know this.

Some words that are well entrenched in the language are abbreviations. These include *sport* (from *disport*) and *fence* (from *defence*). *Bus* is from *omnibus*, Latin for 'for all', and *mob* is from *mobile vulgus*, Latin for 'fickle people'.

Recent abbreviated additions to the anatomical vocabulary of English include *pecs* (pectoral muscles), *abs* (abdominal muscles), and *glutes* (gluteal muscles, i.e. the bum!).

There are words that involve compounding of abbreviated forms. These are called 'clipped compounds'. Examples include *sitcom* (situation comedy) and *sci-fi* (science-fiction).

Alphabetisms and acronyms

In a written language it is possible to abbreviate a compound word or a phrase by using the initial letters. Examples with proper names include *ATM* (Automatic Teller Machine), *CIA* (Central Intelligence Agency), and *FBI* (Federal Bureau of Investigation). Other examples include *FAQ* (frequently asked questions), *ott* (over the top), *tlc* (tender loving care) and *to OD* (take an overdose of drugs).

It is common in contemporary English to pronounce a series of initials as a word. An example that goes back to the Second World War is *radar*, which derives from 'radio detection and ranging' where the first two letters of *radio* have been taken to provide a vowel. *Laser* derives from 'light amplification by stimulated emission of radiation' (quite a mouthful!). Some linguists use the term **acronym** for examples like *CIA* where one names the letters and also for examples where one pronounces the sequence as a single word. Others reserve the term 'acronym' for the latter type, and would refer to examples such as *CIA* and *tlc* as **alphabetisms** or **initialisms**. I will follow the latter practice. Acronyms have become very popular over the last few decades. Examples include *scuba* (self-contained underwater breathing apparatus), *ram* (random access memory: the computing power of your computer), *rom* (read-only memory: the storage capacity of your computer) and *eftpos* (electronic funds transfer at point of sale). This last example illustrates how the sequence of words need not exist independently of the acronym. One assumes 'electronic funds transfer at point of sale' was thought up just to provide the acronym.

The word *yuppify* involves adding the suffix *-ify* to the fairly new word *yuppie*, itself a diminutive with *-ie* of an acronym *y*(oung) *u*(pwardly mobile or urban) *p*(rofessional). It refers to upgrading something such as a shopping centre to make it attractive to yuppies by putting in latte lounges and the like (and putting up the prices!).

Reduplication

A large number of languages use reduplication or doubling as a means of inflection or to form new words. In Indonesian, for instance, *kuda* 'horse' can be reduplicated to form the plural: *kuda-kuda* 'horses'. This is equivalent to inflection and does not really represent a new word, but *kuda-kuda* can also be 'a trestle', 'an easel', or 'a saw-horse', where we clearly have a new word. Reduplication is often iconic and this is clearly so where it indicates plural. It is not so clear in formations such as *kuda-kuda* 'trestle' where the reduplication seems to indicate 'similar' or 'having a property of', but it is interesting to note that it has this function when used with nouns in a number of languages. For example, in Paamese, an Austronesian language of Vanuatu, *tupas* is 'smoke' and *tupaspas*, with partial reduplication, is 'smoky'. In the Australian language Pitta-Pitta *ngapu* is water and *ngapungapu* is 'wet'.

Flying creatures in various languages sometimes have reduplicated names. 'Butterfly' is *kupu-kupu* in Indonesian, *balam-balam* in Woiwurrung (Australian) and *cho-cho* in Japanese (opera buffs will recall Madame Butterfly was *Cho-cho-san*). This may be iconic, aimed at capturing the flapping of wings. Words for oscillation are sometimes represented by reduplicated roots. In Thai, a language that favours reduplication with a change of vowel, the word for 'oscillate' is *yôok-yêek* (the root is *yôok*). In English we have practically no pure reduplication, but we have a number of examples with vowel alternation, and again the notion of oscillation appears: *criss-cross*, *flip-flop*, *ding-dong*, *ping-pong*, *see-saw*, *tick-tock*, and *wig-wag*. The idea is more abstract in *dilly-dally* and *shilly-shally* where the oscillation is of the *will-I-won't-I* type, and in *mish-mash* and *wishy-washy* 'neither one thing or another'.

Reduplication with verbs can indicate ongoing action, repeated action, intense activity, or a number of actors. In Nama (a Niger-Congo language), for instance, *go* means 'look' and *go-go* means 'scrutinize'. In Motu (Austronesian) *mahuta* is 'to sleep' and *mahuta-mahuta* 'to sleep constantly'.

Proper names to common noun

Quite a number of common nouns in English derive from the shifting of names of people or products. *Cardigan* derives from Lord Cardigan (1797–1868) and *macintosh* from Charles Macintosh (1766–1843) the inventor of the waterproofing process. *Diesel* takes its name from Rudolph Diesel (1858–1913), the inventor of the diesel engine, and *braille*, the system of representing letters by a pattern of raised dots for the benefit of the blind, takes its name from the inventor, Louis Braille (1809–1852).

A recent example of a different character is the American colloquial term *oreo*. It is the tradename of a chocolate biscuit with cream filling and it has come to mean a black person with white values.

Trade names are often taken as generic. *Biro* was a prominent brand when ball-point pens first appeared and came to be used as a general name for ball-points, not only in English, but in a number of other languages as well. The brand name comes from the name of the inventor of the ball-point pen,

Lázló Bíró (1899–1985). *Band-Aid* is a trade name, but people often use it for products from rival firms; similarly with *Kleenex*, which can be used for any paper tissue. *Hoover* is a brand of vacuum cleaner, but it has not only become a generic word, it is used as a verb, so one can say, 'I *hoovered* the floor with my Electrolux.'

The names of people, real or fictional, who were famous for some particular activity are often used as common nouns. You can call someone *a Casanova*, *a Judas*, *a Matahari*, *a doubting Thomas*, *a Romeo*, or *a Scrooge* and we can say someone has *a Jekyll-and-Hyde* character. Presumably the significance of historic names is not universally known. I have heard of boys called Tarquin, after Lucius Tarquinius Superbus, who raped Lucrece, and girls called Jezebel, after the infamous bad woman of the Bible (I Kings 16–31).

The names of units in physics are often taken from the names of scientists: *ohm*, *amp(ère)*, *joule*, and *pascal*, for instance. These words are not confined to English.

Taboo and euphemism

It is typical of human cultures that certain topics or terms are **taboo** in certain circumstances or even in all circumstances. Taboo is borrowed from Polynesian *tabu* and means 'forbidden' or 'untouchable'. It is common for there to be taboos to do with religion, death, and sex.

Certain subject matter can be taboo or just certain words. Until the 1970s the subject of menstruation was under a pretty strict taboo. There were products advertised as giving relief for 'the pain you can't explain'. Sex and excretion were taboo in a variety of situations, but within this area certain words were especially taboo, notably *fuck* and *cunt*. *Fuck* has been emerging from its taboo over the last few decades and is now heard regularly in movies. However, these words are not used in newspapers, and in fact the relevant computers are programmed so that they can't print these words. This prevents naughty staff deliberately omitting the *o* in *count* and claiming it was a typo.

The main significance of taboo in the context of word building is that it gives rise to **euphemisms**, nice-sounding alternatives to existing expressions. Words for things that are unpleasant or thought of as inferior or unattractive tend to acquire unpleasant connotations. This leads to a quest for fresh terms and leads to frequent lexical replacement. Today's euphemism becomes tomorrow's ordinary term. Euphemisms are common with sex and excretion. We find expressions such as *sleep with* or *make love to* for sexual intercourse, which is itself a euphemism, *derrière* for bottom, and expressions like *to pass water*, *to do your business*, and *to go to the bathroom* for excretory functions. Pregnancy was a taboo area for our forebears and expressions such as *she's in* *a family way* or *she is with child* were used, as well as the literary French borrowing *enceinte*.

Death is a subject where euphemism is prompted by a desire to spare the feelings of those close to the dead person. Thus we talk of *the deceased*, and someone *passing away*, and a funeral is handled by someone with the very vague title of *undertaker*. Firing or sacking is another area where there is an understandable desire to put the dismissal in a favourable light. Employers often speak of having *to let someone go*, or of *downsizing* or *rightsizing*, or of arranging a *negotiated departure*.

One factor that can lead to euphemism is homophony with a rude word. The word *cock* can still be used in Britain for the male domestic fowl, despite the potential embarrassment of saying a word that sounds the same as a colloquialism for 'penis', but in the US it has been replaced by *rooster*. The American equivalent of the rude British word *arse* is *ass*. This has led to the horse-like animal being renamed *donkey* in that country.

Euphemisms are also to be found in the domains of disease and disability. Over the past generation we have seen a move to institute 'politically correct' language, and a lot of this activity has been aimed at replacing the ordinary terms for disabilities. For instance, people with some kind of physical disability were once called 'crippled' or 'handicapped', but more recently they were referred to as *disabled*, then *differently abled*, and later again as *physically challenged*. People with mental disability were once often referred to as 'retarded', but nowadays they are *mentally challenged* or *people with learning difficulties*. Some radio and television stations have banned the word *spastic*, which is ironic in light of the high frequency of the colloquial abbreviations *spaso* and *spaz* applied loosely to anyone who falters in some small way. Most of the euphemisms and politically correct terms are compounds, many of them like *mentally challenged* with a modifying adverb in *-ly*.

The use of euphemisms and politically correct language has engendered a backlash, and some examples such as *differently hirsute* for 'hairy' appear to be parodies, but sometimes it's hard to tell the serious examples from the parodies as with examples like *socially challenged* used to describe a recluse.

Big business is good at euphemisms. Goods may be *affordable*, but not *cheap*; they may be *standard size* but not *small*. Second-hand cars and houses (sorry, *homes!*) are *pre-owned* or even *pre-loved*. The list of ingredients in some cosmetics features a substance called *aqua*. If that's not 'water', what is it?

Race is another area where there is frequent replacement. This presumably reflects negative views of races other than one's own resulting in existing terms taking on negative connotations. In general the words that acquire these negative overtones are not in themselves derogatory. *Nigger*, for instance, is the Latin word for 'black', but its use by non-blacks is taboo in the United States, and its use can be subject to legal penalties.

We usually can't identify who first produced a new word, but in a few cases prominent people are responsible for a creation that has caught on:

agnostic	Thomas Huxley 1869
Bible Belt	H. L. Mencken (1880–1956), journalist, satirist, author of *The American Language*
catch 22	From the novel *Catch 22* by Joseph Heller 1961
Cold War	The columnist Walter Lippmann 1947
cyberspace	William Gibson, science fiction writer 1982
fifth column	General Mola in the Spanish Civil War (1936–1939)
Iron Curtain	Winston Churchill 1946
Shangri-La	From the novel *Lost Horizon* by James Hilton 1933

Other methods of dealing with new content

Languages do not always use their word-building resources to cope with things that are new to them. They often borrow words from other languages. English does this a lot, and it has borrowed from over fifty languages. Examples include *graffiti* (Italian), *genre* (French), *enchilada* (Mexican Spanish), *mulligatawny* (Tamil), and *tsunami* (Japanese). Another way to cover new content is to extend the meaning of an existing word. Borrowing of words and extensions of meaning are discussed further in chapter twelve.

Sources and further reading

A good introduction to morphology is provided in Carstairs-McCarthy, *An Introduction to English Morphology: Words and their Structure*. For word formation in English there is Adams, *An Introduction to Modern English Word Formation*, and Bauer, *English Word-formation*. For up-to-date examples consult the Web. A number of sites feature new words, especially examples that are clever or cute.

Problems

1 On page 24 it was mentioned that the distinction between a compound and a regularly used phrase was not absolutely clear. Readers might like to think about where the line should be drawn. Here are some examples that are relevant:

(i) Examples where the plural is not at the end of the word: *mother-in-law* (with plural *mothers-in-law* or *mother-in-laws*), *attorney general* (again with two possible plurals), *runner up* (I think *runners up* is the normal (only?) plural).

(ii) Examples with phrase stress rather than compound stress: *designated driver*, *executive stress*, and *grey area* (check how you pronounce this one).

(iii) Names like *Serena Williams* or *Cate Blanchett*.

(iv) Numbers like *thirty-six*, *seventy-two*, or *Five hundred and forty*. And what about *747* as in *I've often flown in a 747*?

Names and numbers can be considered to be compounds containing cells where an entry in a particular cell has a certain significance. First cell in a Western personal name is the given name, second position from the right in a number involves multiplying by 10, and so on.

2 Label the affixes in the following words as inflectional [I] or derivational [D].

postage   [ ]   unwind   [ ]   lionesses [ ] [ ]
wisdom   [ ]   swelled   [ ]   engages   [ ]
delouse   [ ]   criteria   [ ]
glamorous [ ]   pancakes [ ]

3 In words like *tables*, *chairs*, and *bushes* we have inflection for plural, i.e. for 'more than one'. But what is the function of the suffixes in baby-talk words like *dindins*, *beddiebyes*, *wee-wees*, and *cuddles*, and in colloquial forms like *gramps* (grandpa) and *turps* (turpentine)?

4 As I write this, reports are appearing in the media in Melbourne of men arrested for taking pictures up women's skirts with hidden cameras and the practice is called *upskirting*. Radio presenters refer to it as a new word. Sometimes you come across a word that is new to you, but which is not new in the language. Recently I read, 'The crocodile started to *alligator-roll*'. The word *alligator-roll* was new to me, but I wondered if the word had originated in the US where there are alligators and had travelled to Australia where there are crocodiles. Think about new words that you have come across over the last year or so. What kind of word-formation processes do they illustrate (compounds, blends, suffixation, etc.)? How often do you encounter new words, one per week, perhaps? Where are you likely to come across them? In newspapers or magazines? On radio or television? In conversation? How do you think new words get disseminated? You might type 'new words' into your search engine. This will give you some material to think about.

5 The following words are based on proper names from Ancient Greek. Identify the persons or places involved:

sisyphean, sybaritic, herculean, titanic, colossal, stentorian

6 Identify the person whose name is perpetuated in the following:

boycott, fuchsia, guillotine, macadamize, sandwich, silhouette, leotard

7 What are your feelings about euphemisms? New euphemisms can arouse strong feelings. Some people are annoyed by them, while others fall over themselves in their rush to adopt them. I suspect some people have different attitudes to different types of euphemism, e.g. whether they are to do with sex and body effluvia on the one hand, or race or disability on the other.

4. Meaning of words

Words, in their primary or immediate signification, stand for nothing but the ideas in the mind of him that uses them.

John Locke, *Essay Concerning Human Understanding*

Words and meanings

Semantics is the field of linguistics that deals with meaning, the relationship between words, phrases, and sentences on the one hand and entities such as objects, properties, relations, and situations on the other. In this chapter we shall deal with the meaning of words. But first we need to say something about the notion of 'word'. *Book* is a word in English and so is *books*, but you wouldn't consider them separate words if you were compiling a dictionary. We take them to be two forms of the same word, but here we are using word in a more abstract sense. A word in this sense is called a **lexeme** and *book* and *books* are two inflected forms of the lexeme BOOK. Now you might think that we could simply say that *book* is the base or root and *books* the plural form, which is true enough, but in some languages a root never appears without some inflection. In Latin the word for 'wall' can be represented by *murus* when it is the subject of a sentence, *murum* when it is the object, *muros* when it is an object in the plural, and so on, but never by the root alone. There is another complication too. In English *go* and *went* are forms of the same lexeme, since *went* is the past tense of GO, but they represent different roots. Similarly *am, is, are, was, were,* and *be* (as in 'I want to be the winner') are all forms of the lexeme BE, which we usually refer to as the verb *to be*. In what follows I shall be talking about lexemes, but I will simply write 'word'.

Most words **refer** to some entity, process, action or whatever. As we saw in chapter two, these are **lexical** words. They belong in the lexicon rather than the grammar. A minority of words have a function rather than a meaning. We saw some examples in chapter two, words such as *the, of,* and *not,* which are typically unstressed. These are function words or grammatical words.

There are also words and phrases that function as **discourse markers**. Some of these, like *please, thanks,* and *You're welcome,* play a part in negotiation, while others such as *well* (*Well, I wouldn't say that exactly.*), *still* (*Still, he's good at sport.*) and *anyway* (*Anyway, I'm still going to go.*) indicate the speaker's attitude and how the following statement is to be taken in relation to the context (see also p. 112).

There are also **deictic** words, words that have variable reference according to the speech situation. Deictic words may be functional such as *this* and *that* or lexical like *yesterday* and *tomorrow.* They are treated on pp. 44 and 45 below.

At first we might think of the meaning of lexical items as whatever they **refer** to, what they **denote**. However, this is not so. There is a well-known example from the philosopher Frege illustrating the difference between meaning and reference. It involves Venus (the planet, not the goddess). A person could learn about the planets at school or from a book on astronomy and be able to tell you that Venus is the planet nearest the sun. The same person might be familiar with a large star that is visible in the eastern sky just before dawn and the western sky just after dark, where it is known as the Morning Star and Evening Star respectively, but not know that the large star is Venus. It makes sense to say *Venus is the Evening Star,* or conversely *The Evening Star is Venus.* This is not at all vacuous.

To take another example. In the Olympics athletes compete over 1,500 metres. This is 1.5 kilometres, but one would not necessarily equate the two. We understand 1,500 metres in the context of the other Olympic distances of 100, 200, 400, 800, 5,000, and 10,000, whereas we understand 1.5 km in the context of road signs and the like. It is not vacuous to say that 1,500 kilometres is 1.5 kilometres. The meaning is what a word or expression signifies for speakers of the language, and, incidentally, this may not be the same for every speaker.

Lexical items not only have denotations, they also have **connotations**. Indeed, there are everyday expressions such as *I don't like the connotations*, or *That has unpleasant connotations*, or even just *That has connotations*. Connotations are associations. What is evoked or brought to mind by the use of a word is a connotation. A word might have different connotations for different people. See if you agree with my feelings about *naked* and *nude*, both of which refer to having no clothes on. For me *naked* suggests someone unwillingly deprived of clothing (*The guards stripped the prisoner naked.*), whereas nude suggests the tradition of depicting unclothed persons (mainly women) in art and pornography. The word *spry* is defined in various dictionaries as 'active', 'agile', 'brisk', and 'nimble', but it is used only of old people, that is, where there is an expectation of unsprightliness. It has connotations of old age.

Some words have associations with certain texts. The word *glean*, meaning 'to gather the bits of grain left by the reapers' must have been known to many over the years from its prominence in the biblical story of Ruth. Nowadays it is mainly used with reference to gathering scraps of information. It is used in contexts such as *From what I could glean, the Government hadn't come to a decision yet.* The word *manger* does not come up much outside the Christmas story, and the words of the carol *Away in a manger*. Words may also have associations based on frequent collocations rather than specific texts. *Thud* is likely to bring to mind *sickening*, because of the cliché *to fall with a sickening thud*.

A number of words can have the same reference but belong to different styles. Besides the basic word *horse* there is the old-fashioned poetic *steed*, the colloquial *nag*, and the baby-talk *horsie* and *gee-gee*. Words with the same reference can belong to different dialects. The word *wee* covers the same range as *little* and *small*, but it is basically Scottish, though used elsewhere.

When people talk of connotations, they normally mean connotations based on contexts of use, but words can also have associations based on their form. A word might remind you of a rhyming word or expression or an alliterative word or expression, especially if it contains a distinctive feature. A word like *sphere*, for instance, might remind one of some of the other *sph-* words: *Sphinx* or *sphincter*. There is evidence that people associate words on the basis of form when you find people hesitating between similar words such as *prostrate* and *prostate* or misusing *mitigate against* for *militate against*. People are conscious of words that resemble taboo words. Recently I used the word *infarcts* and someone said jokingly,

Please, not in front of the children! This unusual word obviously evoked the f-word.

Hyponyms and hypernyms

All languages have words of different degrees of generality. I can refer to a tree simply as *tree*, or as a type of tree, say *oak*, or as a type of oak, say *pin oak*. The word *tree* covers numerous types of tree including *ash, oak, beech, elm*, and *maple*. These names for particular types of tree are **hyponyms** of *tree*. The word *oak* covers several species of oak such as *live oak, pin oak*, and *scarlet oak*. These are hyponyms of *oak*. Similarly *poodle, Pekingese, Dalmation*, and *fox terrier* are hyponyms of *dog*. Almost every word is a hyponym of some other wider term even if it is only of general words such as object, thing, entity, idea, notion, action, or process. The more general term that embraces a number of more particular terms (the 'superordinate' term) is a **hypernym**. *Tree* is the hypernym of *oak, sycamore, elm, pine*, and so on; *dog* is the hypernym of *collie, red setter, golden-haired retriever, Labrador*, and *Great Dane–Chihuahua cross*.

Synonyms

Words that have the same meaning are called **synonyms.** Examples include *hard/difficult, fast/quick, couch/sofa, perplexed/bewildered, hackneyed/trite*, and *help/assist/aid*. Most people are conscious of the existence of synonyms, and synonymy is the basis for crosswords. Nevertheless, when we look closely at groups of synonyms, we almost always find that there are some differences of meaning or usage. If we are in trouble, we might shout, *Help!* but certainly not *Assist!* The word *aid* is another synonym of *help* and *assist*. If we are injured or fall ill in a public place, we might call for *First Aid*, but not *First Assist* or *First Help*.

Synonyms may differ in that one is more formal. *To receive a letter* is more formal than *to get a letter. Pusillanimous* means 'faint-hearted', but *pusillanimous* is a learned word and likely not to be understood by many, whereas *faint-hearted* is common enough.

As mentioned above, words have connotations as well as denotations. *Deferential* and *obsequious* have very similar meanings, but while *deferential* is neutral in its connotations, *obsequious* has negative connotations. It implies criticism.

Antonyms

If two words are opposite in meaning, they are **antonyms**. There are two types of antonym. The first is illustrated by pairs such as *alive* and *dead* or *male* and *female*. In general one is either alive or dead, not somewhere in between. Alive means 'not dead' and dead means 'not alive'. Much the same applies to *male* and *female*. It is true that one can be in a state that is somewhere between life and death, and it is true that some animals, including humans, are not completely male or completely female. However, there is still a contrast between antonymic pairs such as *alive/dead* and *male/female* and antonymic pairs such as *fast* and *slow*, *heavy* and *light*, or *easy* and *hard*. *Fast* and *slow*, for instance, represent the ends of a scale and there can be degrees of speed in between. Moreover, the estimation of fast or slow depends on whose speed is under discussion. What is fast for a Labrador would be slow for a greyhound. Antonyms of the *alive/dead* type are called 'complementary antonyms'. Those of the *fast/slow* type are called 'gradable antonyms'.

Some pairs of words are converses of one another. *Buy* and *sell*, and the nouns *buyer* and *seller*, are converses in the sense that if A buys goods from B then one can say B sells goods to A. *Teacher* and *pupil* are similarly related as are *employer* and *employee*. These pairs are sometimes called 'relational opposites'. The words *husband* and *wife* are opposite within the field of spouses in the sense that one complements the other; they are co-hyponyms of *spouse*. When children are introduced to antonyms in games, they some-times take *Mummy* to be the opposite of *Daddy* and *dog* to be the opposite of *cat*. While a mummy implies a daddy and vice versa (though both might not be around), *dog* does not imply *cat*, so the idea of antonym is somewhat extended.

Antonyms are not always of equal status. *Heavy* and *light* are antonyms, but in most contexts we would say *How heavy is it?* rather than *How light is it?* We talk about the heaviness of an object rather than lightness. An analogous point could be made about *long/short* and *wide/narrow*.

Polysemy

The word 'good' has many meanings. For example, if a man were to shoot his grandmother at a range of five hundred yards, I should call him a good shot, but not necessarily a good man.
                                                                    G. K. Chesterton

Many words develop multiple meanings, quite often by metaphorical exten-sion. A number of common body parts have extended meanings: *head of the school*, *mouth of the river*, *eye of the needle*, *leg of the table*, and *foot of the hill*.

Affixes too can be polysemous. The *-ette* in *kitchenette* indicates 'small', the *-ette* in *leatherette* indicates 'imitation' and the *-ette* in *usherette* indicates 'female'. The suffix *-er* is polysemous, at least according to dictionaries, in that it can indicate an 'agent' as in *reader*, an 'inhabitant of' as in *New Yorker*, and 'having the property of' as in *double-decker (bus)*. I would prefer to recognize two separate suffixes, one indicating agent and the other covering the other functions.

Homonyms (homophones and homographs)

Languages are not designed by any particular person or by a committee. They evolve, and it can happen that two or more words can come to sound the same such as *bear* (the animal) and *bare* (uncovered). We call groups of words that sound the same **homophones**. Sometimes it happens that two or more words coincide in spelling as with *lead* (the metal) and *lead* (the verb). Groups of words that are spelt the same are **homographs**. The cover term for homophones and homographs is **homonym**. Some pairs of words are both homophones and homographs: *bear* (the animal) and *bear* (carry). I should add that some authorities use the term 'homonym' for cases like *bear*, where words are alike in both sound and spelling.

Homophony and polysemy: profit and loss

A glance at any dictionary suggests that the majority of words are polysemous, and that homophony is not uncommon. Sometimes it is hard to tell polysemy from homophony. Dictionaries distinguish the two on historical grounds. Consider the word *butt* as in 'the stump of a tree', 'the thick part of a rifle', 'the end of a cigarette', and 'the buttocks'. Dictionaries consider these to be four meanings of one word, but it is not obvious to the present-day reader, though on reflection one can see 'non-pointy end' as a common thread of meaning. On the other hand dictionaries take *butt* (object of ridicule), *butt* (cask), the verb *butt* 'to strike with the head' and *butt* 'thick end' to be a set of homophones. The conjunction *but* is also homophonous with the others, but spelt differently. Where words are pronounced alike, but spelt differently, they almost always have a different origin.

On the basis of a dictionary sample, I estimate that English has nearly 10,000 examples of homophony or of polysemy involving a readily noticeable difference in meaning. In theory this means there is a lot of scope for ambiguity, but in practice problems are few and far between, and there is a positive side to homophony and polysemy, namely that it allows for puns. There are also clever expressions based on one or the other that form part of the language. For example, a business that appears to charge unreasonably high prices is said to *charge like a wounded bull*, but *charge* in this expression means 'rush at' not 'demand a price'.

However, homophony can sometimes be a problem. It can cause confusion. In Old English there was a verb *lætan* 'to allow, to set free' and a verb *lettan* 'to hinder, to obstruct'. In Early Modern English these two words had come to be *let*. When Hamlet says *By heaven, I'll make a ghost of him that lets me*, he means 'him that tries to prevent me'. This homophony caused a problem since a sentence such as *I won't let you* could have two quite opposite interpretations. So what happened? Well, the word *let* 'to hinder' dropped out of use, though curiously it survives in the legal phrase *without let or hindrance*, and in tennis where a *let* or *let ball* is one that touches the net on its way to the intended service court.

A similar problem can arise with polysemy. *Hot* 'high in temperature' and *hot* 'spicy' regularly lead to confusion in the context of curries and the like. How often do you hear people say, 'No, I mean hot-spicy.' The word *pepper* presents the same problem. This word can refer to the pungent, spicy powder from plants of the Piper genus or to capsicums. Some capsicums (the larger bell capsicums) have very little peppery flavour, while others (usually quite small) are extremely hot. Dictionaries consider *pepper* in the sense of spicy powder and in the sense of capsicum to be an example of polysemy rather than homophony, presumably because of the hot capsicums, but it would be difficult for the average speaker to see a connection between the spicy powder and the innocuous bell capsicum. Anyway, whatever the dictionary says, an annoying ambiguity can arise with the word *pepper* in discussions of food.

Deictic expressions

Some words, and indeed some bound morphemes, have a variable reference related to the place or time of the communication and the parties taking part in the communication. Take the words *this* and *that*, for instance. If I say *Take this one. I'll keep that one*, then you interpret *this* as referring to one nearer to me, and *that* as referring to one further away, or you might be guided by my pointing, first to one and then to the other. Words like *this* and *that* are **deictic** words or pointing words.

Pronouns make up a system of **personal deixis**. All languages have a pronoun for the speaker (the first person) and one for the addressee (the second person). Some languages lack a third person singular pronoun, so the absence of a form for 'I' or 'you' is interpreted as referring to a third person. On the other hand a number of languages have more than one third person pronoun. English has three in the singular: *he*, *she*, and *it*. These refer to sex or natural gender, though some people tend to use *she* for inanimates. Most languages have plural pronouns as well as singular pronouns. English has *we*, *you*, and *they*, though *you* is also used to refer to one addressee. Some languages have dual pronouns to refer to two people.

A large number of languages make a distinction in first person non-singular forms between those that include the addressee and those that exclude it. In Malay and Indonesian the **inclusive** 'we' is *kita* and the **exclusive** *kami*. In English 'we' covers both possibilities. Suppose there are three people present: Alice, Celia, and Mary. Alice might say to Mary *We* (she and Mary) *are going down the street* or she might say to Mary *We* (she and Celia) *are going down the street*. The first *we* is **inclusive** (addressee included), the second **exclusive** (addressee excluded).

Words like *this* and *that* and *here* and *there* belong to a system of **spatial deixis**. The *here/there* distinction is also found in pairs of verbs such as *come/go* and *bring/take*. I might ring you up and say *Would you like to <u>come</u> over and have a drink? <u>Or</u> I could <u>come</u> over and pick you up and we'll <u>go</u> off somewhere for dinner*. One *comes* to where the speaker is or where the addressee is, but *goes* everywhere else. In many languages the deictic system has more than two

terms. In Latin *hic* 'this' and *ille* 'that' are opposed, as they are in English, but there is a third term *iste*, which can refer to an intermediate distance, in particular to the area near the addressee.

There is also **temporal deixis** found in words like *now, then, yesterday,* and *tomorrow,* and in phrases such as *last month* and *next year.*

Set phrases: idioms and clichés

Our mental lexicon and the practical dictionary contain thousands of set phrases, that is, fixed sequences of words that must be learned by heart. These include phrases such as *on the whole* and *up to date.* Such phrases are often referred to as idiomatic and it is certainly true that being a fluent speaker of the language involves knowing such phrases, but an **idiom** in the narrower sense is a phrase where one cannot work out the meaning from the meaning of the parts as with phrases such as *to be in a rut, to look daggers,* and *it rained cats and dogs.* A number of idiomatic phrases are available for use in particular situations such as *Were you born in a tent?* addressed to someone who has failed to shut the door, or *Is your father a glazier?* addressed to someone blocking your view.

English has a lot of **phrasal verbs** such as *take down, take up, take over, take in, put down, put up, put over,* and *put in.* They consist of a **verb** and **verb**

particle. They are phrases rather than compound words in that a direct object can be placed between the verb and particle. One can say *She put the basket down*, as well as *She put down the basket*. Many of these phrasal verbs are idiomatic. The combination *take in* has a literal meaning in *Because it looked like rain, Kim took the washing in*, but *Kim takes washing in* refers to doing other people's laundry as a means of earning income, and the combination has an idiomatic meaning of 'understand, absorb' in *Because the lecturer went too fast, Kim couldn't take it in*.

Some set phrases are called **clichés**. Cliché is a word of negative connotation. It implies triteness, a history of overuse and subsequent weakening. It is a matter of opinion which set phrases deserve to be called clichés. I have never heard of anyone objecting to established phrases such as *by and large* or *part and parcel*. What is more likely to raise objections is the new cliché. This might seem like an oxymoron. How can a relatively new phrase suffer from overuse? Easy! Some expressions become popular overnight and it is these that are often noticed and castigated rather than the centuries-old examples. The following example is from the manager of a sales team talking to one of his reps. It is a composite example containing at least twelve clichés, some that have been around for a few generations and some that have come into vogue during the last decade. I hope the reader will recognize the style. We have probably all heard people who overuse the overused!

> *I think you've got what it takes. You're not the sort who's going to drop the ball, but let's face it, your performance hasn't been up to scratch. You need to lift your game. You need to try something new, you've got to think outside the box, push the envelope. At the end of the day it's up to you. The bottom line is that if you do your homework and are prepared to go the extra mile, the sky's the limit. One day you might even be sitting in my chair.*

Among set phrases are proverbs. These usually contain advice and are usually whole sentences. Examples include *A stitch in time saves nine, Too many cooks spoil the broth*, and *That's the pot calling the kettle black*. Often one can quote an abbreviated form: *a stitch in time, too many cooks, pots and kettles*.

Conscious connections between morphemes

Dictionaries are a great source for information about the history of the language. As we noted above, the border between homophony and polysemy is decided on historical grounds. But it is interesting to think about what connections speakers actually make between words and parts of words. Some evidence comes from misspelling. I confess to having hesitated over *surname*, wondering whether it was **sirname*, since it seemed reasonable that it was connected with *sir*. In fact the *surname* is from the French *surnom*, literally 'on-name'. In borrowing this word from French the English have changed *nom* to *name*, but left *sur*. Most misspellings are of the type **accomodate* for *accommodate*, which do not make a connection with another word, and some are doubtless just one-off slips of the pen, but consider examples like the following. They suggest non-standard identifications.

> *'He was self scented (self-centred) and cared little for the feelings of others.'*
> *'The city was raised (razed) to the ground.'*
> *'They missed out by a hare's breath (hair's breadth).'*

The word *crayfish* is interesting in this regard. It came into English from French as *crevasse*, but was altered to *crayfish* through a process known as **folk etymology**. This refers to cases where ordinary people make a connection between words or parts of words. The folk supply an **etymon** or **root** that is not justified historically. Of course we usually only find out about such a misidentification when it is reflected in a change of pronunciation and ultimately the spelling. A crayfish does not have a fish-shape, but its flesh is fish-like. In past generations it was common practice for conservative branches of the Christian church to eat fish on Fridays and crustaceans counted as fish.

The term **folk etymology** also applies to cases where the pronunciation and/or spelling is changed to a more familiar form without there being an association of meaning. The effect is the same, namely to create a folk or false etymology. The word *avocado* provides a good example of what can happen. The word comes from Nahuatl, the language of the Aztecs. The original form is *ahuacatl* and meant 'testicles' or 'scrotum'. It was borrowed into Spanish as *ahuacate*. This unfamiliar form was then turned into *avocato* (our word *advocate*), an earlier form of *abogado* 'lawyer'. The word was then borrowed into English as *avocado*. In this instance the change did not involve any association of meaning between testicles and lawyers (despite what one might think), but simply the substitution of a familiar form for an unfamiliar one.

Another example involves *titmouse*. It is a kind of tit in the sense of small bird, but it is not a mouse. In **Middle English** it was *titmase*, pronounced 'tit-maahs', but the unfamiliar part was altered to 'mouse'. Similarly *bridegroom* was originally *bridegoom*, where *goom* meant 'man'. *Goom* did not exist independently and was therefore unfamiliar. It was changed to *groom*, though a *bridegroom* does not normally groom the bride. A more recent example is the expression 'to give somebody short shrift', which often comes out as 'to give somebody short shift'. Again *shrift* is unfamiliar, so it gets replaced by *shift*, despite the fact that *shift* does not make any sense. *Shrift* was a noun from the verb *to shrive* which meant 'to forgive formally as in confession in church'. *To give short shrift* is to give a short, peremptory hearing.

Speakers can not only make false associations between morphemes, they can also fail to identify morphemes. Have you ever had the experience of suddenly realizing the root of one word shows up in another. I had been speaking English for decades before it hit me that *graze* and *grazier* were based on the same root as *grass*, and that *glaze* and *glazier* derive from the same root as *glass*.

How do the vocabularies of languages differ?

When people talk about translating from one language to another, they often give the impression they believe the words in one language correspond to those of another, that is, if language A has a word for some entity or notion, then language B will have a corresponding word. Obviously the language of a people living in the highlands of New Guinea or the upper reaches of the Amazon will not have words for television or computer, let alone DVD or iPod, at least not until they come into contact with mainstream civilization. Conversely, languages like English and Portuguese will not have words for all the fauna, flora, artefacts, and cultural practices found in these areas. But what about the world that is common to speakers of all languages? The heavens and the earth are part of universal experience. It is natural to think that this world of common experience is there cut up into chunks to which each language just supplies its own set of labels. To a great extent this is true. You would expect all languages to have words for 'bird', 'stone', 'moon', and 'water', and you would be surprised to find a language where one word covered 'bird' and 'stone' or 'moon' and 'water'. We would take for granted that birds and stones are very different entities, easily distinguishable, even by creatures that have no language. The same applies to moon and water. However, there are differences between languages in the way they break up the world and name it. The human body is universal, along with its properties. (Human behaviour is universal too, unfortunately!) You would be surprised to find a language that did not have words for 'eye', 'ear', 'nose', and 'tooth', but some features of the body can be classified differently. Some languages, for instance, have different roots for 'head hair' and 'body hair', and the latter term covers the fur of an animal. Some, including Fijian and Samoan, have one word for 'forearm' and 'hand'.

Language encodes the world view of its speakers, not always the same world view for all speakers, and subject to change. For most human beings who have ever lived and for many today the world is flat. We speak of the sun rising and setting, we do not refer to the spinning of the earth making the sun appear to rise and set. Even for most of us who know the earth is more or less a sphere, the earth is still flat for most everyday purposes. Many of us refer to heaven being up and hell down. Even when we are thinking globally we find the earth is almost always shown in atlases with a certain orientation that perpetuates a view that the North Pole is at the top of the globe and a country like Australia is 'down under'.

There is a Middle English poem that begins like this:

> *Cethegrande is a fis [fish],*
> *The moste that in water is.*

A *cethegrande* is a whale. Now it is common knowledge today that a whale is a mammal, but that may not have been widely known in the past. A whale has a sort of fish-like shape, and the word might have been taken to refer to any water-dwelling creature with that shape. It is common for people to pooh-pooh any classification of nature that deviates from what we might find in a reference work on flora or fauna, but folk classification has its own legitimacy. Reference books will distinguish insects and arachnids and under arachnids are classified spiders and scorpions. Most people would distinguish three classes of 'creepy crawlies', namely spiders, insects and scorpions. We have words for these. Arachnid is not a word in common use. There is no widely known concept 'arachnid'.

There are differences between languages when it comes to describing kinship. English has the words *grandmother* and *grandfather*. The former covers mother's mother and father's mother, and the latter covers mother's father and father's father. I find that when it comes to speaking about my forebears, I have to use more precise terms such as *my father's mother* or use a more cumbersome phrase such as *my grandmother on my father's side*. In the majority of languages this distinction is ready made. In Swedish, for instance, there are terms for the four grandparents made up by compounding the words for mother (*mor*) and father (*far*):

mormor	'mother's mother'
morfar	'mother's father'
farfar	'father's father'
farmor	'father's mother'

In many languages there is a single root for each of the four grandparents. Here are the Thai terms:

ya:y 'mother's mother'
ta: 'mother's father'
pù: 'father's father'
yâ: 'father's mother'

We classify our siblings on the basis of sex and talk about brothers and sisters, but many languages classify siblings into older or younger than the speaker, or classify according to both sex and relative age.

The colour spectrum is universal, but languages differ greatly in the number of colour terms they have. In the natural world each feature has its own fixed colour, so colour terms are hardly needed. In modern civilization we can have cars, clothing, curtains, and a host of manufactured goods of different colours, so naturally we have lots of colour terms ranging from basic ones like red and blue to fancy ones used only in the context of this year's clothing or last year's cars.

Linguistic determinism: the Sapir–Whorf hypothesis

Since languages vary in terms of what they have words for and what grammatical categories they express, it is not surprising that over the centuries philosophers and linguists have from time to time raised the question of whether language determines the way we think. This view is often known as the Whorfian hypothesis or, more often, as the **Sapir–Whorf hypothesis.** Edward Sapir (1884–1936) was a famous anthropological linguist and Whorf (1897–1941) was his pupil. Both worked on native American languages. The following quotation from an article 'Science and linguistics' published in 1940 encapsulates Whorf's views:

> When linguists became able to examine critically and scientifically a large number of languages of widely different patterns, their base of reference was expanded; they experienced an interruption of phenomena hitherto held universal, and a whole new order of significances came into their ken. It was found that the background linguistic system (in other words, the grammar) of each language is not merely a reproducing instrument for voicing ideas but rather itself the shaper of ideas, the program and guide for the individual's mental activity, for his analysis of impressions, for his synthesis of his mental stock in trade.
>
> We dissect nature along lines laid down by our native languages. The categories and types that we isolate from the world of phenomena we do not find there because they stare every observer in the face; on the contrary, the world is presented in a

kaleidoscopic flux of impressions which has to be organized by our minds—and this means largely by the linguistic systems in our minds. We cut nature up, organize it into concepts, and ascribe significances as we do, largely because we are parties to an agreement to organize it in this way.

(Whorf, *Language, Thought and Reality*, pp. 212–14)

Virtually all linguists reject the strong version of the theory, namely that language absolutely determines thought, but a weak version of the theory is widely accepted, namely the idea that language can influence the way we see things. Arguments against the strong version of linguistic determinism are not hard to find. Although the words of one language do not always correspond to those of another, we can always translate a word into another language, even if we have to use a phrase or two to do it. In fact we can do this in defining or paraphrasing within a particular language. Another objection can be found by considering the origin of language in the human race. If language completely determined thought, how could language ever have begun?

Most of Whorf's ideas stem from his work on Hopi, a language of Arizona. He was impressed by some of the semantic differences between Hopi and European languages. For instance, he pointed out the borderline between noun and verb can vary from one language to another and he noted that the equivalents of the English nouns *lightning, wave, flame, meteor, puff of smoke,* and *pulsation* are all verbs in Hopi. These words all refer to events of short duration. He also claimed Hopi was 'timeless' and expressed aspect but not tense. The term **aspect** comes up in the next chapter. It refers to making a distinction such as between whether an action or process has been completed or not.

It is probably fair to say that sixty years on some of Whorf's observations about semantic differences between languages have become commonplace. We know, for instance, there are plenty of languages that express aspect but not tense. Some languages have the same word for 'bark' (of a tree) and 'skin' (of an animal) and we can see how the two entities are similar in that they are both outer coverings, but we cannot argue that a speaker of a language with the same word for both fails to see the difference. The same applies with languages that have the same word for 'arm' or 'front paw of an animal' on the one hand and 'wing of a bird' on the other. We can see that the wing and forelimb are homologous, but one would imagine that speakers can tell them apart.

Our perception may not be constrained by language, but it is plausible to suggest that our perception is influenced by the categories of our language. Consider how our perception can be coloured by the connotations of alternative labels. It is commonplace in linguistics to note that one person's *terrorist* is another person's *freedom fighter*. Consider too the effect of a particular classification. In Melbourne, as in most cities, there are posh suburbs, middle class suburbs, and working class suburbs. The distribution of these types is not random, the better suburbs mainly lie to the east and the not-so-good to the west, but that is just a rough generalization. However, in the media they will find reports headed like the following:

> Rapist found. Police arrest man from western suburbs.
> Toxic fume scare. Residents in western suburbs evacuated.
> New crime figures. Western suburbs top the list.

The regular use of the term 'western suburbs' in the media creates a well-defined category that is not well-defined on the ground, and its use in contexts like those quoted creates a negative category. It is plausible to suggest that this will influence people's thinking. In the first two examples the report could have been more specific. Presumably the rapist came from a particular suburb, and the toxic fumes were certainly released into the atmosphere of a certain suburb.

Sexist language

It is difficult for a woman to define her feelings in a language which is chiefly made by men to express theirs.
                                                                    Thomas Hardy

In the wake of the rise of feminism it has become commonplace to point out there is a bias against females built into English and many other languages. In English the pronoun *he* contrasts with *she*, but up till a few decades or so ago we would write sentences such as *If a student has to go to the toilet during an exam, he must be accompanied by an invigilator*, where *he* was used to cover both sexes. In this particular example, people might have realized this use of *he* was a bit odd, since by convention females have to go to a female toilet and they would have to have been accompanied by a female invigilator. However, in many contexts there was nothing to highlight the oddity, and generations of English speakers and writers were happy to use the 'generic *he*'. Some examples occur in the quotations at the heads of chapters in this book.

The word *man* or *Man* was used to cover both sexes. In discussions of the evolution of humans we find references to Early Man, Cro-Magnon Man and cave man, and I think it is fair to say that the image that comes to mind is of a male. Cartoons about cave men depicted males, and females only figured in scenes where they were being hit over the head with a club by cave males. Nowadays discussions of the development of our race use the term *humans*, though the term *cave man* lives on, and in an increasingly vegetarian age we talk about the *cave man diet*. One could make out a case for saying that the use of the generic 'he' and the generic 'man' not only reflected culture, but influenced our perception and perpetuated a notion that males were normal, unmarked humans and females a special marked category.

English makes a sex distinction in the titles of various occupations and the term for the female is the marked one: *actor/actress, usher/usherette,* and *waiter/waitress* (though *widow* (female) and *widower* (male) shows the male as marked). Over the last few decades it has become majority usage to use the basic term for females as well as males. Some names of occupations contained the generic 'man', e.g. *policeman, fireman,* which was presumably appropriate enough when all personnel in these services were male, but as females began to be employed terms such as *police officer* and *firefighter* were introduced. Some terms such as *doctor, lawyer,* and *engineer* had never acquired a feminine form, but when females began to appear in these professions, they were often referred to as a 'lady doctor' or 'woman lawyer'. This raised objections in that it continued the notion of markedness. However, two female doctors in my suburb advertise themselves as 'lady doctors', presumably recognizing that many females prefer to be treated by a female doctor, particularly for an intimate medical problem.

In linguistics it was pointed out that where sentences were made up to illustrate a grammatical point the subject was almost always a male and the object quite often a female. This was part of a larger stereotyping found in the media. In both fiction and educational literature boys were depicted as active and enterprising while girls just tagged along.

Arbitrary relationship between form and meaning

As noted in chapter one, it is obvious that since words are made up of strings of sounds, there is not likely to be any connection between sound and meaning. This is a commonplace observation and it is usually illustrated by pointing out that different languages have different words for the same referent, as we did in chapter one. For instance, English *horse* is *Pferd* in German, *cheval* in French, mǎ in Mandarin Chinese, and so on. However, it is also commonplace to note there are some connections between sound and sense. First of all, there are **onomatopoeic** words, words that seem to echo the sense such as *gong* and *twang*. Then there are groups of words that exhibit what is called **sound symbolism**. These groups have in common an initial consonant or consonant cluster or a particular rhyme that corresponds to a particular meaning. Consider the following group:

hump, lump, mumps, plump, rump, stump

These all have a rhyme -*ump* and they all refer to a rounded, or at least non-pointy, protuberance. Now consider what *bump* means. It can refer to contact involving something weighty whether it be hips, bottoms, or shoulders, or a slow-moving vehicle or vessel, but not the contact of a point with a surface, such as a pencil tapping a window pane. The *crump* of an exploding shell fits in here, as does *thump*. You might also consider *rumble*, and possibly *mumble* and *tumble*, though admittedly this is -*umble* rather than -*ump*. One has to allow that there can be words with -*ump* that do not fit the correlation. *Trump* is an example. However, there are enough examples to suggest there is a connection between sound and meaning in one set of words. You might also note that *Humpty-Dumpty* was no stick insect, and *Forrest Gump* wasn't too sharp.

Other onsets and rhymes that have been claimed to play a part in sound symbolism include the following:

fl: *flame, flare, flash, flicker*
gl: *glare, gleam, glimmer, glint, glisten, glitter, gloss, glow*
-ash: *bash, clash, crash, dash, gnash, mash, smash, dash*

The -*ash* group has been augmented by blending. *Bash* is thought to be a blend of *bang* and *smash*, *clash* is a blend of *clap* and *dash*, *smash* is probably a blend of *smack* and *mash* and *crash* is a blend of *craze* and *mash*.

Some correlations between initial consonants or rhyme and meaning are simply etymological, that is, the same etymon or root is involved. It is fairly obvious that *two*, *twice*, and *twin* share the same root (though it would not be obvious if we spelt *two* phonetically), but the same root appears in *twig*, *twist*, and probably *twill*. It may also be present in *twitch* and *tweak*, which come from Old English *twician* 'to pluck', and plucking involves two things, namely the thumb and the forefinger.

There have been claims that the vowel we find in words like *beet* or the one in words like *bit* is associated with smallness as in *little*, *itsy-bitsy*, and *teeny-weeny*. Obviously *big* and *small* do not fit the pattern, but there may be some substance to the claim. The word *tiny* was once pronounced 'teeny' and the present pronunciation reflects a general change in English whereby all ex-amples of the 'ee' vowel came to be pronounced with the vowel of words like *bite*, and it is significant that we retain or recreate a form with the 'ee' vowel as an emphatic form, one that we use to stress the littleness. The vowels of words like *bit* and *beet* have a prominent high-frequency component in their acoustic spectrum, and the vowel of a word like *boot* has a spectrum where lower frequency components are prominent. This is illustrated on pages 262 to 264 It is no coincidence that the high-frequency speaker on your hi-fi is a *tweeter* and the bass speaker a *woofer*.

Two correlations between sound and sense recur in a number of languages. One is the association of reduplication with names of flying creatures mentioned at the end of the previous chapter. The other is the association of children's early syllables and words for close kin. When children begin making speech sounds, they start with syllables such as *ba, bi, pa, pi, ma, mi, da, di, ta, ti, na, ni*. These are often uttered in pairs such as *mama, dada*, etc. These syllables figure prominently in words for close kin across languages. There is a correlation between word forms such as *mama* and *nana* and meanings such as *mother, father, uncle, aunt, grandmother, grandfather*, and also *breast* or *milk*. However, there is no alignment of a particular syllable with a particular meaning. In English *mama* and *mummy* are 'mother', but *mamma* is 'breast' in Latin, and *mama* is 'father' in the Western Desert Language of Australia; *mam* is 'father' in the Mayan languages of Central America and mê: is 'mother' in Thai. Similarly *dada* or *daddy* is 'father' in English, but *dada* is 'breast' in Indonesian, and *deda* is 'mother' in Georgian. It seems that people attach likely meanings to children's early syllables and these likely meanings are mostly kin terms.

Dictionaries

Dictionaries are like watches; the worst is better than none, and the best cannot be expected to go quite true. **Samuel Johnson**

The principal source of information on word meanings is, of course, the dictionary, so it is appropriate to include some background on the genesis of these useful reference works.

In 1604, a year after Queen Elizabeth I had died and James VI of Scotland had become James I of England, the first English-English dictionary appeared. It was Robert Cawdrey's *A Table Alphabeticall* and it contained 2,521 entries. There had been bilingual word lists going back to the Old English period (fifth century to 1100), but this was the first dictionary devoted to explaining English words in English. Cawdrey claimed on the title page it was 'for the benefit and helpe of Ladies, Gentlewomen, or any other unskilfull persons'. Many of the definitions are quite short, more like what we would expect from a dictionary of synonyms. Here are some examples given in the original spelling, which will doubtless cause my *Spell Check* some considerable consternation.

agglutinate	to ioyne together
assistance	helpe

combustible   easily burnt
deambulation a walking abroade
debonnayre   gentle, curteous, affable
decrepite   very old

Cawdrey's dictionary was soon followed by others. Successive dictionaries plagiarized the work of their predecessors (as they still do!) and grew in size. Nathaniel Bailey's 1730 *Dictionarium Britannicum: a more compleat universal etymological English dictionary than any extant* contained 48,000 entries, and, as the subtitle indicates, it included **etymology** (historical roots or sources). It remained the standard reference until Dr Samuel Johnson's *A Dictionary of the English language* of 1755. This was a two-volumed work of 40,000 entries, but two and a half times larger than Bailey's. It is generally regarded as much superior to earlier dictionaries, but it is fashionable to cite some of Dr Johnson's rather idiosyncratic definitions:

excise: a hateful tax levied upon commodities.
opera: an exotic and irrational entertainment.
oats: a grain, which in England is generally given to horses,
    but in Scotland supports the people.
lexicographer: a writer of dictionaries, a harmless drudge.

In the United States, Noah Webster produced a series of dictionaries culminating in 1828 with his two-volume *American Dictionary of the English language* with 70,000 entries. On his death George and Charles Merriam acquired the rights and produced a series of 'Webster's' dictionaries. The Webster's *Third New International Dictionary* (1961) has 450,000 entries.

The most notable dictionary of all is the *Oxford English Dictionary* (OED). It has its roots in a meeting of the Philological Society in 1857 at which it was decided to collect words not in existing dictionaries with a view to publish a supplement. It soon became evident that a completely new dictionary was called for and in 1858 they resolved to put together a *New English Dictionary on Historical Principles*. They aimed to include all words recorded in literature since the earliest records (except for words that were obsolete by 1150), and to illustrate the spellings, pronunciations, meanings, and usages with quotations. This was an immense undertaking and it required an enormous amount of reading and note-taking. An appeal to the public was successful and volunteers from all over the English-speaking world sent in slips of paper with examples of distinctive usage. There were 800 contributors in all, and the most prolific was Dr W. C. Minor, a murderer, who was incarcerated in an asylum for the criminally insane. The first volume appeared in 1884 and the last in 1928. The dictionary was reissued in 1933 with a supplement under the title *The Oxford English Dictionary* (OED). Further supplementary volumes were published in 1972, 1976, 1982, and 1986. A second edition of twenty volumes was issued in 1989. New material was published in the *Oxford English Dictionary Additions Series,* two small volumes in 1993, and a third in 1997, making a total of twenty-three volumes. The OED is now available in CD-Rom and online, though the cost of accessing OED online effectively limits access to institutions. A third edition is planned, but it remains to be seen whether this will appear in print form.

The main significance of the OED is that it illustrates meanings with quotations at a rate of one per century. It is the main source for the history of English words and most of the material on the history of English words in reference books and text books comes directly or indirectly from the OED.

The OED in particular, and dictionaries in general, aim to be descriptive, but they are usually taken to be authoritative. This is natural enough. One consults the dictionary to find out what is generally taken to be the meaning and pronunciation.

Sources and further reading

There are numerous books on semantics. You could try Cruse, *Meaning in Language,* Hurford and Heasley, *Semantics,* or Lyons, *Linguistic Semantics.* Aitchison's *Words in the Mind* summarizes various psycholinguistic experiments aimed at exploring the mental lexicon. See also chapters thirteen and fourteen of this book.

Whorf's ideas are conveniently available in *Language, Thought and Reality: Selected Writings of Benjamin Lee Whorf.* The circumstances surrounding Dr Minor's contribution to the OED are related in Simon Winchester's *The Surgeon of Crowthorne.*

Problems

1 Do the following groups represent examples of homophony or polysemy?

   (a) *ear* (of corn), *ear* (anatomical)
   (b) salesman's *pitch,* baseballer's *pitch* (the throw), rugby *pitch* (the field), *pitch* (sound), *pitch* (tar)
   (c) *lighter* (in weight), *lighter* (flat-bottomed boat)
   (d) (plum) *jam,* (be in a) *jam* (predicament), to *jam* (between)
   (e) *pickle* (vegetable preserved in vinegar), be in a *pickle* (predicament)

2 The following groups of words have similar meanings, close enough to be listed together in a thesaurus. How do they differ?

(a) *tired, weary, exhausted, spent* (plus various colloquial terms)
(b) *stench, smell, aroma, scent, bouquet, nose* (referring to wine)
(c) *miser, scrooge*
(d) *limp, flaccid*
(e) *abandoned, forsaken, deserted* (adjective)
(f) *soaked, drenched, steeped* (adjective)
(g) *glance, peek* (verb and noun)

3 Some of the phrases that are part of everyday usage owe their currency to the plays of Shakespeare. *Neither rhyme nor reason* can be found in *The Comedy of Errors* and *dead as a doornail* in *Henry VI*. Sometimes the original is distorted. *Comparisons are odious* is derived from *Comparisons are odorous* (*Much Ado about Nothing*) and *All that glitters is not gold* deviates from the original *All that glisters is not gold* (*The Merchant of Venice*). The following phrases are also from Shakespeare's plays. It is not certain that he was the first to use them, but their appearance in his much-read plays probably helped make them popular. See if you can identify the sources. Try the Web.

Love is blind.
We have seen better days.
Give the devil his due.
At one fell swoop
The world's my oyster.
The game is up.

4 Pick out the semantic problems in the following:

(a) 'If we bring a little joy into your humdrum lives, it makes us feel our work ain't been in vain for nothin'.'   **Jean Hagen, *Singin' in the Rain***

(b) 'Cheaper prices.'   **Supermarket ad**

(c) 'The statues will stand there in perpetuity for one year exactly.'

Sports commentator

(d) 'We are all unanimous.'   **Politician**

(e) 'The future is still to come.'   **Politician**

5 Personal names have connotations, some evoke a certain era or age group, others a certain cultural background. How do you feel about the following names?

Abraham, Alice, Beatrice, Brian, Britney, Buffy, Clarissa, Debbie, Helene, Homer, Horace, Maria, Marilyn, Mildred, Solomon, Virgil, Wayne

PART II

Syntax and discourse

5. The simple sentence

Who climbs the grammar tree, distinctly knows,
Where noun and verb and participle grows.   **Dryden**

Ideas of grammar

A mental lexicon is not much use on its own if we want to talk about our experiences. We need **syntax**, a set of rules to combine words into phrases and sentences. Syntax is also called 'grammar', but grammar is used in a number of different senses. It can refer to a comprehensive description of a language. If I buy a Spanish grammar I would expect some information about pronunciation and word building as well as syntax. In its most common use in the community at large 'grammar' refers to syntax and inflection, particularly to a set of rules for guidance as to what is 'right' and what is 'wrong'. People consulting a grammar of English would expect to find something about double negatives, for instance. They would expect to be told that one should not say *I never did nothing* if one means *I didn't do anything*. The point comes up for consideration because some speakers do say, *I never did nothing* or even *I never done nothing*. A professional, scientific description of a language would aim at describing whatever people say, so it would include the double negative and note that it was non-standard and considered incorrect. But the notion of correct grammar is concerned with only a score or so of constructions on which there is divided usage, whereas a truly descriptive grammar would be comprehensive and would cover hundreds of points of grammar that no one bothers to think about. It would mention that *this* and *that* have plural forms used with plural nouns as in *these books* and *those pens*. As far as I know, nobody deviates from the standard usage on this point, so it would not come up for mention in a grammar concerned only with what is 'correct'.

The remainder of this chapter is devoted to the simple sentence. The following chapter deals with compound and complex sentences, and the last section of that chapter reviews the notion of 'correct grammar'.

Predicate and argument

In any language we are going to want to make statements, ask questions, and tell people to do things. Let's just consider statements for the moment. One can safely assume that in any language one can talk about a creature sleeping, coughing, yawning, urinating, and so on, and one can talk about a creature seeing, liking, or biting some thing or some creature. Let us think of notions such as sleeping, yawning, seeing, and biting independently of any particular language. Logicians make a distinction between **predicates** and **arguments**. A predicate expresses a property of an entity or a relationship between entities. These entities are the arguments of the predicate. Notions such as SLEEP, YAWN, COUGH, URINATE, GO, and DIE are one-place predicates, that is, predicates that take just one argument. I will put (all) predicates in small capitals to indicate that I am referring to these notions independently of any language. Thus YAWN implies a creature that yawns, COUGH implies a creature that coughs, and so on. Now consider predicates such as SEE, LIKE, HIT, BITE, CUT, and KIDNAP. They are two-place predicates since they imply two arguments. SEE, for instance, implies a seer and a seen entity, HIT implies a hitter and an object or creature that is hit, and so on. Lastly consider GIVE. It is a three-place predicate since it implies a giver, a gift, and a recipient.

1-place predicates: SLEEP, YAWN, COUGH, URINATE, GO, DIE
2-place predicates: SEE, LIKE, HIT, BITE, CUT, KIDNAP
3-place predicates: GIVE

The predicates listed above are all realized as verbs in English, but predicates can be prepositions, adjectives, or nouns. A preposition like *with* realizes a two-place predicate (*Sally is with Henry*), an adjective like *proud* can be a one-place predicate (*Lucy is proud*) or a two-place predicate (*Lucy is proud of her achievements*), and similarly with a noun like *father* (*George is a father, George is the father of Harry*).

The essential feature of a sentence is that it contains a predication.

Stephen Sondheim writes numerous songs.

In this sentence the verb *write* expresses a predicate. In chapter two the term 'predicate' was introduced in the context of saying that a sentence can be divided into subject and predicate. This is the way 'predicate' is used in traditional grammar, but note that the predicate of traditional grammar is wider than 'predicate' as opposed to 'argument' and takes in all of the sentence except the subject. Some authorities describe the predicate (as opposed to argument) as head of the predicate (as opposed to subject).

In English, and in some other languages, a valid sentence must not only contain a predicate, it must also contain a finite verb. The term 'finite' is explained on page 75 below, but suffice to say for the moment that forms like *write(s)* and *wrote* are finite but not *writing* or *written*. One can't substitute *writing* or *written* in the sentence above, at least not without adding a finite auxiliary verb form such as *is* or *has* (explained on p. 74).

> *Stephen Sondheim is writing numerous songs.*
> *Stephen Sondheim has written numerous songs.*

Where the predication is other than a verb then a form of the verb *to be* must be used to meet the finite verb requirement. Here are some examples from the Michael Douglas character (Gordon Gekko) in *Wall Street*. They illustrate in turn a noun phrase, an adjective phrase, and a prepositional phrase.

> *'The most valuable commodity I know of is information.'*
> *'Greed is good.'*
> *'Lunch is for wimps.'*

The verb *to be*, when used to link the subject and predicate is referred to as the **copula**.

English does allow noun phrases, adjective phrases, and prepositional phrases to be used as predicates without a verb where they are not the main predicate and relate to a direct object.

> *The Orioles made her (to be) captain.*
> *They considered him (to be) mad.*
> *They elected her (to be) party whip.*

In many languages there is no finite verb requirement and nouns, adjectives, or prepositional (or postpositional) phrases can be used as a predicate on their own. The following examples are from Indonesian.

> *Ali guru.* 'Ali is a teacher.'
> *Kapal itu besar.* 'That ship is big.' (lit. 'ship that big')
> *Mereka di Jakarta.* 'They are in Jakarta.' (lit. 'they in Jakarta')

Phrase Structure

Some of the basic ideas of syntax were introduced in chapter two, namely that words cohere into phrases and that the ordering of phrases is significant. Here are two sentences illustrating the significance of order in English.

The snakes bit the dogs.
Hospitals give nurses patients.

In the first example, we interpret *the snakes* as the agents who do the biting and *the dogs* as the victims because of the word order. Similarly in the second example we take *nurses* to be the recipient on the basis of the word order (*Hospitals give patients to nurses*). If the sentence had been *Hospitals give patients nurses*, we would have taken the patients to be the recipients (*Hospitals give nurses to patients*).

Order also plays a part in English in cases where one noun modifies another. We interpret the sequence *garden gnome* as a kind of gnome found in gardens. We take *gnome* to be the **head** and *garden* to be the **modifier**, i.e. we take the first word to modify the second. Suppose we encountered the sequence *gnome garden*. We would interpret this to mean a kind of garden, probably one with a big gnome population.

A sentence is not just a string of words. It consists of a **hierarchy** of phrases, each one being a **constituent** or part of a larger one. Consider the following sentence:

The young man picked the best bloom.

The noun *man* is modified or qualified by the adjective *young* and the determiner *the*. As we saw in chapter two, a sequence like *the young man* is a **noun phrase** (**NP**), in other words, a group of words consisting of a noun as head and any other modifying words. The noun *bloom* is modified by the adjective *best* and the determiner *the*. It is another noun phrase. In everyday parlance the word 'phrase' implies more than one word, but in describing language we use the term 'phrase' even where there is just a single word (the head word) and no modifier, so if we had had just *John* instead of *the young man*, we would still have talked about a 'noun phrase'.

In introducing pronouns in chapter two it was mentioned that they are so-named because they were traditionally thought of as standing for nouns. In fact they are heads of noun phrases. The term 'noun phrase' is thus a misnomer. Pronouns tend to occur on their own. They cannot be modified by a determiner and only rarely by adjectives (*Silly me!*), though they can take various types of following modifier including prepositional phrases (*Hey! You in the armchair; We in the media have to be careful about what we say*). Nouns and pronouns belong to the broader class of **nominals** and a better term would have been 'nominal phrase'.

Now consider the expanded version of our example:

The young man picked the best bloom from the very delicate orchid.

The sequence *from the very delicate orchid* is a **prepositional phrase**. The prepositional phrase consists of a noun phrase and a preposition. One can demonstrate that the sequence *from the very delicate orchid* is a coherent group of words by moving it as in:

From the very delicate orchid the young man picked the best bloom.

The word *very* is an intensifying adverb and it modifies *delicate* to form an **adjective phrase** within the noun phrase within the prepositional phrase. This phrase-within-a-phrase structure is shown by bracketing below:

[The young man] picked the best bloom [from [the [very delicate] orchid]].

We could add *very carefully* to this sentence. Since *carefully* is an adverb and *very* is an intensifying adverb modifying it, *very carefully* would be an **adverb phrase**.

In general the break-up of a sentence into phrases is straightforward and when we give slow dictation we normally put pauses at the breaks between phrases without needing any instruction as to where these phrase breaks should go. One phrase that is not so obvious is the **verb phrase**. In the example above *picked the best bloom from the very delicate orchid* is a verb phrase. One piece of evidence that the verb phrase exists can be found in sentences such as the following answers to a question:

What did the young man do?
Picked the best bloom from the very delicate orchid, he did.
Picked the best bloom from the very delicate orchid. That's what he did.

In the first reply, which illustrates a construction you might hear in the north of England, the verb phrase is moved to the front of the sentence. That's one bit of evidence that it is a phrase. The second reply, which is likely to seem a more familiar way of doing things to most readers, illustrates the same point. The verb phrase in this case is uttered as a phrase on its own and the pronoun *that* refers to the phrase.

At this point we might show the complete break-up of the sentence into phrases. One convenient way of doing this is the labelled tree diagram as in Figure 5.1.

Two different grammatical structures may appear as the same sequence of words. For example the sequence *French history teacher* could refer to a teacher of French history or a history teacher of Gallic extraction. For the

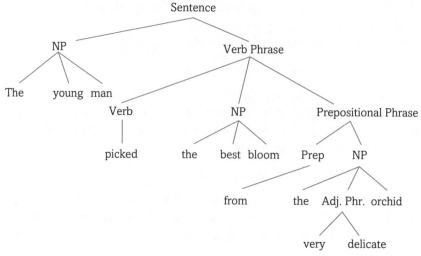

Figure 5.1 Phrase structure.

first meaning the structure would be [[*French history*] *teacher*] with the adjective *French* modifying *history* and the noun phrase *French history* modifying *teacher,* and for the second meaning the structure would be [*French* [*history teacher*]] with the adjective *French* modifying the compound noun *history teacher.*

The same ambiguity can arise with sentences. When I turned on the radio recently, the first sentence I heard was *We discussed the snakes in the office.* I pricked up my ears. Snakes in the office! This sounded alarming. But perhaps it was just a discussion of snakes that was taking place in the office. This sequence of words is ambiguous. You can take *in the office* to be a prepositional phrase that is within the noun phrase: *the snakes in the office* (Alarm! Call the snake handlers!). Or we can take *in the office* to be a prepositional phrase within the verb phrase. (Relax. Everything's ok.) The two possibilities are illustrated in Figures 5.2a and 5.2b respectively,

One way of showing there is a difference in phrasing is to try moving putative phrases. For the first interpretation, we can move the noun phrase *the snakes in the office* to the front of the sentence: *The snakes in the office we discussed.* (*The ones in the garden we didn't worry about.*) For the second interpretation, we can move the noun phrase *the snakes* to the front of the sentence: *The snakes we discussed in the office.* (*The crocodiles we discussed in the boardroom.*) Or we can move the prepositional phrase *in the office: In the office we discussed the snakes.* (*In the boardroom we discussed the crocodiles.*) For the second interpretation we cannot move the whole post-verbal part of the sentence to the front.

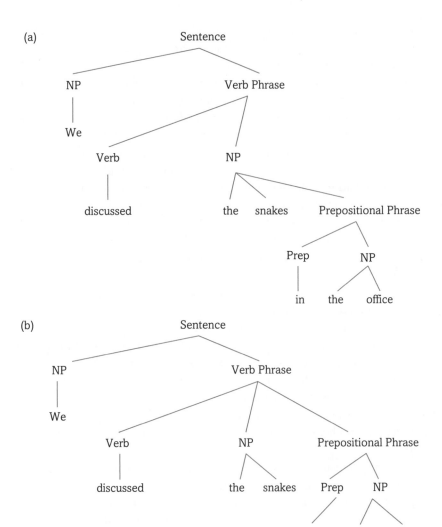

Figure 5.2 We discussed the snakes in the office.

Grammatical relations

Phrase structure, as described in the previous section, is not sufficient to capture the way a sentence is constructed and understood. Consider the following pair of sentences:

Sharapova defeated several opponents.
Sharapova grunted several times.

These two sentences both have a noun phrase following the verb, but the noun phrase *several opponents* in the first sentence is essential. It cannot be omitted. It is implied by the verb. The notion of 'defeat' implies a victor and a vanquished, a winner and a loser. In semantic terms the predicate DEFEAT takes two arguments. On the other hand, the noun phrase *several times* in the second sentence is optional. It can be omitted. It could even be added to the first sentence.

Constituents that express arguments (mostly noun phrases) are **complements**. Constituents that don't express arguments are **adjuncts**. They are mostly prepositional phrases or adverbs, though they can be noun phrases as with *several times* in the second example above. Adjuncts normally supply information about place (*at the airport, in San Francisco*), time (*in the morning, every year*), manner (*with care, thoughtfully*), etc. A general rule that applies across languages is that complements are closer to the verb than adjuncts.

The distinction between complement and adjunct can apply within noun phrases. Consider the phrase *a student of linguistics with a ring in his nose* (an example that does not seem so strange nowadays as it would have a decade or so ago). The verb *study* and the related noun *student* imply a subject of study. The phrase *of linguistics* is a complement since it specifies what the student studies. The phrase *with a ring in his nose* is an adjunct just giving some additional information not implied by *study* or *student*. The general principle that complements come closer to their head than adjuncts applies here too. One can't say *a student with a ring in his nose of linguistics*.

The complement that normally precedes the verb is the **subject**. The complement that normally follows the verb is the **direct object**. Subject and object are **grammatical relations**. The notion of subject was introduced in chapter two where it was mentioned that the subject normally expresses what is to be talked about, what is the subject of the predication. Most two-place verbs are action verbs like *to cut, to mince, to rub*, and *to scratch*. These verbs have agent and patient arguments, and the agent is encoded as the subject and the patient as the object. If all verbs were like this, we could simply talk of agent and patient, but a verb of emotion like *to love* does not have an agent and a patient, yet the experiencer of the emotion is treated in the same way as an agent. Verbs of sensory perception such as *to see* and *to hear* do not have agents, but the perceiver is treated like an agent. It is for this reason that we need a term that is wider than agent, experiencer, and perceiver, we need a term for the relation borne by the noun phrase preceding the verb and that is **subject**. For analogous reasons we need a term wider than patient for the noun phrase that follows a transitive verb, and we call this grammatical relation **direct object**, or sometimes just **object**.

In the following sections, we shall see that in many languages the subject has distinctive morphological marking. In some languages it controls agreement on the verb. In the next chapter we shall see that the subject figures prominently in various syntactic rules in complex sentences. The object does not figure so prominently in the grammar of languages, but in many it has distinctive inflection, and in some it determines marking on the verb.

In a sentence such as *Henrietta gave all her money to her sister* the recipient is usually referred to as the **indirect object**. This applies to English and to analogous complements in various other languages. However, in traditional descriptions of English the term 'indirect object' is also applied to the recipient in the alternative construction *Henrietta gave her sister all her money*, even though the recipient has very different grammatical characteristics in this construction. Where the term 'indirect object' is used in this text it refers to a recipient marked differently from a direct object, for example by a preposition or by the dative case (see next section).

Not every complement noun phrase that follows the verb is a direct object. Consider the following:

Johnson became the president in 1963.
Frieda felt a fool.

These verbs look like normal transitive verbs, but they are significantly different. Compare *Frieda felt a fool* with *Frieda patted a jester*. What follows the verb is described as a **predicative complement**, not a direct object. Note that these sentences can be paraphrased as follows:

Johnson came to be the president in 1963.
Frieda felt herself to be a fool.

Inflection

Inflection on nominals

Case
In a large number of languages nouns and pronouns are inflected to show the relation they bear in a particular sentence. This is **case** inflection. In Turkish, for instance, nouns have six cases as shown in Table 5.1. The undotted *ı* in some of these examples is like the [u] sound of an English word such as *pool*, but made with the lips spread instead of rounded.

The **nominative** is used for the subject of a sentence and the **accusative** is used for the object (providing it refers to a specific entity). In Turkish the

Table 5.1. Turkish cases

nominative	adam	the man (subject)
accusative	adamı	the man (object)
genitive	adamın	of the man, the man's
dative	adama	to or for the man
locative	adamda	with the man, on the man
ablative	adamdan	from the man

word order is subject–object–verb, so there are two ways of distinguishing the subject from the object, namely word order and case.

Adam   adres-imiz-i   buldu.
man   address-our-ACC   found
'The man found our address.'

The **genitive** corresponds with English -'s as in 'the man's dog' or *of* as in 'the possessions of the king'. The **dative** expresses 'to' and 'for (the benefit of)' and the **ablative** 'from'. The **locative** expresses location in general and corresponds to a number of prepositions in English including 'on', 'in', and 'at'.

Case systems tend to be small and on their own they are insufficient to be able to express all the relationships a noun phrase might hold. Case systems are usually supplemented by prepositions or postpositions. Turkish has postpositions including some that govern the ablative such as *dolayı* 'because of': *toplantı-dan dolayı* 'because of the meeting', and *sonra* 'after' : *tiyatro-dan sonra* 'after the theatre'. The term **govern** means 'to determine'. A head may determine the presence of a **dependent** and require that it be in a particular form.

Most of the languages of Europe, including English, are related and belong to the Indo-European family (see also chapter twelve, Figure 12.1). This family had case marking, though it has been almost entirely lost in English. Latin, the language of Ancient Rome, the language from which modern Romance languages such as Italian, French, and Spanish have descended, is an Indo-European language and it has six cases. In the following example the nominative is unmarked and the accusative is marked by -*m*.

Livia Flavia-m monuit.   'Livia warned Flavia.'
Flavia Livia-m monuit.   'Flavia warned Livia.'

Word order in Latin tended to be subject–object–verb, but it was fairly flexible, so the first sentence could have been *Livia monuit Flaviam*, or *Flaviam monuit Livia* and so on, and the second sentence could have had similar variations. The other cases in Latin were genitive, dative, and ablative plus a vocative used in addressing someone. The vocative of *Brutus* was *Brute*, as in Shakespeare's *Julius Caesar* where Caesar says, *Et tu, Brute*, 'Even you, Brutus', as he sees his friend among those stabbing him to death.

In Old English (fifth century to 1100) there were four cases: nominative, accusative, genitive, and dative. Only one survives in Modern English with nouns and that is the genitive, which is reflected in -'s (the apostrophe s). However, -'s in English is not a typical suffix; it is unusual in that it can be put at the end of a phrase rather than with the word marking the possessor. In *the Sheriff of Nottingham's cousin*, the suffix goes on *Nottingham*, but it is the sheriff who has the cousin, not the town.

In English there is a two-way case distinction in personal pronouns (see Table 5.2). There is a **nominative** form used for the subject of a sentence (*I go*) and an **accusative** used for the object of a verb (*Bill saw me*) or object of a preposition (*Bill sat with me*). The case inflection with pronouns is mostly in the form of completely different roots as with *I* versus *me*, though one can see a suffix -*m* in *he /him* and *they/them*.

Table 5.2. English personal pronouns

number	person	nominative	accusative
singular	1st person (speaker)	*I*	*me*
	2nd person (addressee)	*you*	*you*
	3rd person	*he*	*him*
	3rd person	*she*	*her*
	3rd person	*it*	*it*
plural	1st person (speaker plus)	*we*	*us*
	2nd person (addressees)	*you*	*you*
	3rd person	*they*	*them*

While many languages have an accusative case serving to mark the object of a transitive verb, some languages distinguish subject and object by using an **ergative case** to mark the subject of a transitive verb, while the subject of an intransitive predicate and the object of a verb remain unmarked. The following example is from Greenlandic Eskimo where the ergative case marker is -*ip*.

Angut   autlarpuq
man   went.away
'The man went away.'

Angut-ip   iglu   takuvaa.
man-ERG   house   saw
'The man saw the house.'

Number
Many languages use inflection to mark singular-versus-plural number as English does. Some languages make a three-way distinction between **singular, dual** (two) and **plural**. This was a feature of Indo-European and the dual can be

found in Sanskrit and Ancient Greek. In Old English there were dual pronouns such as *wit* 'we two' as well as *we*, which referred to more than two people.

In most languages with marking for both case and number the number marking is usually closer to the root, with case marking forming an outer layer. In Turkish, for instance, *adam-lar-a* is 'for the men' where *-lar-* is the plural marker and *-a* the dative **case marker.**

Number marking in English plays a minimal part in the grammar. The marking appears only on nouns and pronouns, but the demonstrative *this* has a plural *these* and *that* has a plural *those*. In a phrase such as *these books* or *those desks* there is **agreement** in number. Many languages with number marking exhibit the marking on determiners, and often on adjectives, as well as nouns, and agreement serves to bind the noun phrase. In Old English determiners, and in some circumstances adjectives, agreed with their head nouns in number and case. The phrase 'after a few days' was *æfter feaw-um dag-um* and 'with my friends' was *mid min-um freond-um*. The prepositions *æfter* and *mid* governed the dative case, and the suffix *-um* in these examples is the dative plural, that is, a **fusion** of plural number and dative case in a **portmanteau morph.**

Gender

Some languages divide nouns into classes on the basis of broad semantic distinctions, though there are often assignments of nouns to classes the reasons for which remain obscure. Indo-European developed a distinction between masculine, feminine, and neuter classes, and these classes are generally known as **gender** classes. The noun 'gender' was borrowed from French in the Middle Ages (compare modern French *genre*) and is ultimately from Latin *genus* 'race, kind, sort'. Because of the prominence of the masculine/feminine distinction the word 'gender' came to refer to sex distinctions, not only with reference to language, but more generally (see also pp. 191–2). The masculine/feminine/ neuter distinction was found in Old English, but was lost in Middle English (1100–1500). A masculine/feminine distinction is retained in Italian. All nouns are either masculine or feminine, including inanimate and abstract nouns, so it is a matter of grammatical gender not natural gender. The term 'grammatical gender' means that the system is arbitrary and must be learned independently of sex. The term 'natural gender' means the distinction is based on sex. The distinction between the pronouns *he, she*, and *it* in English is based on natural gender (sex), except for a certain propensity for some speakers to refer to certain inanimates as 'she'. In Italian gender marking and number marking are **fused**, that is, there are portmanteau forms for number and gender, and there are three patterns of marking as shown in Table 5.3. Almost all nouns in *-a* are feminine (exceptions include *il dentista* 'the dentist' and *il fonema* 'the phoneme', which are masculine) and almost all nouns in *-o* are masculine (exceptions include *la mano* 'the hand', which is feminine).

Table 5.3. Number and gender marking in Italian

	singular	plural
feminine	-a	-e
masculine	-o	-i
either	-e	-i

Determiners and adjectives show gender agreement with the noun they modify, so although gender is not apparent in those nouns that follow the -e/-i pattern (last row in Table 5.3), it shows up in the determiner and in a large class of adjectives that takes the -a/-e marking for feminine and the -o/-i pattern for masculine.

il cappello rosso (masc)	'the red hat'
i cappelli rossi	'the red hats'
la màcchina rossa (fem)	'the red car'
le màcchine rosse	'the red cars'
il legume fresco (masc)	'the fresh vegetable'
i legumi freschi	'the fresh vegetables'
la chiave nuova (fem)	'the new key'
le chiavi nuove	'the new keys'

Inflection on verbs

Tense and aspect

Verbs are often inflected for categories such as **tense**, which refers to time. In English there is a two-way contrast between **present tense** forms, which are unmarked, and **past tense** forms, which are mostly spelt -*ed* and pronounced as [t] in words like *kissed* and *wrapped*, [d] as in *ebbed* and *rolled*, and [əd] in words like *patted* and *kidded* (see p. 157). However, there are many verbs with an irregular past tense form such as *see/saw, run/ran,* and *buy/bought* plus *go/went,* where a completely different root is used in the past tense. Some languages have three tenses: past, present, and future. English does not have a future tense. In English we usually indicate the future by using *shall, will,* or *be going to: Helen is going to see 'Memoirs of a Geisha' tomorrow.* In general parlance these forms are referred to as 'future tense', but linguists reserve the term 'tense' for the inflected forms.

Another category frequently marked on verbs is aspect. Examples appear below.

Person and number marking

A large number of languages, a majority in fact, mark the person (I, you, or he/she/it) and number (singular, plural, and sometimes dual) of the subject on the verb. Some languages also mark the person and number of the object. Marking the person and number of the subject on the verb is traditional in Indo-European languages, but English retains only a few vestiges such as the -*s* we find on verbs with third person singular subjects: *She runs* vs. *They run*. Marking for the person and number of the subject can be illustrated from Italian.

Table 5.4. Italian verb inflection

Io parlo	'I speak'	*Noi parliamo*	'We speak'
Tu parli	'You speak' (sg)	*Voi parlate*	'You speak' (pl)
Lùi, lei parla	'He, she speaks'	*Loro parlano*	'They speak'

An important difference between English and Italian (between English and a great majority of languages, in fact) is that in Italian one can omit the subject. One can simply say *parla* for 'he or she speaks'. One need use a pronoun only for emphasis. In English, on the other hand, one cannot just say *speaks* on its own.

At this point it might be worth introducing the notion of the auxiliary verb. If we think of words with meaning such as 'break', 'conclude', 'translate', 'demolish', and so on as verbs, we need to recognize that it is common for inflection for tense and for person and number to appear not on these words, but on what is generally called an **auxiliary verb**. In modern spoken Italian the past tense is expressed by a combination of an auxiliary verb and a lexical verb. Some examples are presented in Table 5.5.

Table 5.5. Italian auxiliaries

Io ho parlato	'I have spoken, I spoke'	*Io sono arrivato*	'I have arrived, I arrived'
Tu hai parlato	'You have spoken, you spoke'	*Tu sei arrivato*	'You have arrived, You arrived'
Lùi ha parlato	'He has spoken, he spoke'	*Lùi è arrivato*	'He has arrived, He arrived.'
Lei ha parlato	'She has spoken, she spoke'	*Lei è arrivata*	'She has arrived. She arrived.'

Some intransitive verbs and all transitive verbs form their past tense with the help of *ho, hai*, etc. These are inflected forms of the verb *avere* 'to have', but the verb does not have its lexical meaning here. It is performing a grammatical function, namely, facilitating the expression of the past tense. Some intransitive verbs use *sono, sei*, etc., to form the past tense. These are inflected forms of the verb *essere* 'to be'.

The person/number inflection on the verb is somewhat arbitrary in Indo-European languages, and indeed the origins of the inflections are obscure. However, in many parts of the world the person/number marking for the subject and object are transparently derived from free pronouns. This makes sense if you think of English sentences such as *She hit her* or *I like him*. The pronouns are next to the verb and they are unstressed and pronounced just like unstressed syllables of a polysyllabic verb. Swahili, a Bantu language of East Africa, provides a good example of agreement within the noun phrase and with the verb. In the following example notice the resemblance between *wao* 'they' and *wa-* the first prefix on the verb. Swahili has a number of **noun classes**. In the second example below you can see *wa* marked on each of the words in the subject noun phrase. Here *wa* is marking nouns of the human plural class. The form *vi*, which appears in both examples, marks the plural of a class of items, mainly utensils. It appears on the words that make up the object noun phrase and it represents the object on the verb. The subject and object noun phrases could be omitted and you would still have a complete sentence *wa-na-vi-nunua* 'They buy them' where *wa-* would be understood as referring to humans and *-vi-* as referring to any of a certain class, mainly utensils.

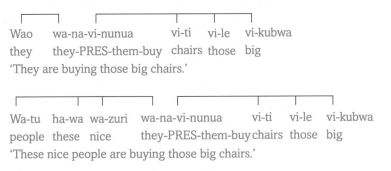

Wao   wa-na-vi-nunua   vi-ti   vi-le   vi-kubwa
they   they-PRES-them-buy   chairs those   big
'They are buying those big chairs.'

Wa-tu   ha-wa wa-zuri   wa-na-vi-nunua   vi-ti   vi-le   vi-kubwa
people these nice   they-PRES-them-buy chairs those   big
'These nice people are buying those big chairs.'

In the grammars of European languages the verb forms marked for person and number are called **finite** forms. These contrast with forms where there is no such marking. Forms like *parlato* and *arrivato* are non-finite, in particular they are **past participles** (sometimes 'perfect participles'). There are two other non-finite forms in Italian. The **present participle** can be used with the verb *stare* to indicate ongoing activity. The lexical meaning of *stare* is 'to stand', but here it has a grammatical function. It is an auxiliary verb.

Present participle: *Sto parlando.*   'I am speaking (at this moment).'

There is a third non-finite form and that is the **infinitive**. It can occur as a complement to various verbs including *volere* 'to wish, to want':

Infinitive: *Voglio parlare.*   'I want to speak.'

These non-finite forms have parallels in most of the languages of Europe. English has finite verb forms and non-finite verb forms, but for most verbs the only evidence of finiteness is the *s*-ending in the third person singular present tense (*she sleeps, they sleep*). If one goes back to Old English one finds separate forms for first, second, and third person singular plus a plural form (illustrated in Table 12.5). The verb 'to be' has some more inflection for the person and number of the subject than other verbs: *I am, you/we/they are, he/she/it is; I/he/she/it was, you/we/they were.*

Like Italian, English has three non-finite forms, the present participle, the past participle, and the infinitive.

Present participle:	I am <u>sleeping</u>. (Not something you say often, at least not truthfully!)
Past participle:	I have <u>slept</u>.
Infinitive:	I hope to <u>sleep</u> tonight.

However, the infinitive is different from the basic form of the verb only with the verb 'to be': *I hope to <u>be</u> asleep by midnight.* The reason for recognizing an infinitive in English is syntactic. Like the participles it can occur without a subject of its own. In the examples above it takes its subject from the finite verb. And like the participles it cannot form a sentence. You can't simply say **Jane running down the street, *The town cut off by floodwaters,* or **She to earn money.* The non-finite forms need to be accompanied by a finite auxiliary.

The infinitive in English is normally preceded by *to* and it is common to quote verbs with this *to*, a useful convention when one considers that in English many words can be used as both noun and verb.

There is one minor class of sentences in English where a finite verb is not required and that is the exclamatory sentence, often preceded by *what!* In the following examples the verb is in the infinitive form.

What! Me be the one to tell him!
What! Her take all the credit!

Note that the subject is accusative not nominative, and note too that exclamatory sentences do not require a verb.

What! Me a liar!
What! Me in a dress!
What! Me fat!

English uses a combination of the verb *to be* and the present participle to express ongoing or **continuous** activity as in

I am writing this letter to you from Earls Court.

It uses a combination of the verb *to have* and the past participle to express the **perfect**:

I have written to you twice in the last few weeks, but you haven't replied.

The terms **continuous** and **perfect** refer to **aspect**, the way the action is viewed. The continuous is ongoing. The perfect is completed, but still relevant. There is a contrast between the perfect and the past tense.

I'm sorry to hear that the authorities there incarcerated you.
I'm sorry to hear that they have taken away your passport.

In the first sentence the incarceration is over, so the past tense is appropriate, but in the second sentence the situation initiated in the past is still in force, still relevant, so the perfect is appropriate. To take another example. You can say *Queen Elizabeth has visited Canada,* because she is still alive, but you can't say *Queen Victoria has never visited Canada,* because she is dead. You have to use the past tense: *Queen Victoria never visited Canada.* The terms 'perfect' and 'continuous' are traditional in describing European languages, but the terms **perfective** and **imperfective** are now in widespread use for an aspect distinction of this type.

English does not have a future tense, at least not as an inflectional category. As mentioned above, future time is expressed by *will, shall,* or *be going to.*

'I'll be back.'   Arnold Schwarzenegger, *The Terminator*

'In five years the Corleone family is going to be completely legitimate.'
                                                              Al Pacino, *The Godfather*

Will and *shall* belong to the class of **modal** verbs, which includes *may, might, must, can, and could.* These modal verbs belong to the general class of auxiliary verbs. They are finite and they are followed by the infinitive. Both these points are hard to see. Most modal verbs are invariable and show no signs of being finite, though in some instances one can see that they are inflected for tense:

Long John could do it in the rehearsals, but he cannot do it now.

As noted above, the infinitive in English is the same as the base or root form of the verb except with the verb 'to be':

I will be the best. I can be better.

English allows up to three auxiliaries in a sentence, four in a passive (see problem 7 at the end of the chapter). The first must be finite and the others non-finite. In the following example we have a modal followed by *have* followed by the past participle of the verb 'to be':

'I could've been a contender.'   Marlon Brando, *On the Waterfront*

Mood

The term **mood** refers to a system of verb inflection marking distinctions such as indicative, imperative, and subjunctive. The **indicative** form is used in statements and does not carry any special marking. The **imperative** is used in commands and the **subjunctive** in wishes. In Latin there was imperative inflection. For instance, *veni* means '(You) come' as a command, whereas 'you come' or 'you are coming' in a statement would be *venis*. In English there is no inflection for imperative, except with the verb 'to be': *Be good!* With other verbs we simply use the base or root form. Here are some imperatives from the movies. Readers might like to try their hand at identifying the sources.

'Round up the usual suspects.'
'Make my day.'
'Show me the money.'

Syntactically imperatives are distinguished by the fact that the subject (*you*) need not be mentioned and usually isn't.

In Early Modern English (sixteenth and seventeenth centuries) one could form a negative imperative by simply adding *not* after the verb as in Hamlet's wish,

Let not the royal bed of Denmark be
A couch for luxury and damned incest.

But in present-day English one must put *not* or *n't* after *do* as in *Don't be a fool!* or as in Basil Fawlty's famous injunction to his staff, when Fawlty Towers was expecting German guests,

'Don't mention the war!'

The other mood inflection, common in European languages, is the **subjunctive**, which expresses wishes. In Latin there were subjunctive forms, at least one of which is used in English, namely *Caveat emptor!* 'Let the buyer beware'. In a statement such as 'The buyer is taking care' the verb form would have been *cavet: Emptor cavet*. In English the subjunctive shows up, at least in the singular, by the absence of the sibilant inflection of the third person present tense. Compare *God save the queen* with the statement *God saves the queen*. Most of the examples we encounter in English in simple sentences are fossilized expressions such as *Heaven preserve us* or *God forbid*.

The term 'subjunctive' might strike the reader as odd since it means 'subjoined'. The explanation here is that in languages like Latin, where the term was coined, it was common in subordinate clauses (explained in the next chapter). This is true of English too. Consider an example like the following:

Ferrari suggested that Rick meet him at 'The Blue Parrot'.
They demanded she come early.
We required that they be there by nine.

Note in these examples the verb lacks the sibilant inflection we would normally have with a third person singular subject, and note that the verb 'to be' has a distinctive subjunctive 'be'. (We have now seen the form 'be' turn up as an infinitive, an imperative, and a subjunctive.)

Another fossil of subjunctive inflection is *were* rather than *was* in sentences such as the following:

If I were rich, I would buy a villa in Tuscany.
Were I to tell him of my past, he would be shocked.

Questions

In English a question can be indicated simply by rising intonation: *Warne smokes?* However, with questions of the type that require a yes-or-no answer, it is more common to use the construction with the auxiliary verb in initial position:

Barbara can go.	*Can Barbara go?*
Barbara is considering their offer.	*Is Barbara considering their offer?*
Barbara has gone.	*Has Barbara gone?*

Where there is no auxiliary required by the content, then *do* is used,

'Do you feel lucky, punk?'

With content questions, those asking *who? what?* and so on, the interrogative word is usually placed first. This does not result in any change of word order where it is the subject that is being questioned:

Which boy wanted more?	*Oliver wanted more.*
Who won the Men's Singles?	*Federer won the Men's Singles.*

Where a constituent other than the subject is questioned, it is moved to the front of the sentence and is followed by the auxiliary:

Who(m) may I see?

To whom have you spoken?
Who have you spoken to?

With what could you buy it?
What could you buy it with?

If there is no auxiliary, then the verb *do* is used:

What do you want?
Which one do you want?
Who did you give it to?

Where the complement of the copula is questioned, the questioned complement is usually placed first followed by the copula and then the subject.

What vintage is this?   *This is a Kanga Rouge 2006.*

Negatives

It will come as no surprise if I say all languages have ways of saying 'no' or 'not'. In Early Modern English the word *not* was placed after the verb as in the following line from Shakespeare's *Othello*:

'I found not Cassio's kisses on her lips.'

This possibility lives on in fossilized expressions such as *I think not*, but in modern English we have to add *not* or the abbreviated *n't* after the first auxiliary verb, and if there is no auxiliary, then we have to put *do* in and place *not* or *n't* after *do*:

Anna will win.	*Anna will not win.*	*Anna won't win.*
They might have seen it.	*They might not have seen it.*	*They mightn't have seen it.*
Hewitt lost.	*Hewitt did not lose.*	*Hewitt didn't lose.*

Where an auxiliary is fronted in a question, the abbreviated form *n't* must follow its host, but *not* may remain.

Henrietta hasn't turned up yet.   *Hasn't Henrietta turned up yet?*
Henrietta has not turned up yet.   *Has Henrietta not turned up yet?*

Passives and other valency changes

At the beginning of this chapter we introduced the related notions of predicate and argument. The set of arguments a predicate takes is often referred to as its **valency** (American **valence**), a term borrowed from chemistry. As pointed out there, the verbs *die, carry,* and *give* are examples of one-place, two-place, and three-place predicates respectively and their basic valency is illustrated in the following sentences.

The little girl died.
The man carried the baby.
The woman gave the water to the old man.

However, languages often allow for rearrangements of the basic valency, as well as additions and subtractions.

One of the most common valency rearrangements is the passive. English has a passive, but it does it in a complicated way, namely by using the verb 'to be' plus the past participle. The first example below is in the basic construction, the **active voice**, and the second in the **passive voice**.

The Sri Lankans beat the Pakistanis.
The Pakistanis were beaten by the Sri Lankans.

The passive allows whatever role was expressed by the object to be expressed by the subject, and the old subject to be expressed via a prepositional phrase or simply be omitted.

In a number of languages there is a morphological passive. In Latin there was a morphological passive in those tenses and aspects not formed on the perfect stem.

a. Catullus   Clodia-m   ama-t.
    Catullus   Clodia   love-3sG
    'Catullus loves Clodia.'

b. Clodia   a   Catullo   ama-t-ur.
    Clodia   by   Catullus-ABL   love-3sG-passive
    'Clodia is loved by Catullus.'

Passives are usually referred to as inflectional. They are regular in their function and one would not consider entering passive forms of verbs like *amatur* in Latin or *beaten* in English as separate entries in a dictionary, but note that they are derivational-like in that they mark a change of valency. There is also some semantic irregularity in that not every transitive verb can be passivized. For example, you can't passivize *have* as in *Lachlan had a dog*.

Another valency rearrangement is one in which an argument is promoted to become an object of the verb. This happens regularly with the verb **to give**:

Uncle Bill gave his old golf clubs to his nephew.
Uncle Bill gave his nephew his old golf clubs.

Give in the sense of 'give to a cause' allows deletion of the recipient: *What did you give? We gave $500.* In limited circumstances it also allows omission of the gift as well as the recipient. When people call at your door asking for a donation to *The Society for the Preservation of the Letter r*, you can say, 'I'm sorry. I gave at the office.'

In many languages a beneficiary in a transitive clause can be promoted to object, and there is marking on the verb to show the change of valency as in the following Indonesian example:

a. Ali   me-masak   ikan   untuk   Hasan.
    Ali   ACT-cook   fish   for   hasan.
    'Ali cooked fish for Hasan.'

b. Ali   me-masak-kan   Hasan   ikan.
    Ali   ACT-cook-BEN   Hasan   fish
    'Ali cooked Hasan fish.'

The prefix *me-* on the verb is one that occurs on most transitive verbs in the active voice. The suffix *-kan* in this instance marks the promotion of *Hasan* from being an object of the preposition *untuk* to being an object of the verb.

It is characteristic of English that these valency rearrangements are made without any morphological marking, as can be seen from the translations of these examples. Most languages would mark these valency changes. English still has some remnants of such marking with *be*-verbs such as *bemoan, besprinkle, besmear:*

> *He moaned about his fate.*   *He bemoaned his fate.*
> *He smeared paint on the wall.*   *He (be)smeared the wall with paint.*

A majority of languages allow an agent to be added to the valency, some entity that causes an action or process or at least allows an action or process. These verbal derivations are called **causatives**. Here is an example from Turkish where the suffix *-dür* expresses the causative notion:

a. Hasan   öl-dü.
    Hasan   die-PAST
    'Hasan died.'

b. Ali   Hasan-ı   öl-dür-dü.
    Ali   Hasan-ACC   die-CAUS-PAST
    'Ali killed Hasan.'

English uses a completely different lexical item, *kill*, to yield the causative of *die*, but for a number of verbs it usually just allows the same verb form to be used in both causative and non-causative constructions:

> *The butter melted.*
> *The sun melted the butter.*

There are a few fossilized causative forms such as the final syllable of *suckle* meaning to 'let suck'. The verb *fall* has a causative *fell* restricted to bringing about the downfall of opponents and trees. *To lay* is the causative of *to lie*, though this is obscured in modern usage. See examples on page 191.

English also allows the object to be omitted with some verbs. For instance, we can say *Helen wrote last week*, though this can only refer to penning correspondence. It could not be used to refer to Helen's professional work for the *Californian Calligraphic Corporation,* for instance. English also allows for the agent of a transitive verb to be omitted. We can say things like *This shirt irons well* or *This book reads well.* In this construction the patient is promoted to subject. In English every independent sentence has to have a subject.

Summary

English has naturally been the focus in this chapter, so I will conclude with a few words about variation across languages, mainly with respect to morphology.

Languages are sometimes classified according to the extent to which they use inflection. Some languages like Chinese and Vietnamese are called **analytic** (or 'isolating') languages, because there is practically no affixation. In Mandarin Chinese there are just a few grammatical suffixes including a marker for plural -*men*, which is obligatory with pronouns and optional with humans, a suffix -*de* with a genitive function as in *wŏ-de* (me-of) 'my' and a few verb inflections for aspect. English is relatively analytic. For instance, there is practically no case inflection, at least with nouns, and there is not the extensive system of person/number inflection across various tenses and aspects that one finds in the more traditional Indo-European languages.

Some languages have a number of derivational and inflectional suffixes, and a word may contain several suffixes. Languages in which words can be broken up into a root plus suffixes in a straightforward way are called **agglutinating** or **agglutinative** languages. A band of such languages runs from Turkish eastwards through central Asia and takes in Mongolian, Korean, and Japanese.

In other languages where there is affixation involving a number of morphemes per word, there are **portmanteau morphs** and it is not always possible to find separate segments for the various grammatical categories. Most Indo-European languages are of this **fusional** type and examples of the fusion of number and gender in Italian were presented on page 73. The distinction between agglutinating and fusional languages is one of degree. Most languages fall between the two extremes. Latin is predominantly fusional in that it does not have separate marking for number, gender, and case, but some verb forms exhibit separate morphs as with *ama-ba-m* 'I was loving' where -*ba*- marks past imperfect and -*m* marks first person singular.

A number of languages are described as **polysynthetic** or 'very synthetic'. They have verbs that bear pronominal markers for subject and object as well as markers for tense, aspect, etc. and they often incorporate a noun object. This means that what would be a multi-word sentence in less synthetic languages often translates into a single word. The following example is from Southern Tiwa, a Tanoan language of New Mexico.

Men-mukhin-tuwi-ban.
you.two-hat-buy-PAST
'You two bought a hat.'

Sources and further reading

The Greenlandic Eskimo examples are adapted from Woodbury 'Greenlandic Eskimo, Ergativity, and Relational Grammar'.

The Swahili examples are adapted from Hinnebusch 'Swahili'.

The immediate source of the Southern Tiwa example is Whaley, *Introduction to Typology*, page 131.

Although the sentence structures shown in this chapter are not really controversial, readers who progress beyond this book will find that different authors have different theories of sentence structure and use somewhat different conventions and terminology. Some not-too-difficult texts are Brown and Miller, *Syntax: A Linguistic Introduction to Sentence Structure* and Huddleston, *English Grammar: an Outline*. For a better cross-language perspective try Comrie, *Language Universals and Linguistic Typology*; Payne, *Describing Morpho-syntax*; Song, *Linguistic Typology*; Tallermann, *Understanding Syntax*; Van Valin, Jr, *An Introduction to Syntax*; and Whaley, *Introduction to Typology*. These suggestions for further reading are relevant to Chapter 6 as well as this chapter.

Problems

1 In the text one-place, two-place, and three-place predicates are mentioned. How many arguments do you think weather predicates take, as in *It rains a lot* and *It's cool*? You might note that in some languages there is no word corresponding to *it* in these expressions. In Italian, for instance, we find *Piove molto* 'It rains a lot' and *Fa fresco* 'It's cool' (lit. *It makes cool*).

2 The following examples are structurally ambiguous. Show this by using brackets.

(a) *Free coffee and mini-bar*   (Hotel ad)
(b) *Left turns out*   (headline)

3 Show the structure of the following by drawing a tree diagram. Examples (d) and (e) admit of two interpretations and require two trees.

(a) *The woman in the leopard-skin coat hailed a cab.*
(b) *She missed forever the scent of the highlands in summer.*
(c) *Very neatly arranged vases of flowers adorned the room.*
(d) *The police officer saw the boy with the binoculars.*
(e) *The head mistress discussed sex with the sixth formers.*

4 On page 68 it was stated that the subject preceded the verb, but that is not the whole story. The subject does not always precede the verb, but it can be identified on the basis of other characteristics. It **controls** (determines) agreement on the verb (*she goes/they go*), and if the subject is a pronoun it is in the nominative case (*she goes/*her goes*). With a tag question as in *Mary's*

going, isn't she? or *Tom's in favour, isn't he?* the pronoun subject in the tag question refers to the subject of the preceding sentence. With these criteria in mind, identify the subject in the following:

The first slice [of ham] they don't use.
Here comes the bride.
There is a child still trapped under the rubble, isn't there?
Into the channel runs a huge volume of water.
There before you stand the real villains.

5 In the following example *dare* is an auxiliary verb, a modal auxiliary to be precise. There are two pieces of evidence for this. What are they?

'How dare he make love to me and not be a married man!'

Ingrid Bergman, *Indiscreet*

6 On page 80 it is stated that in Early Modern English the negative could be added immediately after the lexical verb. This is not the full story. How would you qualify the statement in light of the following examples? The first three are from *Hamlet*, and (d) and (e) from the *Authorised Version* of the Bible.

(a) *Let not thy mother lose her prayers, Hamlet.*
(b) *Let her not walk i' the sun.*
(c) *Pity me not, but lend thy serious hearing*
     To what I shall unfold.
(d) *I know him not. (Luke 22:57)*
(e) *I know not the man. (Matthew 26:74)*

Now if you've figured out a suitable amendment to the statement in the text, you might be troubled by the last sentence in the following lines from *Othello*, but think of the sense and where the stress would have fallen.

(f) *What sense had I of her stolen hours of lust?*
     I saw it not, thought it not, it harmed not me.

7 Put the following active sentences into the passive. In the model example on page 80 the auxiliary *be* is used, but keep in mind the possibility of using *get* in place of *be*.

The flood will isolate the town.
The rats could have eaten the cheese.
The guards may have been mistreating the prisoners.

8 The following sentences have been taken from field notes of the Lhanima language once spoken in western Queensland. See if you can identify the meaning/function of all the bound morphemes and supply the appropriate label. There are no allomorphs. You will need to start by comparing sentences

so that you can identify the lexical words. There is no established label for suffixes like -*tha*. One label is 'proprietive'. Note that there are two separate suffixes with the form -*nga*.

  a.   Malhu muwa-rru kima-nga-nya kutha-nha. Kima-nga-nya kanga-nha.
       'The man used not to drink water. He used to drink rum.'

  b.   Muwa-rru thuka-nya needle-nha wima-tha-nha mingka-tha-nha.
       'The man took the needle with the big hole.'

  c.   Muwa wiya-ngi.
       'The man is laughing.'

  d.   Warra-tji-rru wiya-la-ngi muwa-nha.
       'The women are making the man laugh.'

  e.   Warra mutji-nya Mt Isa-na.
       'The woman slept in Mount Isa.'

  f.   Wama nhangka-nga-nya mingka-na.
       'The snake was (sitting) by a hole.'

  g.   Warra-rru thala-nya muwa-tji-nga-nha kawara-nha.
       'The woman saw the men's dog.'

  h.   Muwa-tji-rru thuka-nya kawara-nga-nha pirna-nha.
       'The men took the dog's bone.'

  i.   Muwa-rru thala-nya kawara-nha Bedourie-na.
       'The man saw the dog in Bedourie.'

  j.   Wara-nga kawara?
       'Whose dog?'

  k.   Kanga-tha-tji-rru thuka-nga-nya kawara-tji-nga-nha pirna-tji-nha.
       'The drunks used to take the dogs' bones.'

  l.   Kawara-rru muwa-nga-rru patja-nya warra-nha.
       'The man's dog bit the woman.'

6. Compound and complex sentences

Grammar. n. A system of pitfalls thoughtfully prepared for the feet of the self-made man, along the path by which he advances to distinction.

Ambrose Bierce, *The Devil's Dictionary*

The following sentence contains two strings each of which qualifies as a sentence as described up to this point. The two strings are bracketed.

[Virginia went to Richmond] and [Vanessa stayed in Bloomsbury].

It is a **compound sentence**. It contains two independent sentences or independent **clauses**. The word **clause** refers to a sentence that is part of a larger sentence.

Now look at the following sentences, each of which contains two clauses, an independent **main clause** and a dependent or **subordinate clause**.

Vanessa knew [that her sister was depressed].
The two sisters talked, [while the children played in the garden].
Virginia knew the man [who married her sister].

These are **complex sentences** where one clause is subordinate to another. In the first of these three examples the clause [*that her sister was depressed*] is a complement of the verb *knew* in the main clause. In the second example the clause [*while the children played in the garden*] is an adjunct. In the third example the clause [*who married her sister*] modifies *the man* in the main clause. Each of these types will be treated in the remainder of this chapter.

Compound sentences

Sentences can be joined together or co-ordinated to form a compound sentence. The co-ordinating conjunctions in English are *and*, *but*, plus *or* on its own or the combination *either...or*.

> *The girls played on the old court and the boys played on the grassed area.*
> *The Democrats would probably support the bill, but the Republicans would surely*
> *oppose it.*
> *Please clean your room or I will have to do it for you.*
> *Either you clean your room or you don't get any lunch.*

In these examples each clause is a full sentence that could stand on its own, but it is possible to omit the subject of a non-initial clause in a compound sentence:

> *She looked hard, but [ ] failed to find the ring within a few minutes and [ ] gave up.*

Co-ordinated clauses that lack a subject cannot stand on their own in English, but they are co-ordinate, not subordinate, that is, they have equal standing in the structure of the overall sentence. As mentioned in the previous chapter, in many languages the subject is not necessary even in simple sentences, since it is incorporated in the verb.

Students are taught not to begin a sentence with *and* or *but*, and that is probably sound advice for beginners, but there are circumstances where it is appropriate. Read the following passages:

> *Jo picked up the kids from the crèche, fed them, bathed them, read them stories, and*
> *put them to bed. And after all that she had to do her history assignment.*
> *Bill checked the oil, put water in the radiator, topped up the battery with distilled*
> *water, and added some detergent to the container for the windscreen washers. But he*
> *forgot to put petrol in the tank.*

In the first example it would be inappropriate to tack the *and*-sentence onto the previous one, since this sentence expresses an addition, not to the last item in the list of chores, but to the sum of the chores. Similarly in the second example, the *but*-sentence expresses a major oversight, one that is ironical in light of the full set of minor checks that have been listed. In these examples where the *and* or *but* introduces a full sentence, there is no syntactic difference between having separate sentences and having a compound sentence.

The only difference is one of grouping by intonation and pause in speech or full stop plus sentence break in writing.

Complex sentences

Complement clauses

It will be recalled from page 68 that a complement is a constituent that expresses an argument of a predicate; it completes the meaning of the predicate. A clause can perform this function.

> *She said [that [she wanted a red sports car]].*
> *[That Australia could win the America's Cup] amazed almost everyone.*

In the first sentence the clause *she wanted a red sports car* is a complement clause introduced by *that,* which could be described as a **subordinator,** a form that introduces a subordinate clause. In this context *that* can be omitted. The complement clause could be compared to a direct object, though it is not really a direct object. In the second example the clause *that Australia could win the America's Cup* functions as subject. It is an unusual type of sentence, even for written English. It would be more normal to make the pronoun *it* the subject and move the clause to the end of the sentence:

> *It amazed almost everyone that Australia could win the America's Cup.*

In the previous chapter the non-finite forms of verbs were introduced. These forms figure prominently in complement clauses. Let us look at the infinitive first.

> *I want to [ ] go.*

In this example the missing subject of the infinitive (indicated by [ ]) is taken to be the same as that of the governing verb *want.* Now compare that with the following,

> *I urged John not to [ ] invest in gold.*

The object of *urged* is *John* and it is this object that is understood to be the subject of *invest.* Other verbs such as *told, persuaded, asked,* or *begged* could be substituted for *urged* without altering the syntax.

The next example looks like the previous one, but what is the object of *like?*

> *We like England to beat Australia.*

This sentence does not state that *we* like *England,* rather what *we* like is victory for England over Australia, in other words, the whole clause *England to beat Australia.* We might represent the difference between the *urge*-sentence and the *like*-sentence by bracketing as follows and using our convention of marking the understood subject by [ ]:

> *I urged John [[ ] not to invest in gold].*
> *We like [England to beat Australia].*

Other verbs that could be substituted for *like* without altering the syntax include *dislike, prefer,* and *want.*

If we use complement clauses with the present participle, we can also add other verbs such as *see* and *resent.*

> *I resented [the customs officials searching my handbag].*
> *The police saw [Wanda chatting up a guy at the bar].*

As with the *like*-sentence, the object of *resented* is the whole clause. Examples with the verb *see* are tricky. At first blush you might think that this sentence says the police saw Wanda, but in fact it does not state that the police saw Wanda, at least not directly. It says that the police saw an event, namely Wanda chatting up a guy at the bar. Wanda is the subject of chatting and the subordinate clause can be put into the passive with no change in the basic meaning:

> *The police saw [a guy being chatted up by Wanda at the bar].*

But there is a further complication. We can also passivize the main verb *saw* to yield

> *Wanda was seen by the police [[ ] chatting up a guy at the bar].*

This suggests that *Wanda* has been taken to be the direct object of *saw*. Some linguists would describe this as an example of **raising**. This term is motivated by the idea that a subordinate clause is always lower than the clause that governs it, and that where the subject of a non-finite verb is interpreted as the object of the governing verb it moves up from a lower to a higher clause.

The same kind of thing happens with *expect*:

> (a)   *The guests expected [Frances to pay for the dinner].*
> (b)   *The guests expected [the dinner to be paid for by Frances].*
> (c)   *Frances was expected by the guests [[ ]to pay for the dinner].*

The (b) sentence confirms that Frances belongs in the subordinate clause, but the (c) sentence indicates Frances has been interpreted as the object of *expect*. One would expect *expect* to behave like *like*, but perhaps *expect* is given an alternative interpretation analogous to verbs like *urge* and *persuade* because an expectation can put moral pressure on the patient to perform!

A straightforward type of raising can be found with verbs like *seem* and *appear*. The following example with *seem* is grammatical, but it does not make sense:

The stones seem to like drugs.

It does not make sense, because stones don't have likes or dislikes. The noun phrase *the stones* is grammatically the subject of *seems*, but it is understood as the subject of *like*. Semantically it belongs with *like*, not with *seems*. In fact we can say the following:

It seems the stones likes drugs.

In this sentence *the stones* is grammatically the subject of the verb it belongs with, namely *likes*. Some modern theories would suggest that the two more or less synonymous constructions found with *seem* can both be derived from an underlying semantic structure like the following:

seems [the stones like drugs]

This structure shows *seems* as a verb with one argument, namely the clause [*the stones like drugs*]. One can derive a grammatical sentence either by putting in a dummy *it*, that is, a meaningless, non-referential *it*, in order to satisfy the grammatical requirement that a verb needs a subject, or by **raising** the subject of *like* to become the subject of *seems*.

seems [the stones like drugs]   →   *It seems [the stones like drugs]*

seems [the stones like drugs]   →   *The stones seem [[ ] to like drugs]*

Raising also plays a part in sentences like the following,

Bruce is eager to see Cats *when he is in New York.*
Bruce is easy to see in bad light, when he wears his yellow safety vest.

Focus on *Bruce is eager to see* and *Bruce is easy to see*. The rest of the sentences just provides context. These two sequences look the same except for the substitution of one adjective for another, but in fact they are understood in quite different ways. The subject of *to see* in the first sentence is understood to be the subject of *is eager*, but in the second sentence the subject of *to see* is not understood to be the subject of *is easy*. The understood subject of *see* in this sentence is indefinite (compare *Bruce is easy for people to see*). *Bruce* is understood to be the object of *see* (*It is easy to see Bruce*). We can bring out the semantic difference between the two apparently similar sequences with the following structures in which *x* stands for an unspecified subject.

Bruce is eager to [ ] see.
is easy[[x] to see Bruce].

To derive a grammatical sentence from the semantic structure posited for *easy*, we can put in a dummy *it*:

>   *It is easy to [x] see Bruce.*

or we can raise *Bruce* to become the subject of *is easy*:

>   *is easy [[x] to see Bruce]. → Bruce is easy [x] to see [ ].*

Adjunct clauses

The simplest type of adjunct clause is the finite adverbial clause introduced by a subordinating conjunction. Here are some examples of adverbial clauses of time.

>   *He left [after the meeting concluded].*
>   *[Before the rain came], the ground was like iron.*

Some of the subordinating conjunctions such as *before* and *after* can occur as prepositions (*after the ball*) or adverbs (*What comes after?*). You could consider these words to be just prepositions that can govern a clause as opposed to a noun phrase. You could also consider that where these words are used without a following noun phrase, they are intransitive prepositions rather than adverbs as they are traditionally designated:

Intransitive preposition (adverb):	They came after.
Preposition with NP complement:	They came after the game.
Preposition with clause complement	
(subordinating conjunction):	They came after the game was over.

Here are some other types of adverbial clause with their traditional labels:

Concession: ~~We managed to win although our star players were all out injured.~~
Reason: Because our star players were out injured, we lost.
Condition: If we soften up the opposition in the first half, we can probably kick a winning score in the second.
Purpose:
   finite: The ants work hard during the summer, so that they might have enough food for the winter.
   non-finite: I shot a rabbit to provide a decent meal for the kids.

Non-finite adjuncts with the present participle are common in English. However, there is no grammatical rule that determines the missing subject. It is a matter of reasonable interpretation. The missing subject need not even be in the sentence in which the participial clause occurs. In the following example, the missing subject is presumably the writer, who is not explicitly mentioned, but the construction raises the possibility that the zebras were at the wheel.

Driving across the plains, the zebras made a strange sight.

The following is a real example. Who has been lying in bed for weeks?

'The accident broke his back and he also had internal injuries. After lying in bed for weeks, the doctor decided to operate.'

Presumably it is the patient who has been lying on his back for weeks, but anyone familiar with the regular identification of the subject of the main clause with the missing subject of a preceding participle is likely to take it to be the doctor at first, before then having to do a recalculation.

Adjuncts with past participles occur, but mainly in formal written English:

Beaten by the champ in three rounds, Rocky despaired of ever winning the title.
Rocky, beaten by the champ in three rounds, despaired of ever winning the title.
Rocky despaired of ever winning the title, beaten by the champ in three rounds.

Relative clauses

A relative clause typically modifies or qualifies a noun just as an adjective does and in traditional grammar a relative clause was called an adjectival clause. Suppose I want to say two things:

1. *The car-park attendants are a waste of money.*
2. *The car-park attendants will be fired.*

It would be quite unnatural to make the two statements as given above, and almost as unnatural to simply join the two statements with *and*. I could substitute *they* for *car-park attendants* in the second sentence, and if I did this and then joined the two sentences with *and*, I would have a perfectly good sentence.

The car-park attendants are a waste of money and they will be fired.

I could also omit the subject of the second clause:

The car-park attendants are a waste of money and [ ] will be fired.

However, there is another way. I could incorporate the first clause into the second by making it a **relative clause** modifying car-park attendants. As in the examples of co-ordination given above, I would not want to repeat car-park attendants, so I would substitute *who*:

The car park attendants, who are a waste of money, will be fired.

The commas around the relative clause indicate that it is parenthetical, something I would indicate by intonation if I were saying this sentence. A relative clause of this type that applies to all of whatever the head refers to, all the car-park attendants in this case, is called a 'non- restrictive relative clause'. If I were to omit the commas (and the pauses), the relative clause would be taken to apply only to those car-park attendants who were considered a waste of money. This kind of relative clause is a 'restrictive relative clause'.

The car park attendants who are a waste of money will be fired.

Here is a pair of examples to bring out the contrast between the two types of relative clause.

restrictive:
Movies which feature sex or violence don't get a 'general exhibition' rating.
non-restrictive:
Movies, which provide entertainment for millions, are big business.

Who is a relative pronoun. It applies to humans and often to animals, but not normally to inanimates. The relative pronoun *which* is used for flora, inanimate objects, and abstract ideas. Incidentally linguists usually use the label *inanimate* to include plants, so one could simply say *which* is used for inanimates. A relative pronoun has an **antecedent**, usually the head noun of the phrase in which the relative clause appears. This specifies the entity the relative pronoun refers to. In *the man who came to dinner,* the noun *man* is the antecedent of *who*.

A relative clause, usually only a restrictive one, may also be introduced by *that*. In fact the grammar check in Word has just put a green line under my example *Movies which feature sex or violence don't get a 'general exhibition' rating.* If I switch to *that*, the green line goes away. This accords with my own preference, but I notice that not everyone shares my preferences. *That* in this context is not considered to be a relative pronoun, but simply a subordinator. It can be used with humans as well as other animates and with inanimates.

The fella/puppy/dress that caught your eye is attracting a lot of attention from the other members.

The subordinator *that* can be omitted where the relativized function is not the subject of the relative clause. In the example just quoted, where the relativized function is the subject, *that* could not be omitted since the hearer/reader would get no clue as to the start of a relative clause and would take *caught* as the verb of a main clause only to be confused when getting to *is*. However, where the relativized function is the object of a verb or preposition, then *that* can be omitted without confusion.

I saw the fella/puppy/dress (that) you picked up.

I saw the fella/puppy/dress (that) you spilt your drink on.

English allows subjects, objects, objects of prepositions, and possessors to be relativized.

subject:

I saw the man who stole the computer.

object:

I saw the man who(m) the police caught.

object of a preposition:

I saw the man who you gave the money to.

I saw the man to whom you gave the money.

I saw the student you wrote the assignment for.

I saw the student for whom you wrote the assignment.

possessor:

I saw that chap whose car was stolen at the supermarket.

I inspected two houses the rooms of which were incredibly small.

I inspected two houses whose rooms were incredibly small.

The last example illustrates that *whose* can be used with inanimates to avoid the bookish 'of which'.

If we look at other languages, we find that a majority have relative clauses. Some relativize subjects only, some relativize subjects and objects and others relativize other functions as well. This hierarchy is also reflected in English. When we look at non-standard usage, we find that practically everybody relativizes subjects in text-book fashion, but when it comes to objects, we sometimes find the following where an object pronoun is retained in the relative clause:

That's the guy I told you about him yesterday.

In the following example a noun phrase object is repeated:

'Thorpe is going to try to break the 49-second barrier, which no more than nine or so swimmers have broken 49 seconds.'

When it comes to relativizing objects of prepositions, we find that quite a large number of people either supply the preposition with a pronoun object or omit the preposition altogether. These aberrations from the standard may be influenced by the traditional rule that one should not end a sentence with a preposition (see p. 98 below), but on the other hand many of the 'offenders' are unlikely to have heard of the rule.

That is something I'm interested in. (standard version)

'That is something I'm interested in it.'

'That is something I'm interested.'
'There's one thing I'm really interested.'
'..in the review which I wasn't impressed he said...'
'...after the meeting which I'll tell you about it in a minute.'
[These are] *'works that he collected and found inspiration.'*
'I'm looking forward to the meeting which they are present.'

The 'superfluous' pronoun also occurs in examples like the following where we have a non-finite relative clause:

'He is impossible to put your finger on him.'

I mentioned above that relative clauses usually modify nouns, but a non-restrictive relative clause can refer to events:

He got there too late to post it, which was just as well.

Fused relatives

One complication with relatives in English is that the antecedent and relative may be **fused** as in the following memorable quotation from *When Harry met Sally* (1989):

'I'll have [what she's having].'

This could be paraphrased bookishly and unidiomatically as *I'll have that which she is having* where *that* is the antecedent and *which* the relative pronoun. In this example *what* corresponds to *that* plus *which*.

When and where

When and *where* are interrogative adverbs in sentences such as *When will you get back?* and *Where are you going?* They can occur as relative pronouns as in the following.

I remember the day when [on which] you left home.
I remember the film where [in which] you played a villain.

An alternative for the first of these would be to omit *when* and for the second to omit *where* and retain the preposition as in *I remember the film you played a villain in.*

Nominalization

In many languages a verb can be used as a noun. In English we often use a verb as a noun without any special marking, as when we say *She gave him a push* or *Piggott started his run two furlongs from home.* Most languages mark the derivation of a noun from a verb, and English does too in some instances, mainly with words borrowed from Latin: *reduce/reduction, permit/permission,* and so on. A verb expresses a predicate with one or more arguments, so the question arises of what happens to these when a verb is **nominalized**. English provides for the subject and object to be retained.

> *The government released its five-year plan today. This took many by surprise.*
> *The government's release of its five-year plan today took many by surprise.*

Here we see the subject expressed as a 'possessor' of *release* and marked with the apostrophe *-s,* and the object of *release* in an *of*-phrase. The adverb *today* has been retained also.

Manner adverbs such as *quickly, happily, wantonly,* or *indiscriminately* can be retained as adjectives.

> *The troops slaughtered the civilians indiscriminately. This disappointed their allies.*
> *The troops' indiscriminate slaughter of the civilians disappointed their allies.*

The sole argument of one-place predicates can be expressed either by the apostrophe *-s* or via an *of*-phrase. In general animates are expressed by *'s* and inanimates via a *by*-phrase:

> *The baby's crying woke me.*
> *The dripping of the tap woke me.*

'Correct' grammar

'I heard a scream, and I didn't know if it was me who screamed or not—if it was I or not.'
Olivia De Havilland, *The Snake Pit*

In the Hitchcock movie *To Catch a Thief* (1955) there is the following exchange:

> *Cary Grant: That sounds more like your mother than you.*
> *Grace Kelly: There's not much difference between us really, just a few years and some grammar.*

The reference in this quote is to the popular conception of grammar, a set of rules laying down what is correct. Grammar in this sense is usually incomplete inasmuch as it concentrates on what readers are likely to get 'wrong', i.e. non-standard. Such grammars do not have rules telling us that we must put an adjective like *tall* in front of a noun like *boy* since no one gets this wrong. Traditional writers on language tend to be **prescriptive,** telling people what they 'should' say or write, and often recommending constructions that are out of date or hardly used. Modern professional linguists see themselves as scientific and descriptive, recording what occurs. Just as botanists describe weeds as well as roses, and for the most part refrain from telling people what they should grow in their gardens, so linguists are interested in the range of language usage and generally do not prescribe what people should say.

Colin Dexter's fictional detective, Inspector Morse, corrects his sergeant for saying things like *It is me* or *It's me* instead of *It is I*. A prescriptive grammar will tell readers they should say *It is I* rather than *It is me*, because the verb 'to be' is not a transitive verb and the pronoun following it, though a complement, is not a direct object. In making this claim a prescriptive grammarian is likely to be influenced by languages like Latin where the complement of the verb *esse* 'to be' would be in the same case as the subject. If the subject was nominative, then the complement would be nominative. 'Tarquin is king', for instance, would be *Tarquinius est rex* with both *Tarquinius* and *rex* in the nominative. However, almost everyone says *It is me*. The prescriptive grammarian believes in grammatical right and wrong and that he (yes, he, I think all of them are 'he') can lay down what is right. Now we all accept grammatical correctness, after all, we all accept that one says *this bottle* and *these bottles* not *these bottle and *this bottles. But we need to ask how we decide which of these forms is correct and the answer is that *this bottle* and *these bottles* are correct because that's what everyone says. That's common usage. If you ask any speaker of any language about grammatical correctness, you will find they have definite ideas about what is right and what is wrong (though typically they cannot make explicit the reasons for their judgements). These ideas about correctness are based on usage. But a problem arises where usage is divided, and in western society usage is often split on social lines. Ultimately speakers and writers have to decide which group they want to identify with. They need to make decisions about what is appropriate for a particular context just as they would in matters of dress or behaviour.

Inspector Morse also corrects his sergeant for saying things like *Who is she thinking of?* instead of *Of whom is she thinking?* The prescriptive rule involved here is that a sentence should not end with a preposition. One could ask, 'Why not?'. Is it because the word *preposition* involves the prefix *pre-* meaning 'before' and therefore the preposition should always precede a noun phrase? When Winston Churchill was rebuked for this supposed solecism, he replied *That is the sort of English up with which I shall not put*.

In the film *Pillow Talk* Doris Day (the virgin) rebukes Rock Hudson (the wolf) with the line, 'There are men who don't end every sentence with a proposition.'

Another well known rule of prescriptive grammar is that one should not split the infinitive as in something like the line found at the beginning of episodes of Star Trek *To boldly go where no man has gone before* (*no one* in later series) where the adverb *boldly* comes between *to* and the verb. As explained in chapter five there are forms of the verb called infinitives to be found in numerous languages and they translate into English as *to* plus an infinitive, not that the infinitive is different in form from the base form of the verb. Simply because *to*-plus-a-verb corresponds to a single word in certain other languages is no reason to refrain from splitting the corresponding phrase in English.

Those advocating correct grammar often invoke logic. A sentence such as *He didn't say nothing* is castigated as being illogical since it contains two negatives and one cancels the other and that therefore the sentence really means he said something. Well obviously it doesn't mean that. Everyone knows what it means. It just happens that in non-standard English two negative forms are used to express negation. In many languages it is standard to use two negative forms as in Italian *Non ha detto niente* 'S/he said nothing', literally 'not s/he-has said nothing.'

In Standard English grammar, the object of a verb or preposition is always accusative so we say *She saw me* not **She saw I* and *He sat with me* not **He sat with I*. However, many people, probably a majority, use a nominative form for the second of two conjoined pronoun objects: *She saw him and I*, *He spoke with her and I*. Logic has some claims here, or at least consistency. One would expect the rule about pronoun objects to apply to all pronoun objects so that

She saw him and me would prevail. But it is still a matter of usage, and usage is divided. Some speakers use the nominative form of the pronoun after a preposition if the pronoun is modified in any way. They would say *any of us*, but *any of we married people*. Some genuine examples are provided in problem 9 below.

Just to finish off this chapter, I present an example of how one can have rules of grammar without them being standard. This is a conversation I overheard in Normanhurst, New South Wales, in 1969. A father is keen to check whether his young son has seen an unusual plane that has just flown by.

Father: *Did you see that?*

Child: *Daddy, I seed it*

Father (with exaggerated expression of horror): *What?*

Child: *Daddy, I sawed it.*

Father (more horror): *What?*

Child: *Daddy, I seen it.*

Father (much relieved): *That's better.*

Sources and further reading

The suggested reading given for chapter five applies to this chapter too. There is also Brinton, *The Structure of Modern English*. For a comprehensive reference on every aspect of English grammar dip into the monumental *The Cambridge Grammar of the English Language* by Huddleston and Pullum.

Problems

1 Pick out the subordinate clauses in the following and label them as complement clauses, adjunct clauses or relative clauses.

'If I did [sleep with anyone], you would be right up there with Michelle Pfeiffer and River Phoenix.'   **Stephen Fry to Emma Thompson in** *Peter's Friends*

'Do you think it will ever take the place of baseball?'
Deborah Kerr, *An Affair to Remember*

'When you've got it, flaunt it.'   **Zero Mostel,** *The Producers*

'It would be tragic if you realized too late, as so many others do, there's only one thing in the world worth having—and that is youth.'
George Sanders, *The Picture of Dorian Gray*

'You mustn't think too harshly of my secretaries. They were kind and understanding when I came to the office after a hard day at home.'   **Claude Rains,** *Mr Skiffington*

'We used her cloak [to make love on], her being in the Salvation Army.'

First episode of TV series, *A Touch of Frost*

'What if this is a dream?'

'Kiss me quick then before it goes away.'

Rachel Ticotin and Arnold Schwarzenegger, *Total Recall*

2 In chapter five present participles of the verb were introduced. These are marked by *-ing* (*Red Rum is running at Aintree*). However, these *-ing* forms can be used as adjectives (*The property has running water*) and *-ing* also marks nouns derived from verbs (*The running of the race was delayed by bad weather*). Identify the word class of the *-ing* forms in the following examples. Some examples admit of two interpretations.

Growers stop eating apples.

The growers increased their plantings of stewing apples.

Emergency services are monitoring river levels and flooding roads.

Entertaining women can be fun.

3 What is the source of ambiguity in these examples?

Murderer sentenced to die twice

He said he would speak to Sister Rita in the men's room.

She told me she was going to have a baby in the middle of Oxford Street.

'The staff… were ordered not to place themselves in danger and to call the police.'

4 The following contain adjuncts. Some adjuncts are participial phrases and some prepositional phrases. In each case there is an ambiguity, although certain interpretations such as one involving flying elephants would be unlikely. Identify the ambiguities.

Tom saw a ghost on his way home from the cemetery.

I saw elephants flying over Kenya.

Are there dolphins in the bay? 'Oh, yes, you see them coming in on the ferry!'

He came to his son's wedding with Mr Brown.

5 Supply the covert arguments in the following. Some examples admit of more than one interpretation.

I want to teach.

I want men to train as nurses.

It's hard to get boys to wash.

The rabbit is ready to eat.

6 Pronouns can be a problem, particularly **anaphoric** pronouns, ones that refer back to something mentioned before or just implied before. They can refer to a particular noun phrase or sometimes a whole sentence. What do the underlined pronouns in the following examples refer to? Allow for more than one possibility.

> Patient: *My breathing still troubles me.*
> Doctor: *Mm! We must put a stop to <u>that</u>.*
>
> *Keep all poisons in the bathroom cupboard. If there are children in the house, lock <u>them</u> up.*
>
> *The ladies of the parish have cast off clothing. <u>They</u> can be seen in the church hall after 1.00 pm.*
>
> *Mother, I've just found out that my fiancé has a wooden leg. Do you think I should break <u>it</u> off?*

7 Each of the following sentences contains a relative clause. Pick out the relative clauses and determine the following:

   (a) which grammatical relation has been relativized (subject, object, object of a preposition)
   (b) the antecedent of the relative pronoun, i.e. what it refers to
   (c) whether the relative clauses are restrictive or non-restrictive.

> *'That's the most fun I've had without laughing.'*   **Woody Allen, *Annie Hall***
>
> *'I'm being sunk by a society that demands success when all I can offer is failure.'*
>   **Zero Mostel, *The Producers***
>
> *'I have loved, with all my heart, 100 women I never want to see again.'*
>   **Anthony Quinn, *Viva Zapata***
>
> *'Remember: you're fighting for this woman's honour, which is probably more than she ever did.'*   **Groucho Marx, *Duck Soup***
>
> *'If there's anything in the world I hate, it's leeches.'*
>   **Humphrey Bogart, *The African Queen***
>
> *'Laura considered me the wisest, the wittiest, the most interesting man she'd ever met.'*
>   **Clifton Webb, *Laura***
>
> *'Make him an offer he can't refuse.'*   **Marlon Brando, *The Godfather***

8 Here are some real-life relative clauses. Consider how you might rephrase the examples so that they would not earn a pedant's censure.

> *'I don't like giving my work number which I don't like people ringing me at work.'*
> *'There are some things I didn't know what they were.'*
> *'. . . those tins, which I think there's still some around.'*
> *'. . . which P.H. told us he was capable of doing that.'*

9 Consider the choice of pronoun form in the following examples from the point of view of 'correct grammar' and usage. Consider both case and the use of the reflexive.

'Myself and the leaders will discuss . . . '
'My sister and myself will . . . '
'Like we in the media do'
'Any of we individuals'

'I want to take this opportunity of thanking you on behalf of the Duchess of Windsor and I.'   **Duke of Windsor, 1965**

10 The following example was given to illustrate a finite complement clause.

She said [that [she wanted a red sports car]].

Compare this with the following examples and see if they contain complement clauses. Note the position of the verbs of 'saying' and 'thinking' and ask yourself whether 'that' could be used.

I mean to say, he's not exactly God's gift to women.
I say, isn't the weather beastly?
The first candidate on the list has got good credentials, I think.
Tom wouldn't be the first cashier to have had his hand in the till, you know.
Joanne's got personality, I reckon, but she's not so good with difficult customers.
He goes like, I couldn't care less, so I decided to look elsewhere.

7. Using language

The world is so full of dissimulation and compliment, that men's words are hardly any signification of their thoughts.

Richard Steele, *The Spectator*

Types of communication

While it is true that language serves to exchange and accumulate information, another pervasive function is to maintain harmony or cohesion between people, or simply to put one human in touch with another. Where relations between people are cordial, talk is exchanged, and failure to talk or to respond to talk can be quite upsetting. People who feel that someone in their group has betrayed them, may 'send them to Coventry', that is, refuse to talk to them. Some strict religious groups will 'shun' a member who fails to live up to the required code of behaviour. Oftentimes an individual will refuse to talk to a friend, a lover, or a member of the family who has offended them. All of this 'no speaks' can be quite disconcerting to the person who is cut off from accustomed interchange. People imprisoned in jail and subjected to physical abuse by other inmates often prefer to put up with bad treatment rather than to be in solitary confinement.

A lot of conversation involves making obvious statements, about the weather, for instance, recounting shared experiences, or whingeing about poor health, poverty, or the failings of the government. Even where information is conveyed it often consists of people relating trivial incidents. The interaction is more important than the content. People who do not talk trivia are unpopular. 'He's (or she's) got no small talk,' is a damning judgement.

Throughout human history the major way language has been used is in conversation, usually between two or more people, though talking to oneself is pretty common too. Nowadays, conversation can be via telephone, including the use of a mobile phone (cell phone), talk-back radio, or video-conferencing.

A lot of oral communication is one-way: someone speaks and hopefully one or more listen as in speeches, lectures, sermons, eulogies, news reports, and sports descriptions. All these can be delivered by radio and television.

In modern literate societies a lot of communication is via writing where writing and reading newspapers and magazines account for most of the activity, but there are also novels, non-fiction of various kinds, and personal correspondence.

For the last decade or so we have been able to send letters by e-mail, and read texts transmitted to our computers. One can 'text' from a mobile phone using a special texting register full of abbreviations such as CUL8R for 'See you later'. We can also have conversations by on-line e-mail or via chat rooms, where an oral style is committed to writing.

A good deal of language interaction involves the exchange of pleasantries, quips, and puns or the telling of jokes. Reports from various cultures suggest that banter or raillery is common, that is, the exchange of smart insults aimed at eliciting smart repartee. Sometimes these are seemingly offensive, but the exchanges are often between friends or kinfolk, and in the context of this kind of ritual gross insults, like you get when you call someone *sonuvabitch*, can be acceptable. Various forms of humorous exchange once mostly the preserve of the spoken medium are now often exchanged electronically.

As mentioned in chapter one, language can also be communicated via signs. In modern society we think of sign language as the primary means of communication used by the deaf, but quite a lot of cultures use signs as well as spoken language. It is useful in hunting, where silence is imperative, and it is useful in communicating over distances too great for speech, particularly where there is noise, across a river or a highway, or even 'across a crowded room'.

Whatever the purpose of our communication and regardless of the medium we use to communicate, we need to be able to assess what our audience knows already and does not know, and we need to be able to compose an elaborate message with various details and make it cohere. These requirements are the subject of the remainder of this chapter. In order to communicate successfully we also need to know which style to adopt. This is covered in chapter eleven.

Given and new information

Consider the following. Mary looks out the window and sees her brother, Mark, driving off in her car without permission, leaving her stranded. She is alarmed at this 'theft' and shows her distress by uttering a few appropriate obscenities that cast aspersions about the legitimacy of his birth and express a desire that he suffer some form of sexual penetration. Her mother hears her and asks her what's wrong.

> Mum: *What's happened?*
> Mary: *Mark's taken my car.*

Other members of the family are in other rooms and hear something of this exchange, but not the full story. They ask the following questions and receive the following replies.

> Fred: *What did Mark do?*
> Mary: *He took my car.*
>
> Anne: *What happened to your car?*
> Mary: *Mark's taken it.*
>
> Dad: *What did Mark take?*
> Mary: *My car.*
>
> Pauline: *Who took your car?*
> Mary: *Mark (did).*

In terms of grammar Mary could have used the reply *Mark's taken my car* for all the questions, but this would not have been appropriate language usage. To explain how the various replies are appropriate it is necessary to make a distinction between **given** and **new** information. When Mary's mother asks *What happened?* she does not know about the taking, nor who the taker is, nor what has been taken. All parts of Mary's reply represent new information. Now Mum will obviously know of the existence of her errant son Mark, and the fact that her daughter Mary has a car. They are not new to her general knowledge, but they are new as participants in the taking incident.

When Fred asks *What did Mark do?* he is taking it as given that Mark did something, so in her reply Mary substitutes *he* for *Mark* because it is given information as opposed to *took my car*, which is new.

When Anne asks *What happened to your car?* she takes the car as given, so Mary is able to substitute *it* for *the car* in her reply.

Dad has overheard the bit about Mark taking something, so all this is given. All he wants to find out is what was taken. Mary could have answered *He took my car*, but she gives just the new information, namely *my car.*

Pauline missed only the identity of the car-taker, so Mary gives just this bit of new information, namely *Mark*. She could have said *Mark did*. Just as words like *she*, *he*, and *it* are pronouns (they stand for nouns, or strictly for noun phrases) *do* is a pro-verb (not a proverb!). It stands for a verb phrase.

In general, given information is expressed in some kind of reduced form, by a pro-form, or simply omitted. New information is normally made explicit. That part of the new information that you would want to emphasize most is the

focus. The focus is resistant to ellipsis (omission) as in Mary's reply to Dad, where Mary simply gives the focus. This is appropriate in answers to questions, where the distinction between given and new is clear cut. This is not always the case. Suppose I read about Hannibal and I am impressed that he invaded the Romans in Italy by travelling from Spain through the Alps with elephants. If I am particularly impressed by the fact that he took elephants with him, I might relay the fruits of my reading to a friend by saying *Did you know Hannibal invaded Italy via the Alps with elephants?* with a strong emphasis on *elephants*. In producing this sentence I assume my friend has heard of Hannibal (this is given information), but I present the rest of the sentence as new information and I see *with elephants* as the focus so I emphasize *elephants*.

English has some alternative constructions for expressing focus. Suppose your football team has won and you attribute their success to Viduka's performance. You could say one of the following:

> *It was Viduka who won the game for us.*
> *The one who won the game for us was Viduka.*

These constructions enable us to make Viduka the focus, by making him the complement of the verb 'to be'. They are particularly useful in writing where you can't use stress. In speech you could simply say *Viduka won the game for us.*

Where all the information in a sentence is presented as new, there are more natural and less natural ways of presenting the information. Suppose a passing motorist runs over the family pet. It could be reported as in (a) or as in (b), but (a) is more natural. There is an association between subject and what we might call 'point of view'. We would see such an event from the point of view of the familiar victim and make that victim the subject of the sentence. The passive construction is a useful way of doing this.

> (a)   *Flossie's been run over by a car.*
> (b)   *A car has run over Flossie.*

Suppose you suffer the misfortune of finding a fly in your soup, you are unlikely to report it as in (a) below, but rather as in (b) or possibly (c). This event is not likely to be presented from the point of view of an insignificant fly. It is likely that the *there*-construction would be used, although one could take the 'soup' as the subject.

> (a)   *A fly is in my soup.*
> (b)   *There's a fly in my soup.*
> (c)   *My soup's got a fly in it.*

There has no meaning in a sentence like (b). It is used simply because English grammar requires a subject. The *there*-construction is useful for describing an action, a process, or a state without presenting any particular participant as subject.

There is a natural point of view where the relationship between entities of different size or importance is involved. If a kiosk and a cathedral stand on opposite sides of a street, you are more likely to say *The kiosk is opposite the cathedral* than to say *The cathedral is opposite the kiosk*. Sometimes the choice of point-of-view is not so obvious. I once learned that the family home of one of my colleagues was across the road from that of a famous nouveau-riche millionaire (who eventually landed in jail). I said to her, 'I hear you used to live near X.' She replied, 'He used to live near us.'

Another way of presenting what you want to talk about is to place it in first position outside the sentence proper. Suppose I am talking about spring bulbs. I could say *Tulip bulbs need to be planted about four inches deep* or I could say *Tulip bulbs, they need to be planted four inches deep*. The phrase that is placed outside the sentence proper announcing what you are going to make a statement about is called the **topic**. It is picked up in the clause proper by a **resumptive pronoun**, in this instance *they*.

Languages vary a lot in how strictly word order is controlled by grammatical rules. English is at one extreme. We cannot vary the order of words in a sentence much, but certain other languages allow a lot more flexibility including Russian and Finnish, where the basic order is subject–verb–object (SVO), and Latin, where the basic order was subject–object–verb (SOV).

Discourse

Chapter five dealt with simple sentences and chapter six dealt with compound and complex sentences. However, we do not communicate just in sentences. On the one hand, most communication consists of more than one sentence, thousands of sentences in the case of a novel. On the other hand, communication, particularly conversation, typically involves a sequence of utterances many of which are less than a full sentence. We often respond with isolated words such as *yes* and *no*, phrases like *on the bus* and *in a minute*, or elliptical sentences such as *I might*.

We have already illustrated some of the features of conversation in the previous section in the course of explaining given and new information. In general, language provides us with the means to avoid redundancy, to avoid repeating full specifications of referents. Some strategies apply within the sentence, others apply outside the sentence, others again apply in both domains.

As we noted in chapter six, we can omit the subject in co-ordinated clauses. Here is a multiple example:

Before going to the beach, David shaved, dabbed his face with aftershave, applied some sunscreen, and sprayed himself with insect repellent.

This strategy is common across languages, but English is a language that has strict rules about filling the subject slot. It does not allow this strategy in a series of separate sentences (except in diary style—see example on p. 194).

Omission of the verb phrase is common in conversation. In the replies in the following examples we have elliptical sentences consisting of a subject and an auxiliary:

> *Can anyone here read Sanskrit?*
> *Krishna can.*
>
> *Will someone take my truck and go and pick up some beer?*
> *I will.*
>
> *Would anyone like to pick up Wilma from the gym?*
> *Meg might.*
>
> *Abigail works fifteen hours a day.*
> *She does?!*

In the first two examples there is a modal auxiliary in the question, so this is retained in the elliptical reply. In the third example there is a modal auxiliary in the question, but a different modal is used in the reply. In the last example, where there is no auxiliary, the grammatical verb *do* is used. It can be considered a pro-form that stands for 'works fifteen hours a day' or as a grammatical verb that facilitates omission of the verb phrase just as the other auxiliaries do.

Where co-ordinated clauses potentially share the same verb, it is common to omit the verb from all but the first clause, though this strategy is mostly confined to writing.

> *Betty watched the tennis, Beatrice [watched] the golf, and Bertha [watched] the football.*

All languages have pro-forms, the most prominent type being pronouns. In English we have **reflexive pronouns**, which apply within a clause, and ordinary pronouns that apply outside the clause. Obviously we would not say *The man in the grey overcoat injured the man in the grey overcoat*, but if we substitute *him* for the object (*The man in the grey overcoat injured him*), we change the meaning since *him* cannot refer to the subject. In this context we must use the reflexive pronoun and say *The man in the grey overcoat injured himself.*

This distinction between reflexive and non-reflexive pronouns is a contribution to the problem of keeping track of referents in narrative. In English we have three third person singular pronouns *he*, *she*, and *it*, so in a story involving a male, a female, and an animal it is easy to keep track of who is doing what to whom.

The dog took an instant dislike to Brian. It growled at him and then began nipping at his heels. On seeing this Tania called it, but to no avail. She had to go and drag it off him.

However, where there is more than one individual of the same sex, it is not so easy to strike a balance between avoiding redundancy and creating confusion. In many languages there is no gender distinction in third person pronouns, but there are other strategies such as using the equivalent of 'this one' for the last-mentioned and the equivalent of 'that one' for the earlier-mentioned. This is like the use of the terms *the former* and *the latter* in English, but these are used only in a formal or written style. Some languages have a pair of affixes, one to show that the subject of a clause is the same as that of the preceding clause, and another to show that the subject is different.

Besides pronouns there are various other pro-forms such as *so*, *same*, and *likewise*, as well as *do*, which, as mentioned above, can be considered a pro-verb or just as a grammatical verb that allows one to omit a verb phrase.

Stephanie has a BA, work experience, and good character references, and Louise does too.

When the vending machine failed to produce the cigarettes, Buffy swore and kicked the machine, and Topsy did the same.

Harry failed physics, Paul likewise.

Pro-forms can substitute for a whole sentence. In the next set of examples we have *which* and *this* performing that function. *Which* introduces a non-restrictive relative clause loosely attached to the preceding clause, while *this* is the subject of a separate sentence.

James did a hamstring during the warm-up and could not play, which threw the coach's carefully planned strategy into confusion.

James did a hamstring during the warm-up and could not play. This threw the coach's carefully planned strategy into confusion.

One of the most obvious ways of achieving cohesion in discourse is to use some kind of linking word or affix. At the beginning of chapter six we noted that both clauses and sentences could be co-ordinated by the conjunctions *and*, *but*, and *or*. We probably think of these words as basic, but it is interesting to note that not all languages have words for 'and', 'but', or 'or', though they all appear to have linking words similar to 'then'.

The choice of an adversative linker such as *but* or *however* can reveal the speaker's or writer's attitude towards the relation of one proposition to another. Imagine the next pair of examples spoken by mothers hoping to have their daughter find a good husband. The mother of Tiffany regards being a member of the armed forces in a positive light, whereas the mother of Gertrude thinks membership in the military is a disadvantage.

> *Fred would make a good husband for Tiffany, and he's in the army.*
> *Leo would make a good husband for Gertrude, but he's in the army.*

A word like *but*, and indeed a word like *and* as used here, come under the heading of **discourse markers**. This is not a part-of-speech category but a functional category and it covers a variety of words and phrases that serve to link the discourse and/or to express the speaker's attitude. Consider the following dialogue:

> A: *The handle on my screen door has snapped off.*
> B: ***Let's see now***. *You could try gluing it.*
> A: ***Actually***, *I was thinking of trying that.*
> B: ***Well***, *it doesn't always work.*
> A: ***Anyway***, *it's worth a try.*

The discourse markers are in bold. Note that they play no part in conveying the content. The basic meaning would be the same if they were omitted, but the result would be somewhat unnatural. We usually use discourse markers to show how what we want to say is related to what has gone before. *Let's see now* indicates B is having a breather and thinking about the problem. With *Actually* A is telling B that she had thought of glue independently. *Well* indicates reservation or doubt, and *anyway* indicates that gluing is worth a try even though there is doubt about its efficacy.

Another way of achieving cohesion is to substitute a word or phrase that has the same or similar reference as one used earlier rather than a pronoun. How often have you seen an article on Shakespeare that uses *Shakespeare* in the first sentence, but *the bard* or *the Stratford bard* in some of the succeeding sentences. This kind of thing is common in news reports of sports where a team will often be referred to by its regular name on first mention, but then by its nickname thereafter, a practice that renders many a sports report incomprehensible to the uninitiated.

The terms *Shakespeare* and *the bard of Stratford-upon-Avon* are synonyms, but there can be semantic links in a text that are indirect. Speakers and writers make use of the audience's knowledge of situations and procedures. The following passage from a western of yesteryear illustrates the main cohesive devices: pro-forms, omission (indicated by [ ]), and linking words, plus an example of a semantic link between *The sheriff drew* and *Colts*. Readers of westerns are expected to know that sheriffs were armed with Colt 45 revolvers.

Bart began to reach for the knife on the bar behind him, but as he did so, he knocked over a glass. The sheriff drew. His twin Colts spat fire. Bart gave one brief convulsion and [ ] slumped to the floor.

Co-operative principle

If language be not in accordance with the truth of things, affairs cannot be carried on to success.
Confucius, *Analects*

Normal language use depends on shared culture, everyday logic, and co-operation between speaker and hearer. If you learn the grammar of a language (phonology, morphology, and syntax) plus the lexicon, you will still not be able to interact with the natives unless you learn something about their culture. You need to be able to pick up on references. Life in the US would be very confusing for anyone unfamiliar with Halloween, Homer Simpson, Mickey Mouse (and Micky Mouse courses!), the Primaries, the Yankees, and Thanksgiving.

At school we are taught logic and we accept its validity, but in everyday life we work on what I call 'everyday logic', which involves probability. Suppose I know my friend Pauline never goes out unless she is driving her car. I go past her apartment and I see her car is not in the carport, so I conclude that she is out. It could be that her car has been stolen or is in for repair, but I operate on the balance of probabilities. This everyday reasoning plays a big part in using language. We often have to sort our way through lexical ambiguities and work out who 'he' and 'she' refer to by assessing what is most likely to be what the speaker has in mind.

The third thing we need for successful communication is co-operation. The speaker must try to be clear and truthful, and the addressee must assume the speaker is being honest and straightforward when it comes to interpreting what has been said. The philosopher H. Paul Grice put forward what he called the **Co-operative Principle** governing verbal interaction. This he breaks down into four maxims:

Quantity   Give just the information required, no more no less
Quality   Don't lie or make claims for which you have no evidence
Relation   Be relevant
Manner   Be clear and orderly, avoiding ambiguity

These maxims may seem rather obvious requirements for successful communication, but they serve as a useful standard against which to judge deviations.

Quantity
When you attempt to communicate you need to estimate how much detail to include. You need to be able to calculate what your audience already knows.

If you give too little information, you run the risk of being obscure. If, on the other hand, you include too much information, you are likely to bore or insult your audience. As an example of including too much information, take the following. I once shared a compartment on a train out of London with two music professionals of African descent, she a singer, he a saxophonist. At one stage the singer said to the saxophonist, 'After Glyndebourne, I thought I would just teach for a while, but they were casting *Porgy and Bess* and they wanted someone black, so I auditioned and got a part in the chorus.' Now I would have thought most people are familiar with the fact that Gershwin's opera is for an entirely black cast, and *a fortiori* musical people would not need to be reminded.

People can flout the maxim of quantity in an attempt to deceive. If a man comes home from the casino and his partner asks him how much he lost and he replies $50 when in fact he has lost $500, he is violating the maxim of quantity. If he lost $500, then it is true that he lost $50, but the natural assumption is that a full disclosure is being made. Our gambler has flouted the maxim of quantity by providing insufficient information.

Quality

When we say things like *So I've been told, I'm pretty sure that...*, or *I'm absolutely certain that*, we are making an effort to observe the maxim of quality and indicate the strength of our evidence. It is interesting to note that in a number of languages the grammar requires an obligatory indication of the strength of evidence, usually in the form of a marker on the verb. In Tariana, a language of northwest Amazonia, there is a range of evidential markers from which one must be chosen. In the following example, *-ka* indicates that the speaker actually saw Jose playing football.

Jose	irida	di-manika-ka.
Jose	football	he-play-VISUAL

'Jose played football (We saw it).'

But in place of *-ka* there could have been *-mahka* 'we heard it', *-nihka* 'we inferred it from things we saw', *-sika* 'we inferred it from general knowledge', or *-pidaka* 'we were told'.

Relation

Consider the following exchange:

A: *Did you know that Bolivia has invaded Peru?*
B: *My daughter has a toothache.*

B's reply is obviously irrelevant, bearing no relation to A's statement and such gross irrelevance is unlikely from anyone with a normal grasp on reality. But calculated irrelevance is common in argument. Politicians, for instance, and Public Relations personnel are good at failing to answer questions put to them and answering another question or 'going off on a sidetrack'. Calculated irrelevance can also be used to indicate politely that you don't want to discuss a certain topic. If Donna says to Hal over a Friday after-work drink, 'Didn't I see you with one of the girls from the office the other night?' he might reply, 'Would you like another drink?' A direct, relevant reply nowadays is to say, 'Don't go there.'

When faced with an apparently irrelevant reply, addressees will normally make some effort to see a connection between the question and the reply. Suppose two supporters of the Melbourne Football team meet in Melbourne:

> A: *Are you going to the game on Saturday?*
> B: *We're playing in Sydney.*

At first glance, B's reply might seem irrelevant, but B estimates that A will be able to conclude from the fact that attendance would require a return journey of over 1700 kilometres that he (or she) is not going. In fact to have said just, 'No!'' would have violated the maxim of quantity (insufficient information). If B had said something like, 'No, we are playing in Sydney and it would take too long and be too expensive for me to go', he would probably be judged to have given too much information. In fact B's reply is a good example of the way language can work.

At a school reunion a woman identified a man who had been in her class and said, 'Ah, yes. I remember you. Weren't you smart?' He replied, 'I still am.' He was trying to be smart in another sense by picking up on the past tense, which was irrelevant in this context. The woman could have said, 'I remember you, a smart one.'

Manner

Sibyls and soothsayers are notorious for being vague and ambiguous. Croesus, the ancient king of Lydia, approached the Delphic oracle to ask whether he should attack the Persian Empire. He was told that he would destroy a great empire. He went ahead and attacked, and was defeated. He had destroyed a great empire, his own.

Most of us find it convenient from time to time to exploit ambiguity. Suppose a military commander is told that his troops have captured an enemy spy. He might say, 'Find out what he knows, but I don't want to hear of any torture being used.' The natural interpretation is that his troops are not to use torture, but there is also a literal reading, namely that the commander just doesn't want to hear about the torture. His troops can then torture to their hearts' content and if reprimanded, can appeal to the literal interpretation. If the commander is reprimanded by a higher authority, he can appeal to the natural interpretation.

Up till a generation or so ago respectable hotels would not allow a male and female to share a hotel room unless they were married. There is a story about Mr Brown who approached the reception desk with Mrs Jones in pursuit of a night of adulterous lust. The clerk asked them both were they married and they both said 'yes' and were given a room. They were married all right, but not to one another!

Sometimes a breach of co-operation can involve a failure to observe more than one maxim. In the film *Night Shift* (1982) Henry Winkler shows Michael Keaton a picture of his girlfriend and asks him what he thinks. Michael Keaton replies, 'Nice frame'. He flouts the maxim of quantity by giving insufficient information and the maxim of relation by mentioning the frame. Obviously Michael Keaton is not too impressed with the appearance of the girlfriend, but at least he is not openly derogatory.

Speech Acts

Actions that are carried out by words are called **speech acts**. One can make an assertion, a hypothesis, a promise, or a judgement. One can ask a question, direct someone to do something, or even bring about a new state of affairs: *I hereby pronounce you husband and wife*. Typically there is a correspondence between form and function. We use an interrogative form for a question, an imperative for a command, and the indicative for other functions such as making a statement, a threat, an apology, and so on.

function	form
Question	*Does it rain much here?*
Command or request	*Water those vegetables!*
Other	*We get a lot of rain during the spring.* (statement)
	I'll get you, you bastard. (threat)
	I am sorry for the inconvenience. (apology).

When the form and function match, we have a 'direct speech act'. Now all this is worth saying only because we can deviate from the match of form and function and produce what is called an 'indirect speech act'. Many indirect speech acts are aimed at softening the force of a command. Instead of saying *Pass the salt*, you might say *Could you pass the salt?* And it would be a pretty unco-operative person who answered *Yes* and left you without any of the requested condiment.

Suppose you take a job as a doctor's receptionist. A patient comes in and you know that he or she will have to wait. On the basis of your grammar book and lexicon you might feel that it is ok to say *Sit!* Well that might be all right for Fido, the dog, if you are working at the vet's, but it will seem strangely abrupt to a human patient. You might try, *Sit, please!* but that's not much better. The normal thing to say in this situation is to use a question form and say something like *Would you like to take a seat for a moment?* or *Would you like to take a seat? The doctor will see you shortly.* For some sitting situations there are fixed expressions available. If you find yourself in charge of an audience who have stood up for the national anthem and you want them to resume their seats, you say *Please, be seated.* If you want them to rise to drink a toast, you ask them to *Be upstanding.* These are formulaic imperatives, but they are imperatives of the verb *to be*, so these are not quite direct speech acts.

Sometimes requests are made indirectly via statements. You are a guest in somebody's house, you feel the room is a bit cold and you notice that the

window is open. You feel it would be rude to close the window yourself, so you say *It's getting a bit chilly in here* hoping your hosts will take the hint and close the window.

Conversation

Never ask an old man about his health. He might tell you!

As pointed out at the beginning of the chapter, conversation is the most common way language is used. There are fairly ritualized ways of beginning and ending a conversation. These vary across cultures. When English speakers meet an acquaintance they tend to use a greeting word such as *Hello! Hi! Good morning! Good afternoon! Good evening!* (but not *Good Night!*) and ask *How are you?* or *How are you doing?* These questions are meant to be answered in a perfunctory way, but sometimes people take the opportunity to give a resumé of their recent misfortunes. If a conversation is to ensue, then the interlocutors need to negotiate turn-taking. In some instances it will be obvious that a speaker has come to the end of what they want to say from the completeness of the content and the completeness of the syntax. The end of the speaker's turn will be marked by an appropriate intonation cadence, usually a fall, and, if hand movements and facial expression has played a part, there will be an appropriate coda in these modes too. In other instances there will be a question (*Have you seen* The English Patient*?*) or a tag question (*It's an intriguing film, isn't it?*), which invites a response.

If speakers want to hold the floor, they can signal they are continuing by pausing after some kind of connecting word such as *and, but,* or *or.* In the following example the speaker pauses after the second example of *so* (marked by...). Another possibility is to pause in the middle of a construction, for example after the subject. Note the hesitation pause after *they,* which is interrupted by the hesitation marker *er.* Obviously these breaks do not indicate the speaker has finished the turn. The question *Guess what?* invites only a short response and in fact is another means of indicating there is more to come.

> A: *So then they decided to go to the pictures and they... er... couldn't agree on which one to go to, so... so they tossed up between* Basic Instinct *and* The Sound of Music *and 'Guess what?'*
> B: *What?*
> A: *The flippin' penny rolled down a crack in the footpath and stopped on its side, you know, on its edge.*

If one wants to cut in, one can clear one's throat, raise one's hand with the index finger raised, move forward in one's seat, or all three. Where there are more than two people involved, this is a common strategy to 'bags' the next turn.

There are formalized ways of ending a conversation. Obviously there are leave-taking expressions such as *Good bye! Bye! Bye now! See yuh!* and *Ciao*, but one can't politely blurt out one of these expressions straight after an exchange of content. There needs to be a lead up. You might say something like *I'd better be getting along* or *Well, things to do*, or *Better get on*. If you think things have come to a natural end and the participants should be moving on, you might just utter a prolonged *so* or *well*, prompting the other participant or participants to start moving or exchange the customary leave-taking phrases.

The conventions for greeting, opening a conversation, turn-taking, permissible subject matter, and ending a conversation vary from culture to culture and differences of convention can raise problems in cross-cultural communication, usually accusations that the person from the 'other' culture is rude.

Sources and further reading

The Tariana example is from Aikhenvald, *A Grammar of Tariana*.

Useful texts include Bloor and Bloor, *The Functional Analysis of English*, which uses the framework of Michael Halliday, a framework in which a lot of work has been done on discourse in English; Cameron, *Working with spoken discourse*; and Cutting, *Pragmatics and discourse*. Grice's Co-operative Principle is to be found in his article 'Logic and Conversation'.

Problems

1 The following examples are grammatically correct, but in terms of discourse principles they are odd. Explain what is odd about them.

'Although it is against the rules for campers to bring dogs, several are wandering loose and some are with owners on leads.'   **Waikato Times**

John looks like his son.

A draught is here. (No, not a beer!)

Who gave the presentation speech at the dinner?
David gave the presentation speech at the dinner.

The prince went up to the king and he asked him if he was going to address the troops. He didn't reply, so he thought he might have to do it himself, but then he turned to him and said he would, so he didn't have to worry after all.

2 In certain contexts it is convenient to be very brief. This puts the onus on the audience to make a sensible interpretation on the basis of context. How might the following be misinterpreted? They are all written instructions, and I have it on good authority that they have all been misinterpreted at least on one occasion.

Ladies bring a plate, men a bottle.

Traditional instruction to those attending an amateur social function

No standing.

Kerbside sign

Take one teaspoonful after meals. Shake first.   Instruction on bottle of medicine

Wash before eating.

Instruction on lettuces

3 Read the following extract from a short story and then answer the questions below.

It had been a long flight from London to Newark, and then a four-hour wait for my flight to LA. I am not a gregarious man, at least not when I'm flying, and certainly not when I'm tired. So when I finally boarded, I was very pleased to find that I had a good seat, a window seat behind the partition that divided off business class, plenty of leg room, and no one next to me. At least that's the way it looked right up until departure time, but at the last moment I looked up to see a young woman in a white mini-suit scurrying towards my seat. 'Hi!' she said, holding out her hand, 'so you're the lucky guy who's got me. I'm Claudia. What's your name?'

I give her my name and immediately bury myself in the airline magazine, but to no avail. I have to hear her life story. She's leaving New Jersey to take up a job in LA. She's been waiting on standby all day, and she appears to have had the odd drop of vino, to judge from her breath. The job's only to keep her going until she makes it big in the soaps. That's her ambition, but she's not going to 'fuck' her way to the top. She's no 'slut'. She wishes she could smoke on the plane. She smokes two packs a day, just to control her 'hyperness'.

Now we are going through her snaps. Do I think she is pretty enough to make it in soaps? I am gracious about this, and to tell the truth she is quite good looking. What do I think she weighs? Now this is an awkward one. I know I can't guess too high, and I really don't know much about women's weights. But then I remember a number from South Pacific with the line, 'A hundred and one pounds of fun, that's my little honey bun.' I risk an estimate of 102. Fortunately, it turns out to be pretty close.

She chatters on endlessly, fidgeting in the seat like a bird, and when she isn't grabbing my arm, she's prodding me. I pray that Continental will take her away and stow her in some quiet place for the rest of the journey.

(a) Pick out all the discourse markers. This is not easy. One criterion you could use is to look for words that could be omitted without any loss of content. You could try to say something about the function of the discourse markers. Their function will probably be clear to you, but it will be difficult to make this explicit.

(b) What part does the choice of tense play in this narrative?

(c) Can you find any examples where the cohesion depends on the reader's knowledge of situations or settings rather than grammatical devices?

(d) What is the significance of the inverted commas around certain words? How might the force of the inverted commas be captured in speech?

4 In the last section of the chapter, it was mentioned that there are cross-cultural differences in the conventions for conducting conversation, but no examples were given. You might like to discuss your relevant experiences. Consider opening sequences including greetings, questions about health, and remarks on the weather. Consider how close the participants stand or sit. Do they touch? Does one person grab the wrist or forearm of the person sitting next to them? Does one person tap the lapel area of the other in making a point? Are long pauses allowed or does all space have to be filled? How loudly do the participants speak? What about subject matter? Some people are uneasy about discussing politics or religion. There are almost always some restrictions on sexual content. Finally, consider the closing sequences of a conversation.

You are likely to find that there are differences between male-to-male and female-to-female conversations and between the parts females and males play in cross-gender conversations.

Finally, be careful about making negative judgements about a culture or a gender. If there is a convention you don't like, that does not mean the convention is inferior to the one you are used to. On the other hand there are individual differences and you might be justified in condemning the practice of some who deviate from the norm for their group. I recently heard a sports commentator criticized for spraying interviewees with saliva.

PART III
Speech and writing

8. Phonetics

Colonel Pickering: *I rather fancied myself because I can pronounce twenty-four distinct vowel sounds; but your hundred and thirty beat me. I can't hear a bit of difference between most of them.*
Professor Henry Higgins: *Oh, that comes with practice.*

G. B. Shaw: *Pygmalion,* Act II

Syllables

There are two main kinds of speech sound: vowels and consonants. Virtually every word in every language contains at least one vowel. If you came across words like *pfft* or *skz* in a language, you would be surprised. You would wonder how they could be pronounced. There was a film called *Phffft,* starring Jack Lemmon and Kim Novak (1954). It referred to 'the sound made by the sudden disintegration of a marriage'! The sequence is pronounceable, but try conveying it so someone some distance away. You would find it pretty hard. You wouldn't be able to pronounce it loudly. To make a successful word you usually need at least one vowel. Vowels have carrying power. Vowels are made with **voice**, the sound made by vibrating the **vocal cords** in the voice-box, and letting this sound out through the mouth unimpeded. Voice is explained below, but first a word about syllables.

In all languages words are made up of syllables. The **syllable** is the smallest sequence of sounds a person will break a word up into in giving very, very slow dictation. The syllable usually contains a vowel as its **nucleus** and there may be one or more consonants preceding or following the vowel. Here are a few lines from Longfellow broken into syllables. I believe all readers will break up these words into the same number of syllables, but we may not all agree on where the boundaries are. Some readers might break *mighty,* for instance, into *migh-* and *-ty.*

Un-der a spread-ing chest-nut tree
The vill-age smith-y stands
The smith a might-y man is he
With large and sin-ew-y hands.

The consonant or consonants that precede the nuclear vowel constitute the **onset** of the syllable, and any consonants following the nucleus constitute the **coda**. The nucleus and coda together make up the **rhyme**, so called because this is the bit that rhymes in pairs like *stands/hands* and *stop/hop*, where the *st* and the *h* are the onsets and *-ands* and *-op* are the rhymes. If the rhyme consists only of a vowel, the syllable is said to be **open**. If one or more consonants follow the vowel, the syllable is said to be **closed**. Thus *meat*, *boot*, and *doom* are words consisting of a single closed syllable. *Me*, *boo*, and

The author, aged five, at the doctor's. Obviously a boy who knew his letters

do are words consisting of a single open syllable, as is *thigh* because we are talking about sounds, not letters of the alphabet.

In this book, and in linguistics generally, the words 'consonant' and 'vowel' refer to sounds, not letters. It is important to be aware of this, particularly in English where there are numerous discrepancies between letters and sounds. There are five vowel letters used in English, namely *a, e, i, o,* and *u,* plus *y,* which can represent a consonant as in *yes* or a vowel as in *smithy.* In some instances vowels and consonants are represented by a **digraph**, a pair of letters. For example, in the first syllable of the word *spreading* one vowel sound is represented by *ea,* and in *tree* one vowel is represented by *ee.* In many words such as *mane, cope,* and *bite* a vowel sound is represented by a combination of vowel letter plus 'silent e' flanking a consonant letter. Consider how these words would be read if the 'silent e' was lacking (*man, cop, bit*). It is common for a pair of consonant letters to represent a single consonant as with the *ll* in *village* and the *th* in *smithy.* On the other hand, the letter *x* in words like *box* and *extra* represents two consonants, namely a *k*-sound and an *s*-sound. *Box* sounds the same as *bocks,* and in advertising *socks* is often spelt *sox.*

In the following sections, we shall describe how vowel sounds are made, confining ourselves mainly to English, and then we will describe how consonants are made. In the course of these sections and in later chapters we will make frequent reference to the syllable.

Vowels

Speech sounds are made with breath from the lungs. To understand how these sounds are made it is necessary to consider first of all the **larynx** or voice box, which sits at the top of the trachea or wind-pipe. The larynx is larger in males than in females and is visible as a bulge in the throat known as the Adam's Apple. As you read this section, you will need to keep an eye on Figure 8.1, which shows the vocal organs. In the larynx are two flanges of tissue called the **vocal cords** (Figure 8.2). The opening between them is called the **glottis**. These cords can be brought together and set vibrating by the air coming from the lungs. This produces what we call **voice**, the sound that is common to all vowels. When you whisper, you let the air from the lungs pass through a narrow opening between the cords. This produces a weak noise. If we simply vibrate our vocal cords and open our mouth wide we get an *ah*-sound, the one doctors ask for when they want to examine our throat. Try making the *ah*-sound and then whispering the *ah*-sound. The difference is that the whispered version is **voiceless** and the ordinary one is **voiced**.

The various vowels are differentiated by moving the jaw, the tongue, and the lips. If we close our mouth somewhat and put our tongue near the roof of

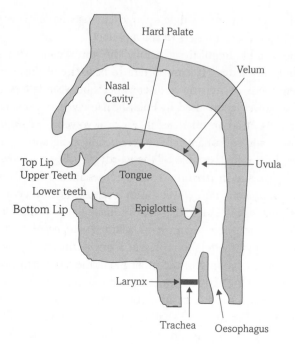

Figure 8.1 The vocal tract.

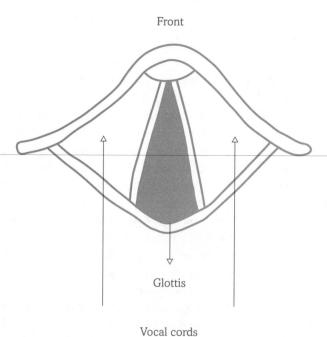

Figure 8.2 The Vocal cords.

the mouth, we get an *ee*-sound as in words like *meet* and *feet*. If we round our lips and put the back of our tongue near the back part of the roof of the mouth, we get an *oo*-sound as in words like *shoot* and *root*.

English is particularly inconsistent in representing vowel sounds. The letter *u*, for instance, represents one sound in *but*, another in *bush*, a third in *Lulu*, and a fourth in *use* (which sounds the same as *youse*, the non-standard plural of *you*). In any case the alphabet does not contain enough letters to represent all the speech sounds there are in English and other languages. Linguists need a way of representing speech sounds that is independent of the alphabetic conventions of any particular language and comprehensive enough to cater for all the sounds that humans use in one language or another. They use the **International Phonetic Alphabet** (**IPA**). From here on, as each speech sound is introduced, its IPA symbol will be given. By convention phonetic symbols are enclosed in square brackets. There is an American version of IPA. Standard IPA uses a number of special symbols, the American version uses fewer special symbols and makes more use of ordinary letters and diacritics to facilitate typing. Both systems are introduced below. The differences are mainly in the representation of the consonants. See Table 8.3.

As mentioned above, different vowel sounds can be made by moving the tongue to different positions, and they can be described in terms of where the highest point of the tongue is (see Figure 8.3). In terms of tongue height vowels can be described as **high**, **mid**, or **low**. In terms of forward and back the tongue is described as **front**, **central**, or **back**. If the tongue is raised as high as it can go and as far forward as it can go without touching the roof of the mouth or being close enough to cause audible friction, we get the high, front vowel of words like *beet* or *beat*. It is written as [iː] in IPA, where the [ː] indicates that it is a long vowel. In the American version of IPA a colon is used to indicate vowel length. If the tongue is low and central, we get the vowel of *hut* or *but* or the vowel of *ha* or *baa*. These vowels are similar in quality except that the vowel of *hut* and *but* is short and is written either with [a] or an upside down *v* symbol [ʌ], whereas the vowel of words like *ha* and *baa* is long and is written [aː]. If the tongue is raised as high as it will go and retracted so that the back of the tongue is close to the soft palate, the vowel [uː] of *Lulu*, *Lou*, or *do* is produced. This vowel is produced with rounded lips. There is a universal association of roundness of the lips with backness of the tongue, the higher the back vowel the more rounding there is. In virtually every language you will find a high, back, rounded vowel (Italian *la luna* 'the moon', French *un coup* 'a blow', etc.). However, unrounded high, back vowels do occur in various languages including Turkish and Cambodian (Khmer), and it must be said that lip rounding among some English speakers is not very strong, and in some varieties such as Cockney and Australian English, there is little rounding.

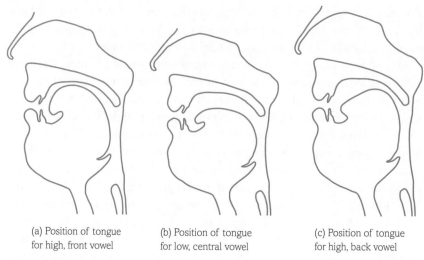

(a) Position of tongue for high, front vowel

(b) Position of tongue for low, central vowel

(c) Position of tongue for high, back vowel

Figure 8.3 Tongue positions.

   The full set of the English vowels is set out in Tables 8.1 and 8.2. Two major varieties are taken into account. For British English we refer to a contemporary version of **Received Pronunciation** (**RP**), which was also known as BBC English. This was a variety that arose among the educated class in south-eastern England and came to be recognized as a standard in Britain and throughout the Commonwealth countries. It was spoken only by a minority, though imitated to various degrees by a much larger number. Language is constantly changing, vowels in particular, and over the last few decades RP has changed towards an accent spoken over a wider social spectrum in south-eastern England. Some further discussion of this interesting social phenomenon is contained in chapter eleven. For American English we refer to **General American**, sometimes called 'Standard Midwestern' or simply 'Midwestern' (see chapter eleven, especially Map 11.2). An important difference between Received Pronunciation and General American is that in General American there is an *r*-consonant in the pronunciation wherever there is an *r* in the spelling, whereas in RP an *r*-consonant occurs only before a vowel. All speakers of English pronounce the *r* in words like *red* and *hairy*, but in RP there is no *r*-consonant in words like *hard* and *car*, though the [r] does appear where a word-final *r* is followed by a vowel at the beginning of the following word as in *The car overturned*. In fact among many speakers of RP and similar varieties an [r] occurs wherever a word ends in any vowel other than [iː] or [uː] and the following word begins with a vowel. Thus one hears *the idea*[r] *of it* and *I saw*[r] *it*.

   In listing the vowels we list just the vowels that are distinct from the point of view of conveying meaning. We list [iː] as in *beat* and [ɪ] as in *bit* because these

Table 8.1. The vowels of British English

	front	central	back
high	iː *meet, read* ɪ *hit*		uː *hoot, boot* ʊ *hood, put*
mid	e or ɛ *red, head* ɛː *bare, dare*	ɜː *heard, herd, word* ə *the*	ɔː *all, law, caught*
low	æ *hat*	ʌ or a *hut, butt* aː *baa, hard, laugh, path, glass*	ɒ *cot, hog*

Table 8.2. The vowels of American English

	front	central	back
high	iː *meet, read* ɪ *hit*		uː *hoot, boot* ʊ *hood, put*
mid	e or ɛ *red, head*	ɜː *heard, herd, word* ə *the*	ɔː *all, law*
low	æ *hat, laugh, path, rather, glass*	ʌ or a *hut, butt*	ɑː *baa, hard, cot, hog (caught)*

vowels distinguish these two words as well as numerous other pairs such as *neat/ knit* and *feet/fit*. We ignore the fact that these vowels show some variation in pronunciation from speaker to speaker and according to where they occur in a word, how rapidly they are spoken, and so on. The speech sounds that are distinguished by their ability to distinguish meanings are called **phonemes**. We shall explore the concept of the phoneme further in the next chapter.

The symbols used for the vowels require some comment. The letter [a] in IPA is for a low, front vowel, a little lower than the [æ] in *cat* and [ʌ] is for an unrounded mid-low back vowel. In practice these symbols are also used for a more central low vowel found in words like *but* and *up*, and that is how these alternatives are used in this book. The symbol [ɑː] is used for a low, back vowel. In transcribing words like *baa* or *ma* in RP, one could use [aː], or one could use [ɑː] for a more conservative RP pronunciation. For American English [ɑː] is generally more appropriate. With words like *hard* where the [r] is retained in American English, we would transcribe [haːd] or [hɑːd] for RP and [hɑːrd] for American English.

The main difference between the vowels of RP and of General American is that in General American [ɑː] is used not only for those words like *ha* and *hard*, which have [aː] in RP, but also for words like *cot* and *hog*, which have [ɒ] in RP, and for some words like *caught*, which have [ɔː] in RP. Another important difference is that words like *laugh, raft, bath, rather, fast, last, glass,* and *pass,* which have [aː] in RP, have [æ] in American English, or, more accurately [æː]. In Table 8.1 a vowel [ɛː] is included for words like *bare* and *dare*. This vowel occurs only in words with an *r* following the vowel in the spelling, and it arose as a consequence of the loss of the [r] in Received Pronunciation and indeed in most of England (see Map 11.1). This vowel sound occurs in American English too, but since the [r] is retained in General American, there is no need to consider [ɛː] as a distinct vowel, that is, as a vowel phoneme. A word like *bared* can be considered to have the same vowel as a word like *bed*, with any difference in quality or length attributable to the following [r].

The mid, central vowel [ə] shown in Tables 8.1 and 8.2 is different from all the others in that it is found practically only in unstressed syllables such as the first and last syllables of words like *arena* or *marina*. It is called **schwa**. Some speakers stress [ə] when contrasting the words *a* and *the* as in *I said a book not the book*. Other speakers have special stressed pronunciations for these words so that *a* rhymes with *hay* and *the* sounds the same as *thee*.

There is one further complication with [æ]. Readers are invited to think about this in problem 5 at the end of chapter nine.

Diphthongs

In making the [iː] vowel of words like *bee* or *bead* or the [ɔː] vowel of *all* or *law*, the tongue remains in a particular position. These are **pure vowels**. However, in making the vowel of words like *bay, buy, boy, bough*, and *bow(-tie)*, the tongue moves from one position to another. These are **diphthongs**. The IPA representation of diphthongs consists of two symbols, one for the starting point of the tongue movement and one for the end point. The course of the tongue movement is shown in Figure 8.4 where the quadrilateral defines the possible vowel space.

There are differences in the course of the tongue from one variety of English to another. We will ignore these for the moment, except to point out that the use of [oʊ] for the diphthong in words like *hope* and *home* follows a convenient convention. For many speakers the starting point of the tongue movement will be more central and it would be appropriate to write [əʊ].

Traditional descriptions of RP include the diphthongs [ɪə] (as in words like *fear, here*, and *deer*), [ʊə] (as in words like *tour* and *lure*), and [eə] or [ɛə] (as in words like *bare, chair*, and *there*). Words like *fear* and *here* tend nowadays to be pronounced with [iə] and can be interpreted as two syllables, one syllable with the vowel [i] and the other with the vowel [ə]. In the same way words like *tour* and *doer*, which tend to be pronounced with [uə], can be interpreted as having two syllables. The diphthong [ɛə] was often pronounced as [ɛː], particularly in closed syllables (i.e. where the vowel is closed by a consonant, e.g. *bared* as opposed to *bare*) and this is now the common pronunciation. Note that all these words have an *r* following the vowel in question and this *r* is pronounced in General American and in some varieties of British English (see Map 11.1). Where the *r* is pronounced, there is no diphthong.

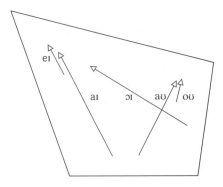

[eɪ] as in *hate, bay, rain, rein, eight, they, great*

[aɪ] as in *I, bite, my, rye, sigh, height, lie, buy, eye, aisle, eider*

[ɔɪ] as in *boy, buoy, boil*

[aʊ] as in *how, house*

[oʊ] as in *so, old, home, folk, road, soul, low, toe*

Figure 8.4 English diphthongs.

Some American writers on American speech consider the amount of tongue movement in the diphthongs of words like *mate* and *rose* to be negligible and they would simply write these words as [met] and [roz] respectively. If one follows this convention, one needs to use [ɛ] to distinguish the vowel of words like *met* from the diphthong of words like *mate*.

met [mɛt]   mate [met]

Consonants

Consonants are normally of shorter duration than vowels and occur at the edges or margins of syllables. Whereas vowel sounds are made with no obstruction to the breath stream, most consonants are made by blocking the breath stream at some point or constricting it. Let us look at various types of consonant starting with those that involve the maximum obstruction to the breath stream.

Stops
Stop sounds are made by blocking off or stopping the breath stream. The [p] sound as in *Peter* and [b] as in *Bill* are stops made by closing the mouth and blocking off the breath stream with the lips, a closure that can be easily observed. These **labial** sounds are the bane of ventriloquists whose aim it is

to conceal the movement of their articulators so that you associate the speech sounds they make with the lip movements of their dummy. The [t] sound as in *Tom* and [d] as in *Dick* are made by blocking off the breath stream with the tongue against the upper gum ridge. This ridge is also called the alveolar ridge and [t] and [d] are called **alveolar** stops. The [k] sound of *Kit* and the [g] sound of *Garry* are made by blocking the breath stream with the back of the tongue against the soft palate or **velum,** that is, the back part of the roof of the mouth. [k] and [g] are called **velar** stops.

The members of these three pairs of stops are distinguished by voice. The sounds [p], [t], and [k] are voiceless in that the sound is made just by the sudden blocking of the breath stream, while [b], [d], and [g] are voiced, that is, made with vibration of the vocal cords as well. Some further information on how this distinction is made is given in the following chapter. See also Figure 9.1 in chapter nine.

Fricatives

Fricatives are noise sounds made by squeezing the breath stream through a narrow opening. The sounds [f] and [v] are made by putting the upper teeth against the lower lip. This is something you can easily see. Another problem for the ventriloquist! The [f] is voiceless and [v] voiced. There are two *th*-sounds in English made by putting the tip of the tongue between the upper and lower teeth. The voiceless one is represented by [θ] (theta) and is found in *thistle, theology,* and *breath.* The voiced one is represented by [ð] (eth) and is found in *these, there,* and *breathe.* [s] and [z] are made by putting the tip of the tongue near the upper gum ridge. [s] is voiceless and is found in words like *sin, hiss, basic, kisser,* and *ice.* [z] is voiced and is found in *zebra, buzz,* and words like *music* and *amusing* where it is spelt with 's'. The *sh*-sound is voiceless and is made by putting the front of the tongue near the gum ridge and the front part of the roof of the mouth (the hard palate). It is found in words like *shut* and *bush.* The IPA symbol is 'long s' [ʃ], or [š] in the American version. The voiced equivalent is mainly found in the middle of words like *pleasure* and *division.* It is represented by [ʒ] (yogh) in IPA and [ž] in the American version. Some speakers have an initial [ʒ] in *genre* [ʒɒnr] and a final [ʒ] in *rouge* [ruʒ], both words being borrowed from French. Some speakers also have a final [ʒ] in [kæʒ], an abbreviation of *casual.*

The [h] sound of words like *hat* and *hide* is essentially whisper, that is, it is made by bringing the vocal cords close together and producing noise in the glottis. In English [h] occurs only at the beginning of a syllable as in *hot, hate, be-head,* and *be-hind.*

Affricates

An affricate is a combination of a stop and a fricative. There are two in English. One is the voiceless *ch*-sound found in words like *chap* and *catch* and at both ends of the word *church*, and the other is the voiced *j*-sound found in words like *jam, Roger,* and at both ends of the word *judge.* The *ch*-sound is represented in IPA by [tʃ], which captures the stop-plus-fricative nature of the sound, and the voiced equivalent is represented by [dʒ]. In the American version of IPA the ch-sound is represented by [č] and the *j*-sound by [j].

The fricatives [s], [z], [ʃ], and [ʒ] and the affricates [tʃ], [dʒ] are collectively known as **sibilants**.

Nasals

Nasals are made by blocking off the breath stream in the mouth and letting it escape through the nose. Take the [m] sound in words like *mum.* You can see the breath stream blocked off at the lips. Try making a prolonged *m*-sound and while you are making *mmmmm,* pinch your nose with your forefinger and thumb and you will cut the sound off. The velum or soft palate, the back part of the roof of the mouth, can be raised or lowered. In normal breathing it is lowered to allow the breath stream to escape through the nasal passage. In making most speech sounds it is raised to block off the nasal passage, but with nasals it is lowered.

The [n] sound of words like *nun* is a nasal made with the tongue against the upper gum ridge and the [ŋ] sound that occurs in words like *hang* and *singer* is made with the back of the tongue against the soft palate or velum.

Liquids

The [l] sound of words like *lily* is made by putting the tip of the tongue against the upper gum ridge and letting the breath stream pass over the sides of the tongue. It is called a **lateral** from the Latin *later-alis,* the root of which is *later-* 'side'. The [r] sound of words like *run* and *carry* is made by curling the tongue just behind the gum ridge and letting the breath stream pass over and around it. Both the *l*-sound and the *r*-sound are voiced and collectively they are known as **liquids**. It is possible to make an *r*-sound by flicking the tongue up to the gum ridge or even flicking it back and forth, that is, trilling it. Such an *r*-sound occurs in Scottish English and other English speakers often use it in certain circumstances such as declaiming poetry or trying to be very clear. In IPA the symbol [r] is used for the **trilled-*r*** and an upside down-*r* for the sound found in the mainstream pronunciation of words like *Garry*; however, we shall just use [r] for both. In Table 8.3, [r] is shown as a **rhotic**, which is a convenient label derived from the name of the Greek letter *rho*. It covers any of the sounds represented by letter *r*. The term **rhotic** is also applied to those accents such as General American that have [r] before a consonant or at the end of a word. Such accents are also sometimes called 'r-ful'.

Glides

There are two glides in English. One is the *y*-sound of words like *yes*. It is vowel-like in that the tongue is in the position for the vowel [i], but consonant-like in that it occurs on the margins of a syllable. In IPA it is represented by [j], but by [y] in the American version. To appreciate how it is like [i] but filling a consonant position, say *Iago* very slowly [iːaːgoʊ] and then say it faster keeping the stress on [aː]. You will find that [iː] reduces to the *y*-sound to yield [jaːgoʊ].

The other glide is the *w*-sound of words like *Wednesday*. It is vowel-like in that the tongue is in the position for [u], but it is consonant-like in that it occurs on the margins of a syllable. It is represented by [w] in IPA. To appreciate how it is like [u] but filling a consonant position, say *uakiri*, a word borrowed into English from Tupi for a type of monkey found in the Amazon Basin. Start by pronouncing each letter slowly [uakiri] and then say it faster aiming to keep the [a] vowel. You will find that [u] reduces to the *w*-sound to yield [wakiri]. In the normal English pronunciation the stress is on the second last vowel, so the pronunciation is [wəkiri], but the point remains, namely that [u] is vowel-like in articulation, but consonant-like in terms of syllable structure. You could also consider words like *distinguish* and note that *u* before a vowel is pronounced [w]. The [w] glide is made with rounded lips, so it has two points of articulation. It is velar, but it is also labial. It is described as a labio-velar glide. It is placed twice in Table 8.3.

The glides [j] and [w] are also called **semi-vowels** since they are articulated like [i] and [u] respectively.

Some speakers have a voiceless labio-velar fricative in *wh*-words like *white* and *whales*. The symbol for this is [ʍ]. This sound is found in Scotland and Northern Ireland, for instance, and among some speakers of American English. It is found sporadically in other parts of the English-speaking world, usually among speakers aiming to maintain a distinction found in the spelling.

I mentioned that [j] is like [i] and [w] like [u] except that the glides appear in the margins of the syllable and the vowels in the nucleus. All linguists agree that there is a [j] (or [y] in the American version of IPA) in words like *yeast*, *yes*, *yacht*, and *yuppie* and a [w] in words like *win*, *wan*, and *won*. In all these words the glide occurs in the onset of the syllable. But what about the coda of the syllable? Can a glide occur there? Linguists describing American English usually interpret the diphthongs of words like *high* and *how* as ending in a glide, so they would notate these words as [hay] and [haw] respectively, whereas linguists describing other varieties of English would transcribe these words as [haɪ] and [haʊ] respectively. The American practice makes sense if you consider cases where a vowel follows as in words like *buyer, Maya, cower, Howard, coir,* or *lawyer*. Take the word *Maya*. There are two syllables and the sound that comes in the middle is the same as the sound at the beginning of *yes*, so transcribing the word as [mayə] is appropriate.

Stops, fricatives, and affricates are known collectively as **obstruents** and nasals, liquids, glides, and vowels are called **sonorants**.

It was stated on page 125 that the nucleus of a syllable is a vowel. However, a liquid or nasal can be syllabic. In a word like *muddle* there are two syllables, but in normal pronunciation there is no vowel in the second syllable. The [l] fills up the syllable and we would notate the word as [mʌdl̩] where a subscript vertical line indicates a syllabic sound. Similarly in a word like *button* the [n] fills the second syllable [bʌtn̩]. In very slow dictation, syllable by syllable, a schwa would be the nucleus of the syllable in words like these, so we would have [mʌdəl] and [bʌtən].

The consonants of English are displayed in Table 8.3. They are laid out according to a general convention with **place of articulation** on the horizontal dimension with the sounds made at the front of the mouth to the left and those made at the back of the mouth to the right. **Manner of articulation** is shown on the vertical dimension with the sounds that are least vowel-like at the top of the chart and those that are most vowel-like at the bottom. Where two symbols are given in the palatal column, the first is general IPA and the second American.

Table 8.3. The consonants of English

		labial	labio-dental	dental	alveolar	palatal	velar	glottal
stops	voiceless	p			t		k	
	voiced	b			d		g	
fricatives	voiceless		f	θ	s	ʃ š		h
	voiced		v	ð	z	ʒ ž		
affricates	voiceless					tʃ č		
	voiced					dʒ ǰ		
nasals		m			n		ŋ	
lateral					l			
rhotic					r			
glides		(w)				j y	w	

A further alternative for the affricates is [tš] for the voiceless one and [dž] for the voiced.

What's in a name, phonetically speaking?

People often say things like, '*Mark*, that's a strong name.' They also say it of names like *Brad*, *John*, *Luke*, *Scott*, and *Zac*. Can you imagine them saying it about *Amanda*, *Melinda*, or *Melanie*? You might object, 'Ah, but they are names for females!' Yes, they are, but that is not coincidental. Where surveys of 'favourite words' or 'nice' words have been conducted, the results have shown a semantic preference for peace and quiet (*peace*, *twilight*, etc.) and a marked phonetic preference for polysyllabic words ending in a vowel and containing liquids (*l*, *r*), nasals (*m*, *n*) or glides. Stops occur but mainly in **homorganic** nasal-stop clusters or homorganic liquid-stop clusters. Homorganic clusters are those made at the same point of articulation such as the nasal-stop clusters [mp], [mb] (labial), [nt], [nd] (alveolar), and [ŋk], [ŋg] (velar). Homorganic liquid-stop clusters in English are [lt] and [ld] and, in American English, [rt] and [rd].

It is common for males to be given names that are monosyllabic and contain stops, names such as *Brad*, *Bruce*, *Clark*, *Craig*, *John*, *Rick*, and *Tom*. Judgements about 'strong' names may be based on associations, but phonetic properties seem to be relevant. Females are more likely to be given polysyllabic names ending in a vowel, and with the preferred consonants and consonant clusters mentioned above. Think of names such as *Angelina*, *Annabelle*, *Barbara*, *Cecilia*, *Elizabeth*, *Emma*, *Emily*, *Gabrielle*, *Laura*, *Linda*, *Mia*, *Olivia*, *Rhonda*, and *Wendy*. The difference between the male and female names is neutralized with abbreviated forms such as *Barb*, *Beth*, *Gab*, *Kate*, *Liz*, and *Pat*. As a group these are phonetically indistinguishable from the male names given above or shortened male names such as *Dan*, *Joe*, *Matt*, or *Mike*.

More speech sounds

All languages have stop sounds and most include labial, dental (or alveolar), and velar stops. A stop sound can also be produced by blocking off the breath stream in the glottis. It is represented by [ʔ]. In Cockney English, it is found in the middle of words like *batter*, where it corresponds to the [t] of standard pronunciation [bæʔə]. In contemporary RP a glottal stop can sometimes be found in words like *football* [fʊʔbɔːl] and *atlas* [æʔləs], that is, where an expected [t] precedes a consonant in the following syllable.

In Scottish English, there is a voiceless velar fricative [x] found in words like *loch* [lɒx]. This sound also occurs in German in words like *Bach* ('brook' or the name of the composer). German also has a voiceless palatal fricative [ç] as in *ich* 'I'.

In French there are four nasalized vowels. These are made with the velum down to allow the breath stream to escape through the nose as well as the mouth. In IPA these nasalized vowels are written with a tilde as in *un bon vin blanc* [œ̃ bɔ̃ vɛ̃ blɑ̃] 'a good white wine'. The symbol [œ] is like the vowel in English words such as *bet* [ɛ] but made with rounded lips. To produce [œ̃] you need to lower the velum as well.

In all languages the pitch varies over the course of an utterance, but in some languages like Chinese, Vietnamese, and Thai and in numerous African languages a particular vowel can be pronounced with a higher-than-normal pitch or a lower-than-normal pitch to yield a word with a different meaning. There is also the possibility of rising or falling pitch. These distinctive pitch levels and contours are called **tones**. The following illustration from Thai shows the diacritics used to mark them.

mid level tone	kʰaː	1. to be stuck
	kʰaː	2. species of grass
high level tone	kʰáː	to trade
low level tone	kʰàː	galangal (aromatic rhizome used in cooking)
rising tone	kʰǎː	leg
falling tone	kʰâː	1. price
	kʰâː	2 (a) slave, servant (b) I, me

There are numerous other speech sounds found in various languages around the world and there is no space to describe them all here, but perhaps **clicks** are worth mentioning. They are a regular feature of the Khoesaan (Khoisan) languages and some Bantu languages of southern Africa such as Zulu. They are used in English, but not as parts of words. The *tsk tsk* sound used to express disapproval is a type of click. The back of the tongue is pressed against the velum and the tip of the tongue is pressed against the teeth. As the middle of the tongue is lowered, a low pressure pocket is formed and as the tip of the tongue is moved from the teeth, the inrushing air produces a click. Another type of click is used to express encouragement (usually accompanied by a thumbs-up sign), and yet another to tell horses to 'giddy-up'.

Markedness

At this point we will introduce the notion of **markedness** in relation to speech sounds. It is an important concept, which has relevance to the make-up of words, to syntax, semantics, and language use. Some languages have a high, front rounded vowel. It occurs, for instance, in French *tu* 'you'. To make this sound you raise your tongue as if you were going to say [i], but you round your lips. This sound occurred in Old English where it was written with *y* and this is how it is represented in IPA, so French *tu* would be [ty]. In the American version of IPA this vowel is written [ü] as it is in the normal orthography (spelling) of German, e.g. *übung* [ybʊŋ] 'exercise'. The vowel [y] is marked with reference to [i] in that it has an extra feature, namely rounding. It is less common than [i] in the languages of the world, and any language that has [y] has [i]. In other words the presence of the high, front rounded vowel implies the presence of the high front unrounded vowel. Of the pair [i] and [y] the vowel [i] is **unmarked** and [y] is **marked**.

The nasalized vowels of French are marked with respect to the ordinary oral or non-nasalized vowels. Rounded front vowels are marked with respect to unrounded front vowels, so the nasalized, rounded, front vowel of French introduced above, namely [œ̃], is doubly marked.

A good example of markedness can be found in the marking of singular and plural as in English *book* and *books*. The singular is literally unmarked and the plural literally marked in that it bears an extra form to mark plural, namely -s.

The unmarked alternative in an opposition is the basic one. The term 'unmarked' is sometimes equated with natural. For instance, it is unmarked for nasals, liquids, glides, and vowels to be voiced.

Alert readers may have noticed that in the discussion of sexist language on pages 52 and 53, the terms 'marked' and 'unmarked' were used with reference to language practices that treat males as unmarked and females as marked. This extended usage of the terms is fairly standard.

Sources and further reading

Basic information on phonetics is available in numerous sources. A good, authoritative book is Ladefoged, *A Course in Phonetics*. A comprehensive list of phonetic symbols is available in *The Handbook of the International Phonetic Association*.

Cruttenden, *Gimson's Pronunciation of English* (6th edition) is a good guide to British English. Up-to-date information on contemporary Received Pronunciation is available aplenty on the Web. Just type 'Received Pronunciation' into your search engine. In particular look for an article by J. C. Wells entitled 'Whatever happened to Received Pronunciation?' Some sites include recorded samples that enable you to hear the sounds.

A number of web sites offer information on the pronunciation of American English. Try 'Phonetics: The sounds of English and Spanish – The University of Iowa'. You can hear the sounds and see an animated picture of the production of each one.

Problems

1 Go through the vowels and consonants of English one by one. Pronounce each slowly and see if you can tell where the tongue and lips are. Whatever variety of English you speak, you will find that you will probably have the set of consonants listed in this chapter (with [ʍ] perhaps an exception], but there is a good deal of variation with vowels. As you go

through the vowels and diphthongs, list examples of each sound from your own English.

2 A useful exercise is to listen to examples of different accents, your fellow students or presenters and interviewees on the radio and television. You also hear different accents in dramas, but these are more often than not imitations. With any accent you hear try to identify what marks it as different from your own. Pay attention to the vowels, particularly the long vowels and diphthongs.

3 Transcribe the following words into IPA. You can aim at any accent you are familiar with. Beware of traps for young players. For instance, don't put letter-*c* for the first consonant in *cat*.

cat	[ ]		knee	[ ]	
knit	[ ]		promise	[ ]	
bottom	[ ]		kitchen	[ ]	
usual	[ ]		Thomas	[ ]	
ewes	[ ]		music	[ ]	

Breathe with slow breaths.   [   ]

She judges churches harshly.   [   ]

An English film   [   ]

4 Transcribe the following words from IPA into normal orthography (spelling).

(a) [sɪŋ]   ....   [sæŋ]   ....   [sʌŋ]   ....
(b) [ðæt]   ....   [θɪsl̩]   ....   [θæŋks]   ....
(c) [ɪz]   ....   [aɪs]   ....   [aɪz]   ....
(d) [reɪt]   ....   [raɪt]   ....   [raʊt]   ....
(e) [wʊmn̩]   ....   [wɪmn̩]   ....

Now try some sentences. They are all quotes, misquotes, or thought-to-be quotes from films.

5 In this first batch there are spaces between the words.
(a) [juː eɪnt hɜrd nʌθŋ̩ jɛt]
(b) [pleɪ ɪt əgɛn sæm]
(c) [huː wəz ðə θɜːd mæn?]
(d) [eləmentriː diə wɒtsn̩]

6 Now try some phrases and sentences with no spaces between words.
(a) [kʌmʌpn̩siːmiːsʌmtaɪm]
(b) [meɪðəfɔːsbiːwɪθjuː]
(c) [wiːlɔːlweɪzhævpærɪs]
(d) [ʃeɪkn̩bʌtnɒtstɜːd]

7 The following are in the American version of IPA and represent General American pronunciation.

   (a) [ðərʌšn̩zɑrkʌmɪŋ]

   (b) [ændaɪgɛsðætwəzyɔrəkɑmpləsɪnðəwʊdčɪpər]

   (c) [ðɛlɔːizəjɛləsmɪstrəs]

   (d) [yuːdoʊntnoʊwɑtlʌvmiːnz təyuːɪtsjʌstənʌðərfɔːrlɛtərwɜːrd]

   (e) [wɛlnoʊbɑdiːzpɜːrfɪkt]

   (f) [wɑtkn̩aɪduːoʊldmæn? aɪmdɛdɑːrntaɪ?]

8 Read the following joke and then consider the last two words. Has the discussion of glides and their relation to vowels in this chapter thrown some light on how this joke works?

> *Two boll weevils grew up in Arkansas. One went to New York and became a famous actor. The other stayed behind in the cotton fields and never amounted to much. He became known as the lesser of two weevils.*

On the same point, you might consider the name *Aloysius*. In my experience it is pronounced [æləwɪʃəs]. Where does the [w] come from? You need to assume an earlier pronunciation with a full (non-reduced) vowel in the second syllable.

9 The order of frequency of occurrence of the consonants of English is as follows:

[n] [t] [d] [s] [l] [ð] [r] [m] [k] [w] [z] [v] [b] [f] [p] [h] [ŋ] [g] [ʃ] [j] [dʒ] [tʃ] [θ] [ʒ]

With an eye on Table 8.3 see what generalizations you can make about the first half dozen or so and the last half dozen. The appearance of [ð] in sixth position spoils a promising generalization; it owes its position to the high frequency of the word *the*.

9. Phonology

A ghost! I'm aghast! I should've guessed!

Take It From Here, **BBC radio comedy programme 1948–1960**

The phoneme

Speech sounds are regularly affected by neighbouring sounds. We described [n] as an alveolar nasal and [l] as an alveolar lateral, but in words like *tenth* or *plinth* the [n] will be dental and in words like *health* and *wealth* the [l] will be dental. The *th*-sound [θ] is dental and the tongue anticipates the dental position in making the preceding [n] or [l]. It would be hard not to do this. It is difficult to detect any difference in sound between a dental and an alveolar nasal or lateral, but you can trying saying *tent* slowly and feel where your tongue goes, and then try saying *tenth* and feel where your tongue goes. Dental-n and dental-l are represented in IPA as [n̪] and [l̪].

Some speech sounds exhibit a certain variation independently of neighbouring sounds. For example, some speakers pronounce the [r] in *three* with a trill in an attempt to be very clear in giving phone numbers, etc. This is called **free variation**. In the previous chapter it was mentioned that among some speakers of contemporary Received Pronunciation a glottal stop appears in words such as *Gatwick*, which may be pronounced [gæʔwɪk]. In fact some speakers alternate between [gæʔwɪk] and [gætwɪk]. This variation is limited to a particular position (before a consonant at the beginning of the next syllable), but it is not determined by neighbouring sounds, and it has the potential to signal something other than basic meaning. The choice of [t] in this environment could indicate an attempt at being careful.

In the previous chapter we said that humans are capable of making over 100 different speech sounds and that each language selects some of these. We then listed forty-two sounds for British English, but in doing that we ignored differences between alveolar [n] and dental [n̪] and between [ɛə] and [ɛː] in words like *care* and *bare* because these differences do not affect meaning. When we say that RP has forty-two speech sounds, we mean it has forty-two distinctive speech sounds or **phonemes**. We ignore differences between the actual sounds or **phones** if they do not affect meaning. Typically a phoneme is pronounced in a number of different ways in different environments and these different types of phone are called **allophones**. When we want to distinguish phonemes from allophones we enclose the symbols for phonemes in slashes (obliques). Thus we might say that /n/ has allophones [n] and [n̪].

To appreciate the difference between phones and allophones we might think of advertisements for new houses. A builder might advertise the Casa Grande, the Hacienda, the Mansion, and the Villa. At a particular point in time the builder might have thirty-four actual houses under construction. The four models the builder advertises correspond to phonemes and the actual structures of timber, bricks, and mortar correspond to phones. If the Casa Grande is to be built on a lot that slopes down to the left, there will be a sub-floor area on the left; if the Casa Grande is built on a block sloping down to the right, the sub-floor area will be on the right. These are analogous to allophones conditioned by the environment. The Hacienda might be offered in double-tumbled beige bricks, Brazilian Brown bricks, or Alaskan White bricks. The different coloured versions are also analogous to allophones, but they can be chosen freely just as one might choose [ɛː] or [ɛə] in the mainstream British English pronunciation of words like *there* or *care*.

Spelling is based on phonemes. English spelling is irregular, but it never shows differences that do not matter from the point of view of meaning. Native speakers are attuned to those distinctions that affect meaning and oblivious to others. When you learn a new language, you can expect to have difficulty distinguishing sounds that are allophones in your own language. As mentioned above, the alveolar [n] and dental [n̪] both sound the same to English speakers. In some languages these sounds belong to different phonemes, that is, the distinction between alveolar and dental is relevant to meaning. Learning to hear this distinction presents a challenge for an English speaker.

Minimal pairs

Suppose you are presented with the problem of learning a language that does not have a written form, a language of Brazil or New Guinea, for instance. How would you work out which distinctions were phonemic? The first rule of thumb is to look for **minimal pairs**, words that have a different meaning, but which differ minimally. In Kalkadoon (Kalkutungu), a language spoken until recently in Queensland, Australia, there is a word [n̪aː] 'this' and a word [naː] 'to stand'. This is a minimal pair and we can conclude that the difference between the dental nasal and the alveolar nasal is responsible for the difference in meaning. The second rule of thumb is to see if two phones (sounds) can occur in the same position. In the Kalkadoon example the dental and alveolar nasals both occur in word-initial position, so there can be a minimal pair. But what if one occurred only in one position (say, between vowels) and the other occurred only in another position (say, word-initially)? In that case there couldn't be a minimal pair based on [n] and [n̪]. The technical term for this kind of distribution is **complementary distribution**: the distribution of one speech sound complements that of another speech sound. This of course is the situation in English referred to above. The dental nasal [n̪] occurs only before the voiceless dental fricative [θ] and the alveolar nasal [n] occurs elsewhere, that is, only in various other positions. The dental nasal and the alveolar nasal cannot contrast.

Minimal pairs are sometimes elusive, but often a near minimal pair will suffice. At the head of this chapter there is a line from an old radio program, 'A ghost! I'm aghast! I should've guessed!' The words *ghost* and *guessed* are a minimal pair, but *aghast* is for practical purposes the same as if it had been *ghast, since the schwa [ə] in the first syllable of *aghast* is unlikely to have influenced the following vowel. It is difficult to find minimal pairs for [ʃ] and [ʒ] in English, mainly because, except in a few foreign words, [ʒ] occurs only between vowels. We would normally take a near minimal pair such as *thresher* and *treasure* to be evidence that these two sounds belong to different phonemes.

Stops: phonemes and allophones

Let's look at another example of allophones. In listing the speech sounds of English we described the stops [p], [t], and [k] as voiceless and the stops [b], [d], and [g] as voiced, but the labels 'voiced' and 'voiceless' in this context need some qualification. In pairs of words like *pill/bill, pat/bat,* and *putt/butt* [p] differs from [b] in that with [p] there is aspiration, a puff of air following the release of the stop. The voicing of the vowel does not begin immediately the stop is released, but it does with [b]. The same point could be made about the pairs [t]/[d] and [k]/[g]. If we write the words *pat, tat,* and *cat* in a narrow phonetic transcription, they would be [pʰæt], [tʰæt] and [kʰæt], where the superscript *h* represents the aspiration. (A narrow transcription is one that shows more detail than a broad one.)

Now let us look at what happens when stops appear at the end of a word as in *rip/rib, right/ride,* and *luck/lug.* In this position the voiceless stops are differentiated from their voiced counterparts by the fact that the whole syllable is shorter before a voiceless stop. The vowel in *rip* is shorter than the vowel in *rib*, the vowel in *right* is shorter than the vowel in *ride*, and the vowel in *luck* is shorter than the vowel in *lug*. This shortening occurs before voiceless fricatives like /s/ and voiceless affricates like /tʃ/ as well as before voiceless stops, and it affects 'long' and 'short' vowels. In other words, whatever the natural length of a vowel or diphthong, it will be shorter before a voiceless stop or fricative, and, strange to say, in English it is this difference in vowel length that is the main clue to whether a syllable-final stop is voiced or voiceless.

The point is illustrated in Figure 9.1, which displays waveforms for the words *bit*, *beet* (or *beat*), *bid*, and *bead*. The waveform is a record of the rise and fall of amplitude or intensity over the course of the word. Note that the sound of the vowels dies away with the occlusion or blocking of the breath stream leading into the final stops. The /t/ in *bit* can be seen just before the 8.8 mark, and the /t/ in *beet* can be seen just past the 10.0 second mark. The main point of the illustration is to show length differences in the syllable. In the second row we have *bid* and *bead* with the expected difference in vowel length between the short vowel /ɪ/ in *bid* and the long vowel /iː/ in *bead*, which has

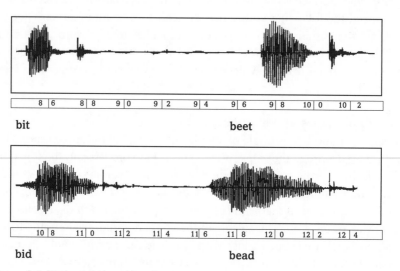

Figure 9.1 Bit, beet, bid, and bead.

the same length as the vowel in words like *bee* where no consonant follows. The difference in length between the short vowel /ɪ/ in *bit* and the long vowel /iː/ in *beat* is maintained, but note the vowels in these two words are much shorter than in *bid* and *bead*.

At this point we can see that the notion of a phoneme is quite abstract. A phoneme can have allophones (variant pronunciations), and its presence can sometimes be detected more by its effect on a neighbouring phoneme than in itself.

In the film *Mickey Blue Eyes*, James Caan, an American gangster, tries to teach the English art auctioneer, Hugh Grant, to speak like like he does. He gets him to say *Hey, forget about it.*

Hugh Grant: *Hey, forget about it.*
James Caan: *Change the t's to d's.*
Hugh Grant: *Hey, forged aboud id.*
James Caan: *Id?*
Hugh Grant: *But you said change the t's to the d's.*
James Caan: *But not the last one.*

This is an instructive example. First of all it shows that an American can see this particular difference between British and American English, but when James Caan gives the correspondence of [t] and [d], he overgeneralizes, and realizes his mistake only when he hears *id*. (The correct environment is between vowels where the following vowel is unstressed.) It is also interesting that he considers that /t/ is to be changed to /d/, though not having had the benefit of reading a book like this one, he expresses the rule in terms of letters of the alphabet. It is a moot point as to whether an **intervocalic** /t/ pronounced by flicking the tongue up to the alveolar ridge, with continuous voicing, sounds like /d/ or is actually pronounced the same as /d/. In other words is /d/ pronounced with a flap of the tongue rather than as a true stop? Readers familiar with this *d*-like pronunciation might like to think about it. The phenomenon is not unknown in Australian English, though it has not always been as common as it is nowadays. When I was at primary school, the standard way of asking someone to desist from applying a Chinese burn or an Indian headlock or whatever was to say *Quit it up!* I learned this as *Quid it up!* and never connected *quid* with the comparatively rare word *quit* until I was an adult.

Now let us look at words like *spat*, *stick*, and *scout*, words that begin with a consonant cluster with [s] followed by [p], [t], and [k] respectively. In such words there is no aspiration, no puff of breath, no delay in the onset of voicing. But note that in this environment you can't have [b], [d], and [g]. In this position you don't need to differentiate the pairs [p]/[b], [t]/[d], and [k]/[g]. The voiced stops cannot occur. The distinction between voiced and voiceless stops is **neutralized** in this environment.

You can check the presence of aspiration in words like *pat*, *tat*, and *cat* and the lack of aspiration in words like *spat*, *stick*, and *scout* or *bat*, *dot*, and *gull* by taking a sheet of A4 paper and holding it in front of your mouth while you say these words. Hold the sheet about half way down and a couple of inches away from your lips. The sheet will move when you pronounce an initial /p/, /t/, or /k/, but not when an /s/ precedes, and not with initial /b/, /d/, or /g/. The difference is very noticeable with the labials. You will notice a big puff with /p/, no puff with /sp/ or /b/.

As mentioned above, speakers of different languages employ a certain set of the sounds from the range that the vocal apparatus is capable of producing. When it comes to bilabial stops English chooses the sounds [p], [pʰ] and [b], but only two bilabial stop phonemes because [p] and [pʰ] are variants or allophones of the one phoneme. In some languages these three sounds [p], [pʰ], and [b] are separate phonemes. Thai is such a language as the following set of words illustrates. The sounds [p], [pʰ], and [b] can all occur in the same word-initial position and switching from one to the other produces a change in meaning. This cannot happen with [p] and [pʰ] in English since both cannot occur in the same position. In English [p] and [pʰ] are in **complementary distribution**: one variant occurs in one position and the other in another position.

English

/paː/	[pʰ aː]	Pa
/spaː/	[spaː]	spa
/baː/	[baː]	baa (of sheep), bar (RP)

Thai

/pʰàː/	to split
/pàː/	forest
/bàː/	shoulder

It is common for languages not to distinguish voiced and voiceless stop phonemes at the ends of words. This happens in Thai, for instance, and in German. The German words *der Bund* 'the league', *das Bund* 'the bundle', and *bunt* 'colourful' are all pronounced [bʊnt], though the voiced and voiceless stops are distinguished where a vowel follows as in the plural, so *das Bund* has a plural *die Bunde* [bʊndə] 'the bundles'.

Languages can have one, two, three, or four phonemically distinct sets of stops:

• Some languages have just one series of stops. Neither voicing nor aspiration is phonemic. Finnish is like that, as are many Australian languages.
• Many languages have two sets of stops. Many are like English in having voiceless and voiced sets. Mandarin Chinese has an unaspirated set (written

with *b*, *d*, etc., in the official romanization) and an aspirate set (written *p*, *t*, etc).

- Some languages have three sets. Ancient Greek had voiceless, voiceless aspirate, and voiced stops. Thai has this three-way contrast in labials (as illustrated above) and dentals, but only a two-way aspirate/non-aspirate contrast in palatal and velar stops. Cambodian (Khmer) is the same.
- In some languages spoken in India, such as Hindi, there is a series of voiced aspirate stops written *bh*, *dh*, etc., as well as voiceless stops, voiceless aspirate stops, and voiced stops, i.e. four series of stops.

Natural classes

It is common for classes of sounds to behave in similar ways. The class of nasals, for instance, /m/, /n/, and /ŋ/, all behave alike in that nasalization tends to spread to neighbouring vowels. In a word like /liːn/ 'lean', for instance, the velum will lower just before the tongue blocks off the breath stream at the alveolar ridge, so that the last part of the vowel will be nasalized. It will also be obvious from much of the discussion up to this point that the three voiceless stops, /p/, /t/, and /k/, behave alike. Common behaviour is linked to manner of articulation and point of articulation and these properties are picked out in Table 8.3 by the rows and columns. In descriptions of language constant reference is made to these columns and rows, which pick out natural classes of phonemes.

Of course, a particular phoneme may exhibit distinctive properties. We have seen in the last chapter that /t/ can be pronounced as a glottal stop, and it can also be pronounced as a flap (see the panel).

Summary

The phonemic principle involves picking out similar sounds and seeing if they contrast in various positions. If they contrast in any one position, then they belong to separate phonemes. They need not contrast in every possible position. An example was given above showing that there was a three-way contrast in bilabial stops in Thai. This contrast holds for syllable onsets, but stop contrasts are neutralized in Thai in syllable-final position so there is only one possible bilabial stop as in a word like *ráp* 'receive'. Some sources use *p* in the romanization, some use *b*, and some even use *bp*.

If two similar sounds are in complementary position (the distribution of one complements the distribution of the other), then they cannot contrast and we assign them to the same phoneme. Examples were given above of dental-n [n̪], which occurs only before a dental, and alveolar-n [n], which occurs elsewhere. There may be complementary distribution between sounds that are quite unlike as there is with [h] (always syllable initial) and [ŋ] (always syllable final), but we would not assign two sounds that were quite different to the same phoneme.

The notion of the phoneme is fundamental and the phonemic principle is implicit in all systems of writing. As we shall see in the next chapter, writing has pictographic origins, but in all cases it comes to represent phonemes or combinations of phonemes, usually syllables.

Putting the sounds together

Languages vary in what sequences of sounds they allow and what word shapes they allow. In chapter one it was pointed out that a visitor to New Zealand quickly gets to recognize Maori place names. Maori has ten consonants, namely /p, t, k, m, ŋ, f, h, r/, and /w/. The velar nasal /ŋ/ is written with the digraph *ng* and the /f /is written with the digraph *wh*. There are five vowels /i, e, a, o/, and /u/, each of which can be long (or double) or short. There are no consonant clusters; all syllables are open, that is, they end in a vowel. Words vary in length. Most have two or more syllables. Monosyllabic words (those of one syllable) tend to be grammatical words corresponding to English words such as 'the' and 'shall'.

kahawai	'type of fish'
kauri	'type of tree'
pakeha	'European person'
kumara	'sweet potato'
Mahuru	'September'
ahurea	'culture'

Now contrast these words with the following representative sample of words from Mandarin Chinese. They are given in the official Pinyin romanization where *ng* represents a velar nasal, *j* a palatal affricate [tʒ], *z* a dental affricate [ts] and *zh* a **retroflex** affricate. (Try [ts] with the tip of your tongue curled back.)

liăn	'face'	*diàn-yĭng*	'movie'
mă	'horse'	*wŏ-men*	'we'
yăn	'eye'	*Bĕi-jīng*	'Beijing'
yí	'to suspect'	*zhōng-guó*	'China'
míng	'bright'	*píng-zi*	'bottle'

One can immediately see that words tend to be monosyllabic or to consist of a pair of syllables. There are tones and there are only two consonants possible at the end of a syllable, namely *n* and *ng*.

The word shapes or patterns of syllables a language allows are called **phonotactics**. The phonotactic patterns of English are not easy to describe. English allows a great range of consonant clusters between vowels and at the

Table 9.1. Initial consonant clusters in English

/pl/	play	/tl/	*					/kl/	clay
/pr/	pray	/tr/	try					/kr/	crane
/pw/	*	/tw/	twine					/kw/	quick
/bl/	blade	/dl/	*					/gl/	gloat
/br/	brine	/dr/	dry					/gr/	grit
/bw/	*	/dw/	dwarf					/gw/	Gwen
/sp/	spot	/st/	stick					/sk/	skite
/spl/	splay	/stl/	*					/skl/	sclerosis
/spr/	spray	/str/	street					/skr/	screw
/spw/	*	/stw/	?					/skw/	squid
/sm/	smile	/sn/	snip						
/fl/	flea	/θl/	*	/sl/	sleep	/ʃl/	*		
/fr/	free	/θr/	through	/sr/	*	/ʃr/	shrill		
/fw/	*	/θw/	thwart	/sw/	swing	/ʃw/	*		

ends of words, but the clusters found at the beginning of words are simpler to describe. They are laid out in Table 9.1.

A number of regularities become apparent when the various clusters are laid out like this.

(i) Note first of all that the two-consonant clusters are made up of a stop or voiceless fricative followed by a sonorant, or by /s/ plus a voiceless stop (but see (viii) below).

(ii) Three-consonant clusters are made up of /s/ plus a voiceless stop plus a liquid or glide (but see (vi) below).

(iii) There is no /sŋ/ and that is because /ŋ/ occurs only at the end of a syllable. The velar nasal was once only a variant or allophone of /n/ occurring before a velar stop in words like ink [ɪŋk] and king [kɪŋg]. When the /g/ was lost in mainstream English from words like king, the velar nasal became a phoneme in its own right. A word like king /kɪŋ/ formed a minimal pair with kin /kɪn/. Incidentally, some speakers retain /g/ in words like king, and some retain it only where a vowel follows as in The Last King of Scotland.

(iv) The table reveals a number of regular or **systematic gaps.** There are no clusters of labials though English speakers can pronounce /bw/ in words like Swahili bwana 'master' and /pw/ in words like Spanish pueblo 'people'. Also there are no clusters of an alveolar and /l/, nor of a dental and /l/. The absence of the cluster /stw/ is an **accidental gap.** I have been told that at some universities Student Week (the week before the end-of-year exams) is abbreviated to Stweek [stwiːk], which fills in the gap.

(v) The alveo-palatal /ʃ/ has a very limited distribution in initial clusters. It occurs with /r/ in words like *shrill* and *shrimp*, but /ʃl/ does not occur in ordinary words, only in a few words borrowed from German such as *schlieren* 'streaks in igneous rocks' or from Yiddish (which is a sister language of German) such as *schlemiel* 'awkward, unlucky person'. The cluster /ʃw/ occurs in the linguistic term *schwa* for the mid-central vowel [ə] and in the brand name *Schweppes*, both borrowed from German, though *schwa* ultimately comes from Hebrew. These borrowed words along with other German and Yiddish borrowings such as *schmaltz* and *schnauzer* are not really part of mainstream English and are not used at all by a large proportion of the population. If we confine ourselves to words well established in English, we find an interesting pattern between the /s/ clusters and the /ʃ/ clusters as displayed in Table 9.2.

Table 9.2. Sibilant–sonorant clusters in English

/sl/	slip	/ʃl/	*
/sr/	*	/ʃr/	shrill
/sw/	swim	/ʃw/	*

The sole cluster with ʃ is /ʃr/ and it complements the /sr/ gap in the s-clusters. Some linguists would take words like *shrill* to be phonemically /sril/ with [ʃ] being the pronunciation of /s/ that occurs in this cluster. It is interesting to note that a majority of English speakers, including newsreaders, pronounce the *Sri* of *Sri Lanka* as [ʃriː]. They presumably aim at [s] and don't notice that it comes out as [ʃ].

(vi) There are also clusters with /j/ as the final member such as in *pew* [pjuː], *view* [vjuː], *cute* [kjuːt] and *spew/spue* [spjuː], but the following vowel is always /uː/ and some would consider the /j/ part of the nucleus of the syllable.

(vii) The voiced fricatives are not included. They do not appear in any regular words. One can have /vl/ in the Russian name *Vladimir* and /vr/ in *vroom! vroom!*

(viii) There is one other cluster, namely /sf/, which occurs in a few words of Greek origin such as *sphere*, *sphincter*, and *Sphinx*, and possibly also in *svelte*, a word borrowed from French, but ultimately from Italian *svelto* 'plucked'. This cluster stands outside any generalizations that can be made about initial consonant clusters in English. It is quite an exceptional cluster, though well established. It is interesting to note that some unsophisticated speakers do not have this cluster. They put [ə] between the /s/ and the /f/.

Connected speech

On my first day in linguistics the lecturer asked how I pronounced *sandwich.* It was not surprising that he picked me, since I was the only student in the class. I dutifully enunciated *sandwich* as /sændwɪtʃ/. He then asked me how I pronounced the phrase 'a couple of sandwiches' and I found myself saying something that sounded like 'samwidges', that is, I said /sæmwɪdʒəz/. It was an instructive example since it illustrated two features of any but ultra slow speech, namely **elision** (I omitted the /d/) and **assimilation** (I had pronounced /n/ as /m/, anticipating the bilabial position of the following /w/). I think most speakers of English would exhibit the same elision and assimilation in this phrase. I also pronounced /tʃ/ as /dʒ/. This is another kind of assimilation. I made the consonant voiced in the context of vowels, which are voiced. I'm not sure if other speakers of English do this, but it is a regular feature of my pronunciation.

When we speak, there are no breaks between words as there are in writing: *a tack* sounds like *attack,* and *like 'er* sounds like *liker* or *Leica.* We do not sound out every segment of every word clearly. The closest we get to this is in giving a speech to a largish audience or visiting elderly relatives, where we are likely to speak slowly and loudly. In typical, natural, connected speech we find assimilation, elision, and vowel weakening, which is where a vowel becomes shorter and more central, approaching [ə]. These reductions are particularly noticeable in short function words like *and, of, to,* and so on.

Assimilation is common with a sequence of nasal and stop. In a phrase such as *the sailors in Plymouth* the *n,* an alveolar nasal, is likely to come out as an *m* in anticipation of the labial /p/ in *Plymouth.* Similarly a phrase such as *ten kings* is likely to be pronounced as [tɛŋkɪŋz] with the /n/ being pronounced as a velar nasal in anticipation of the /k/ in *kings.*

Elision is common in words like *p(o)lice, choc(o)late* and *libr(ar)y* even in fairly slow speech, and Henry Higgins himself would be hard pressed to detect a vowel between the *r*-sounds in *terrorist.* Awkward consonant clusters often suffer elision in running speech so that *facts* sounds like *fax* and *next* sounds like *necks.* I and my fellow lecturers are often referred to by students as /lɛtʃərəz/ and since we are all persons of the highest probity, I take it that this pronunciation is an example of elision plus some fusion of /t/ and /j/ to form /tʃ/. The following sentence illustrates elision and vowel reduction with function words,

He went to his mum's and had a cup of tea.
[hiːwɛntʊɪzmʌmzn̩ædəkʌpətiː]

The phrase *cup of tea* is regularly pronounced [kʌpətiː], which is recognized in the abbreviation, 'Would you like a cuppa?'

Assimilation, elision, and vowel weakening increase as one speaks more informally and more rapidly. A phrase such as *It's only half past two* is likely to undergo a series of 'shortcuts' the more rapidly one speaks. Note in reading this example that [aː] as in *half* and *past* reduces in length and is transcribed [a]. This vowel sounds the same as [ʌ] in *shut*, but as noted in the previous chapter [a] is an alternative way of transcribing this vowel.

[ɪtsoʊnliːhaːfpaːsttuː] → [ɪtsoʊnlihafpastuː] → ['tsoʊnliapastuː] → [tsaniapastuː]

Spoken language is a very rapid means of communication. A sentence like *The train's coming* or *Fred's taken my keys* takes less than two seconds. Something like *I've got it* or *Give it to 'em* can take less than one second. Newsreaders average 3.33 words per second, but someone speaking rapidly can double or treble this rate in a burst. Given the speed of natural speech, it is remarkable that we understand what is being said to us, especially when we have to compete with noise. Successful communication depends a lot on predictability. When the content of a message is really new, then communication is likely to break down. How often have you been introduced to someone at a noisy party and missed the name. You hear the bit that goes *I'd like you to meet . . .* because it's predictable, but you miss the name if it is at

all unusual. Of course once you do pick up a name, you are more likely to remember an unusual one like *Engelbert* rather than *Peter* or *John*.

There is recognition of the fact that we cannot interpret accurately without some help from context in the use of words to illustrate letters where flight numbers, licence numbers, and the like are being transmitted. Anyone who has ever seen movies and television programmes will be familiar with *alpha*, *bravo*, *Charlie* for *a*, *b*, and *c*, and in everyday life when we are spelling a name for someone, we often have to say 'M for Mary' or 'N for Nancy'.

Stress and intonation

The noun *insult* in phonemic notation is /ɪnsʌlt/, but so is the verb *insult*, yet the noun and verb do not sound the same. Clearly something is missing and that is **stress**. The noun has a stress on the first syllable and the verb has a stress on the second syllable. We can indicate this with an acute **accent** on the vowel of the stressed syllable. For the sake of simple presentation we will put accents over the normal written form. Thus we write *ínsult* (noun) and *insúlt* (verb). People tend to think of stress as being a matter of loudness, but higher pitch plays a part too in the realization of stress, at least in most varieties of English. Also a stressed syllable tends to be a little longer than any other unstressed syllables in the word, and the pronunciation is likely to be clearer and fuller, that is, there is less likelihood of elision and vowel reduction. This is more obvious in pairs such as *rébel* and *rebél* where the vowel of the unstressed syllable is reduced to [ə].

Words of three or more syllables usually have a strong stress and a weaker stress as in *ìntonátion* where the grave accent indicates the weaker stress. The weak stress is normally separated from the strong stress by one or more unstressed syllables. There are differences between British and American English in the placement of stress. British English often has a single stress where American English has a stronger and a weaker stress. For example, British *labórat(o)ry* versus American *láboratòry*, and British *sécret(a)ry* versus American *sécretàry*.

Besides word stress there is pattern of stress that runs across phrases, or in the case of short sentences, across the whole sentence. Take a sentence like *I handed the report to the senator*. There are three stressed syllables as shown:

I hánded the repórt to the sénator.

Over the sentence there is a strong–weak–strong pattern of loudness, so the stress on *report* is a little weaker than the other two. The last stressed syllable, the first syllable of *senator*, bears the strongest stress, not through extra loudness, but more through a rise in pitch on the stressed syllable followed by a rapid fall.

Of course any syllable can be given an extra strong stress where there is a contrast or a clarification. This is shown below by underlining.

I didn't just send it through the mail. I handed the report to the senator.
I handed the report to the senator, moi, me, myself!
You handed a report to the senator? No, I handed the [ðiː] report to the senator.

Morphophonemics

When a prefix or suffix is added to a stem, there is often some adjustment required so that the sequence of affix and stem does not violate any of the constraints on what phonemes can form a sequence. As mentioned on page 73, the plural in English has three forms: /s/, /z/, and /əz/. There are also some irregular plural forms such as *mice*, the plural of *mouse*. If English speakers are presented with made-up words such as *gluck*, *snab*, and *grooch* and asked to describe more than one of these, they unhesitatingly come up with the correct plural. This means there must be a rule that they have subconsciously learned. Well, what is it? Let's look at some examples of words that take the regular plural markers:

/s/:   lip, cat, pack, chef
/z/:   club, cad, dog, dove, bell, room, day, bee
/əz/:   bus, bush, church, buzz, rouge (assuming /ruʒ/), judge

The general principle is as follows:

/əz/ after sibilants: /s, z, ʃ, ʒ, tʃ, dʒ/
/s/ after other voiceless phonemes
/z/ after other voiced phonemes

This principle makes good sense. Try putting /s/ or /z/ immediately after a sibilant. Pretty awkward, isn't it? Now look at the distribution of /s/ and /z/ after other phonemes. The /s/ is used after voiceless phonemes and /z/ after voiced phonemes. Try putting /s/ after a voiced stop or fricative or try putting /z/ after a voiceless stop or fricative. Unless you go very slowly, you finish up getting the voicing to assimilate: voiced with voiced and voiceless with voiceless. An /s/ can be added to words ending in a nasal or /l/ (or /r/ for those that have it), but you finish up with pronunciations that fit words like *pence* or *pulse*. So why do we have /z/ in this position? The explanation here is historical. If you go back to late Old English, say around the time of the Battle of Hastings in 1066, there was only one regular plural form and it had come to be [-əz]. In the Middle English period (1100–1500) the [ə] in the final syllable of words was lost, but it could not be lost where [-əz] came after a sibilant since this would have produced an almost unpronounceable sequence, so [-əz] remained. Where /z/ came up against a voiceless stop or fricative it became /s/, but it did not need to change after a nasal or liquid, hence [penz] not [pens] for the plural of *pen*.

Keen readers will wonder about plurals like *pence*, *twice*, and the old-fashioned *thrice*. Before the plural in late Old English was /əz/ it was /əs/ and so was the genitive. The genitive was used in words like *hennes* and *twies* to form an adverb, and this adverbial /əs/ escaped the change to /əz/ that occurred with genitives. The /ə/ dropped out to yield *hens*, later re-spelt *hence*, and *twis*, later re-spelt *twice*. This pronunciation later spread to *pence*, which must have been considered a measure of quantity rather than a plural. The pronunciation also spread to *dice*, which was originally the plural of *die*, but came to be taken as a singular.

A number of words have irregular plurals. Some like *tooth/teeth* and *mouse/mice* go back to Old English, others are borrowed from other languages such as *criterion/criteria* from Greek. It may seem odd to form a plural be changing the vowel of a word as with *mouse/mice*, but originally the singular was [muːs] and the plural [muːsiː]. The [iː] vowel of the inflection caused the rounded back vowel of the stem [uː] to become a rounded front vowel [yː] (or [üː]), which eventually become [iː]. The vowel of the inflection then was lost. This left a singular [muːs] and a plural [miːs] and subsequent sound changes gave us modern [maʊs] and [maɪs].

The past tense in English has three allomorphs. There is an /əd/ form used after /t/ and /d/ as in *patted* and *kidded*, a /d/ form used after other voiced phonemes as in *rubbed, loved, judged, killed, rained*, and *booed*, and /t/ used after other voiceless phonemes: *wrapped, kicked, watched*, and *kissed*. The general principle is the same as with the plural. An earlier /əd/ lost its /ə/ except where it would have produced an awkward cluster of /tt/ or /td/. The /d/ then assimilated to the voiceless property of voiceless stops, fricatives, and affricates. Some Old English past tense forms are shown in Table 12.5.

Underlying forms

In introducing morphophonemic alternation we explained something of how the alternation got there by looking at the history of the forms. We cannot explain why late Old English had a plural [-əz] and a past tense [-əd] and we cannot explain why the vowel in the final syllable dropped out, but given these forms and the vowel loss, we can account for the distribution of the forms in Modern English. Some linguists like to describe morphophonemic alternations in terms of an underlying form that exhibits a set of realizations (allomorphs) determined by the environment. If, for instance, a prefix shows up as *om-* before words beginning with *b*, and as *on-* with words beginning with any other phoneme, then one would naturally assume that the basic form was *on-* and that *om-* arose through assimilation in place of articulation to the following *b*. When linguists posit an underlying or basic form, it is often a form that existed at an earlier period, but not always. The allomorphs of the regular English plural could be derived from /-əz/, the actual original form, or from /-z/. If we take /-əz/ to be the basic form, the derivation of the allomorphs looks like this. The underlying forms are shown in the first line and the effects of schwa deletion and assimilation shown in subsequent lines.

	cats	pigs	leeches
underlying form	kæt-əz	pɪg-əz	liːtʃ-əz
delete /ə/ except after sibilant	kæt-z	pɪg-z	liːtʃ-əz
z → s after a voiceless phoneme	kæt-s	pɪg-z	liːtʃ-əz

If we take /z/ to be the underlying form, we can derive the phonemic forms as follows.

	kæt-z	pɪg-z	liːtʃ-z
insert ə after a sibilant	kæt-z	pɪg-z	liːtʃ-əz
z → s after a voiceless phoneme	kæt-s	pɪg-z	liːtʃ-əz

Sometimes a morpheme will have a fuller allomorph in one environment and a reduced one in another. Consider the following,

damn   damnation
hymn   hymnal

A common way of describing an alternation like this is to take the fuller form to be the underlying form. In this instance one would take /dæmn/ and /hɪmn/ to be the underlying forms with a rule to delete the final /n/ word-finally, that is, in an environment where it was not permitted by the phonotactics of English.

In those varieties of English such as RP where there is alternation in words like *sore* with /r/ being pronounced only where a vowel follows as in 'sore and sorry', it makes sense to ascribe the /r/ to the underlying form and to delete it except where a vowel follows. For those speakers, the vast majority, who use an [r] in words like *saw* as in /aɪsɔːrɪm/ 'I saw him', the same treatment would be appropriate. In terms of contemporary phonology there is no difference between *sore* and *saw*, despite the fact that the /r/ is historical in *sore* but an addition in *saw*.

It is not always possible to establish an underlying form where there is a phonologically conditioned alternation. In some Australian languages there are some phonologically conditioned alternations with case markers where the markers are so different it is impossible to suggest an underlying form from which the allomorphs can be derived. The following words are from Kalkadoon (Kalkutungu) and are nouns in the locative case, which expresses location and could be translated 'at', 'on', 'in', etc. according to context. The digraph *th* represents a dental stop and *t^y* a palatal stop.

mat^yumpa-thi	'kangaroo'	*kupu-pia*	'spider'	*utingarr-pia*	'emu'
pint^yamu-thi	'sun'	*kunka-pia*	'stick'	*kalpin-pia*	'young man'
warluwa-thi	'shade'	*putu-pia*	'stomach'	*thuarr-pia*	'snake'

The allomorph *-thi* is used with vowel-final stems of more than two syllables. The *-pia* allomorph is used with vowel-final stems of less than three syllables and all consonant-final stems. The two allomorphs are so different that it would be totally implausible to derive both from a single form.

Sources and further reading

The study of phonemic distinctions and their distribution is called **phonology**. There are numerous books on phonology. They are all about theories of phonology, about ways of describing phonological systems. Carr's *Phonology* is a relatively easy introduction to a range of theories with data from various languages, and his *English Phonetics and Phonology: an Introduction* is good for English. Those who would like to read more about the phoneme without going deeply into theories of phonology will find useful articles on the Web. Just type 'phoneme' or 'phonology' into your search engine.

Problems

1 Here are some words from an Australian language Pitta-Pitta in broad phonetic notation. Try to establish whether alveolar and dental consonants contrast by looking for minimal or near-minimal pairs and complementary distribution. Check word-initial position and intervocalic position. No words were recorded with initial [n]. Note that [c] in [laca] represents a voiceless palatal stop, which sounds similar to the voiceless, palatal affricate of English.

[takuku]	baby	[maṇa]	bad	[maḻu]	no
[kuṭi]	pull	[ina]	you	[ṇala]	bark, skin
[ṯina]	foot	[ṯana]	they	[ṭarri]	crawl

[pala]	rain	[tala]	if	[laca]	ok, all right
[kuti]	swan	[laiŋuru]	again	[tarri]	to boil

2 The following words are transcribed phonetically from Old English. Look at the distribution of the voiced and voiceless pairs of fricatives ([f], [v]; [θ], [ð]; and [s], [z]) and see whether they contrast or are in complementary distribution.

[kuːθ]	known	[huːs]	house	[fiːf]	five
[foːda]	food	[luvu]	love	[baðian]	to bathe
[θorn]	thorn	[goːs]	goose	[nozu]	nose
[sunu]	son	[fæðom]	fathom	[saːr]	sore, wounded
[over]	over	[bæθ]	bath	[driːvan]	to drive

3 If we write *pea stalks* and *peace talks* as a string of phonemes, they both come out as /piːstɒːks/. Try saying each phrase slowly. You should notice a difference. This shows that the syllable boundary between the words is significant, since it is relevant to how the adjacent syllables are pronounced. Read over the section of this chapter on the phoneme, and find two pieces of information on the pronunciation of stops and fricatives that are relevant to the distinction.

If you pronounce these phrases quickly, the difference between them is greatly reduced and context would be the listener's best guide to telling them apart, such a good guide in fact that if someone said *She's off to the pea stalks in Brussels*, I'm sure no one would notice anything odd.

4 It was stated in the previous chapter that the affricates consist of a combination of stop-plus-fricative. If they were taken as consonant clusters, what consequences would this have for general statements about possible initial consonant clusters in English?

5 There is one phonemic distinction that is not recognized by the English spelling system and that is one between [æ] and [æː]. Admittedly it is somewhat marginal, but some words such as *bad, glad, mad,* and *sad* have [æː] whereas others such as *add* and *pad* have [æ]. As explained above, all vowels are shorter before a syllable-final voiceless obstruent, so there are three possible lengths:

bad, mad, sad, glad	long vowel, i.e. as long as a recognized 'long' vowel
add, pad, lad, brad	normal length for a 'short' vowel before a voiced consonant
at, pat, fat, brat	normal length for a 'short' vowel before a voiceless consonant

Since the distinction between [æ] and [æː] is lexical, that is, it depends on particular words, we have to recognize the distinction as phonemic, albeit on marginal grounds. There are also some other irregularities. Grammatical words like *am* and *can* (be able) have the short vowel, whereas *ham* and *can* (tin) have the long one. Make a list of all the phonemes that can close a syllable with [æ], think of a few words illustrating each possibility, and then see if this distinction occurs in your speech and what the distribution of [æ] and [æː] is.

For American English [æː] occurs in words like *laugh, lava, path, rather,* and *pass*. In these words the vowel is followed by a fricative, and in British English it has become [aː]. Some reports indicate that there is a contrast between [pæːθ] 'path' and [pæθ] as an abbreviation of *pathology*.

I should add that not all linguists accept that there is a phonemic distinction involved, though all accept there is some lexical irregularity in the distribution of length with [æ]. The facts differ from one variety of English to another.

6 Here are some Indonesian verbs involving a prefix that begins with /mə/. This prefix appears on most transitive verbs in the active voice. What principle determines the allomorphs of the prefix?

pukul	*məmukul*	'hit'	*buka*	*məmbuka*	'open'
tulis	*mənulis*	'write'	*dapat*	*məndapat*	'get'
kirim	*məŋirim*	'send'	*ganti*	*məŋganti*	'change'

With vowel-initial verbs the prefix is /məŋ/ as in /məŋambil/ 'take'. What does this suggest about the underlying form of the prefix?

7 Here are some Spanish nouns and their plural forms. The vowels are written phonetically, not phonemically. Treat [e] and [ɛ] as allophones of the phoneme /e/ and [o] and [ɔ] as allophones of the phoneme /o/. Now the first question is to determine when the plural is formed with /s/ and when with /es/. [x] stands for a voiceless velar fricative.

fruta	*frutas*	'fruit'	*muxɛr*	*muxerɛs*	'woman'
karta	*kartas*	'letter'	*mes*	*mesɛs*	'month'
mesa	*mesas*	'table'	*rasɔn*	*rasonɛs*	'reason'
parte	*partɛs*	'part'			
vino	*vinɔs*	'wine'			

There are five vowel phonemes in Spanish. As noted above, the vowels [ɛ] and [e] are allophones of a single phoneme and so are [ɔ] and [o]. See if you can work out the basis for the complementary distribution. (It is the same for the front and back vowels.) Intervocalic consonants form the onset of the following syllable, i.e. a word like *fruta* breaks up into two syllables *fru-* and *-ta*.

10. Writing

The Egyptians

Humans have been drawing pictures for tens of thousands of years, and the earliest examples of writing are **pictograms**, small, often stylized, representations of anything that can be seen: people, body parts, animals, plants, heavenly bodies, and so on. The best-known examples are the **hieroglyphs** of Ancient Egypt, which date back to the fourth millennium BC.

The word 'hieroglyph' is from the Greek *hieros* 'sacred' and *glyphein* 'to carve'. The original hieroglyphs were carved in stone, but later these symbols were used on other materials, especially papyrus, a writing material made from the pith of the papyrus reed. The formal written form was called 'hieratic' (sacred), and there was a 'demotic' (common) version, a running hand version, in which the pictographic origin was pretty much lost. The hieroglyphs were written either in columns to be read from top to bottom or in rows to be read either from left to right or right to left.

Pictographic symbols shade into **ideograms**, symbols that represent an entity indirectly by representing an associated notion. The symbol for 'head' in Figure 10.1 is pictographic, and the symbols for 'mountain' and 'mouth' are stylized pictograms, but the symbol for 'house' is based on the plan of a simple house and is not an attempt at depicting a house.

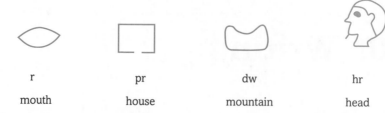

r	pr	dw	hr
mouth	house	mountain	head

Figure 10.1 Egyptian pictograms.

The Egyptian system started off as a **logographic** system, that is, one in which the pictograms and ideograms represented words (Greek *logos* 'word'), but obviously there are numerous concepts for which no pictographic or ideographic representation suggests itself, including grammatical forms both bound and free. The Egyptians solved this problem by using some symbols just for their phonetic value. This is called the **rebus principle**. Rebuses are sometimes used in parlour games or games for children where participants have to represent words by pictures. They might, for instance, write a symbol for a bee to represent the verb 'be', or a symbol for '8' to represent 'ate'. The Egyptians also took a number of words with a single consonant and used them to represent consonants wherever they occurred. These are called 'phonograms' and some examples are shown in Figure 10.2. The word for 'mat', for instance, had the consonant [p] and it was chosen to represent [p], the word for 'loaf' contained the consonant [t] and it was chosen as a phonetic symbol for [t], and so on.

The Egyptians also took some words with two and three consonants and used them phonetically. The word for 'house', for instance, contained the consonants [p] and [r], and it was used to represent various words with these two consonants. The Egyptians did not represent vowels, and in fact we do not know the quality of the vowels of the words we find in the hieroglyphs. In fact, we do not always know where the vowels occurred. Suppose in English we were to write just the consonants, then *pt* would represent *pit, pet, pat, pot, put, pity, potty, putty*, etc. This would be confusing, and indeed the rebus system raised problems for the Egyptians, which they solved mainly by adding a 'determinative', a symbol chosen for its semantic value. The hieroglyphs chosen as determinatives usually had a generic meaning such as divine, human, animal, plant, etc. Some examples are shown in Figure 10.3. Note that each determinative usually had a meaning more abstract than what was represented in the pictograph.

Some examples of the use of determinatives are given in Figure 10.4. In the first row the vulture is represented phonetically by three phonograms (*nrt*)

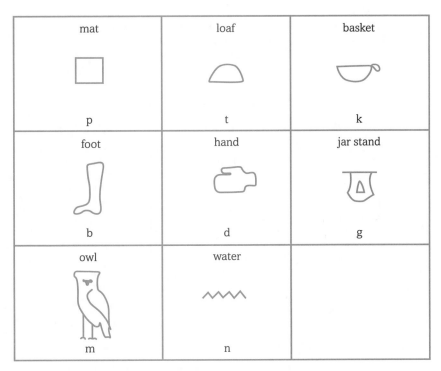

mat	loaf	basket
p	t	k
foot	hand	jar stand
b	d	g
owl	water	
m	n	

Figure 10.2 Egyptian phonograms.

plus the symbol for 'vulture' as a determinative. In rows two and three the consonants for 'knee' [pd] and 'foot' [rd] are represented by phonograms (*pd* and *rd*) plus a symbol for 'leg' as a determinative. This serves to pick out the correct reading for *pd* and *rd*, each of which could stand for a number of words. In the bottom row the verb *prt* 'go out' is represented by phonograms for [pr] and [t] plus an ideographic determinative for 'walk' consisting of a pair of walking legs.

In the final example in Figure 10.5 we have the symbol for 'chair' or 'seat'. It is a symbol that admits several readings including [st] and [ws]. In the first line it is supplemented by the phonogram for [t], which narrows the reading down to [st]. The determinative pins down the meaning to 'seat' or 'throne' (the value of the first symbol) or 'place'. In the second line the pictogram for 'eye' is used as a phonogram [jr], which, in connection with the determinative for gods, indicates that the appropriate reading for the chair symbol is [ws]. This gives [wsjr], the name of the god known to us as 'Osiris'.

Egyptian hieroglyphs were used until near the end of the fourth century AD. The Roman emperor Theodosius ordered all non-Christian temples closed in 391, which meant the end of the public use of hieroglyphs.

Hieroglyph	Basic Referent	Extended Meaning
	papyrus scroll	write teach know
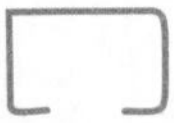	house	building
	penis	urinate procreate male
	woman	female
	man	male
	god	divine

Figure 10.3 Egyptian determinatives.

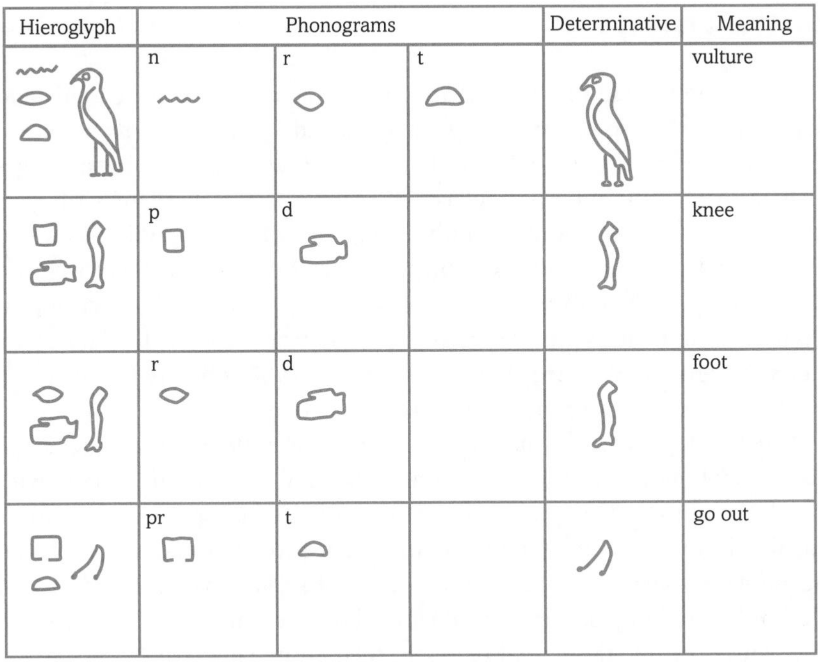

Hieroglyph	Phonograms			Determinative	Meaning
	n	r	t		vulture
	p	d			knee
	r	d			foot
	pr	t			go out

Figure 10.4 Egyptian phonograms and determinatives.

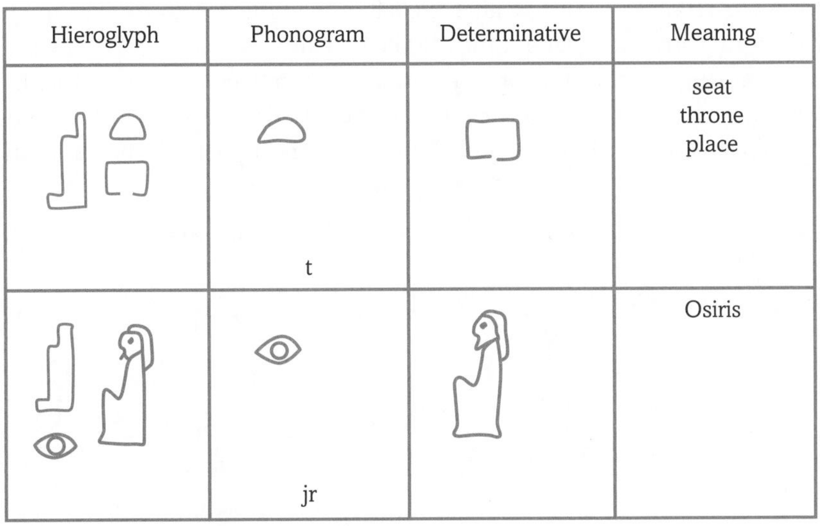

Hieroglyph	Phonogram	Determinative	Meaning
	t		seat throne place
	jr		Osiris

Figure 10.5 Disambiguating hieroglyphs.

Cuneiform

In Mesopotamia (southern Iraq) the Sumerians also used pictograms and ideograms. In Mesopotamia the pictograms and ideograms were simplified over time and by around 3400 BC they were produced by pressing a wedge-shaped 'pen' into soft clay tablets. The term for this kind of writing is **cuneiform** from the Latin *cuneus* 'wedge'. This method of writing pushed the conventionalization in a certain direction; for instance, there were no curved lines, and scribes found it convenient to switch from writing in vertical columns to writing in rows, top-to-bottom and left-to-right as we do, and signs were rotated 90 degrees, which further obscured their iconic properties. Some examples are given in Figure 10.6.

Like the Egyptians, the Sumerians came to adopt the rebus principle and use symbols not only for objects but also for words homophonous with words for objects. This provided a means of representing numerous words for which no pictographic representation suggested itself. Sumerian was an agglutinative language with a limited range of syllable patterns and a good deal of homophony between morphemes, both free and bound, so by using the rebus principle they could represent their entire language.

Around 2500 BC the Akkadians succeeded the Sumerians as the dominant power in Mesopotamia. They adopted cuneiform and adapted it to their language, while at the same time using it for Sumerian, which was retained as a language of culture, just as Greek was retained in the Roman Empire and Latin was retained in Europe after the fall of the Roman Empire. The use of cuneiform spread throughout the Middle East and was used for a number of different languages. It developed into a kind of alphabetic system, at least a system for representing consonants. The Semitic languages, which include Akkadian, Aramaic, Hebrew, and Arabic, have mostly triconsonantal roots,

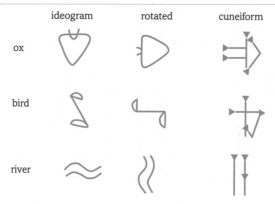

Figure 10.6 Development of cuneiform.

and inflection and derivation often involve a change of vowel as with English *sell/sale* and *run/ran*, though there are also prefixes, suffixes, and infixes. A much quoted example is *k-t-b*, the root for 'writing'. In Arabic, this root forms the basis for *kitāb* 'book', *kutub* 'books', *kutiba* 'it was written', *maktub* 'written', etc. In a language with such a structure one can represent just the consonants and anyone familiar with the language can work out what the vowels are from the context. This works to some extent in English. Try reading this:

Cnfrm wrtng sprd thrgh th Mdl st

You probably had no trouble working out what this is, though you might think I cheated by relying on a number of silent consonants.

Towards an alphabet

Cuneiform ceased to be used around the first century AD, but another development in alphabetic writing was to be the mother of all the alphabetic scripts of the world. Semitic people in the area of modern Israel and Lebanon had developed a consonantal alphabetic system on the basis of Egyptian pictographic forms by around 1900 BC. They would have been familiar with consonantal-alphabetic cuneiform as well as the Egyptian system of phonograms for consonants. Among the peoples who used this form of consonantal alphabet were the Phoenicians who lived in an area corresponding to modern Lebanon. They had a system of twenty-two characters.

True alphabetic writing arose when the Greeks encountered the Phoenician system and adapted it to Greek. In the Mycenaean period (1500–1100 BC), Greek had been written in a syllabic script known as linear B (so called because it was preceded by an as yet undeciphered script Linear A). A syllabic script is not suitable for Greek because there is a large number of syllable patterns and numerous consonant clusters. When the Greeks adopted the Phoenician consonantal alphabet, they used some of the signs to represent vowels. They used the symbol *aleph*, for instance, which represented a glottal stop in Phoenician, to represent [a]. Figure 10.7 shows the development of some letters of the Greek and Roman alphabets from Egyptian hieroglyphs via Phoenician consonant symbols. The figure does not show the numerous variants that existed, but it does show how symbols become distorted over time so that their origin can become completely disguised.

The Greek system was the first alphabetic system, one in which each phoneme is represented, though by the latter part of the first millennium BC

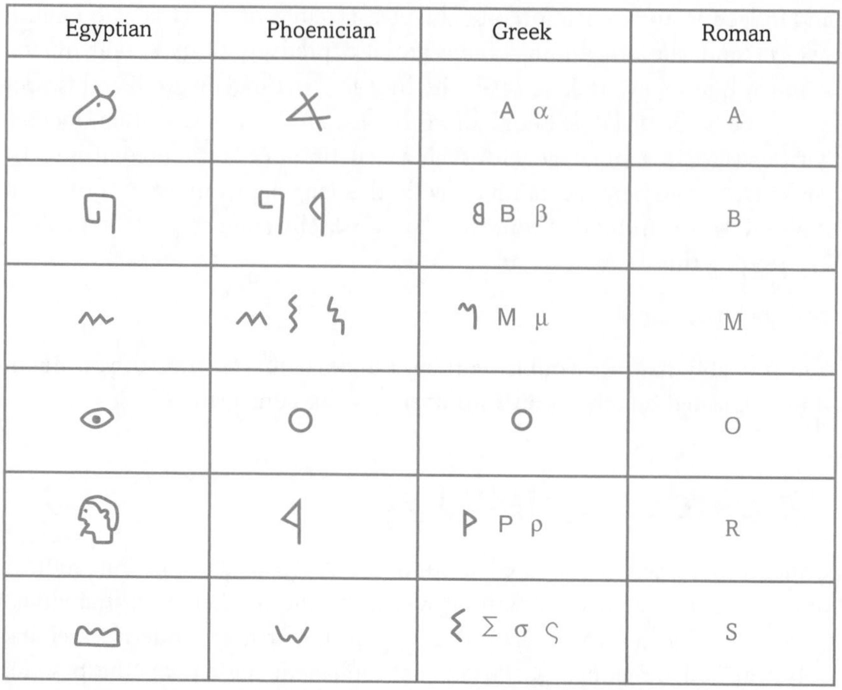

Egyptian	Phoenician	Greek	Roman
𓌉	𐤀	A α	A
𓉐	𐤁 𐤁	B B β	B
〜	𐤌 𐤌 𐤌	𐤌 M μ	M
👁	O	O	O
𓁹	𐤓	Ρ P ρ	R
𓈖	W	Σ σ ς	S

Figure 10.7 Pictograph to alphabets.

the Phoenicians themselves had begun adding diacritics for vowels. The Greek system was adopted by the Etruscans in central Italy and then the Romans adopted it. The Roman alphabet later became the alphabet of Western Europe. A derivative of the Greek alphabet, namely Cyrillic, was adopted in Eastern Europe and is used for Russian.

All alphabetic writing systems can be traced back in some measure to the consonantal system of the Phoenicians, though there are great differences in their appearance. Hebrew script, Arabic script, and the Devanagari of India look nothing alike, but they have a common origin.

Beyond the Mediterranean and Near East

The Chinese writing system has its roots in pictograms dating back to the fourth millennium BC, and a fully developed writing system was in use in the second millennium BC. As with any pictographic system, the iconic aspect gets reduced as the symbols are written with different instruments and on different materials, sometimes with haste. However, a few characters still preserve a recognizable resemblance to their referent, or at least a resemblance that can be seen once the meaning is given:

木 mù 'tree'   門 mén 'gate'   川 chuān 'river'   日 rì 'sun'   口 kǒu 'mouth'

There are also some obvious ideograms:

二 èr 'two'   三 sān 'three'

Many characters are compound. For instance, the character for *jiān* 'sharp' consists of the character for 'small' combined with the character for 'big' below it 尖. The idea is that a sharp point involves a narrowing from big to small. The character for *míng* 'bright' consists of the character for 'sun' (see above) combined with the character for 'moon' 明.

As with other writing systems the rebus principle was used to cope with words that could not easily be represented by a pictogram or ideogram. For instance, the symbol for *lái* 'wheat' was used for *lái* 'come'. However, there are many homophones and these are distinguished by forming a compound character in which one element, the radical, generally indicates the meaning, at least in generic terms, and the other, the phonetic, indicates the pronunciation. For example, the character that was originally used for 'wheat' occurs as a phonetic with radicals for 'mountain', 'water', and 'eye' as in the following example:

來   character originally used for *lái* 'wheat', subsequently used for the homophonous *lái* 'to come' and still used for that verb.

崍   Mt Lai in Szechuan province (The first character is the mountain radical.)

淶   Lai, a river in Hebei (The first character is the water radical.)

睞   1. glance at 2. squint (The first character is the eye radical.)

To take another example. The characters for 'cat' and 'dog' are shown below. Each contains the animal radical as the left-hand component. The character for 'cat' has a phonetic that indicates that the pronunciation is *māo*. On its own this character represents 'seedling'. The character for 'dog' has a phonetic that indicates the pronunciation of the word for 'dog' is *gǒu*. On its own this character represents 'phrase' and is pronounced *jù*. The pronunciation has changed over time, but the old pronunciation is fossilized as the phonetic for 'dog'. Note in passing that the voiced symbols in the romanization of Chinese represent non-aspirate voiceless obstruents.

貓   māo 'cat'
狗   gǒu 'dog'

A large number of Chinese words are disyllabic, being compounds of monosyllabic roots. In many cases the disyllabic words consist of near synonyms and their creation is motivated by a desire to avoid homophony. The root for 'peace' is *ān,* and the character is a compound one showing a woman under a roof. I leave it to the reader to work out the motivation for this combination. Anyway, *ān* generally appears in disyllabic words rather than on its own. One such disyllabic word is *ān níng* where one can see the roof as the upper part of the left-hand component with the woman below it. The roof also appears as the upper part of the right-hand component:

安寧　ān níng 'peaceful'

The Chinese writing system requires memorization of thousands of characters. Chinese dictionaries list around 50,000 characters, but a knowledge of 5000 suffices for most purposes. The Chinese government has issued lists of simplified characters plus an official romanization called Pinyin (used in the examples above). Chinese characters were once used for Vietnamese until Portuguese missionaries introduced the Roman alphabet.

The Japanese use a writing system introduced from China in the fourth century AD. They currently use up to about 3000 Chinese characters (kanji) for the roots of content words plus a syllabary of forty-six members made up of Chinese characters chosen for their sound. These syllabic characters have been simplified and they now exist in two versions, hiragana and katakana. Hiragana is used mainly for function forms both bound and free, and katakana for foreign names. For instance, the Japanese verb form *nobo-ru* 'go up' is written 上る where the first symbol is the Chinese character for 'up' (*shàng* in Mandarin) and the second character is the hiragana representation of the syllable -*ru.* Similarly the verb form *kakimasu* is written 書きます where the first character represents the root and the other three are the hiragana forms for -*ki-ma-su.* In fact the root or base is *kak-* 'write', but the *k* at the end of the root is the initial or onset of the second syllable and is treated as such in the written representation. Japanese lends itself to a syllabic representation since it has mainly CV syllables as in words like *haiku* 'a type of poem' and *kimono* 'traditional gown'. The only exceptions are syllables ending in nasals as in *sensei* 'teacher' or syllables in which the coda is the same as the onset of the succeeding syllable as in *yatto* 'finally'.

An alphabet for Korean was introduced by King Sejong in the fifteenth century. Before that Chinese characters were used, and the use of Chinese characters persists alongside the alphabet.

Writing also developed independently in Central America. On present evidence it appears that the Zapotec were using writing by 400 BC. The system was basically pictographic and logographic, but there were some symbols for syllables. The most elaborate Central American writing system was that of the Mayan people used throughout the first millennium AD. Their pictographic, logographic system was augmented with a syllabary, and they

a.   b.

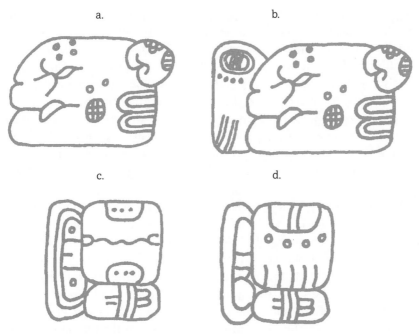

c.   d.

Figure 10.8 Mayan writing.

would add symbols for affixes around the main symbol for the root. In Figure 10.8 the first example (a) is a pictographic logogram of a jaguar. Words could be represented phonetically using the syllabary and sometimes a logogram was augmented by one or more syllabic signs. In (b) there is a syllabic sign for *ba* in front of the sign for jaguar, which indicates the word *balam* as opposed to one of the other words for 'jaguar'.

The syllabic signs were used for grammatical affixes, and in (c) a sign for *u*, which in this context indicates a third person possessor, is placed in front of a logogram for 'prisoner'. In (d) the word for prisoner, namely *bak*, is represented phonetically by symbols for *ba* and *ki*. The syllabic signs represent open syllables and where a syllable ends in a consonant, as in this case, the vowel represented by the symbol is disregarded. The reader will notice that the symbol for *u* is somewhat different from the one in (c). This is incidental or free variation and is common in Mayan writing.

Writing in general

Writing systems that aim at representing sounds rather than meaning represent phonemes or combinations of phonemes (syllables), rather than

allophones. This is only to be expected since the people involved in adapt-
ing the alphabet to their language are normally oblivious to allophonic
variation. In many languages there is a good fit between the spelling system,
or **orthography** as it is sometimes called, and the pronunciation. Italian,
Spanish, and German have few pitfalls for anyone trying to read aloud.
French has more discrepancies between spelling and pronunciation, but
these are largely predictable. In general a final written consonant, other
than those representing a liquid (*l* and *r*), is silent. English has the worst
relationship between spelling and sound, an unfortunate characteristic for
a language that has the greatest number of people learning it as a second
language.

As pointed out in chapter one, comparatively few of the thousands of
languages in the world and the thousands more that once existed have ever
been committed to writing, but this is obscured by the fact that national
and international languages are written languages. Writing has obvious
advantages, particularly in commercial transactions in large-scale societies,
and it facilitates the cumulative growth of knowledge. The Chinese were the
first to invent printing and were using movable wooden block type by the
eleventh century. Printing was invented in Europe in the fifteenth century,
possibly independently of the Chinese, possibly not. Gradually after that
more and more people managed to acquire literacy and access to reading
materials, mainly in Europe and her colonies. At the present time the
majority of people around the world can read, but there are anomalies
even in societies that pride themselves on being advanced and sophisticated. Some people manage to go through the educational system without
learning to read and others lose what skill they have through lack of
practice. Although writing is based on spoken language, written language
has properties not found in spoken language. For instance, you might write
Her parents having gone out, Roxanne invited her boyfriend over but would
you actually say that? Writing also allows the use of long sentences with lots
of subordinate clauses, constructions that would tax the short-term memory of a speaker and hearer. Learned, literary German abounds in long
sentences with one clause embedded within another, and, since all clauses
with an auxiliary and all subordinate clauses are verb-final, there can be an
accumulation of verbs at the end of a sentence. The following parody is
from Douglas Hofstadter.

> *The proverbial German phenomenon of the verb-at-the-end about which droll tales of
> absentminded professors who would begin a sentence, ramble on for an entire lecture,
> and then finish up by rattling off a string of verbs by which their audience, for whom
> the stack had long since lost its coherence, would be totally nonplussed, are told, is an
> excellent example of linguistic recursion.*

Spelling English

In the Middle English period people wrote in their local dialect. In this period spelling was not fixed. By the beginning of the sixteenth century printing had come into general use, and, except for a few northern Scottish texts, only the dialect of the London area appeared in print. By the middle of the seventeenth century a fixed spelling system emerged. Not everyone kept to the standard spelling, and a survey of private correspondence reveals numerous deviations from the standard. These deviations are a good guide to pronunciation. Here are some examples from the fifteenth to eighteenth century: *adishon* (addition), *corrup* (corrupt), *Injan/Injean/ Injun* (Indian), *offen* (often), *soger* (soldier), *Wensday* (*Wednesday*), *wood* (would), and *writin* (writing). Some of the pronunciations indicated are current standard, such as *Wensday*, but others are not, for example *corrup*.

As noted above, English has the worst relationship between sound and spelling of any language. First of all there are silent consonant letters as in *wring* and *knee*, and in words borrowed from Greek such as *psychology* and *pneumonia*, although the silent letters in these words are predictably silent and not a major source of annoyance. Vowel sounds are represented in unusual ways in words such as *aunt, build, bury, eye, friend, journey, move, people, pretty*, and in both *woman* and *women*. The pronunciation of words with the *gh*-digraph needs to be learned from speech. In Middle English it represented a palatal fricative as in German *ich* 'I' or a velar fricative as in German *Bach* or Scottish *loch*. In Modern English it is silent after *i* as in *high* and *mighty*, but *-ough* words are unpredictable: /af/ (or /ʌf/) in *tough, enough, slough* (*off*), /ɒf/ in /*cough, trough* (/ɑf/ in General American), /u/ in *through*, /ə/ in *thorough*, /oʊ/ in *though*, silent in *Edinburgh*, and /aʊ/ in *bough* and *Slough* (the place and the Slough of Despond in *Pilgrim's Progress*).

Some words such as *come, love*, and *son* have *o* where we might have expected *u* on the basis of the pronunciation. In the Middle English period (1100–1500) these words had a *u* and were spelt as *luu/luue, cum/cumme* and *sun/sune, sunne*, but sequences involving two or more of the letters *i, u, m*, and *n*, which were made up of short vertical strokes in the writing of the time were hard to read, so *o* was introduced to help the reader sort out where one letter ended and the next began. Figure 10.9 shows these three words as they might have looked in a Gothic script of the Middle Ages before and after *o* was introduced.

Incidentally the word *sun* also acquired an *o* with some writers, but *u* became standard. It should be noted too that *v* was not a letter separate from *u* (that's why we call *w* 'double u' though it looks like a double v). One read the letter *u* as [u] or [v] according to whether a consonant or vowel followed.

Some words were respelt to indicate their Latin origin. *Dette* was respelt *debt* (Latin *debitum*), *vitailles* was respelt *victuals* (Latin *victualia*), and *endite* was

cume   lune   sune

come   lone   some

Figure 10.9 Gothic script.

respelt *indict* (Latin *indictus*). However, these new spellings created marked discrepancies between pronunciation and spelling, since people still pronounced the words in the traditional way. The three words just quoted are pronounced [dɛt], [vɪtl̩z] and [ɪndaɪt]. A conservative spelling system has one advantage, namely that it indicates morphemes that are disguised in pronunciation such as *dictate* in *dictation*, and it indicates something of the origin of the word. However, the geniuses who introduced the new Latin-type spellings managed to make a few mistakes. For instance, they respelt *iland* as *island* in the belief that it came from Latin *insula*, when it fact it came from Old English *iglond*, and they respelt *sissors* as *scissors* in the belief it came from Latin *scissus*, past participle of *scindere* 'to cut', whereas it came from Old French *cisoires*, ultimately from Latin *cisoria*, which is based on the root *caes-* 'cut', 'slain'.

Some inverse spellings also arose to complicate the picture. For example, the sequence *-ight* occurs in *night, right, fight*, etc. The word *delight* comes from French *delite*, ultimately from Latin *delectare* and was spelt *delite*, but it acquired the *gh*-spelling by analogy with *night*, etc.

In the early nineteenth century Noah Webster introduced a number of new spelling conventions for America. Some were adopted such as dropping the *u* in *colour, favour*, etc., replacing *-re* with *-er* in words like *centre*, and replacing *-ce* with *-se* in *defense, offense*, etc. One innovation was accepted in Britain as well as in America, namely dropping the final *-k* in words such as *musick* and *optick*.

The discrepancies between sound and spelling give rise to two features of language that are largely peculiar to English. One is that even among educated people there is often uncertainty about how to pronounce some unfamiliar words, mainly those encountered in writing rather than speech. The other is the phenomenon of **spelling pronunciation**, i.e. the use of a pronunciation that is based on the spelling rather than in accordance with the accepted pronunciation. Words borrowed from French such as *hour, honour*, and *honest* came into English without an initial [h] as did *hospital, habit*, and *heretic*, but the latter have acquired an [h] from the spelling. The word *herb* is pronounced with an [h] and without one (the latter mainly in the US), and though *hotel* has an initial [h], one still sometimes hears *an (h)otel*. With words like *anthem, catholic*, and *theatre*, which came into English from French (most of them ultimately from Greek) the digraph *th* was pronounced [t], as it still is in *Thomas*, but a [θ] was introduced on the basis of the spelling. The [t] pronunciation lives on in the familiar forms of some personal names: *Anthony* (*Tony*), *Catherine/Kathryn* (*Kate*), and *Arthur* (*Artie*).

The traditional pronunciation of *forehead* is 'forrid', but it is common nowadays to hear 'fore-head', particularly in the US. This is an example of reversing a sound change on the basis of the spelling. *Midwife* was once pronounced 'middif', but is now 'mid-wife'. *Housewife* became 'hussif', a pronunciation that lingers on for a needle-and-thread kit issued to personnel in the armed services, though 'house-wife' is now the majority pronunciation among those few familiar with the referent, as it is for the wife of the house, though this referent is obsolescent. The word *hussy* is a reduced form of *housewife*. It has undergone semantic pejoration as well as phonetic reduction.

Many people believe that the spelling is a guide to the correct pronunciation and argue, for instance, that it is wrong to include an intrusive *r* in *the idea of it* or *I saw him*, because there is no *r* in the spelling. They do not suggest changing the spelling to fit the pronunciation. However, the question of spelling reform is raised seriously from time to time, and there would obviously be a big advantage to learners of English, both native and non-native, if spelling were as trifling a matter as it is in Italian or Spanish. However, there are some disadvantages. First of all, there would be the problem of deciding which pronunciation to represent in cases where there was variation, for instance, with words like *word* and *beer* in which *r* is pronounced in the US, but not in mainstream UK English. Second, there would no longer be a clear indication of the root *music* in a word like *musician* or the root *electric* in a word like *electrician*. A further point concerns reduced vowels. At present we have a common representation of the root *photo-* in *photograph* and *photography*, but this would be obscured if we wrote *fotograf* and *fetografi*. These concerns are part of the larger question of how valuable it is to retain spellings that give a good guide to etymology, a good guide to Latin and Greek origins. Many would prefer to keep the present system for just this reason.

One curious feature of English spelling that is causing comment at the present time is the 'apostrophe -*s*'. According to the standard rule, which was adopted in the nineteenth century, the apostrophe is not used to mark plurals, just possession as in *the girl's name* (one girl has a name) and *the girls' room* (a room for a number of girls). However, it is frequently used nowadays for the plural. There are two situations that seem to prompt this usage. One is with abbreviations whether in letters or figures: *CV's* (plural of *curriculum vitae*), *the 22's* (.22 bore rifles), *the 1950's*. The other is with the plural of words ending in a vowel such as *echo*, *logo*, *solo*, and *visa*. Adding an -*s* makes these look like foreign words and, at least for those ending in -*o*, suggests a pronunciation of the final syllable that rhymes with *boss*. This usage is sometimes referred to as the 'greengrocer's apostrophe' because of its frequency on placards advising of the availability of *potatoe's* and *tomatoe's*, but the usage is not confined to greengrocers, and although it is more common with vowel-final words, it is often used with consonant-final words as well. To most people the greengrocer's apostrophe seems to reflect a declining standard of education among vendors of fruit and vegetables and anyone else who uses the apostrophe for plurals, but in fact Dr Johnson had plurals like *grotto's* and *innuendo's* in the eighteenth century.

Sources and further reading

The quote from Douglas Hofstadter can be found at <http://www.sysprog. net/quotwrit.html>. Dr Johnson's apostrophe is mentioned in David Crystal's *Words, Words, Words*, page 88. Chapter eleven of that work contains interesting information about English spelling.

The examples featuring *lái* in Mandarin Chinese are from De Francis, 'The Ideographic Myth'.

Data on Mesoamerican writing comes from Harris and Stearns, *Understanding Maya Inscriptions* and from Marcus, 'Mesoamerica: Scripts' in volume 8 of K. Brown (ed.), *Elsevier Encyclopedia of Language and Linguistics*. Figure 10.8 was redrawn from those sources.

For information on writing systems try Daniels and Bright, *The World's Writing Systems*; Campbell, *Handbook of Scripts and Alphabets*; or Coulmas, *Writing Systems*.

Problems

1 It is sometimes remarked that scripts are spread with religions. To what extent is this true? You will need to go beyond this text to find an answer.

2 What are the limitations of a pictographic or ideographic system of writing? How are these limitations overcome?

3 Consider each of the following words and see if you can work out how the discrepancy between sound and spelling arose. The best way to go about this task is to use a history of the English language—Pyles and Algeo, for instance.

ballet, bury, college, damn, know, love, one, rendezvous, two

4 One defence of the English spelling system is that it preserves the identity of the stem in derivations, e.g. one can see *critic* in *criticize* even though there is an /s/ in *criticize* corresponding to the second *c*. Find more examples of this kind of thing and try to estimate how extensive the phenomenon is.

PART IV
Variation and change

11. Varieties

Yankees are 'pretty much like Southerners—except with worse manners, of course, and terrible accents'.

Rhett Butler to Scarlett O'Hara in the novel *Gone with the Wind* by Margaret Mitchell

Variation

Speakers of a language don't all speak the same, nor do individuals speak the same in every situation. In most languages there are different varieties spoken in different areas. In many cultures there is language variation correlated with social position, sex, or age, or with the setting or situation. In this chapter we shall look at some of these types of variation.

Languages and dialects

Languages change over time. Most of us are aware of changes in vocabulary as new words come into use, mainly for new inventions such as computers, and other words fall into disuse, but all aspects of language change including pronunciation, word-building, syntax, and the meaning of particular words. These types of change are described more fully in chapter twelve. Suppose a particular language is spoken over an area such that the speakers are not all in regular contact. In fact let us imagine the case where speakers of a language settle on two islands, too far apart for regular contact. Some changes will occur on Island A and independent changes will occur on Island B, so that after a period there will be two local varieties of the language, or two **dialects**.

It is likely that after a very long period of separation the two dialects would diverge so much that they would be mutually unintelligible and we would have to recognize two separate languages.

The criterion of mutual intelligibility is used to decide whether we have dialects or separate languages, but it often happens that dialects form chains so that speakers of dialect A can understand dialect B, and speakers of dialect B can understand dialect C, but speakers of dialect A cannot understand dialect C. Where there is a long chain of dialects it is hard to answer the question of how many languages there are. In one sense there is only one language, but this is unrealistic if the majority of speakers can understand only neighbouring dialects. It is common to think of everyone in a particular country as speaking the national language or speaking a dialect, but it is often the case that within a particular country there are a number of closely related languages each with its own dialect chain. In Italy, for instance, Neapolitan and Sicilian are separate languages, each with their own dialects. They are not mutually comprehensible, nor are they comprehensible to anyone who knows only standard Italian.

A dialect chain can cross national boundaries. Thai, the national language of Thailand, and Lao, the national language of Laos, are members of a dialect chain, but they are recognized as separate languages on political grounds. This pair also illustrates a difficulty in applying the criterion of mutual intelligibility. Lao speakers claim they can understand Thai, but Thai speakers are not so ready to claim they can understand Lao. This is partly because the Lao are exposed to Thai in the media, and partly because Thai speakers have a negative attitude towards Lao.

A single language crosses the borders of Serbia, Croatia, Montenegro, Bosnia, and Herzegovina. When Yugoslavia was a single political entity the language was called Serbo-Croatian. One name that is used nowadays is Bosnian/Croatian/Serbian, as well as separate labels such as Serbian. While linguists may seek to determine the difference between language and dialect by objective criteria such as a measure of mutual intelligibility, people tend to recognize languages on the grounds of what is common to a particular group, whether it be a nation or a smaller group.

For many people in the world there is a choice between dialect, local language, national language, or international language. Suppose I am a native of Singaraja on the northern coast of Bali in Indonesia. I will speak the local dialect of Balinese, but also be familiar to some extent with other dialects. Balinese is a local language in Indonesia along with Sundanese, Buginese, Javanese, and various others. Like most Indonesians, I will also know the national language, Bahasa Indonesia, or simply, Indonesian. I may also know English, an international language.

In England there were dialects right from the outset, because what was to become the English language was brought to Britain in the fourth and fifth centuries AD by three separate groups, the Angles, who settled in the Midlands and North, the Saxons, who settled in the south, and Jutes, who settled in Kent. In the Middle Ages people in Britain wrote in their own dialect. There were six broad dialect areas: Scottish, Northern, East and West Midland, Southern and Kentish. In the fifteenth century a standard form of the language began to emerge based on the language of the southeast, and this became the sole medium for written work. The main focal points for the emerging standard were London, the seat of government and main centre of commerce, and Oxford and Cambridge, the two great centres of learning.

Speakers of a language are cognizant of dialects, at least neighbouring dialects, but it has been common since the nineteenth century for scholars to investigate dialects by going around gathering data on pronunciation, word choice, morphology, and syntax in an attempt to build up a complete picture. The results of their surveys are plotted on a map. Lines of demarcation are drawn between different pronunciations or different words for a particular meaning (e.g. *bucket* or *pail*). These lines are known as **isoglosses**. Where a number of isoglosses coincide, we have an indication of a dialect boundary. Of course we do not always get neat borders between dialects, and when we do, we often get dialects within dialects. For instance, Scottish English is a dialect within Britain, but within Scottish there are northern, central, and southern sub-dialects, and within these sub-dialects there are smaller dialects, sub-sub-dialects if you like.

However, these traditional, essentially rural, dialects, like dialects elsewhere in Europe, are now dying under the impact of mass media and education, which promote the standard. There is greater social and geographical mobility, though that includes a lot of migration to cities, which to some extent become focal points for new dialects. One feature that distinguishes a dialect is the overall pronunciation or **accent**, and accents live on. One salient marker that separates the South of England from the Midlands and North of England is that the latter retain [ʊ] in words like *chum*, *luck*, and *putt*, so that *putt* sounds the same as *put*. Another salient marker occurs in words like *path*, *after*, *pass*, and *dance*. In the south the vowel is [aː] or [ɑː]. In the north it is [æ]. A readily observable difference separates West Country from other dialects and that is the use of initial voiced fricatives in words like *farm*, *thumb*, and *summer* where others have voiceless fricatives. The /r/ is retained in words like *car* and *card* in this area, and indeed across a wider area of the south and west. Isoglosses for these salient regional differences in pronunciation are illustrated in Map 11.1.

In the United States there are three broad dialect areas (see Map 11.2). The Northern dialect takes in New England and stretches west along the US–Canada border, with Eastern New England as a significantly different sub-division. The Southern dialect area runs south from Delaware and Maryland down to the Gulf States. The Midland area takes in the rest of

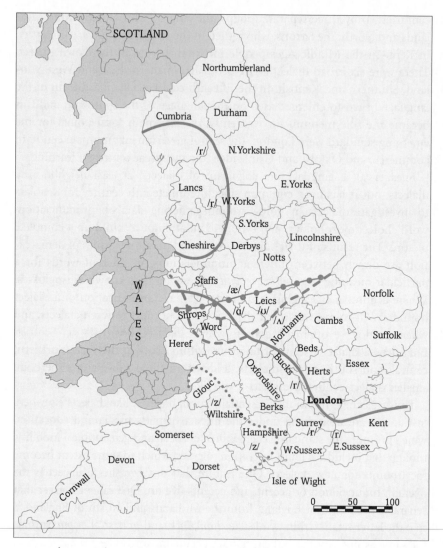

——— marks areas where /r/ is pronounced in words like *car* and *card*, i.e. where there is no
following vowel.

– – – separates area to the north where /ʊ/ is retained in *but, chum*, etc. from area to the south
where these words have /ʌ/.

...... separates area to the west where an initial voiced fricative is found in words like *fox, summer*
and *shilling* from area to the east where an initial voiceless fricative occurs.

• • • • separates area to the north which retains /æ/ before a voiceless fricative as in *path, laugh* and
grass from the area to the south where these words have /ɑː/ or /aː/.

Map 11.1 Some isoglosses in England.

the country. It is sometimes called 'Midwestern' and it is the basis for 'General American' as referred to in various publications including this one. It has a prestige emanating from its spread. It is the accent most often adopted by newsreaders since it is area-neutral and considered 'accentless'. Southern American English is the second largest dialect. It is distinguished by various features including the use of *you-all* or *y'all* as a second person plural pronoun and by a distinctive accent, including the use of [a:] or [ɑ:] in words like *rice*, *night*, and *mine*, which have the diphthong [aɪ] elsewhere. The Southern accent has negative connotations for speakers of other forms of American English. This is partly the result of a long-standing negative attitude on the part of the North that goes back before the Civil War, and it is not helped by the persistently negative portrayal of Southerners in Hollywood movies.

Besides local varieties and sub-varieties of a language, there are national varieties. Many people make a broad distinction between American and British English, even though there are obvious variations within these countries. These distinctions are primarily based on vocabulary and accent. Numerous differences in vocabulary are well known. Take the motor car, for instance, which has an alternative label *automobile* in American English. We find British *windscreen* versus American *windshield*, British *bonnet* versus American *hood*, British *boot* versus American *trunk*, and so on. A prominent feature of pronunciation that distinguishes the national varieties is that mainstream British English has lost /r/ except where a vowel follows, whereas it is retained in America in words like *bar*, *beer*, *card*, and *carton*. However, there are exceptions on both sides of the Atlantic. As can be seen in Map 11.1, /r/ is retained in parts of the west and southwest of England. Conversely in the United States /r/ in the relevant contexts is frequently omitted in the coastal parts of the Southern dialect area and further up the east coast including New York City and eastern New England. The Southern dialect area is illustrated in Map 11.2. Other characteristic features of American English include flapping the /t/ that occurs between a stressed vowel and an unstressed vowel in words like *butter* and *writer* so that it sounds like a /d/, a strong secondary stress in words like *laboratory* and *secretary*, and pronouncing words like *nude* and *tune* as if they were *nood* and *toon* where British English has [njuːd] and [tʃuːn].

Canadian English has a vocabulary that is partly British and partly American. The accent sounds like US English to people outside North America, but to some US observers it sounds like British English. In fact it combines features of both US and British English. As in most US English /r/ is retained before consonants and at the end of a word, the /t/ is flapped in words like *butter* and *writer*, and there is a strong secondary stress in words like *laboratory* and *secretary*. On the other hand Canadian English retains [j] (or [y]) in

Map 11.2 US Dialects.

words like *nude* and *news* and /tʃ/ in words like *tune* and *tube*. Vocabulary is a mixture of British and US, with US influence on the increase especially among the young.

Australia, New Zealand, and the former British colonies in Africa have vocabularies that are basically British with an admixture of distinctive local terms, and an increasing stock of Americanisms. They also have their own accents, but there is little dialect variation.

Social varieties

Class differences

In most small-scale societies, those of hunters and gatherers for instance, all people of the same sex and age have much the same social standing. But large-scale societies or civilizations on the other hand are characterized by social classes based on factors such as birth, wealth, and education. In the democracies of the West class distinctions have reduced over the last century or so, but differences do remain. Class distinctions are a recognized feature in Britain and though the former colonies pride themselves on being more egalitarian, class differences exist there too. The average person recognizes some correlation between class and use of language, and differences of usage frequently give rise to comment in everyday life and in the media. Behind these comments there lurks the notion of a standard. There are recognized standards of correctness in spelling, pronunciation, grammar, and in the use of certain words, and deviations from the standard are often the basis for adverse comment.

Spelling

A standard spelling emerged in the seventeenth century and the notion of a standard is clearer in spelling than in pronunciation, grammar, or lexicon. In Britain and the Commonwealth the Oxford English Dictionary is the accepted standard. The United States has a slightly different standard initiated by Noah Webster in the early nineteenth century. Canada has a mixture of both the British and US standards (e.g. *tire centre*). With spelling the notion of a standard is uncontroversial. Few people in the English-speaking world deliberately deviate from the Oxford or Webster spelling system or their local mixture. There are calls for spelling reform from time to time, not surprising given that English has a poor relationship between sound and spelling, but there are no moves to establish spelling dialects. Deviations from standard spelling abound, as any schoolteacher will attest and a survey of amateur postings on the web will confirm. Some deviations are accidental, others reflect ignorance, but there is general acceptance of what is right and what is wrong. Although the average person might adopt an indulgent attitude towards bad spelling, bad spellers are at a disadvantage in the range of jobs they can successfully apply for (though Spell Check may save some of them!).

Pronunciation

A recognized standard in pronunciation emerged in Britain in the nineteenth century. It is likely that the bringing together of students from all over Britain in the public (i.e. private!) boarding schools of the southeast played a part, particularly as this produced a privileged elite that went on to Oxford and Cambridge and then assumed positions in the civil service, the Foreign Office, the army, the law, and the Anglican Church.

The pronunciation that became the standard was dubbed 'Public School Pronunciation' by the famous phonetician Daniel Jones, but he later introduced the label **Received Pronunciation** (RP) and that is the term used by linguists today. A term in general use is 'Oxford accent', another is 'BBC accent', since RP has been the accent adopted by the BBC from its inception in the 1920s. RP can be described as the accent of the educated in the south-east of England. It is a dialect to the extent that it originated in south-eastern England, but it is more a class dialect than a geographical one, perhaps even more since it has been adopted to varying extents in other areas of Britain and in Commonwealth countries.

For more than a century people who did not use Received Pronunciation in England were made to feel inferior, and many who did not acquire it from their family or milieu sought to imitate it. A classic example is to be found in George Bernard Shaw's play, *Pygmalion*, better known from the musical version, *My Fair Lady*. A cockney flower girl, Eliza Doolittle, who makes her living by selling flowers on the street, approaches Professor Higgins, a professor of phonetics, and asks him to teach her to speak like a lady, so she can get a job in a flower shop. She has heard him boast that he could, with three months' training, pass her off as a duchess at an ambassador's garden party or even get her a place as a lady's maid or a shop assistant, 'which requires better English'. This line picks up on an interesting facet of the correlation between class and language, namely that those catering to the upper classes were often more concerned with correctness than their masters and mistresses, and they aspired 'to speak well'. Higgins succeeds in teaching Eliza to speak RP, but neglects to teach her the standard grammar, so that when she is let loose at a morning tea, she creates a lot of bemusement for her fellow tea drinkers and amusement for the audience by mixing Cockney grammar with RP. Readers might remember her saying things such as *What I say is, them as pinched it done her in* with a 'frightfully proper' accent.

Received Pronunciation is a recognized standard, not only in Britain but throughout the Commonwealth countries. Some people consciously aspire to speak it, just as Eliza Doolittle did. Many more shift from their local accent towards RP, often without being aware of the change. However, many English speakers have a negative view of the 'posh' or 'plummy' accent. It is the accent of the ruling classes and those nearer to the other end of the social scale are not too likely to be particularly enamoured of the 'toffs'. They resent the social injustice that the class system represents and the assumption of superiority that often goes with being near the top end of the social scale. In radio programmes, films, and television programmes RP, often an exaggerated version of RP, is spoken by males who are effeminate, foppish, or effete, and by both males and females who are snobbish or arrogant. Sometimes this is done deliberately for comic effect, as with the Penelope Keith character in *To the Manor Born* or the Joanna Lumley character in *Absolutely Fabulous*, but there is no doubt that many people have an ambivalent attitude towards RP and a negative attitude towards what they hear as its exaggerated form. Over the last few decades there have been signs of some levelling in the accents of south-eastern England with RP being modified 'down' and Cockney being modified 'up' resulting in what has come to be called **Estuary English**, the general accent of the London area, which is spreading in the counties adjacent to London and appearing in other urban centres of England.

Deviations from RP are of two kinds. The first is the positioning of the vowels and diphthongs in what we might call the 'vowel space'. It is this that is responsible for the overall difference of 'accent'. Take Cockney English, for instance. Cockney and RP have more or less the same set of vowel and diphthong phonemes, but realize them differently. For instance, the diphthong in words like *hate, raid,* and *fame* is [eɪ] in RP and close to [aɪ] in Cockney, and the diphthong in words like *tight, kite* and *pint* is [aɪ] in RP but close to [ɔɪ] in Cockney. These differences are shown in Figure 11.1 with the front-gliding diphthongs in Figure 11.1 (a) and the back-gliding diphthongs in Figure 11.1 (b). The RP diphthongs are in black and the Cockney vowels in green. Note that the notation is appropriate only for the RP diphthongs, but is retained for the corresponding Cockney diphthongs. There is little or no lip rounding in the Cockney back-gliding diphthongs, and among some RP speakers there is little lip rounding in the starting point of what is notated [oʊ], so for such speakers [əʊ] would be more accurate.

(a) Front-gliding diphthongs

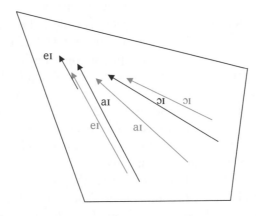

(b) Back-gliding diphthongs

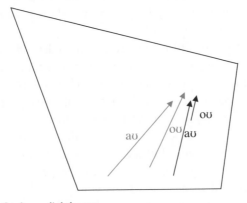

Figure 11.1 RP and Cockney diphthongs.

Sometimes in the tabloid press you will see the Queen's speech mimicked with spellings such as 'May husband and ay'. Of course the Queen does not have the diphthong [eɪ] in these words, but with those diphthongs that glide towards [ɪ] her diphthongs are one place to the left of the corresponding Cockney diphthongs and the 'ay' spelling exaggerates this difference.

The other kind of deviation from RP involves the treatment of particular phonemes in particular contexts. One feature that is stigmatized throughout the English-speaking world is the dropping of /h/ from the beginning of words like *house, horse,* and *hungry.* This is a feature of Cockney English, but not confined to it. When I was young, it was common in working class speech in Australia. However, in RP the /h/ can be dropped from an initial unstressed syllable as in *an historical novel,* and practically all speakers omit it in unstressed words like *his* and *her. She looks after his mother. She asked her old man.* Another widely recognized social marker is g-dropping, that is, pronouncing words such as *running* and *jumping* as *runnin* and *jumpin.* This is an interesting one. Although it is 'low class' to drop the *g,* it was very much upper class well into the twentieth century. The addition of a [k] in *somethingk* (I have also heard *somepthingk*), *anythingk,* and *nothingk* is 'low class' throughout the English-speaking world.

In general one was judged with respect to where one's speech fell on a scale ranging from RP to the local, whether that be Cockney, West Country, or whatever. Much the same applied to the pronunciation of former colonies such as Australia, New Zealand, and the African colonies. Those who spoke with a Scottish, Welsh, or Irish accent were judged somewhat differently. To some extent a Scottish accent is considered to have its own legitimacy, and the same applies to Welsh and Irish accents.

Speakers of RP sometimes condemn other accents as being ugly and difficult to understand. It is difficult to find a rational basis for asserting that particular speech sounds are ugly. Sometimes a particular vowel or diphthong is singled out for attack. For instance, the Cockney or Broad Australian pronunciation of *rate,* which sounds like RP *right,* is said to be 'ugly', but the [aɪ] diphthong is apparently mellifluous when it occurs in the RP pronunciation of a word like *right!*

The charge that non-RP accents are hard to understand relates to the general difficulty of adjusting to an unfamiliar accent. Some Americans are reported as having found RP difficult to understand. Each accent is easy to understand by speakers with that accent. It could not be otherwise. If people were having trouble understanding one another because there were insufficient distance between their vowels and diphthongs, then they would subconsciously adjust to keep the system working. But such a situation never arises. That is not to say that vowels never merge. Among a majority of speakers of General American words like *pin* and *tin* have the same vowel as *pen* and *ten,* and for some American speakers *merry, Mary,* and *marry* are homophonous.

Grammar

With regard to grammar, there is a standard of correct grammar recognized throughout the English-speaking world, at least for written English, but, as explained on pages 97 to 100, in some ways the standard is artificial and out of touch with usage. Deviations from the standard are normally looked on unfavourably. However, one has to be careful of labelling these deviations as errors. One has to allow for an alternative system. Consider African American Vernacular English (AAVE). Almost every sentence in this variety of English contains a deviation from the standard, but it would be wrong to condemn these differences as errors, since AAVE has its own consistent system. A sentence such as *She working* looks like an error for *She is working*, but a form of the verb 'to be' is used in AAVE, namely *be* itself. *She be working at McDonalds* means she is employed at McDonald's. However, although a professional linguist might point out that AAVE has its own system, there is no escaping from the fact that most people will see practically every sentence as ungrammatical. This of course applies to most so-called errors. A person who uses the nominative form for pronouns in phrases such as *between you and I* or *with you and she* has a system. It is just that it is not the textbook system.

As mentioned on pages 97 to 100, in connection with grammar, a lot of deviation from what textbooks prescribe is socially acceptable. Consider the verbs *lie* and *lay*, for instance. The textbook forms for the past tense and past participles look like this:

> *Today I lie (down).*   *Today I lay the books down.*
> *Yesterday I lay down.*   *Yesterday I laid the books down.*
> *I have lain down to rest.* *I have laid the books down.*

Deviations from this pattern are frequent. One hears *Lie them down this way* and *Yesterday I laid down*. These widespread deviations will be perfectly acceptable for many, but condemned by purists.

Word usage

Some deviations from the standard are to be found in the use of certain words. For instance, the word *fortunate* means 'lucky' and the word *fortuitous* means 'by chance', but *fortuitous* is often used in the sense of lucky as in, 'It was fortuitous that you thought to bring the spare key.' This usage is so common that it may come to be accepted.

Sex and gender

An important social factor determining language variation is the biological difference of sex, or **gender**, the different social roles played by the sexes, which varies somewhat from one culture to another, and from one period to another. In English-speaking culture males and females differ in speaking styles. Women tend to exhibit a wider range of intonation and a more expressive body language. Or alternatively, men tend to show less variation in intonation and have a less expressive body language. Studies of language and gender try to avoid taking male behaviour as the standard. Some studies claim that women are more likely than men of the same social class to speak 'better' and use more 'correct' forms, whereas men will often aim at a working-class target in accent, grammar, use of colloquialisms, and swearing. Where there are markers of class difference such as using or not using a velar nasal in words like *running* and *jumping*, surveys show that more men use the *runnin'* and *jumpin'* forms. Though these findings have been taken as evidence that women are comparatively conservative, other studies show that women are leaders in adopting new variants. The sexes also differ in choice of vocabulary; women are more likely to use words like *gorgeous* or *divine*, or expressions like *absolutely fabulous*. There are also different discourse styles. Men tend to report briefly, women more discursively.

The collection of data on male/female differences in language use is still in its early stages and it faces the problem of disentangling variation along gender lines from variation within the genders, which in turn relates to broad class differences and finer grained differences such as those between occupation groups, interest groups, and so on.

In many languages, however, there are well-defined, formal differences between the speech of males and females. In some languages there are regular phonological differences. In Gros Ventre (northeast US) women have palatalized velar stops, as in /k^{y}atsa/ 'bread', corresponding to palatalized dental stops in men's speech, as in /d^{y}atsa/. In Darkhat Mongolian the rounded back vowels in men's speech correspond to central rounded vowels in women's speech and central rounded vowels in men's speech correspond to front rounded vowels in women's speech.

Another kind of difference is found in Thai. A male refers to himself as *phŏm*, both males and females can use *chán*, but only a female uses *dichán*. A male adds *khráp* at the end of a sentence to be polite, a female adds *khâ*.

He: *Sawàtdii khráp.*	Hello!
She: *Sawàtdii khâ.*	Hello!
He: *Phŏm pay talàat khráp.*	I'm going to the market.
She: *Dichán pay bâan khâ.*	I'm going home.

Age

In some societies, certainly in the West, there are differences of language correlated with age. Given that language is constantly changing, it will inevitably be the case that old people will be found using obsolescent features. For instance, a few decades ago you would hear older speakers of RP, and Australian and New Zealand English pronouncing words like *off*, *cloth*, and *cross* with an [ɔ:] vowel as in words like *paw* rather then with an [ɒ] vowel as in *hot*. In Gilbert and Sullivan's comic operetta *The Pirates of Penzance* (1879) there is a lot of humour extracted from the homophony of *orphan* and *often*, but one wonders what future generations will make of it, especially now that /t/ is being restored in *often*. You can still find older people using words like *wireless* for *radio*. However, there are also colloquial expressions that circulate more or less exclusively among schoolchildren and teenagers. Some words and expressions are ephemeral, lasting just for a year or so, often with just a particular age group. Some are old and form part of the permanent vocabulary of young people's speech. A few words start life among the youth and then pass into general circulation. For example, *awesome*, *unreal*, and *bad* (in the sense of 'good'), although primarily associated with the young, are used by middle aged speakers.

There is also a colloquial style peculiar to youth. Take the following passage.

> *This guy comes in and he's, like, cool, sooooo cool. I'm like, 'Anytime, your place or mine.'*
> *And he comes up and goes, 'Would you like to dance?'*
> *And I'm, like, wetting myself, but I play it cool. 'I'm not dancing with you.'*
> *'You are too.'*

It contains a number of features of 'teenspeak'. It consists of a style also associated with popular narrative and jokes (*This guy comes in . . .*), and some long-standing features of young people's speech such as *goes* meaning something like 'says'. It also contains some relatively new uses of *like*. In the first line *like* marks hesitation, but it also serves to highlight the following word *cool*, which is further emphasized by being repeated with a drawn out *so*. The next *like* is the most interesting feature. It can introduce what someone said or thought or it can give an indication of what they might have said or thought, something *like* what they might have said or thought.

Styles

A: He's certainly very good. Where does he come from?
B: He's domiciled in Newcastle.
A: Yes, but where does he live?

Exchange between two sports commentators

In the previous sections we dealt with variation that tended to be fixed for each speaker. A particular person is likely to speak a certain dialect, and speak in a manner determined by social class, sex, and age. But some people will have a command of more than one dialect and most people can vary their speech and writing style to fit different situations. They have a repertoire of **styles** ranging from formal to informal and encompassing special spoken styles such as baby talk and special written styles such as diary style.

Register and jargon

The styles associated with particular activities are called **registers**. A register often goes hand-in-hand with a specialized vocabulary. Various occupations, areas of study, sports and recreational pursuits have their own vocabulary or **jargon**. If I want to talk about my use of a computer, then I can hardly avoid using terms such as *hard disk, floppy disk, download, megabyte,* and *save* (in its special computer sense). Cricket has an interesting jargon in that it contains a number of examples of opaque combinations of familiar words. There are positions on the field with names such as *first slip, long leg, fine leg,* and *silly point.* A batsman can *glance to fine leg* and a bowler who manages to deliver a set of balls without the batsman scoring is said *to have bowled a maiden over.*

If I want to talk about cooking, I will find myself using words such as *simmer, poach, sauté,* and nowadays I might talk of serving meat on a *bed of mash* or perhaps *julienne-ing* the carrots (slicing them lengthways). If, however, I am writing a recipe, I will not only be using the jargon of cooking, but a certain style with lots of short, imperative sentences. This is the recipe register.

Beef stir-fry for two.
Sauce: Take two dessertspoonfuls of oyster sauce, two of soy, two of honey plus a teaspoonful of sweet chilli sauce and mix over a low heat. Add water.
Chop half a white onion fine and slice two Dutch carrots and two sticks of celery.
Cut 350 grams of steak into bite-sized pieces. Brown in oil over high heat. Add sauce.
Add vegetables. Cook for ten minutes over medium heat.
Add capsicum and cashews before serving,

The diary register is well known and easily recognizable, particularly in English where it regularly breaks the rule that main clauses must have a subject. It also represents the case of a register that is not associated with a jargon. The following could have been written by Bridget Jones.

Woke up about 10. Felt wasted. Strange man in my bed. Thought it was Brian? Turned out to be Abdul. Rang Roxanne. No answer. Was probably still out to it. Tried around 11. Still no answer.

Officialese, official language, or bureaucratese is the register used by those in authority when exercising their authority. Officialese can often be pompous, stilted, and obscure, and it invites derision. I never cease to wonder when I'm instructed to 'deplane the aircraft' why I couldn't be told it's all right to get off the plane. What is officially called an *amber traffic signal* is a *yellow light* in common speech. Not long ago it was not uncommon to see signs at railway stations (or 'train stations' as they are called nowadays) *Do not expectorate*. This isn't very helpful when one considers that the sort of person likely to spit in public is hardly likely to know what this unusual learned word means.

```
PLEASE BE ADVISED THAT
THIS BISTRO IS A SMOKE
       FREE ZONE
```

A 'no smoking' sign in officialese.

In modern societies a person will begin by learning the jargon of various school subjects, then the jargon of a few leisure-time activities and sports, and the jargon of various forms of employment, perhaps including military jargon from doing military service. The use of jargon is difficult to avoid. The jargon is there for a purpose. It provides a set of labels for what needs to be talked about in a certain sphere of activity. Nevertheless, the use of most jargons sets off in-groups within society, and some people seem to use more jargon that is necessary, particularly when speaking to 'outsiders'. The same applies to register, even more so, since there is more choice as to whether to use the special register or keep to a mainstream language.

Argot

Whereas jargon and some special registers can be arcane to outsiders simply because they are specialized, there are varieties of language that are designed to be an in-group language. Forms of argot or cant fall into this category. An **argot** consists of an alternative vocabulary of words and phrases circulating within a particular group. The word 'argot' is traditionally associated with thieves, con-artists, grifters, and vagabonds, and is sometimes referred to as 'thieves' slang'. However, types of argot are also used by those who supply goods or services without having a shop, people such as street vendors or market stall-holders. An argot is also in use among itinerant gypsies in Britain, and various forms of English argot contain a number of words from Romany, the language of the gypsies (see chapter twelve). Argots are also in use in gay sub-culture, but much of the vocabulary has been 'outed' over the last few decades.

Argot is similar to jargon in that it consists of a vocabulary mainly of nouns and verbs, and uses regular syntax, but it differs from jargon in that jargon is normally formal and necessary for accurate and succinct communication, whereas argot is informal and not necessary from the purely communicative point of view. The use of argot identifies one as a member of a relatively small, and often oppressed, group. It always serves to bond the in-group, and sometimes it provides a code opaque to authorities.

In horse racing, harness racing, and dog racing there is an arcane form of language consisting of jargon to do with the animals (*hock, fetlock*) and their equipment (*bridle, saddle*), the jargon of gambling (*even money, five-to-two*), colourful expressions found in old style racing papers where jockeys were *postillions* and bookmakers *satchel swingers*, plus an argot of slang expressions such as *a monkey* (500 pounds or dollars) and *morning glory* (a horse who performs well in early morning training, but fails in races).

Secret language

Secret forms of language are not uncommon. They range from ways of disguising every word to just secret passwords. Secret forms of language have been used by priestly castes, secret societies, lodges, criminals, and those whose activites arouse the suspicions of the lawkeepers, rightfully or wrongfully. Secret language is used in religious or religious-type ceremonies, in initiation ceremonies, and to restrict communication to a chosen few. Sometimes the use of secret language is serious business, other times it is used for fun.

The users of argot sometimes employ forms of coded language. In *Back Slang*, which was in use in Britain among hawkers, barrow boys, and other food vendors, each word is said to be pronounced backwards. However, it is based largely on the written form of words, so, for instance, the silent *e* in a word like *police* is treated as a vowel. Note too that an unstressed 'e' has to be added when words like *old* and *lamb* are reversed. The first example illustrates two treatments of *the*, reversal and no reversal.

Evig eth ecnop a tib o the delo bemal.
'Give the ponce a bit of the old lamb.'

Kool tou! I nac ees eth reppock nimoc.
'Look out! I can see the copper coming.'

The French have a 'secret language' called *Verlan*, which is said to be used by the criminal classes among others. The syllables of a word are reversed so that 'un café' becomes *un féca*. The 'silent e' is used, so 'la classe' [laklas] becomes *la cecla* (or *secla*) [lasəkla]. With monosyllabic words the syllable is reversed so that 'un bus' becomes *un sub*.

Secret languages were once popular among children, but they seem to have dropped out of fashion. They are all similar to back slang in that they involve some systematic distortion, usually of the written form of language. The best known and most widely used in English has been *Pig Latin*. It was used just for fun or so that kids could talk in front of outsiders (e.g. their parents or other children) without the outsiders understanding them. The system is so simple that outsiders were likely to cotton on after a bit of exposure, but it still served to mark the in-group from the out-group. There are a number of varieties of Pig Latin. In most of them one takes any consonants that precede the first vowel of a word and puts them at the end followed by -*ay*. If there is no such consonant or consonant cluster, that is, the word begins with a vowel, then one adds -*way* or -*yay*, or just -*ay* at the end of the word. Here is an example where -*way* is used.

> *I will now give you an example of Pig Latin.*
> *Iway illway ownay ivegay ouyay anway exampleway ofway Igpay Atinlay*

In a word like *synod* where 'y' represents a vowel, the Pig Latin form is *ynodsay* (not that this word is much used in Pig Latin circles).

Rhyming slang

A form of in-group communication that is traditional with Cockneys, at least since the nineteenth century, is **rhyming slang**. It has also been popular in Australia, and is not unknown in America. Basically it consists of a rhyming phrase substituted for a word so that, for instance, 'eyes' becomes *mince pies*, 'mouth' becomes *north and south* and 'nose' becomes *I suppose*. It has had a certain social stigma attached to it, and was once associated with the criminal classes, but it has come to be quite widely used. Rhyming slang has something of an argot or secret code about it, since the referent is not always clear to the uninitiated. It becomes more of a secret code when the rhyming element is omitted. In the television series *Minder* Arthur Daley used to talk about getting on the *dog*. The *dog* is the *dog and bone*, that is, the phone. When we talk about someone *rabbiting on*, we are using a word derived from rhyming slang. *Rabbit* is short for *rabbit and pork*, rhyming slang for 'talk'. *Rabbit and pork* started life as a substitute for the noun 'talk', then got to be used for the verb 'to talk'. If someone is *rabbiting on*, they are talking at length. Other examples of expressions that started off life as rhyming slang, but which have come into more general use, include *brass tacks* for 'facts', *chew the fat* for 'chat', and *Dutch treat*. *Dutch treat* was originally rhyming slang for 'eat', but has come to mean a meal in a restaurant where two or more persons pay their own share, that is, they *go Dutch*.

Allusive language

Language can be used in an allusive way. In discussing the use of proper names as common nouns in chapter three *Judas* and *Doubting Thomas* were mentioned. These are characters in the New Testament and knowledge of what they are famous for is part of Christian culture. Some allusions are to pieces of text. Traditional sources for these literary allusions were the Bible and Shakespeare. These allusions are very common nowadays in the headlines of newspaper and magazine articles. So many articles about miserable winters have been called 'The winter of discontent' that it has become trite. The source is the opening lines of *Richard III*: *Now is the winter of our discontent/Made glorious summer by this sun of York*. Titles of novels, plays, and films are often allusive. There is a film *Outrageous Fortune* with Bette Midler and Shelley Long where the title comes from Hamlet's 'To be or not to be' soliloquy. There are also allusions to popular culture. An article about deposed Empress of Iran, Farah Pahlavi, hoping to return to the throne was called *The Empress Strikes Back*, playing on the title of the popular film *The Empire Strikes Back*. The use of allusions is an example of playing with language. It has something in common with argot and other esoteric forms of language in that while it communicates its basic meaning to anyone who knows English, it conveys the hidden meaning to a select few.

Formal and informal

Language is not an abstract construction of the learned, or of dictionary makers, but is something arising out of the work, needs, ties, joys, affections, tastes, of long generations of humanity, and has its bases broad and low, close to the ground.

Noah Webster (1758–1843)

Apart from registers there are styles that are not tied to a particular activity. We all have a natural, informal mode that we use in the family and among our friends, and we all know that a more formal style is appropriate in the prepared text of news reporting and lectures, for instance, and in talking to people in authority and dignitaries such as senators, bishops, presidents, and monarchs. The main difference between formal and informal lies in choice of vocabulary: standard *police* versus informal *cops*, or formal *receive a letter* versus everyday *get a letter*.

In describing informal language two terms come up: **colloquial** (or collo-quialisms) and **slang**. 'Colloquial' simply means informal and covers every-day language and slang, plus vulgar and taboo words. While 'colloquial' has positive or at least neutral connotations, the word 'slang' is generally used negatively. It generally refers to very informal language, so an expression such as 'got a letter from home' would be colloquial, but not slang. Some diction-aries characterize slang as ephemeral, but while many slang expressions are short-lived, others live on. Some definitions include reference to its esoteric character and it is that aspect that figures in the terms 'back slang' and 'rhyming slang'. To 'ephemeral' and 'esoteric' we could add 'socially and geographically restricted'. It is characteristic of slang that it is confined to a particular group at a particular time, and for that reason alone it is unsuitable for formal purposes, which often involve communication with the commu-nity at large. Part of the attraction of slang lies in its esoteric character. It is a good marker of identity. Moreover, slang and colloquial language generally often display a certain cleverness and colour. For instance, someone having to work hard is said to be *flat out like a lizard drinking water* and someone forceful is said to have *more push than a revolving door.*

In some languages there is a distinction between a 'high' form of the language and a 'low' form with the high form used in certain situations such as speeches, news broadcasts, and formal letters, and the low form in other situations such as informal conversation. Where this is generally recognized, with the two varieties having different labels, the situation is called **diglossia**. In Switzerland, for instance, High German is the high form and Swiss German the low form. In Greece Katharevousa is the high form and Dhimotiki the low form. In Arabic speaking countries Classical Arabic is the high form and the local variant of colloquial Arabic the low form. In both Greece and Arabic-speaking countries the low form is used on the radio and in novels, and the high form very much a special form reserved for formal situations.

In some cultures there are marked differences in the styles that must be used in different social situations. In Javanese, for instance, there are three forms of the language: *ngoko, madya,* and *krama.* The differences lie in vocabulary. The basic form is *ngoko,* and this is the form childen learn first. In general people use *ngoko* at home and among friends, and in addressing people of lower social standing, and they use *krama,* the high form, in addressing people of high status in formal situations. They can use *madya,* the middle form, in ambivalent contexts or where they are unsure about what is appropriate. They can also switch to Indonesian to avoid using the wrong style. Table 11.1 illustrates the three levels with three versions of a sentence that means, 'Did you take that much rice?' As can be seen, the differences in some cases consist of an entirely different root and in other cases there are

Table 11.1. Javanese speech levels

	query	you	take	rice	that much
Ngoko	*Apa*	*kowé*	*njuput*	*sega*	*semono*
Madya	*Napa*	*sampéyan*	*mendhet*	*sega*	*semonten*
Krama	*Menapa*	*nandalem*	*mundhut*	*sekul*	*semanten*

variant forms of a root. Not every *ngoko* word has *madya* and *krama* equivalents, and the example is simplified in that it does not show some of the possible alternatives.

In Thai there is a special form of the language to be used in addressing royalty. The difference is mainly in the vocabulary, and the royal language contains more words from Sanskrit-Pali and Khmer (Cambodian) than more demotic varieties of Thai. For instance, the Thai words for 'eat' are *kin* (informal) and *rapprathan* (formal), but the royal term is *sawɔ̌ːy*, a word borrowed from Khmer.

Terms of address

Colonel Pickering: What is his trade, Eliza?
Eliza: Ain't you going to call me Miss Doolittle any more?
Colonel Pickering: I beg your pardon, Miss Doolittle. It was a slip of the tongue.
Eliza: Oh, I don't mind. Only it sounded so genteel.

G. B. Shaw: *Pygmalion*, Act II

In many cultures the formal mode is required for practically every situation outside family and friends, and the choice between formal and familiar begins with greetings and terms of address. In some languages of Europe there are pronouns to be used in addressing intimates as opposed to others. In French the singular pronoun *tu* 'you' is traditionally used in talking to a familiar such as a close friend or family member, and also to a small child, while *vous* is used in talking to anyone else despite the fact that it is a plural form. In German there is alternation between the familiar *du* and the less familiar *Sie*, which is a third person form (though spelt with a capital 's' when used for the addressee). In Italian the alternation is between *tu* and *Lei*, again a third person form. A similar distinction can be found in Dutch, Norwegian, Swedish, Russian, and Spanish. French usage spread to England in the Middle Ages and *thou* (nominative) and *thee* (accusative), the singular forms, began to be used as intimate singular forms, while *ye* and *you*, the plural forms, were used as non-familiar singular forms. This usage continued until the seventeenth century, when *thou* and *thee* dropped out and *you* became the regular singular as well as plural. It is quite noticeable in Shakespeare where close friends and all low characters address one another with 'thou' and 'thee', and address others as 'ye' or 'you'. In Europe the use of the familiar forms has come to be used to a wider circle over the last few decades, along with greater use of given names as opposed to surnames, a change that has also taken place in English.

Identity and solidarity

Language is a strong marker of identity, probably the strongest. All the forms of variation discussed in this chapter serve to identify people as belonging to an area, a social group, a gender, or an age group. If I speak a dialect, a local language, a national language, and an international language I can identify at different levels, with groups of various sizes. At the local level the dialect of my area will be full of words with local connotations, local allusions, it will be the form of language I am most comfortable with when speaking with family and friends. I will probably be able to express my feelings best in my local dialect. My dialect will also serve as a kind of secret language if it is sufficiently different from the language of wider communication. It might be useful if I want to keep things from authorities. Even where there is no dialect available, people can identify at a local level by using more colloquialisms. The colloquial language is less uniform than the standard variety.

I might use the local language, the national language, or an international language for various purposes. Each higher level gives me an entrée to a larger group, and I can identify with groups of different size. Suppose I am a native of Lombok in Indonesia. I identify with locals on the basis of my native Sundanese, and with my fellow countrymen on the basis of Indonesian. I am a Moslem and I have learned Classical Arabic so I can read the Koran. This unites me not only with other local Moslems, but to some extent with Moslems from the rest of the world. I am educated and I can read and speak English. This gives me access to a wealth of practical literature and enables me to keep up regular contacts with English speakers around the world.

Where a standard form of language exists, most speakers accept that it is a standard, but obviously huge numbers choose not to follow the standard. In some instances a speaker will not have access to standard spelling, grammar, and word usage through lack of educational opportunity, but more often than not it is a matter of language users choosing a variety that identifies them with an area or a particular social group. People choose to identify by choice of language, just as they do by choice of dress. Some people might want to identify as a Geordie (from Newcastle) or a Glaswegian (from Glasgow), while others might move towards imitating RP, either subconsciously or perhaps consciously in the hope of enhancing their prospects of employment. Southerners in the United States might prefer to identify as Southerners rather than gravitate towards General American. Many people find that certain non-standard forms are practically obligatory for acceptance in certain social groups.

Some thousands of the world's languages have very small numbers of speakers and are endangered and many of these small communities are taking measures to try to preserve their languages. This is no easy task when the young are attracted to the 'toys' of modern civilization and see the practical advantages of speaking any more widely spoken language that they are exposed to. Where languages have died, it is common for the descendants to try to revive the lost language. This is virtually impossible to do, but the fact that so many communities try is testament to the importance of language as a marker of identity.

Sources and further reading

The Javanese example on page 200 is adapted from Errington, *Structure and Style in Javanese*, pages 90 ff.

There are lots of very readable sources for the ground covered in this chapter. One of the most attractive sources is Crystal, *The Cambridge Encyclopedia of the English Language*, especially chapters 20 and 21. For regional variation in Britain try Trudgill, *The Dialects of England*. For regional variation in American English there is Wolfram and Schilling-Estes, *American English Dialects and Variation*. For world English Trudgill and Hannah, *International English* is useful.

For language and gender Cameron, 'Gender' is a good place to start, and a recent book is Eckert and McConnell-Ginet, *Language and Gender* (2003).

For a good introduction to sociolinguistics there is Holmes, *An introduction to Sociolinguistics*; Romaine, *Language in Society*; and Trudgill, *Sociolinguistics: an Introduction to Language and Society*. For the part social factors play in language change read Labov, *Principles of Linguistic Change*, vol. 2: *Social Factors*.

Problems

1 Standards of correctness vary from place to place and over time. What are the points of correct usage that most often come up for comment in your local English?

2 How many jargons are you familiar with? Think of school and university subjects you have studied, jobs you have had, sports, recreational interests.

3 Identify the registers illustrated in the following examples.

(a)   *A complex body with hints of spice followed on the palate by a dried fruit character supported by subtle oak and smooth tannins.*

(b)   *370,000 on my left. Any advance on 370,000? Will anyone give me 375,000?*

(c)   *Female 45 Rubenesque seeking prof/bus man 40–55 NS GSOH for LTR*

(d)   *Re yours of the 5th inst*

4 What differences do you notice between male and female language usage? Think about word choice, idiomatic expressions, style, syntax, and pronunciation.

Another thing to consider is differences in perceptions of words. For instance, one survey aimed at illustrating differences between the dictionary meaning and what people thought certain words meant revealed differences between male and female subjects. For instance, males presented with the word *sophisticated* thought first of it as applying to inanimate objects such as computers, while females thought first of its application to humans. For many females it had negative connotations and was associated with 'hoity-toity' and 'stuck-up'.

5 In playing Scrabble players will sometimes reject a word put on the board by a fellow player on the grounds that it is 'not a word', or 'not a real word', often on the grounds that the word in question is 'slang'. Such arguments can presumably be solved by appointing a particular dictionary as arbiter, but you might like to think about the notion of what is a (real) word in the variety of English you speak. On what grounds would you disqualify a contender for the status of 'word'?

6 The following are the titles of articles that have appeared in newspapers and magazines. They all contain an allusion. See if you can spot the source.

The force is with them.
Article about the Armed Robbery Squad.

Brave new families.
Article about gay and lesbian families.

Back to the couture.
Article about the new season's fashions.

What's rotten in the Empire State?
Article about problems in the Empire State Building.

7 The following words are at least dated, if not obsolescent or obsolete. See if you know the following and if you can say something about the contexts in which they were used.

bade [bæd], *by and by, banns, bounder, cad, compère, old maid, rotter, smite* (*smitten* is still current), *swell* (as in 'That's swell'), *vouchsafe.*

8 The use of terms of address in English has changed a lot over the last few decades, and probably in other European languages. Here are some facets to think about and discuss. If you can compare experiences from different parts of the English-speaking world or from other languages, all the better.

- When do you address people by their surname? When do you use their given name?
- When do you not use a name at all?
- Do you ever have occasion to use formal titles of address such as *matron, doctor, Your Grace,* etc? What formal titles of address do you know?
- How do you address members of your immediate family (parents, offspring, and siblings) and how do you address uncles, aunts, and grandparents?
- When, if ever, do you use terms of endearment such as *darling, sweetie*?

12. Language change

General

As mentioned at the beginning of the previous chapter, languages change. Over time every facet of a language can change: the sounds, the morphology, the syntax, the semantics, and the vocabulary. Most readers will be familiar with Shakespeare's English of 400 years ago (**Early Modern English**) and realize that the language has changed somewhat over four centuries. Some readers will have been introduced to Chaucer's fourteenth-century English and realize that it can be a little difficult to understand. English from 1100 to 1500 is called **Middle English**, so Chaucer belongs to the 'Late Middle English' period. If we go back beyond 1100, we find that the **Old English** of this period is so different that it needs to be learned like a foreign language. Here is a sample from Aelfric's *Colloquy*. It is written in the form of a transcript of an interview. The extract given here is from an imagined interview with a hunter. The dental fricative in Old English was represented by ð (eth) or þ (thorn), but I have transcribed these as *th*. Try reading the passage aloud. You need to give the vowel letters their IPA values.

Teacher: *Ne canst thu huntian butan mid nettum?*
Not canst thou hunt apart-from with nets?

Hunter: *Yea, butan nettum huntian ic mæg.*
Yea, apart-from nets I can [lit. may]

Teacher: *Hu?*
How?

Hunter:	*Mid swift hundum ic bepœce wildeor.*
	With fast dogs I catch wild beasts.
Teacher:	*Hwilce wildeor swithost gefehst thu?*
	Which wild beasts mostly catch thou?
Hunter:	*Ic gefo heortas, and baras, and ran and rœgan, and hwilon haran.*
	I catch harts and bears and reindeer and roe, and sometimes hares.
Teacher:	*Wœre thu todœg on huntothe?*
	Were you today in hunting?
Hunter:	*Ic nœs [=ne wœs], fortham sunnandœg is, ac gystrandœg ic wœs on huntunge.*
	I was not, because it is Sunday, but yesterday I was in hunting.

If you were transported back in time and set down in Winchester, you would not be able to understand much at first, partly because of the pronunciation, but after a day or so you would be able to understand quite a deal, and you would be able to say a few things, though in a kind of ungrammatical form of Old English, for it would take you more than a few days to master the various inflections such as the infinitive illustrated here in *huntian* and the dative case in *hundum.* You would probably think of *hund* as meaning 'hound', but it refers to dogs in general, and *wil(d)-deor* looks like 'wild deer', but *deor* in Old English could refer to any animal.

The English language was brought to Britain in the fourth and fifth centuries by the Angles and Saxons who settled themselves there forcibly and in great numbers, overrunning the Celtic inhabitants, who remained as dominant only in Wales and Cornwall. The Angles and Saxons came from an area around southern Denmark and northern Germany, so it is not surprising to find that English is related to German and Danish, as well as Dutch, Swedish, Norwegian, and Icelandic. These languages are known collectively as the Germanic languages, and scholars are able to show that they share a **genetic** relationship; in fact, they can reconstruct the proto-language from which these languages sprang, a language that they call Proto-Germanic. We have no direct evidence for this language, which must have been spoken by the Germanic people before they split up, probably about 2500 years ago. The evidence for genetic relationship can be found in numerous cognate words, inflections, and derivational affixes. **Cognate** forms are forms that can be traced back to a common root. Examples are shown in Table 12.1.

Now, just as it is obvious that the Germanic languages are genetically related, it is equally obvious that Portuguese, Spanish, French, Italian, and Romanian are related. They are called the Romance languages. They are descendants of Latin, a language for which we have written records, albeit mostly formal material that does not reflect the spoken language from which

Table 12.1. Some Germanic cognates

English	Swedish	Danish	Dutch	German
to find	*finna*	*finde*	*vinden*	*finden*
to fall	*falla*	*falde*	*vallen*	*fallen*
fish	*fiska*	*fiske*	*visschen*	*fischen*
sing	*sjunga*	*synga*	*zingen*	*singen*
sang	*sjöng*	*sang*	*zong*	*sang*
sung	*sjungit*	*sunget*	*gezongen*	*gesungen*
to sit	*sitte*	*sidde*	*zitten*	*sitzen*
(length)-wise	*-vis*	*-vis*	*-wijze*	*-weise*
(friend)-ship	*-skap*	*-skab*	*-schap*	*-schaft*

Table 12.2. Latin roots and Romance reflexes

English	Late Latin	Portuguese	Spanish	French	Italian
horse	*caballo*	*cavalo*	*caballo*	*cheval*	*cavallo*
to do	*facere*	*fazer*	*hacer*	*faire*	*fare*
smoke	*fumo*	*fumo*	*humo*	*fumée*	*fumo*
they were having	*habebant*	*haviam*	*habían*	*ils avaient*	*avevano*
we sing	*cantamus*	*cantamos*	*cantamos*	*chantons*	*cantiamo*

these languages have derived. Table 12.2 illustrates some Latin vocabulary and verb inflection and the reflexes of those forms in four Romance languages.

If we now compare Latin and proto-Germanic, we find they are related. This is illustrated in Table 12.3, but I will let English stand for proto-Germanic for the purposes of illustration. This cognateness of the Latin and English forms is not immediately obvious until one notices there are regular correspondences. In English the initial voiceless stops [p], [t], and [k] became fricatives: [p] became [f], [t] became [θ], and [k] became [h]. This is part of a wider sound shift known as Grimm's Law, which affected proto-Germanic and is reflected in all the Germanic languages. 'Law' in this context just means regular correspondence, and 'Grimm' is Jacob Grimm, the elder of the brothers Grimm, known throughout Europe for the 'Fairy Tales' they collected. Instead of Latin other languages could have been used in the

Table 12.3. English–Latin cognates

Latin	English	Latin	English	Latin	English
pater	*father*	*ten-uis*	*thin*	*corn-u*	*horn*
pisc-is	*fish*	*tre-s*	*three*	*cord-is*	*heart*
ped-is	*foot*	*tu*	*thou*	*cent-um*	*hund-red*

comparison such as Greek, Persian (Farsi), or Sanskrit, the language of the Hindu scriptures, the language ancestral to Hindi and a number of other languages of the Subcontinent. The Greek for 'father', for instance, is *paté:r* and the Sanskrit *pitár*. Most of the languages of Europe plus a number of languages found further east are related. They belong to the **Indo-European** language family, the name reflecting the fact that the languages of the family are found in Europe and what was India in the days of the British Empire (now India, Pakistan, and Bangladesh).

The correspondences illustrated in Table 12.3 not only provide evidence for the relatedness of Latin and English, they illustrate an important feature of sound change, namely that viewed over a long period of time, it is regular. The distribution can be stated in phonological terms; we do not normally have to specify particular words, though there is in fact an irregularity in the word *thou* since the initial consonant is voiced [ð] whereas the regular sound is voiceless [θ]. However, this falls under another generalization, namely that initial [θ] became [ð] in function words in English.

A simplified tree-diagram showing branches of the Indo-European family is presented in Figure 12.1.

A number of other languages of the world can be shown to be genetically related as members of a language family. Examples include the following:

- The Uralic language family is found in north-eastern Europe extending across northern Russia into north-western Siberia. The Finno-Ugric branch of this family includes Finnish, Estonian, and Hungarian.
- The Afroasiatic family contains a number of branches, the best known of which is Semitic, which contains Akkadian (which was spoken in Meso-potamia from the third to the first millennium BC), Aramaic and the closely related Hebrew (which has been brought back to life as the language of Israel), and Arabic, which, as the language of Islam, has spread over northern Africa and the Middle East.
- The Turkic family includes one well-known language, namely Turkish. It is sometimes linked with the Mongolic and Tungusic languages to the east in an Altaic family, but it is more likely that resemblances between these languages are the result of diffusion (see p. 227).
- There are three language families in the Caucasus, which are sometimes lumped together because of typological similarities. The best-known lan-guage of the Caucasus is Georgian, spoken in Georgia, at the eastern end of the Black Sea.
- The Dravidian family is spoken in southern India and Sri Lanka and includes Telegu, Kannada, Malayalam, and Tamil.
- Austroasiatic comprises two branches, the Munda languages of north-east India, which includes Santali, and the more scattered Mon-Khmer branch,

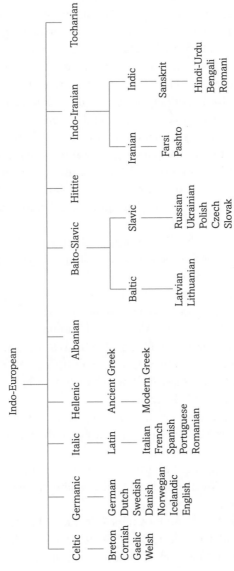

Figure 12.1 Indo-European language family.

which includes Mon in southeastern Myanmar (Burma), Khmer (or Cambodian), the official language of Cambodia, and Vietnamese.

- The Sino-Tibetan family includes the various forms of Chinese (sometimes referred to as the Sinitic languages) plus Tibetan and Burmese.
- The Tai languages are found in Laos, Thailand, Burma, Vietnam, and southern China and include two national languages, Lao and Thai.
- The Austronesian family is noted for its size (about 1,000 languages) and its vast spread. It extends from Madagascar in the west (where Malagasy is spoken) to Easter Island in the east. It includes the native languages of Taiwan in the north and Maori, the native language of New Zealand in the south. Other Austronesian languages include Indonesian-Malay, Tagalog (Philippines), Fijian, Samoan, Tahitian, and Tongan.
- The Niger-Congo family of southern Africa has about 1,000 members including the Bantu group of languages. Swahili, which is a lingua franca in east Africa, is the best known. (A lingua franca is a language that serves as means of communication between speakers of different languages.)
- The languages of the Nilo-Saharan family are found mainly in north-eastern and north-central Africa.
- The Eskimo-Aleut family has two primary branches. The Aleut branch is spoken in the Aleutian Islands and the Eskimo languages are found in Siberia, Alaska, Canada, and Greenland.
- In North America there are a number of well-established language families including the Algonquian languages found in the eastern part of North America and westwards into Alberta and Montana, the Caddoan and Siouan families of the Great Plains of mid-western US, the Iroquoian language family of south-eastern Canada and the eastern US, the Muskogean family of the south-eastern US which includes Choctaw (Mississippi) and Creek (Alabama and Georgia).
- The Na-Dene language family of Alaska and western Canada includes the large Athapaskan branch, which has an enclave in the south-west of the US, which includes Navajo (Navaho).
- The Uto-Aztecan language family is found mainly in the south-west of the United States and Mexico and it includes Nahuatl, the language of the Aztec civilization.
- Language families of Central America include the Mayan languages, spoken in south-eastern Mexico and Guatemala, and the Chibchan languages, which cover an area extending from Nicaragua to Ecuador.
- In South America the most widely spoken native language is Quechua. It is spoken in Peru, Ecuador, and Bolivia, extending north into Colombia and extending south into northern Chile and north-western Argentina. It shares similarities with Aymará and the two are sometimes grouped in an Andean family.

Recognized families include the large, widespread Arawak family, ranging from Honduras in Central America to Brazil in South America, and formerly to Paraguay and Argentina; the large Carib language family found in and to the north of Brazil; the Panoan family of Peru and neighbouring parts of Bolivia and Brazil; and the Tupian family located in Brazil. The Tupí-Guaraní sub-group is also found in Brazil, but various members of the sub-group are found in Bolivia, Paraguay, and Argentina. Guaraní is an official language of Paraguay along with Spanish.

In some instances there are resemblances between languages or language families that are insufficient for linguists to be able to determine whether they are genetically related. Typically such languages or families are in contact, and one cannot determine whether the resemblances are due to genetic inheritance or extensive borrowing (see p. 227 below). The languages of the Australian mainland provide an example. They look as if they are related, but there is insufficient evidence to demonstrate this. Sometimes these larger groupings are called stocks or phyla. An extreme example is the 750 or so languages of the island of New Guinea and surrounding islands that are not Austronesian. These are collectively known as 'Papuan', though some genetic families can be found within this grouping.

Many languages are isolates, that is, they have no known genetic relatives. Examples include Japanese, Korean, and Basque.

Sound change

As noted above, the sounds of a language can change over time. The most common types of change are those that are reductive, that involve a kind of erosion, a wearing away of the difference between morphemes. One such change is **assimilation**, whereby a sound becomes like a neighbouring sound, and the other is the **loss** of a sound. However, as we shall see, reductive changes do not account for the whole picture. Languages obviously do not head *en masse* towards baby talk.

Assimilation is particularly common in nasal-stop sequences. Consider the following Latin words and the forms of these words that English has borrowed:

in = 'not'		*in* = 'in'	
imperfectus	imperfect	*impingere*	impinge
imbecillitas	imbecility	*imbibere*	imbibe
intactus	intact	*intolerabilis*	intolerable
indecorus	indecorous	*inducere*	induce
inconsideratus	inconsiderate	*incursio*	incursion
inglorius	inglorious	*ingressus*	ingress

In the first group there is a prefix *in* meaning 'not'. In the second group the first morpheme is *in* meaning 'in', which occurs as a free form and is cognate with English *in*. Where the alveolar nasal /n/ was followed by a labial /p/ or /b/ it became labial /m/. Where it was followed by a velar stop /k/ or /g/ (letter *c* represents /k/), it presumably became [ŋ] as it has in English, but this does not show up in the spelling.

Another type of assimilation that is common is for a velar stop to become palatal before a high, front vowel. Latin *circa* [kirka] 'around' survives in Italian as [tʃirka], and English *chin* derives from a Germanic *kinn*. In any language the tongue will always anticipate the tongue position of the front vowel in making a velar stop, but sometimes this assimilation goes further.

English has numerous silent letters, and most of these represent the **loss** of a phoneme. Examples include *knee*, *knave*, and *wring*. In the word *knight* two consonants have been lost. The digraph *gh* represented a palatal fricative, which can still be heard in Scottish English, and which is found in the cognate word in German, namely *Knecht*. The German word *Knecht* means 'farm labourer' and Old English *cniht* meant 'boy' or 'servant', but the word later became a title of prestige through being used for the 'king's knights'.

Closely related to loss is vowel reduction in unstressed syllables. This is particularly common in English where various vowels are reduced to schwa [ə] in unstressed positions. Compare *telegraph* /tɛləgræf/ and *telegraphy* /təlɛgrəfiː/. Unstressed vowels are frequently lost as in *choc(o)late*, *p(o)lice* and *We(d)n(e)sday*, and, as was pointed out on page 156, the unstressed vowel was lost in Middle English plurals except where it would have produced an unpronounceable cluster.

Among the less common sound changes is **fusion**, where two adjacent sounds become one. This happens in English with words like *issue* and *tissue* where the sequence /sj/ often becomes /ʃ/, and in words like *division* where the sequence /zj/ has become /ʒ/.

Sometimes words are augmented by the **addition** of a consonant, a vowel, or even a syllable. Where a consonant is added, it is usually homorganic as in *varmint*, a dialect form of *vermin*, or in *thunder*, which has acquired an extra /d/. It was *thunor* in Old English (compare German *Donner*). Speakers sometimes insert a vowel to break up a consonant cluster. From some speakers you hear *elm* pronounced as *elum*, *athlete* as *athalete*, and *film* as *filum*.

Occasionally sounds change because the same sound occurs in a neighbouring syllable. This is **dissimilation**. In Latin there was an adjective-forming suffix *-alis* as in *gener-alis* 'generic, general', *capit-alis* 'of the head, capital (of crime)', *reg-alis* 'of a king, royal', and *ven-alis* 'venal'. It dissimilated to *-aris* if an /l/ occurred in the stem: *milit-aris* 'military', *circul-aris* 'circular', and *regul-aris* 'regular', but not if the /l/ was in the onset of the first syllable of the stem, hence *leg-alis* 'legal', *let-alis* 'lethal', and *flore-alis* 'floral'. A similar dissimilation results in the loss of a second /r/ in some English pronunciations of *secretary* and *February.*

Metathesis is a fancy name for what might more reasonably be called 'transposition'. Ever since the Old English period there has been alternation in the order of *s* and *k* in the verb *to ask*. The form *ask* is standard, but *ax* exists in a number of dialects. In Old English the word for 'three' was *thrie* and 'third' was *thridda,* but the *r* and the high vowel have changed places in *third* (for those who still retain the *r*).

Sometimes the pronunciation of a phoneme will change without altering the overall system of contrasts, but in other cases one phoneme merges with another. In Old English there was a rounded high front vowel. It was represented in the spelling by *y* and this is the letter used in IPA. It occurred in words like *cynn* /kyn/ 'kin' and *cyssan* /kysan/ 'to kiss', but this merged with the unrounded high front vowel in Middle English, so we now say *kiss* with unrounded lips (though we may round them in actual osculation!). The same unrounding happened with the long rounded high front vowel. Old English /dryːgan/ 'to dry' became Middle English /driːgan/. A more recent example of merging can be found among many speakers of General American where the vowels of pairs like *pin* and *pen* have merged.

In Early Modern English a major change took place in the pronunciation of the long vowels in English. This is known as the **Great English Vowel Shift** (**GEVS**; see Table 12.4). It was so named by a famous Danish linguist Otto Jespersen (1860–1943), who is sometimes called the 'Great Dane'. The long vowels were raised and those that were already high became diphthongs.

By and large the GEVS did not affect the overall vowel system. With the back vowels each one just moved up one step, as it were. With the front vowels there was some variation between speakers. In Early Modern English it was common for 'ea' words like *dream* and *meat* to rhyme with words like *name* and *mate,* both having the vowel [eː], but by the seventeenth century the [iː] pronunciation of the 'ea' words that we are familiar with became mainstream usage so the 'ea' words like *meat* and *beat* came to rhyme with 'ee' words like *meet* and *beet.* A few words retained the [eː] (or [eɪ]) pronunciation including *great,*

Table 12.4. The Great English Vowel Shift

Late Middle English	Modern English	Modern Spelling
/liːf/	/laɪf/	life
/seːd/	/siːd/	seed
/drɛːm/	/driːm/	dream
/naːm/	/neɪm/	name
/gɔːt/	/goʊt/	goat
/roːt/	/ruːt/	root
/duːn/	/daʊn/	down

steak, and *break*, plus some pronunciations of the surname *Mclean*. Vowels are relatively unstable compared to consonants. Changes in the pronunciation of vowels are ongoing, and most of the differences of accent between different regional varieties of modern English are to be found in the pronunciation of the vowels, especially the long vowels and diphthongs.

Since a high proportion of changes consist of assimilation and loss, it might be thought that over time languages would finish up with all clusters of consonants matching in place and manner of articulation and words becoming shorter. However, new combinations of morphemes arise from time to time that yield longer words with clusters of consonants that are unassimilated. This happens with *inpatient* (as opposed to *outpatient*), and *input* (as opposed to *output*), though it must be said that some speakers pronounce *input* as *imput*. Sometimes loss of a vowel gives rise to new clusters as with the loss of the unstressed vowel in the *-ed* past tense in Late Middle English, which produced clusters like [bd] in *ebbed* (OE *ebbode*) and [vd] in *loved* (OE *lufode*).

Morphological change

If we use the term 'morphology' to cover all derivational processes and all inflection, then we can say that the principal features of morphological change are the loss of morphology and the acquiring of new morphology. In Indo-European languages there has been a good deal of loss of morphology over the centuries, particularly in English and the Romance languages. This can be seen with case inflection, where the nominative/accusative distinction has been lost from nouns and the distinction between subject and object made by word order, and where other cases have been replaced by prepositions. In the following line from the story of the Prodigal Son the Latin version marks the complement of *adhaesit* 'he adhered', namely *uni* 'one' by the dative case. The word *civium* 'citizens' is dependent on *uni* 'one' and is in the genitive case and *regionis illius* 'that region' is dependent on *civium* so it is also in the genitive case.

Latin	Adhaesit	uni	civium	regionis	illius
	adhere.PERF.3SG	one.DAT	citizen.PL.GEN	region.GEN	that.GEN
OE	He...	folgode	anum	burgsittendum	men	thæs
	he	followed	one-DAT	citizen-DAT	man.DAT	that.GEN
	ric-es.					
	kingdom.GEN					
Italian	Si mise a servizio di uno degli [di + gli] abitanti di quella regione				
English	'He attached [himself] to one of the citizens of that region.'				

Now most of this holds true for the Old English translation. The complement of *folgode* 'followed' is the phrase *anum burgsittendum men*, literally 'a burg-sitting man', and it is in the dative, and *thæs rices* is a dependent genitive. Note in passing that *men* is the dative singular of *man*, and happens to be the same as the plural *men*. If we look at the modern versions we see that English uses the prepositions *to* and *of* in place of the dative and genitive, while Italian uses *a* and *di* in place of the dative and genitive (though it uses a different phrasing 'He put himself to the service of one of the inhabitants of that region').

English has also lost a lot of verbal inflection for person and number. In Old English there were separate inflections for first, second, and third person singular plus a form for the plural, as well as distinctions between present and past and indicative and subjunctive. Table 12.5 shows the present and past inflection of *timbran* 'to build'.

Table 12.5. Old English present and past verb inflection of *timbran 'to build'*

	present	past
I	timbre	timbrede
you (thou)	timbrest	timbredest
he, she, it	timbreth	timbrede
we, you, they	timbrath	timbredon

Early Modern English in south-eastern England retained the second person singular forms and alternative forms for third person singular present tense, namely the *-(e)th* shown in Table 12.5 and *-(e)s*, a northern form that had found its way south. Modern mainstream English retains only this sibilant ending as in *cleans, washes*, etc.

There is a tendency for irregular morphology to be lost. English has acquired an irregular plural from Greek with *phenomenon/phenomena* and *criterion/criteria*, but at present there is a tendency to eliminate these in favour of the regular sibilant plural, interestingly by taking the plural forms *phenomena* and *criteria* as the singular. This kind of regularization can take place on a large scale. In Old English there were numerous 'strong' verbs, that is, verbs that showed vowel alternation in the past tense and past participle. There were in fact several classes of strong verb. Some alternated like *drive, drove, driven* and others like *sing, sang, sung*, and so on. There were also 'weak' verbs, that is, ones that formed their past tense with the form we write as *-ed* (see *timbran* in Table 12.5). The weak verbs have been the majority throughout the history of English and over time strong verbs have lost their vowel alternation and acquired the *-ed* ending. For instance, in Old English *help* was a strong verb *helpan* with a past *healp* (later *holp*) and a past participle *holpen*. The alternation in this word survived in mainstream English until the seventeenth century, but then gave way to *helped* as the past tense and past participle. The older past participle *holpen* may be known to some readers through its occurrence in the Magnificat in the Evening Prayer Service in the Book of Common Prayer of 1662 (*He remembering his mercy hath holpen his servant Israel*) or in the Authorized Version of the same verse: *He hath holpen his servant Israel, in remembrance of his mercy* (Luke 1:54).

These major shifts in morphological marking towards the dominant pattern are often described as levelling analogy. **Analogy** often plays a part in morphological change, and speakers often see analogies even between small sets of words. Against the trend of verbs moving from the strong to the weak type we find the verb *dive* has acquired an alternative irregular past tense *dove* in American English by analogy with *ride/rode, drive/drove, write/wrote,* and *stride/strode*.

If the only direction of morphological change was loss, then we would have a unidirectional change in human language towards the analytic type represented by languages like Chinese where there is little morphology other than compounding, but in fact new morphology can be created. As an example of the origin of a derivational suffix, consider -*dom* as in *kingdom*. The word *kingdom* can be found in Old English, but at that time it was a compound of *cyning* and *dōm*, where *dōm* was a word meaning 'judgement' related to the verb *dēman* (modern *deem*). *Dom*, under the spelling *doom*, is still in the language, but there is no clear connection between *doom* and the -*dom* of *kingdom, serfdom*, and the like, so -*dom* assumes the status of a suffix, a form which cannot stand on its own, but which can be added at the end of a stem to form a new word. The suffix -*dom* is still productive and appears in modern formations such as *officialdom, stardom*, and *gangsterdom*.

As an example of the origin of number inflection, consider the following example from an Australian language Pitta-Pitta. Plural is represented by *parri* or *pitjiri*, which can be free forms or they can be placed between the root and the case inflection as in *walka-pitjiri-nha*.

Nga-thu	walka-pitjiri-nha	thuka-yangu.
I-ERG	child-PLUR-ACC	take-PRES.hither
'I am bringing the children.'		

In the closely related neighbouring language Lhanima, *pitjiri* has been reduced to -*tji*, which alert readers might recall from question eight at the end of chapter five.

Nga-thu	walka-tji-nha	thuka-yangu.
I-ERG	child-PLUR-ACC	take-PRES.hither
'I am bringing the children.'		

We can be fairly certain that -*tji* is a reduction of *pitjiri* since the word *parrkula* 'two' can be used as a suffix like *pitjiri*, and it too appears in Lhanima in reduced form. With a comparison of these languages we can see three stages: free form, form used as a suffix, reduced form used as a suffix.

In general a function form receives less stress than a lexical form. Free function forms tend to be pronounced as if they were unstressed syllables of neighbouring lexical words, and can become part of such words (though that is not what happened in Pitta-Pitta). Where function forms become part of lexical words, they are likely to become further reduced (as did happen in Lhanima). Consider the following example. Nowadays it is common for couples to live together without being married, people have 'partners' instead of husbands or wives. Now if you have a partner, how do you refer to those who would be the in-laws if you were married? One of my colleagues says these are the 'outlaws'. Very funny, but try saying *mother-out-law* or *brother-out-law*, and you will soon see what I mean by function forms within words being subject to reduction. If these formations were to come into use, the form *out* with its diphthong would inevitably be reduced to [ət] or perhaps just [ə].

There are numerous examples of free forms becoming bound forms, and we can safely extrapolate and say that almost all bound forms came from free forms. The only other possibility is for part of a word to be re-analysed as an affix. Humans do not dream up new affixes.

Phonetic reduction plays a big part in language change. Not only does it mean that unstressed function words get attached to neighbouring lexical words, but it also results in many of those irregularities that are so annoying to second-language learners. Consider the way we form yes-no questions in English with *do/does* preceding the subject. The following list shows *do/does* with each of the singular pronouns and indicates how the combination of verb and pronoun is pronounced in rapid speech.

Do I want to go?	[daɪwɒnəgoʊ]
Do you want to go?	[dʒuːwɒnəgoʊ]
Does he want to go?	[dziːwɒnəgoʊ], [ziːwɒnəgoʊ]
Does she want to go?	[tʃiːwɒnəgoʊ]

Of course we can speak slowly and retain a more analytic arrangement where *do/does* and the pronouns are distinct, and we have the more analytic forms represented in writing. But this kind of phonetic reduction is common in languages and can become fossilized and lead to an irregular set of forms, in this instance it would lead to a set of interrogative pronouns /daɪ, dʒuː, ziː, tʃiː/.

Syntactic change

Syntactic constructions can change. Word order provides examples. In Old English word order was fairly flexible, but in a main clause the verb was usually the second constituent, while in subordinate clauses the verb was normally clause-final. This is still the situation in German.

In (a) below, the subject is the first word and the verb follows in second position. In (b) the adverb *tha* 'then' occurs. It occupies first position, as it usually does; the verb comes second, and the subject is relegated to third. In (c) the object noun phrase has been placed first, so again the verb follows and is in turn followed by the subject. There is also a subordinate clause with the order subject–object–verb (SOV).

(a) *Eadric seah thæt scip.*
     'Edric saw that/the ship.'

(b) *Tha seah Eadric thæt scip.*
     'Then saw Edric that/the ship.'

(c) *Thæt scip seah Eadric, ær he thone cyning sohte.*
     'That ship saw Edric, before he the king visited.'

In Modern English the regular order is SVO, so obviously there has been a change, and we can trace this change in Middle English. In most instances the subject was the first constituent in main clauses, so there would have been numerous SVO sentences. This tendency seems to have become a rule, and SVO order was later extended to subordinate clauses. The old verb-second principle lives on in expressions such as *There goes the neighbourhood* and we still put an auxiliary in second position after certain adverbs.

Scarcely had she closed the boot (trunk) than she realized she had left the keys inside.
No sooner had Wilma found her glasses than she lost them again.

One common type of syntactic change is the reinterpretation of one part-of-speech as another. In English prepositions such as *concerning* and *regarding* are derived from the present participle of verbs. Verbs are a common source of prepositions and postpositions. This can be seen most easily in languages that have **serial verb** constructions in which more than one verb is used in a clause for a single predication. Only the first verb can host marking for tense, aspect, negation, etc. so the second verb is preposition-like or postposition-like. Here is an example from Ewe, a language of the Kwa branch of the Niger-Congo family. The form *ná* is a verb. In (a) it is the sole verb and it bears person/number marking for the subject. In (b) we have a serial verb construction where there are two verbs. The first verb bears person/number marking for the subject, but the second cannot. It is functionally equivalent to a preposition and it corresponds to English 'for' in meaning.

a. *Me-ná   ga   kofí*
    1-give   money   Kofi
    'I gave Kofi money.'

b. *Me-wɔ   dɔ́   vévíé   ná   dodókpɔ́   lá*
   1-do   work   hard   give   exam   the
   'I worked hard for the exam.'

A source for local prepositions, postpositions, and affixes is provided by concrete nouns, especially body parts. In English we can say *on the face of*, *at the bottom of*, and *at the back of*, which can be considered compound prepositions. In Jacaltec, a Mayan language of Central America, *sat* 'in front of' derives from *sat* 'face', and *wi* 'on top of' derives from *wi'e* 'head'.

Markers of tense and aspect, whether free forms or bound, derive from a number of sources. In English the auxiliary verb *will* that indicates future time derives from the lexical verb *will* as in *She willed it to happen*. In Thai the lexical verb *dài* 'get, obtain' is the source of the past tense marker. In Tok Pisin, a creole language of New Guinea, the future marker derives from the English adverb *bye-and-bye*. It was adopted as an adverb *baimbai*, then shortened to *bai*:

Bai mi rait.   'I'll write.'

It then took its place among other preverbal 'auxiliaries' indicating modality:

Ben bai i wok tumora.   'Ben will work tomorrow.'

Semantic change

The meaning of words changes from time to time. Types of change can be classified under various headings such as widening or narrowing.

Widening

It is common for the meaning of a word to widen. **Widening** of meaning can happen in fairly trivial ways. A word like *pen* comes to cover various new types of pen over a period of time (fountain pen, ball-point pen, light pen). *Coach* and *carriage* have been extended from horse-drawn vehicles to motorized vehicles and rail cars.

Sometimes the meaning of a word is extended by misunderstanding. The word *transpire*, which literally means 'breathe through' and is applied to the breathing of plants, used to mean 'to leak out of information'. One encountered sentences such as *What had transpired during his absence, he didn't know.* Anyone unfamiliar with this learned word could take it to mean 'happen' and this is the sense in which most people use it today.

Alibi provides another example. It is a Latin word meaning 'elsewhere' and in law it refers to evidence that someone was elsewhere from the scene of a crime. A person can say *I cannot be guilty, because I have an alibi (I was elsewhere)*. This word then gets used for cases where someone is offering some other type of evidence of innocence or just some mitigating factor, some excuse. People now say things like *I got caught on the train without a ticket and I didn't have an alibi (excuse)*.

Perhaps the most common way words acquire new senses is through metaphorical extension. This is a way a language effectively acquires new words. Think of metaphorical extensions of terms to do with electricity such as *to turn somebody on* or *to be switched on*. A person of dual sexual orientation is *AC/DC*. Computer terminology is full of examples where old words have acquired new senses. *Spam*, for instance, formerly referred to canned meat (It is a blend of spice and ham, literally!), but now applies to computer-multiplied junk e-mail. The word *hit* can be used to mean visits to a web site as in *My website receives very few 'hits.'*

Narrowing

On the other hand the meaning of a word can be narrowed. An example of **narrowing** can be found in *meat,* which used to mean 'food', but since the fifteenth century it has become specialized in the sense of 'flesh food'. Old words and old meanings often survive in compounds and fixed expressions. The old sense of *meat* lives on in *sweetmeats* (which are not flesh) and in the expression *One man's meat is another man's poison,* a saying that extends beyond food.

Reinterpretation

In some instances the meaning of a word is reinterpreted drastically. The word *want* used to mean 'lack'. When Browning writes *I want the heart to scold,* he means he lacks the heart to scold. The verb *want* must have occurred frequently in sentences such as *I want a drink.* But if you say you lack a drink, you surely desire a drink, and so the word was reinterpreted as meaning 'to desire'. The old sense lives on in something like *My car wants a wash.*

A famous case of reinterpretation involves *bead.* It is related to the Old English verb *biddan* 'to ask, to bid, to pray' and once meant 'prayer'. From the practice of counting prayers on little balls on a string (a rosary), the word came to refer to the little threaded balls. So a sentence such as *She's telling her beads* meaning 'She's counting her prayers', came to mean 'She's counting her little threaded balls.'

A modern example that seems startling to some, particularly in light of what we said about homophony, involves words like *bad* and *wicked* acquiring the opposite sense of 'very good'. When Venus Williams won Wimbledon in 2001, she complimented her younger opponent, Justine Henin-Hardenne, by saying that with more experience she would be really 'wicked'. This antonymic change is mediated by contexts where to be wicked is considered in a favourable or at least neutral light as in 'wicked sense of humour'. *Bad* has made a similar antonymic switch in some quarters while retaining its basic meaning for all speakers. I recall hearing a character in some forgettable TV programme say, 'Do you mean bad bad, or just bad?'

At the present time a number of people in the media say or write things like *The spectators were literally glued to their seats.* Now if the spectators were literally glued to their seats, they would have difficulty leaving except by easing themselves out of their trousers or skirts. The word *literally* is being used just for emphasis. For the time being we can say that this rates as misusage, but who can tell about the future? One day it may become majority usage and English will have to find a new word for the present meaning of *literally.*

Pejoration and amelioration

Words sometimes take on a worse sense. This usually reflects an unfavourable view of the referent. A number of words for the common people have undergone pejoration. *Lewd* originally referred to lay (non-clerical) people and *vulgar* meant 'ordinary' or 'common'. 'Common' itself has 'gone down-hill' as in *They're quite common.*

Colloquial words for women seem to suffer from a certain pejoration, words like *chick, bird,* and *dame.* They acquire negative connotation from the off-hand way they are used. Some words for women come to imply promiscuity, words like *moll/mole* and *tart.* The word *bimbo* is interesting in this regard. Originally a word for 'baby' in Italian, it came into English for an effeminate male, and then came to be used for a female more notable for her pretensions to glamour than her mental capacities, but already you find people querying whether it refers to a promiscuous woman. In French the word *fille* 'girl' has acquired the 'tart' sense, and has been replaced by *jeune fille,* literally 'young girl'.

Words for country people often 'go downhill'. *Boor* has gone from 'peasant' to 'uncouth person', while *peasant* has gone from 'small farmer' to 'unsophis-ticated person'. In the Middle Ages a *villain (villein)* was a low ranking person in the feudal system. Now it refers to a criminal.

Some words for city people on the other hand have undergone **amelior-ation**. This means they have taken on a better sense. *Urbane* once meant 'relating to the city' as *urban* still does, but it came to mean 'sophisticated'. *Civil* meant 'related to the community or state' as it still does in *civil duties,* but it has an added sense of 'polite' or 'courteous'. *Politic* comes ultimately from the Greek *polis* 'a city', but its meaning ranges from positive senses such as 'wise' or 'astute' to the more negative 'expedient'.

Weakening

Words frequently lose their strong sense through familiarity or overuse. It is not hard to see that *awful* once meant 'full of awe' and *dreadful* meant 'full of dread'. Today they simply mean 'very bad'. A similar change has taken place with *terrible, horrible,* and *shocking. Awesome* has been revived among the young as a term for enthusiastic appreciation: *That's awesome. That's great.*

Phrase abbreviation

Another way a word can acquire a new meaning is through the abbreviation of a phrase or clause. Consider the word *engaged.* We can say 'the line is engaged', 'I was engaged to carry out a survey', or we can say 'I am engaged'. In the last instance this is understood to mean 'I am engaged to be married' without any need for the specification 'to be married'.

The word *wife* used to mean 'woman', but it frequently occurred in phrases such as 'John's wife' or 'Henry's wife'. In this context it means 'married woman' and so the word *wife* on its own took on the sense of 'married woman'. This shift led to a new word for 'mature female human' and it was created by combining *wif* (the older form of wife) with *man* to produce *wifman,* which later reduced to *woman.*

RETRONYMS

One stimulus for lexical change is a new invention. It involves finding a new label, not just for the new invention, but also for what the new invention supersedes. For instance, when e-mail was invented, a new name had to be found for ordinary mail, and the smart label *snail mail* came into use. These new labels are called **retronyms**. Here are some other examples:

original	new invention	retronym
movie/film	talkie	silent movie/film
aircraft/aeroplane	helicopter	fixed-wing aircraft/aeroplane
record	cd	vinyl record
television	colour television	black and white television
razor	safety razor	cut-throat razor

Loan words

At a number of points in the text I have written about loan words, words 'borrowed' into English. I have not explained the term since I feel its meaning is obvious. If I say a word such as *foyer* is **borrowed** into English from French, then I mean it is a French word that English speakers have adopted for use in English. It is the norm to talk of languages 'borrowing words' and of 'borrowed words', but this is an odd usage of 'borrow' when one considers there is never any question of the words being given back.

Languages frequently borrow words from other languages, particularly words for new artefacts and ideas. Borrowing can occur on a large scale.

When the Romans expanded and conquered what was to become the Roman Empire, they took over Greece and Greek-speaking areas in southern Italy and in an area that runs from Turkey around the eastern end of the Mediterranean to Egypt. They embraced Greek culture, and young upper-class Romans were taught Greek. Over time Latin acquired numerous Greek words such as *philosophia*, *theatrum*, and *thesaurus*, and, with the advent of Christianity, words such as *anathema*, *angelus*, and *charisma*. This is a good example of a phenomenon that recurs where languages come into contact with a new culture, though the common situation is for the conquered to learn from the conqueror, not, as with the Greeks and Romans, for the conqueror to learn from the conquered.

By the time of the Norman Conquest (1066) English had acquired a number of Latin words (including some that were originally Greek), mostly words to do with Christianity such as *apostle*, *disciple*, and *epistle*. English also borrowed words from the Vikings who invaded and settled, mainly north of a line running from London in the southeast to Chester further north in the west. The Vikings came from Norway and Denmark and spoke Old Norse, a Germanic language closely related to Old English, and the ancestor of Swedish, Danish, Norwegian, and Icelandic. Borrowings include everyday words such as *skirt*, *sky*, *kick*, *get*, *give*, and *egg*. Old English naturally had its own words for the referents of these words, but given the dominance of Viking settlers in the north of Britain, it is not surprising that some of their words found their way into English.

After the success of William the Conqueror at the Battle of Hastings (1066) England came to be ruled by French-speaking Normans. This is the Robin Hood period of British history, but what the numerous movies of good King Richard and bad King John don't reveal is that these kings and their court and nobles spoke French. During this period English acquired some thousands of words from French. The borrowed words were mainly to do with administration (*government*, *parlement* (later *parliament*), *chancellor*, *minister*), the church (*cardinal*, *sanctuary*, *salvation*), the law (*arraign*, *indictment*), the military (*battle*, *lieutenant*), learning (*geometry*, *grammar*), and the good life (*dinner*, *confection*, *chandelier*, *tournament*).

With these borrowings, many of them learned and long, the character of the language began to change. The division between basic Old English (or Anglo-Saxon) words and learned words borrowed from Greek and Latin, either directly or from French, became even more marked during the Renaissance, in particular during the sixteenth century. The word *Renaissance* means rebirth, and the rebirth referred to is a rebirth of interest in the culture of Ancient Greece and Rome. The Latin language had been held in high regard throughout Europe for centuries and the vernaculars, that is, the local languages such as English and French, were held to be inferior and in need of improving, mainly through borrowing. In the second half of the sixteenth century and the first half of the seventeenth century English borrowed over 10,000 words from Latin, some directly, some from French, which also borrowed extensively from Latin during the same period (even though French is a descendant of Latin). The borrowings of this period include *compensate, emanation, emancipate, expectation, fictitious, malignant, peninsula, susceptible,* and *transient,* as well as others ultimately from Greek such as *democracy, encyclopaedia,* and *parenthesis.* Some words that were borrowed such as *exsiccate* (to dry) and *demit* (to send away) did not survive. There is a passage from Shakespeare's *Macbeth* that illustrates the contrast between the generally long borrowed words and the usually short native words. Compare *multitudinous* and *incarnadine* with *green* and *red.*

> Will all great Neptune's ocean wash this blood
> Clean from my hand? No, this my hand will rather
> The multitudinous seas incarnadine
> Making the green one red.

Adulation of Latin in England, though widespread, was not universal. One scholar, Cheke, made an effort to make up words from English roots rather than borrow from Latin. In translating the bible he used *hundreder* for 'centurion', *crossed* for 'crucified', and *gainraising* for 'resurrection'.

Large scale borrowing is not confined to English. Japanese, Korean, and Vietnamese have borrowed massively from Chinese. In all three languages more than half the lexicon comes from Chinese. Burmese, Cambodian, Thai, and Lao have borrowed numerous words, mostly forming a learned stratum, from Pali, the language of Buddhism. Thai and Lao are similar to English in having an everyday vocabulary of short words, either monosyllabic words or compounds of monosyllables, contrasting with long learned words such as (*prathaanaathíbɔdii* 'president of a country' and *rátchakaan* 'reign'. Languages spoken where Islam has been dominant have all borrowed heavily from Arabic. *Kitab* 'book', for instance, is found from Swahili in east Africa (as *kitabu*) to Indonesian in the Pacific.

English speakers have been in contact with speakers of numerous other languages since the early seventeenth century, and English has acquired words from more than fifty languages, a few thousand in total (in addition to the borrowings mentioned above). French has been the main source. Many of the French borrowings over the last two hundred or so years are often recognizable from accents in the written form. These include *cliché, passé, tête-à-tête,* and *vis-à-vis,* as well as others like *début,* that are sometimes written with an accent. The relationship between sound and spelling gives a clue to French origin in words such as *champagne* (*ch* for [ʃ]), *crochet* (last syllable rhymes with *pay*), and *ravine*, where the vowel letter *i* in combination with a silent *e* is read as [iː] not [aɪ] as in *mine*.

English has borrowed from Spanish mainly in America. Examples include words such as *canyon*, *lasso*, *rodeo*, *stampede*, and the verb *vamoose* from Spanish *vamos* 'let's go'. All of these will be familiar to most of the English-speaking world through American westerns. Recent borrowings from Spanish include *enchilada*, *macho*, *machismo*, *nada*, and *cojones* 'balls' in the literal and metaphorical sense.

Italian loanwords are mostly to do with music (*concerto*, *soprano*, *solo*, *sonata*), architecture and painting (*fresco*, *pergola*, *portico*), and food (*pasta*, *pizza*). Some recent borrowings are *paparazzo/paparazzi* and *graffito/graffiti*.

A few words have been borrowed from Dutch including some terms to do with seafaring such as *buoy*, *cruise*, *deck*, *keel*, *skipper*, and *yacht*. From German we have borrowed a range of words including a number of compounds such as *blitz(krieg)*, *delicatessen*, *festschrift*, *kindergarten*, *poltergeist*, *rucksack*, and *sauerkraut*.

From a large number of other languages English has borrowed a few words. As one would guess, *Bolshevik*, *czar/tsar* (ultimately from Latin *Caesar*), *kopeck*, *sputnik*, and *vodka* are from Russian; *goulash*, *hussar*, and *paprika* are Hungarian; *fez* and *kebab* are Turkish. There are some Arabic loans dating back to the Middle English and Early Modern period such as *alcohol*, *algebra*, *alkali*, *almanac*, all of which contain the Arabic definite article *al*. Biblical Hebrew is the source of *amen*, *cherub*, *rabbi*, *Sabbath*, and *shibboleth*, and Modern Hebrew is the source of *kibbutz*. Borrowings from Persian include *caravan*, *bazaar*, *mogul*, and *shah*. Sanskrit, the ancient language of India, is the source of *avatar*, *karma*, *mahatma*, and *yoga*, while its descendants such as Hindi/Urdu are the source of *bungalow*, *dinghy*, *jungle*, *pyjamas*, *pundit*, and *shampoo*. Tamil, a Dravidian language of southern India, has supplied *catamaran*, *curry*, *pariah*, and *mulligatawny* (pepper water).

There are a few borrowings from Chinese such as *ketchup*, *ginseng*, *kowtow*, and *tea*, while Japanese has supplied a few score of words including *bonsai*, *geisha*, *sake* (rice liquor), *soy(a)*, and *karaoke*.

A number of words have been borrowed from the native languages of the Americas. In North America these include *kayak* (Yupik in Alaska), *igloo* (Inuit in Canada), and *moccasin*, *(o)possum*, and *tomahawk* (the Algonquian languages of north-west US). Further south we find borrowings that have come into English via Spanish. These include *chilli*, *chocolate*, and *tomato* (all Nahuatl) and *potato* (Arawak). Of course we borrowed the referents, not just the words. And a good thing too!

Among other borrowings *rattan* is a Malay word, *tabu/taboo* and *tattoo* (ornamental marking on the skin, not the military *tattoo*, which is from Dutch) are Polynesian, and *kangaroo* is Guugu-Yimidhirr (northern Queensland).

Linguistic areas

While the borrowing of words is an easily recognizable phenomenon, there can also be borrowing of phonological, morphological, and syntactic patterns. This happens where languages are in contact, particularly where there is bilingualism or multilingualism. An interesting case of phonetic borrowing can be found in Western Europe. In the seventeenth century it became popular among the upper class French to pronounce /r/ not as an alveolar tap or trill but as a uvular trill [R] or fricative [χ]. The **uvula** is the appendage you can see hanging down from the back of the roof of your mouth. This pronunciation spread over the next three centuries to Germany, Switzerland, Luxembourg, Belgium, Holland, Denmark, and eventually southern Norway and Sweden.

Chinese and three national languages to the south (Lao, Thai, and Vietnamese) plus a number of minority languages in the area all have monosyllabic roots and are tonal. Chinese would appear to be the source of the similarities. Vietnamese looks like a form of Chinese, but in fact it is related to Cambodian (Khmer) and other languages of the Mon-Khmer language family. It has been sinicized—made like Chinese—following centuries of political and cultural domination by China. Where a number of features of language diffuse across language boundaries and bring about convergence, we have a **linguistic area**, also known by the German name *Sprachbund* 'language union'.

The Balkans is another linguistic area, where languages such as Greek, Albanian, Romanian, Bulgarian, Macedonian, and Serbian share a number of diffused properties. For instance, the infinitive was lost in Greek so that instead of saying something like *Thelō grapsein* 'I want to write', one said *Thelō na grapsō* 'I want that I may write.' This usage spread to Macedonian and the southern dialects of Albanian, where the infinitive has been lost, and to Serbian, Bulgarian, and Romanian, where the infinitive is vestigial or retained in the written language. Albanian, Bulgarian, Macedonian, southern dialects of Serbian, and Romanian share a word-final definite article, as in Romanian *lup-ul* 'the wolf'.

The Indian Subcontinent is a linguistic area. It contains languages from the Indo-European, Dravidian, Munda, and Tibeto-Burman families. Most of these have **retroflex** consonants (*d, n, l* made with the tip of the tongue curled back making them sound like *rd, rn*, and *rl* as in American *murder, burner*, and *pearly* respectively), Subject–Object–Verb (SOV) word order, postpositions, causative suffixes, and various other features in common. A band of languages running westwards from Turkey through central and northern Asia across to Korea and Japan is characterized by SOV word order, postpositions, and agglutinative word structure. The chain includes Turkic, Mongolic, and Tungusic languages, which are sometimes grouped in an Altaic family, but it is more likely that there has been convergence between neighbouring languages over a large area.

Ethiopia is another linguistic area where languages belonging to the Cushitic, Semitic, Omotic, and Nilo-Saharan families share grammatical similarities such as SOV word order and postpositions, and phonological features such as /f/ but no /p/. Most of the rest of Africa forms one large linguistic area where the basic word order is usually SVO. A large number of languages have tones (about 80%); many use the verb for 'surpass' to express the comparative (X is long surpasses Y), and many share certain polysemies such as *drink/ smoke* and *see/hear/understand*. None of these properties is exclusive to Africa but the concentration of these features is suggestive of a linguistic area.

Motivation and direction of change

We can say something about the direction of language change, especially sound change, but it is difficult to know why changes take place. Consider the change from [k] to [tʃ] before a high front vowel in words like *circa* 'around' in late Latin or early Italian. We can see the phonetic motivation for such a change; we can see that it is easier to pronounce the consonant with the same place of articulation as the vowel. Similarly, with those who pronounce English *input* as [ɪmpʊt], we can see there is less effort in using the labial position for the nasal as well as the stop. It was mentioned above that the two most common types of sound change are assimilation and loss. This has lead to the notion that 'ease of articulation' is a cause of phonetic change. While it is certainly a factor, and while it accounts for the direction of many sound changes, it cannot be the cause. The sequence [ki] remained in Latin for a thousand years or more before it changed to [tʃi]. We cannot explain why the change took place at a particular time. With other types of change such as the Great English Vowel Shift we cannot even appeal to ease of articulation, and it has to be said that the reasons for particular sound changes at particular times remains a mystery. One factor that has been posited is the desire for some speakers to differentiate themselves from others. In other words just as people choose certain hairstyles and styles of dress to mark themselves as being young and cool or mature and 'respectable', people choose pronunciations to distinguish themselves. There is always some small variation in pronunciation that usually goes unnoticed. If some speakers happen to favour a particular variant, this then gives the chosen variant a certain sociolinguistic significance. William Labov studied a change that took place on the island of Martha's Vineyard off the coast of Massachusetts (a location featured in a number of films including *Jaws*). The change involved a centralization of the first part of the diphthongs [ay] and [aw] towards [ə]. Labov showed that the change was more marked in those islanders who had a negative attitude towards the mainlanders and that this pronunciation had become a marker of islander identification.

Changes in the morphology are not quite so mysterious. Phonetic weakening can result in free unstressed grammatical forms becoming bound so postpositions become case inflection and pronouns become affixes on verbs. But, as noted above, phonetic erosion wears away some inflection, so a language needs to find more analytic alternatives. In English and in the Romance languages the erosion of case endings led to reliance on word order to distinguish subject and object and greater use of prepositions (see the *Prodigal Son* example above). Erosion of person/number marking on the verb necessitates using free pronouns.

Some syntactic changes are triggered by changes in the morphology. In English and the Romance languages regular subject–verb–object word order developed when the case distinction between nominative and accusative was lost.

There is a theory that syntactic change takes place in the process of acquisition rather than in the grammars of mature speakers. Take the case of word order in English. As noted above, Old English had a principle of placing the verb in second position. The first position could be filled by an adverb, a prepositional phrase, the direct object, or a noun in the dative or a subject. However, the subject would have been by far the most frequent choice and a child exposed to a high proportion of subject–verb–object sentences might well have taken that order to be the result of a subject–verb–object rule rather than a statistical tendency with a verb-second rule. However, we cannot assume that the change was initiated by children.

Sources and further reading

The Ewe example is taken from Heine, Claudi, and Hünnemeyer, *Grammaticalization*, page 1. Data about Africa was taken from Heine's article 'Africa as a linguistic area' in volume 1 of K. Brown (ed.), *Elsevier Encyclopedia of Language and Linguistics*. Labov's work on Martha's Vineyard is accessible in his 1972 book *Sociolinguistic Patterns*, which contains a reprint of an earlier 1965 paper.

For information on a wide range of languages there is Lyovin, *An Introduction to the Languages of the World*, and Comrie, *The World's Major Languages*.

There are numerous books on language change. Aitchison's *Language Change: Progress or Decay?* is an easy read. An authoritative coverage can be found in Campbell's *Historical Linguistics*. For a history of English try Pyles and Algeo, *The Origins and Development of the English Language*. For the part social factors play in language change read Labov, *Principles of Linguistic Change*, vol. 2: *Social Factors*. For a good account of serial verbs see Crowley, Lynch, Siegel, and Piau, *The Design of Language*.

Problems

1 In English letter *a* normally represents the sound [æ] as in *cat*, *sat*, and *mat*, but it represents an [ɒ] sound in the RP pronunciation of *wan*, *wash*, *want*, and *quality*. From what you have read about speech sounds in chapters eight and nine and keeping in mind the tendency languages exhibit towards assimilation, can you deduce what has happened in words like *wan*, *wash*, *want*, and *quality*? The word *swam* is an exception. Can you guess why?

If you have a nice generalization covering words like *wan*, *wash*, *want*, and *quality*, then words like *swag*, *quack*, and *wag* will be exceptions. Can you add a further rider to account for these words?

2 The Great English Vowel Shift was illustrated in Table 12.4, and it was noted that it affected long vowels. Some vowels escaped the GEVS because they had become short. For instance, *wise* [wiːzə] later [wiːz] became [waɪz] 'wise', but the vowel had become short in *wisdom* and was not affected. Here are some more examples of the shortening. Can you determine in what environment the shortening took place?

wise	wisdom	divine	divinity
Christ	Christmas	sublime	sublimity
contrite	contrition	criticize	criticism

3 Some speakers of American English drop the past tense marker with certain verbs as below. Why is the past tense marker dropped with *sweep*, but not with *steep*? Can you spot what the principle is?

keep	kep'	steep	steeped
creep	crep'	heap	heaped
sweep	swep'	step	stepped

4 The following words are of Greek origin. What clues are there in the spelling to suggest a Greek origin?

cycle, psyche, theocracy, parenthesis, philander, echo, pneumatic

5 The following are of Latin origin. They are inflected forms. Find out the original meaning of these words in Latin (not just the meaning of the root).

recipe, credo, exit, imprimatur, placebo, veto, audio, video, posse

6 The following have changed in meaning over the centuries. Label the changes as widening (generalization) or narrowing (specialization).

word	earlier meaning	later meaning
business	state of being busy	occupation, trade
fowl	bird	chicken
wade	go	walk through water
go	walk	move, travel
mill	place for grinding grain	factory
liquor	fluid	alcoholic fluid
starve	die	die of hunger (also 'be very hungry')

7 The following have changed in meaning over the centuries, or have acquired an additional sense. Label the changes as amelioration or pejoration.

word	earlier meaning	later meaning
bitch	female dog	bad-tempered female
crafty	skilled	wily
fame	report, rumour	celebrity, renown
grandiose	grand, stately	pompous
glamour	enchantment, spell	allure
reek	to smoke (intransitive)	to stink
vixen	female fox	bad-tempered female

8 It is common for lexical words to become grammatical, but it hardly ever happens that grammatical or functional words become lexical. English provides some examples such as *He's just a has-been* or *He's a gonna/gunna*, the latter referring to someone who is always 'going to do something'. Can you think of other examples? Perhaps not, there are very few, but there are rather more new words that incorporate a function word.

PART V

The brain

13. Language acquisition

There is in every child a painstaking teacher, so skilful that he obtains identical results in all children in all parts of the world. The only language men ever speak perfectly is the one they learn in babyhood, when no one can teach them anything!

Maria Montessori

Basic requirements

Anyone who has battled to learn a second language through years of secondary school and university must be impressed by the ability of young children to learn language. Most children begin to talk in their second year and can talk a great deal by the time they are four or five and understand even more than they can express. They acquire language without much in the way of specific instruction. They get some help from people talking to them in **motherese** or **caregiver speech**, a special register featuring short utterances spoken slowly and clearly, with exaggerated intonation contours and frequent repetitions. Some repetitions are of single words and phrases, which are presumably a help to the child in identifying words in longer utterances. There are also lots of tokens of sentences like *Are we ready for dindins?* and *Someone has wet their nappy, haven't they?* In English these are not particularly simple from the syntactic point of view, though analogous sentences are simple enough in many other languages. Caregivers often reformulate children's utterances, in particular, they expand telegraphese examples as in the following exchange:

child: *How it work?*
father: *How does it work?*
child: *How it work?*

Children often appear to ignore such expansions, as in this example where the child is not at the stage where he can handle grammatical verbs and agreement, but that is not to say that the expansion has not registered.

The caregiver register is also full of baby-talk forms such as *ta* (thanks), *tatta* [tæta:] (good-bye), *tum-tum* or *tummy*, *mama*, *dada*, *nana*, *choo-choo*, *wee-wee*, and *poo-poo*. These are presumably thought to be easier for the child to pick up, since they reflect the efforts of children beginning to speak. The extent to which motherese helps children is controversial, and it is uncertain that baby-talk is used as much in other cultures as it is in ours. As children reach school age, they are usually spoken to in a way closer to the adult norm, and it is doubtful whether they receive any help with acquiring syntax. Most of the corrections they receive are to do with socially approved alternatives rather than with syntax *per se*, for instance, telling the child to say, 'I did it' not 'I done it.'

Any child can learn any language they are exposed to. A Korean child will learn Korean if they are raised in a Korean-speaking environment, but Greek if they are raised in a Greek-speaking community. A child can learn more than one language, and they learn whatever language or languages they are exposed to pretty near perfectly. This does not mean that they learn to speak textbook grammar. They learn whatever they are exposed to. As we noted in chapter eleven, there are several norms other than the standard. If all the speakers the child is exposed to use *seen* as the past tense of *saw* and *done* as the past tense of *do*, then that's what the child will learn.

Acquiring phonology

There is experimental evidence showing that infants can make fine discriminations among sounds. A baby sucking peacefully while hearing repeated tokens of [pa] will increase its sucking rate dramatically if the stimulus is changed to [ba]. The phonetic difference does not have to be phonemic in the language or languages of the parents. If a baby in an English-speaking environment is exposed to repeated tokens of [pa] and then the stimulus is switched to [pʰa], the sucking rate will increase. However, this ability to make fine discriminations is not confined to speech sounds, and the ability to discriminate speech sounds is not limited to human babies, but can be found in a variety of creatures including monkeys, chinchillas, and Japanese quail (Clark 2003, p. 61). The ability to make fine discriminations between speech sounds does not last into adulthood. Once children have mastered one or more phonological systems, this blinds them to distinctions not present in what they have acquired.

Around six months babies start **babbling**, producing various speech-like sounds, especially strings of open syllables such as [mama] and [baba] and [dada]. As noted on page 55, open syllables with labial and dental or alveolar stops and nasals figure prominently in the languages of the world with meanings such as 'mother', 'father', 'auntie', and 'gran'. Presumably there is a tendency to associate the child's early syllables with a likely referent.

Children then progress from simple syllables like [ma] and [ba] in three ways. They add sounds made at other places of articulation such as velars; they add other manners of articulation, and they produce closed syllables. Glides are produced early, followed by fricatives, liquids, and affricates. Where they aim to produce a word containing a consonant they have not mastered they make a substitution. For instance, they will substitute a stop for a fricative so that a word like *river* comes out as *ribber*, *fat* as *pat*, and *mother* as *mudder*. In early stages glides may be substituted for liquids so that *Lulu* comes out as *yuyu*, and *rye* as *wye*. Children frequently omit syllable-final consonants in the early stages, but they don't normally omit an onset. If they encounter a 'difficult' initial consonant, they substitute an 'easier' one. Where they encounter con-sonant clusters in the onset of syllables, they often omit a consonant so that *snow* might come out as [soʊ] and *smile* as [saɪ] or [saɪl]. Sometimes they make a substitution in a cluster. For example, children often pronounce words such as *play* as [pweɪ], putting the glide [w] in place of the liquid [l]. This is interesting in that clusters of labials do not occur in English.

With polysyllabic words children begin by producing just the stressed syllable, and then they manage a succeeding final syllable in words like *mummy*, *doggie*, and *brother*. They take longer to add a preceding unstressed syllable so that *banana* comes out *nana* and *spaghetti* comes out as *ghetti*.

From the point of view of an adult, children often appear to pronounce different phonemes alike. In some instances, this is the case, but **acoustic** analysis, that is, analysis of the sound by means of laboratory instruments, reveals that sometimes there is a difference, though not sufficient for adults to pick up.

Children are mostly unaware of discrepancies between their output and the target provided by parents or whoever else they are exposed to. If a child tries to say *clean* and you hear it as *queen* and repeat it as *queen*, it is likely the child will say, *I said* [kwiːn] *not* [kwiːn]!

Mastering the full phonology in English takes the child about six years. English is notable for having a large number of word-final consonant clusters and these are learned last, clusters like those in *length* (though this is [lɛŋθ] for many adult speakers), *breadth, next,* and various past tense forms such as *matched,* and *fudged.*

Acquiring syntax

One-word stage

In their second year children usually begin to speak in one-word utterances. These single words are often used to express a predication. For instance, a child might say [æ] looking at some stewed apple. This monosyllable will be interpreted as 'apple', but it might be uncertain whether the child is just letting his audience know that he or she knows the name of that substance or whether he or she would like a few spoonfuls (probably the latter!). These one-word utterances are called **holophrastic** (whole-phrase) since they seem to correspond to a phrase or sentence. At first these words are tied to the immediate situation, but eventually they display **displacement**. A child might say *doggy* when the family dog is not around or *bickie* when no biscuits are in sight.

Two-word stage

The one-word stage can last from a month or so to as long as a year, but usually during their second year children produce some two-word utterances. These express requests, questions, and descriptions of actions, processes, and locations. There are what seem to be nouns, verbs, adjectives, and locational words such as *in,* which can appear as prepositions and adverbs in adult English. There are grammatical words such as pronouns (*me, you*) and deictic adverbs (*here, there*), but there are no function words that serve to join content words such as *of* or parts of the verb *to be* (*is, were,* etc.). There are no inflections either, at least in a language like English where roots can be isolated (see below), so these early utterances can be said to be in telegraphese, that is, in the register of the telegrams of yesteryear which were charged by the word and which therefore led to texts with very few function words. Intonation suggests that many early two-word utterances are genuine phrases or sentences and not just separate words as in a list, but it is possible that some combinations are learned by heart or are based on a pattern in which there is a variable slot, such as *Where X?* or *More X.*

Consider the following sample notated during the first month of two-word utterances. This particular child, Hilary John (HJ) was a late-starter and was 2;9 (two years and nine months) at the time of recording, but though he was slow to develop syntax, his articulation was normal for that age. Each example is accompanied by an interpretation.

1 *Bubble coming* A bubble is coming.
2 *Bubble come* A bubble is coming.
3 *Smack Daddy* I'm going to smack Daddy.
4 *Naughty me* Reply to 'Why did you hit Laurence?'
5 *Gone pencil* My pencil has gone.
6 *Smack Laurie* Smack Laurence!
7 *Sockie here* Your socks are here.
8 *Study bed* He's studying in his bedroom.
9 *Finish tea?* Have you finished tea [evening meal]?
10 *Near Daddy* I will put this chair near Daddy.
11 *Out bed* I want to get out of bed.
12 *Dat, man?* Is that [breakfast you are preparing] for [the work]man?
13 *Clothes wet* Her clothes are wet.

Each utterance is a predication. At this stage there are intransitive sentences (1, 2, 5) and verbless sentences where the adult version would require part of the verb 'to be' (4, 7, 13). With transitive verbs the subject is not expressed (see 3, 8, 9). This is common in the early stages and reflects the fact that transitive subjects very often express given information and are in less need of specification than objects. Some linguists would describe these two-word predications in terms of **topic** and **comment** rather than in terms of subject and predicate, but it is interesting to note that the participant that is not included in these two-word utterances is not just an agent as in (3) above but also an experiencer as in *[I] like chips*, the roles that are encoded as subject in adult grammar. These two-word sentences appear to be novel constructions rather than attempts at imitation; note the word order in (5), for instance. There are, however, sequences learned by heart. One of the first utterances of this child was, 'Three, two, one, zero!' Contrary to the generalization made at the beginning of this section there is one inflection, namely *-ing*, the present participle form (1). This is usually learned early.

It is interesting to think about how the child gets started on syntax. Once one knows some syntax, one can use that knowledge as an anchor and work out word classes from their distribution. But how to get started in the first place? It is likely that the child sees that physical objects behave in a certain way and that actions behave in another, and that that gets them started on the noun and verb classes.

Longer sentences

The child progresses from the two-word stage to producing longer utterances of various lengths, still mostly in telegraphic mode. The rate of development varies from child to child, but each child goes through the same stages of development.

HJ, who started talking late, advanced to longer sentences after just a few weeks. The plural morpheme is usually the next to be produced after -*ing* and HJ conformed to expectation by using regular plurals at 2;10 months. The word *ruff* in (17) below is his idiosyncratic substitute for 'this' and 'that' in demonstrative pronoun function. As with the substitutions that are obviously phonetic, HJ was oblivious to the substitution and did not understand the sadistic adult who used *ruff* as a demonstrative pronoun in speaking to him.

14 *Push Daddy heater*   I'm going to push Daddy into the heater.
15 *In talk Allie*   I'm going in[to that room] to talk to Alice.
16 *Cupboard hard me*   The cupboard is too hard for me [to open].
17 *Ruff like too*   I'd like that too.
18 *Back car in garage*   The car is back in the garage.
19 *Lots dog*   There are a lot of dogs [in that car].
20 *Like chips*   I like chips.

When the subject of a transitive verb is eventually introduced, it is the accusative form of pronouns that is used, as with intransitive predicates (see (4) above).

21 *Me see parrots*   I want to see the parrots.
22 *Her have now*   She has it now.

These examples are not just strings of words, there is hierarchical structure. The following all have phrases within the sentence. Note the object in first position in (24).

23 *[Mine bed] broke*   noun phrase
24 *[Two eyes] Alice got*   noun phrase
25 *Run [around Alice]*   prepositional phrase
26 *You [like ice cream]?*   verb phrase

Negation

Negation is expressed first by *no* used on its own, then by *no* and later *not* usually placed at the beginning of the utterance:

27 *No help me*   Reply to 'Can I help you?'
28 *No catch me*   You can't catch me.
29 *Not me fault*   It's not my fault

At the next stage the negative *not* is placed before the verb:

Me not go outside, me got sore toe.

In many languages negation doesn't involve any more than the addition of the negative morpheme, but in English the child has to learn to use *do*. (See below.)

Not long after *not* is introduced, *can't* is used, possibly as an unanalysed whole, along with *don't*, first in commands and then in statements.

I can't find my other bit [of] scarf.
Don't say, 'Shut up', rude.
Me don't want to stay at Grannie's, stay at home.

Questions

Yes-no questions signalled by intonation are found at the two-word stage (9), (12), and continue on into adult English. Here are some more examples:

30 *Me smack him?* Will I smack him?
31 *Him bit you, that possum?* Did he bite you, that possum?

Content questions occur early, but there is no auxiliary except for the contracted *is* in expressions like *What's that?* or *Where's so-and-so?* It is likely that these sibilants are unanalysed and just taken to be part of the interrogative.

Where chocolate now?
What's ruff? [What's that?]
How [does] it work?
How [did] dat Bingo [dog] came in our back yard, how?
What [did] you say?
What you having [to eat]?
What [have] you been doing? [Note been]

When an auxiliary is introduced, at first there is no inversion. HJ failed to produce a content question with an auxiliary during the period of observation (up to 3;9 years), though he included auxiliaries regularly in other types of clause:

I'm going to give you a bikkie.
When you're at school, let me read it.

Patient subjects

With transitive verbs the agent is typically expressed as the subject and the patient as the object. With some verbs such as *melt*, *move*, and *break* it is possible to express the patient as the subject, particularly where there is no agent involved. Examples of this appear early:

Mine cricket bat broke again, mine.

With most verbs the passive construction must be used to express the patient as subject, but the passive in English is complicated in that it requires an auxiliary verb and a past participle. The passive is acquired in stages. The passive without an agent is acquired before the passive with an agent, and the auxiliary verb is not present in early examples.

You get whole burnt, you too close [to the fire].
You going get burnt.

Agentless passives are by far the most common type in adult English, so it is not surprising they are learned first.

Compound and Complex sentences

Not long after progressing beyond the two-word stage, the child begins to introduce compound and complex sentences. Two propositions can be effectively combined simply by juxtaposition and children begin by doing this (*I saw the rabbits; fed them*). They learn to form compound sentences with *and* about the time they learn to use *and* to join noun phrases.

Relative clauses appear early, but without *who*, *which*, or *that*. A two-and-a-half-year-old girl who saw me taking pictures at a party remarked, 'You ['ve] got a camera like [the one] Daddy ['s] got.' These relative clauses appear at the end of sentences modifying an immediately preceding noun phrase. In the following examples, HJ is asking to be given some easier questions in a word game:

Daddy, write some names me know.
You do some words we know.

Only later do children produce sentences with relative clauses modifying subjects, but such sentences are not common in adult English anyway. Subjects tend to express given information and tend to be simple, often pronominal.

Complement clauses can be finite or non-finite. The non-finite type appears first with *want*:

Me want to go there one day.
Me want [to] tip [it] out [to] see [what] us got.

The second example is interesting in that despite the fact that it lacks any function words and the nominative form of pronouns, it contains a fused relative clause *[what] us got*. The clause *see [what] us got* could be interpreted as co-ordinated or as a non-finite purpose clause.

Here are some examples of finite complement clauses:

Laurie say me pig eater.
I don't know where are my jeans.

Adverbial clauses also appear early, often without the conjunction:

[When] me get bigger, me come.
When you go, Alice cry.

Some linguists claim that by the time a child turns four all the constructions found in speech are in place, but it is doubtful whether that is true for all children. However, production lags behind comprehension. Experiments in which children are asked to manipulate objects or toy animals reveal they can understand differences of word order (*The dog chased the cat* vs. *The cat chased the dog*) or active versus passive (*The dog chased the cat* vs. *The cat was chased by the dog*) before they produce these differences regularly.

Acquiring function forms

As noted above, children begin with telegraphic speech. In English they acquire the present participle in *-ing* early, but use it without an auxiliary as in (1) above. The next inflection to be learned is the plural, then the other two sibilant inflections, the possessive (*Mary's book*) and the third person singular (*She sleeps*), and later the past tense (*He laughed*). Children sometimes use irregular forms such as *teeth* and *went* before they begin using the regular inflections. When they do start using the regular inflections, they tend to overgeneralize regular inflection so we get forms like *bringed* for *brought* and *eated* for *ate* with verbs, and *mans* for *men* and *mouses* for *mice* with nouns. Sometimes they add regular inflection to an irregular inflected form (*two mens, she wented*). With irregular plurals they are usually exposed to a number of baby-talk alternatives that have regular plurals: *toosies, toosie-pegs, mousies, goosies, footsies.*

Nearly breaked it.
When you at school, I haved it [your book].
Drawed something, something for you.

The errors are an indication that the child is using rules and not just repeating an unanalysed inflected form.

The demonstratives *this, that, the,* and *a* are learned early, but *some, every,* and *each* are not fully learned until later.

Even at the two-word stage children use lexical prepositions like *in* and *on*. Only later do they acquire grammatical prepositions like *of.* It is natural that they would acquire concrete notions before abstract ones, and it is significant that they use forms referring to place early. Locative or local notions are fundamental to language. They form the basis for the terminology of time (*at noon, over summer, in winter*) and they are the basis for numerous metaphorical extensions. Consider *abroad, uptight, think through, demystify,* and thousands of other words and set phrases that have a partial or complete locative origin.

As noted in the previous section, children do not use parts of the verb 'to be' in the early stages, but they do use the contracted form of *is* in *What's this?* and *Where's that dog?* It may be that these are unanalysed wholes.

English has very little morphology and the little it has is mostly agglutinative. This means the child can operate with stems and then add the inflections later. In many inflected languages this would not be possible. Every word form of nouns, pronouns, adjectives, and verbs bears an inflection. The child begins with attempts at inflected words, though the inflection may not be produced because of limitations on the child's phonology. When the child produces fully inflected words, it is likely that some forms are unanalysed. As might be expected, languages with regular inflection like Turkish provide fewer problems than irregular ones like Russian.

Acquiring semantics

If you try to learn a language by interrogating a native speaker, you will find yourself pointing to entities and asking the speaker to give you the word for whatever is indicated. This works quite well, but one problem that arises fairly frequently is the precise meaning of the word that is offered. If you point to a three-year-old male child and ask, 'What do you call him?' you might get words with meanings such as 'baby', 'child', 'boy', 'nephew', 'grandson', or 'Charlie'. This is the problem that faces the child. They have no trouble picking up a word for some entity, some activity or process, or some attribute, but it might take them a while to refine the extension of the words they learn. My granddaughter began by using the word 'boy' just for her brother, as if it was his name. This is 'underextension'. More common I think is 'overextension', where a word is applied to a wider range than it does in adult English. Examples I have heard include calling the back area of a station wagon the *boot* (American *trunk*), extending *couch* (which seats more than one) to cover 'armchair' (which seats only one), and using *snow* for 'hail'. Other reported examples of overextension include *daddy* for any man, *ball* for any spherical object, *collie* for any dog, *dog* for various four-legged animals, and *tick-tock* for watches, clocks, scales with dials, and gas meters. These overextensions do not mean that the children who use them fail to distinguish the various referents. Children who call all men *daddy* know which man is their father, and children who use *ball* for apple know you can't eat a ball (though you may chew on it!).

Children also begin using word-building processes early, often producing forms for referents that already have a name. Examples include *brooming the yard* for 'sweeping the yard', *sleepers* for 'pyjamas', and *stepper* or *climber* for 'ladder'.

It is interesting to observe the semantic generalizations children make. One child in trying to describe lengths of drainage pipe that have a series of small slots along their length said 'those pipes with...' and then ran his middle fingers up and down on his stomach to indicate the slots, presumably seeing an analogy between the cylindrical pipes and the cylindrical trunk of the body.

In the first six months of talking children develop a vocabulary of about fifty words, and they can understand perhaps four times that number. During the next six months their vocabulary grows to 200, and after that it quickly runs to thousands. A teenager would probably know 30,000 words. In the early years the passive vocabulary far outstrips the active vocabulary, and remains greater than the active vocabulary throughout life.

The child's early utterances are bare statements, questions, and commands in the sense that there are no discourse markers. Their use of *but* develops some time after the age of three, but only later do they add discourse markers such as *well* as in *Well, he is your favourite teddy* or *now* as in *Now that's an idea*. Later again they master the meaning of logical connections such as *if* and *because*.

Idioms present a challenge for the child, in fact this can be a problem right through life. There are an enormous number of idiomatic expressions, many of them colloquial and restricted in their distribution so that one keeps encountering new ones. Children are puzzled by expressions such as *raining cats and dogs* and *She drinks like a fish*. They are inclined to take idioms literally or not to realize they are idioms. One child, when asked to help look for a lost trowel, replied, 'I'll peel my eyes', taking the verb phrase from the idiom *Keep your eyes peeled*.

Further stages

There is a lot more a child has to learn than is covered above. There are principles of language use in discourse as described in chapter seven, and there is control of varieties as discussed in chapter eleven. There are politeness routines, and so on. There is also more complicated syntax such as sentences like *Who did you say Mum told you she saw in the supermarket?* where *who* questions the object of *saw*, which is the fourth verb in the sentence. I take for granted that any native speaker of English can produce a sentence like that, but there are some constructions in English that seem to lie outside the range that every child acquires. Consider the following:

I watched channel two, and my brother channel seven.
Had I been there a minute earlier, I might have been able to resuscitate him.
The meeting having finished by four, the delegates repaired to the bar.

My guess is that any native speaker could understand these constructions, but that few would actually produce them. They are rather 'bookish' and I suspect that if they are acquired, it is by conscious learning.

Sign language and its acquisition

As mentioned in chapter one signing is an alternative to speaking, and there are a number of sign languages including BSL (British Sign Language) and ASL or Ameslan (American Sign Language). These are true languages and they need to be distinguished from signed forms of language such as **Signed English**, which are systems of signs used to convert written words into signs.

The true history of signing will never be known. There must have been thousands of children born deaf in different societies over the ages, most of them isolated from other deaf children. Recent accounts of deaf children have shown that they can invent signs, and they would have learned gestures that were in use in their community. If they were lucky, the community would have had a secondary sign language in use for special purposes, but many deaf children must have suffered from being unable to communicate. They would have had only an observer's understanding of culture; they would have had no understanding of kinship, of spiritual or religious beliefs, of myth or history.

Until around the 1970s there was widespread ignorance of sign language and educators discouraged its use on the grounds that it hindered learning to lipread and speak (a very difficult task if you can't get feedback from your efforts). In some cases children in schools for the deaf had to pick up sign language from those who knew it (usually those with deaf parents) out of sight of their teachers. This is reminiscent of the situation with ethnic minorities where children would learn in the dominant language, but speak their own language among themselves.

Sign languages do have some signs that are ideographic or iconic, that is, where there is some connection between the sign and a referent. In some sign languages, 'weigh' is indicated by moving upraised palms up and down as with the traditional balance-type scales, and 'umbrella' is signed by imitating the action of opening an umbrella, but most signs are built up from meaningless components just as spoken words are.

Signs can be broken down into four parameters:

- **shape:** fingers extended, fingers bent, hand cupped, fist
- **orientation:** palm up or down, towards or away from signer, fingertip to side of cheek
- **location:** where the sign is placed in the signing space, i.e. the upper body region
- **movement:** hands moving up or down, left or right, twisting

As well as the manual signs facial expression plays a part. For instance, a yes-no question can be indicated by raised eyebrows.

Most signs for a morpheme are short and correspond to a single syllable in spoken language. They achieve this useful brevity through greater use of more than one parameter simultaneously. 'Drink', for instance, is indicated by cupping the hand (shape), bringing it up (movement) to the mouth (location). This, of course, is an iconic sign.

Children acquire sign language in stages analogous to those followed by children acquiring spoken language. They start with single signs, then they combine signs, and they lack grammatical signs in the early stages.

Hearing children of deaf parents acquire both sign and spoken language, with the acquisition of the first signs preceding the acquisition of the first speech sounds.

Theories of acquisition

Noam Chomsky, the most famous living linguist and a linguist who is also known to the public through his political writings, claims that children have a special innate ability to learn language, and that this is not just part of general intelligence, but rather an autonomous language-specific component of intelligence. Since children are able to learn language effortlessly at an age when they cannot learn the principles of organic chemistry, quantum mechanics, or linguistics, the claim is not surprising. Moreover, one can suffer mental impairment that leaves language intact or have language deficiencies and full intelligence (see following chapter). Followers of Chomsky have posited that there are innate principles of **Universal Grammar** (UG) that constrain and guide the child. According to the theory the child does not need to select from an unlimited number of hypotheses about how language is structured. Only certain structures are possible. Chomsky's views have attracted a large following, but the notion is the subject of continuing debate.

Chomsky's views relate to syntax not to language as a whole, in particular to operations involving movement and recursion as in a sentence quoted above:

Who did you say Mum told you she saw in the supermarket?

In this example *who* questions the object of *saw,* which is the fourth verb in the sentence. One could say that *who* has been moved. Compare the echo sentence *You said Mum told you she saw who in the supermarket?* Obviously there is a link between *who* at the front of the sentence and the position of the object of *saw,* whether we call it movement or not, and it is also obvious that this is a sophisticated feature of syntax. This sentence also illustrates **recursion**, which involves embedding a constituent within a constituent of the same type, in this instance one clause within another, with the possibility of long embeddings (in theory infinite embeddings if one can reuse certain verbs). In recent work Chomsky and some of his associates have suggested that at a minimum recursion is part of the innate language faculty.

This special faculty for acquiring language is claimed to operate up till around puberty so the first twelve years constitutes a critical or sensitive period during which the child must be exposed interactively to language if there is to be the effortless, efficient mastery of language we all are familiar with. A number of children have been brought up without normal exposure to language. These include feral children found abandoned and living with animals (like Tarzan) and children confined in near isolation for one reason or another. There is a much quoted case of Genie, a girl who was physically restrained and denied almost all interaction with her parents or anyone else until she was thirteen. When she was freed, it was found that she could acquire only a small vocabulary with difficulty and could not master syntax. There are reports of other similar cases where such children have been restored to normal human contact after the first decade of their life, and have failed to acquire more than a minimum of language, in some cases despite intensive training. This tends to provide support for the notion of a critical period, but there are no reports on the cognitive abilities of these children before they were cut off from normal human interaction, and one has to allow for the traumatic effect of their isolation.

An important theme of arguments for a specialized, innate faculty is 'poverty-of-stimulus'. Chomsky and his followers claim that there is no negative evidence available to the child (i.e. no sentences marked as ungrammatical), but in fact children are corrected and it is common for parents to give full, grammatical versions of children's incomplete or inaccurate attempts. The proponents of the specialized innate faculty also claim that the positive evidence is too weak to account for the fact that any child will arrive at the correct hypotheses about how the language or languages they are exposed to work. One argument for the poverty-of-stimulus position goes like this. To form a question in English one needs to move the auxiliary to a position in front of the subject, but relevant examples are too rare for the child to be able to see that the movement of the auxiliary is structure dependent. The auxiliary does not move over a specified number of words, nor does it always move to the front of the sentence, but it does move over one constituent regardless of the length of that constituent. The point is illustrated in the following examples where the subject has been bracketed and where the position that the auxiliary would have occupied in the corresponding affirmative is shown by a hyphen.

Can [I]—go?

Can [the teddy that lost his eye]—still see ok?

If you see Kay, will [you]—tell her to come early?

Opposed to the Chomskian position are those who believe that children simply learn on the basis of whatever data they are exposed to, and frequency plays a part in what is learned earlier. In this instance they point out that studies of large corpora of English text show that a range of relevant examples does occur and that there is no evidence that they do not occur in the data available to children. One might add that children produce evidence for structure once they are past the two-word stage, and it is not surprising if they see fronting as structure dependent.

Proponents of UG note that the passive is learned comparatively late and they attribute this to the fact that it requires the object to be moved, and this movement cannot be handled until there is a certain maturity. Opponents point out that passives are not very frequent in the speech the child is exposed to, but in languages where the passive is more frequent in adult speech, the passive is learned earlier. These languages include Sesotho (Bantu), Inuktitut (Eskimo-Aleut) and Quiche (Mayan). As noted earlier, the complexity of the passive varies from language to language as well.

Other examples that are sometimes offered as evidence for in-built constraints on grammar include the fact that children do not come out with passive versions of sentences such as *The ice-cream cost three dollars*. Why don't children generalize the passive so that any structure of the form NP [VNP] gets passivized? But one needs to consider discourse principles. The passive is used so that one can talk about an entity that would not normally be encoded as subject. With the verb *cost*, there is little motivation to make the amount the topic.

It is not true that children unerringly select the correct hypothesis at the first attempt. Children sometimes form interesting hypotheses that have to be rejected. I once observed a child who had forgotten his socks say *I got for my socks*. This struck me as amazing. How could the child have analysed *forgot* as *for* plus *got* and then reversed the order? After I observed the child for some time, I discovered that he used *for* in front of the object of transitive verbs that do not refer to impingement on a patient. So though he said things like *He ate the cake*, he said *He liked for the cake*. Presumably the *for* was generalized from verbs like *look for* and *wait for*. It was also the case that this child, like other children acquiring English, dropped initial, unaccented syllables, so *got for* was an an abbreviated version of *forgot* plus a preposition used to denote objects that were not actually impinged on.

The debate between the Chomskians, who believe in a specialized, innate faculty for acquiring syntax, and those of more empirical bent, who believe language acquisition can be accounted for in terms of general cognitive ability, continues. Hopefully, collecting extensive data of adult-child interaction will go a long way towards resolving the poverty-of-stimulus argument.

Those who believe in a dedicated language faculty are normally concerned with syntax only, but syntax is not independent of morphology, and the entries for various classes of word in the mental lexicon, words such as verbs and prepositions, must contain syntactic information. Syntax is obviously not independent of semantics and pragmatics (language use) in actual performance, nor of the medium, whether it be signing or speaking. Of course, it is legitimate for Chomsky and his followers to isolate a syntactic component of language, but a child's mastery of all aspects of language is impressive.

Second-language acquisition

Although children can acquire one or more languages through normal exposure and without much in the way of specific instruction, teenagers and adults find learning a new language difficult. The pronunciation is usually a problem, particularly if there are phonemic distinctions in the target language not found in the learner's naturally acquired languages. This is typically the case unless one is trying to learn Hawaiian or one of a number of other languages with a small phoneme inventory. Even if one masters new distinctions, it is difficult not to carry over all sorts of subtle phonetic habits from one's native language, and thereby speak with an 'accent'. The vocabulary usually requires masses of rote learning, although this problem may be reduced if you are learning a closely related language or if there has been large scale borrowing of words between the learner's language and the target language. English speakers have a start with other Germanic languages such as German and Swedish, where numerous words are similar to their English counterparts, and also with Greek, Latin, or any of the modern descendants of Latin such as Italian and French, since English has borrowed massive amounts of vocabulary from Greek, Latin, and French.

Besides the problem of vocabulary, there can be difficulties in morphology and syntax. Inflection can be a problem. Some languages have very little, some have regular inflection, while others, such as Russian, have a good deal of irregular inflection. As mentioned above, children can acquire any language they are exposed to, though they will take longer to learn the morphology where it is extensive and irregular, but for an older person learning a new language the degree of difficulty is to some extent determined by characteristics of the target language relative to those of the native language.

The circumstances in which one attempts to learn a new language and one's motivation to learn vary from case to case. The situation that most closely resembles the situation of a child acquiring language is one where one enters a new language community, perhaps as an immigrant. Most of us have watched a foreign film in an unfamiliar language. We find we cannot catch the sounds, we cannot break up the stream of speech into words. At first, all we pick up are a few words uttered in isolation, words for 'yes', 'no', 'let's go', and so on. The immigrant's success in learning a new language varies from case to case. Some fail to acquire almost any of the language of the host country, while others master a good deal of the language in a short time. While this variation is partly a matter of circumstances and motivation, it also appears to be a matter of ability. While children show very little variation in their ability to learn, older people show the same kind of variation you find in the learning of mathematics or sociology. Some people are able to learn a number of new languages more quickly than a child can.

Attempts to teach non-native languages have a long tradition. For instance, wealthy Romans employed Greek-speaking tutors to teach their children Greek, and over the centuries governesses of various degrees of proficiency have been given the task of teaching foreign languages, especially French, to privileged children in Europe and its colonies.

The most traditional method of teaching a second language was the grammar and translation method. Students were given specific instruction in grammar through a series of graded lessons, and each lesson was accompanied by exercises in translation into and out of the target languages, often only in the written form. This produced a good understanding of the way the grammar worked, and, depending on circumstances, an ability to read and write the target language. It worked well enough for a dead language like Ancient Greek or Latin, though that is not to say the method could not have been improved, but it worked poorly for French and German, and after six years of high school hardly anyone could speak fluently, even less could they understand rapid conversation.

In the middle of the twentieth century the audio-lingual method was introduced. This involved students listening to recorded samples, mostly individual sentences, and repeating them *ad nauseam*, and answering questions based on them. The language samples were usually genuine colloquial sentences and an improvement on translating *La plume de ma tante est sur la table de Monsieur Duval* 'The pen of my aunt is on the table of Monsieur

Duval', but there was no scope for genuine interaction. Classes were usually held in language laboratories where students listened to tapes via headsets.

More recently there has been a move to the direct approach, which tries to mirror the environment of first language acquisition. Classes are held entirely in the target language and conducted around a series of themes such as asking directions, asking for food and drink, and so on. Teacher and students interact and errors are tolerated, the emphasis being on successful communication rather than grammatical accuracy. The aim is to produce communicative competence whereby the learner acquires a repertoire of styles and is made aware of norms of appropriate usage. This method works quite well if allowance is made for the small amount of time devoted to it, namely a few hours a week for forty or so weeks of the year in the case of high school students and perhaps no more than twenty-four or so weeks in the case of university students. In some cases provision is made for a sojourn in a country where the target language is spoken, and this is obviously a great benefit. The armed forces provide intensive language courses with native-speaker instructors where the students are required to communicate only in the target language. They do this for at least forty hours per week for up to a year, so not surprisingly the graduates are proficient.

One problem with the direct method is that students are left without the slightest notion of how language works. They can graduate without knowing what a noun or a verb is, or what a subject or object is. Given that English has been taught without overt instruction in grammar for a generation or so, a high school graduate or a university graduate can describe the digestive system, the motion of the planets, subatomic particles, and the workings of the capitalist system, but still be unable to describe the workings of the language they use for the other tasks.

From the point of view of understanding language the difficulties facing the second language learner are of interest largely because they highlight the almost miraculous ease with which children acquire language when they are too young to learn any other area of study. Music provides an interesting comparison. At one extreme there is Mozart composing at five, at the other extreme there are people like me who have difficulty singing the national anthem in tune. With language, every child is a Mozart.

Sources and further reading

For a brief, general overview there is E. Lieven's article 'Language Development: an Overview' in volume 6 of K. Brown (ed.), *Encyclopedia of Language and Linguistics*, and E. Bavin's 'Syntactic Development' in volume 12 of that work. Among books there is Clark, *First Language Acquisition*, and Fletcher and MacWhinney, *The Handbook of Child Language*. Aitchison, *The Articulate Mammal: an Introduction to Psycholinguistics*, is presented pretty much in lay terms.

To find out about Chomsky's recent views on the language faculty there is Fitch, Hauser and Chomsky, 'The Evolution of the Language Faculty' (2005), which contains references to earlier papers, but the best way to follow arguments for and against Chomsky's position is to type the names of these three authors into your search engine: you will find a number of downloadable papers.

There is a collection of corpora of child language available on the web at CHILDES (The Child Language Data Exchange System). Besides a database of transcripts there are programs for computer analysis of transcripts, methods for linguistic coding, and systems for linking transcripts to digitized audio and video.

Problems

1 If you are in a group of people with different language backgrounds, make up a list of baby-talk words in a number of languages. What phonological properties do they share? What meanings do they cover? What parts of speech are represented?

2 List pet names such as *Betty* for *Elizabeth* and *Meg* for *Margaret*. What features of child phonology are reflected in them?

3 The following words have been notated from the speech of a two-year old child. Describe how the child expresses the initial consonant clusters of English. The best way is to write rules for converting the consonant clusters of adult English into the child's equivalents. You should strive to make general statements wherever possible. Use the labels for place of articulation and manner of articulation introduced in chapter eight. Remember the label 'labial' can apply to /w/.

[bwiːd]	bleed	[tiː]	tea
[bwɔːt]	brought	[siː]	see
[gweɪt]	great	[kwæːm]	cram
[swɪŋ]	string	[kwiːn]	queen
[tweɪn]	train	[kiː]	key
[siːp]	sleep	[sɪn]	skin
[fwaɪ]	fly	[sweɪp]	scrape
[twaɪn]	twine	[kwiːn]	clean
[faːtiːz]	Smarties	[wab]	rub

[faɪ]	spy	[lɒg]	log
[pweɪ]	play	[fweɪ]	spray
[swiːt]	sweet	[swiːk]	squeak
[gwoʊ]	glow	[seɪk]	snake
[fɪn]	thin	[dwaɪ]	dry
[fwuː]	through		

4 On the basis of the following sample describe how the child's ability to produce content questions differs from an adult's. In the first two examples the child is asking an adult to say what he has just mouthed. In other words, the child is giving the adult a test in lip reading.

What me say?
What me said?
How do my name?
What Mummy said?
What you write/do/eat?
What you writing/taking/having?
How it work?
Where chocolate now?

5 In a sentence such as *I told Dom to ask Mervyn to get Fred to chop the wood* we have a long example of recursion where one clause is within another, but the sentence is easy to follow. The following sentences also contain recursion, but they are difficult to interpret. Why?

The judge gave the man who put the money that members had been saving for a year
on a horse a long sentence (longer than this one!).
The teacher who the headmaster who the minister appointed criticized resigned.

14. Language processing: brains and computers

The words of language, as they are written or spoken, do not seem to play any role in my mechanism of thought. The physical entities which seem to serve as elements in thought are certain signs and more or less clear images.

Albert Einstein

Brains

Lateralization

As everyone knows, the brain is located in the head under the skull. It consists of two halves, the left and right hemisphere, joined by the *corpus callosum.* A curious fact about the working of the brain is that the left hemisphere controls the movements of the organs on the right side of the body and the right hemisphere controls movements of the left side of the body. Language, as we shall see below, is controlled largely from the left hemisphere.

Figure 14.1 shows a scan of the author's brain obtained by Magnetic Resonance Imaging (MRI) in which the two hemispheres can be seen. Figure 14.2 shows a side view of the left hemisphere with an indication of various areas discussed in the text.

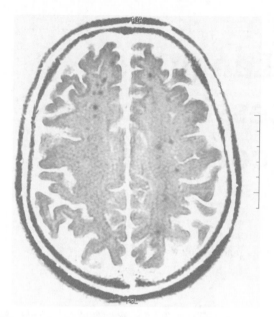

Figure 14.1 MRI scan of author's brain.

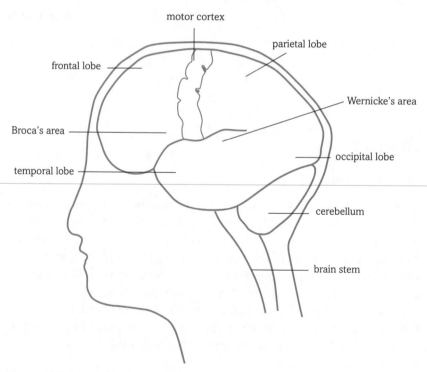

Figure 14.2 Areas of the brain, left hemisphere.

Localization-Modularity

Broca's area

In 1861 Paul Broca reported that an area near the front of the left hemisphere of the brain is crucially involved in the production of speech. He came to this conclusion on the basis of autopsies performed on people suffering from impairment or loss of speech. This area of the brain is now known as **Broca's area** and aphasia that results in speech difficulties is known as **Broca's aphasia** (also 'motor aphasia' or 'expressive aphasia'). **Aphasia** is a language disorder resulting from damage to the brain from a stroke, a tumour, a wound, or infection. Patients with Broca's aphasia have difficulty in initiating speech and in articulating words. There are long pauses, there is lack of intonational contour, and function forms are often omitted, both free forms like *the* and *of* and bound forms like plural marking or past tense marking. Here is an example of a Broca's aphasic speech quoted in the Wikipedia entry for 'expressive aphasia':

> *Yes...ah...Monday...er Dad and Peter H...(his own name), and Dad...er hospital...and ah...Wednesday...Wednesday nine o'clock...and oh...Thursday...ten o'clock, ah doctors...two...an' doctors...and er...teeth...yah.*

Many patients with Broca's aphasia have difficulty with right-side motor control and writing shows misspellings and poor letter formation. Deaf people dependent on sign language show analogous disfluency in using sign language if they suffer damage to Broca's area.

Wernicke's area

In 1874 Carl Wernicke reported that an area towards the back of the left hemisphere was crucially involved in comprehension. This area is now known as **Wernicke's area** and the term **Wernicke's aphasia** is applied to a language disorder that manifests itself in difficulties in understanding language. A person suffering from this disorder can usually speak fluently, but with words that may be inappropriate in context. Some of the substitutions are semantically related (*Mary is my son*), and some are phonetically related (*without playing any attention*). Syntax is affected too. Function words may be used inappropriately, word order is sometimes distorted, and subordinate clauses tend to be absent. While patients with Broca's aphasia are painfully aware of their inability to put their thoughts into words, those with Wernicke's aphasia are unaware of the problem and can speak and write spontaneously, though with errors.

Other types of aphasia

Broca's and Wernicke's areas are connected by a bundle of nerve fibres known as the *arcuate fasciculus*. Damage to this area can result in **conduction aphasia** in which patients have difficulty in repeating words and phrases, though they can utter phrases fluently. They also have difficulty with pronouns and other function words. Comprehension is unaffected.

There are other types of aphasia. For instance, some people suffer brain damage that results in their inability to recognize speech sounds, though they can hear other sounds, while others can recognize speech sounds, but not other sounds. People suffering from various types of aphasia often have difficulty finding words for concepts. This is called **anomia**, and it is something that many of us exhibit to various degrees as we get older.

Modern technology has enabled us to discover more about the workings of the brain. Magnetic Resonance Imaging (MRI) provides pictures of the brain and can reveal infarcts and lesions. It is also possible to stimulate areas of the brain electrically and see what effect that has. One discovery relevant to language is that movement of the body is controlled by the motor cortex and that the part of the motor cortex that lies just behind Broca's area controls articulation.

As research continues, it appears that the neat localization pattern that one might deduce from the discoveries of Broca and Wernicke needs to be modified. There are patients that exhibit symptoms associated with Broca's aphasia without apparent damage to the relevant area and similarly there are patients with symptoms of Wernicke's aphasia without damage to the relevant area. Conversely there are cases where patients have damage to these areas, but do not have the expected language difficulties. Nevertheless, there remains some evidence for localization.

There is ample evidence that the ability to use language is centred in the left hemisphere. Children with lesions to the right hemisphere can acquire language normally, while those with lesions to the left hemisphere display impairment, particularly in their ability to acquire syntax. It sometimes happens that one hemisphere of the brain has to be removed. Humans can survive with just one hemisphere of the brain, but while children with the right hemisphere removed can acquire a full range of language abilities, those with the left hemisphere removed can learn words and their meanings, but they have difficulties in acquiring complex syntax.

Performance errors

Aphasics are of interest to linguists because their problems throw some light on how language is organized in the brain. The same can be said about the **performance errors** or slips that the rest of us make. Some of these slips are discussed below, but first it is worth looking at what we can deduce about language in the brain from reasoning and introspection. It is obvious that a good deal of knowledge consists of files based on sense experience. There are gigabytes of video files in the brain, as well as audio files, taste files, smell files, and touch or texture files. These files are linked. If I think of Uncle Charlie, I might conjure up an image, perhaps an image with the sound of him singing *Champagne Charlie*, with a recollection of the rough touch of the stubble on his chin and his distinctive smell.

The mental lexicon obviously must allow us to go in both directions, from concepts to words, and also from words to concepts. When we speak, we are prompted by some experience based directly or indirectly on sense impressions, or some estimation, deduction, calculation, etc. When we listen to speech, we have to identify morphemes on the basis of their sound, usually with some help from the context, but we have to find the meanings in that part of our mental lexicon that is arranged in terms of sounds.

Difficulties in production

In producing language, the speaker, signer, or writer has to find words for concepts. Let's take a simple example of something concrete and fairly specific, namely a palm tree. In the brain there must be an association of the label *palm tree* with a series of visual memories of palm trees. If I think of a palm tree, I am likely to think of the palm tree in my back yard, the palm tree on the proverbial desert island, palm trees in desert oases, palm trees on tropical shores, and so on. This is illustrated in Figure 14.3, which shows a part of my back garden and a number of other palm tree images in the boxes at the top.

In Figure 14.3 the palm tree and the word *palm tree* are connected by a thick line, a shrub to the right is linked with the label *oleander* by a thin line. The thickness of the lines represents the strength of association between word and referent. I am not likely to hesitate over the name *palm tree* when confronted by an image of one, mentally or visually, but I am likely to hesitate over the name of the less familiar oleander, especially if tired, distracted, or inebriated.

Sometimes you have a concept in your mind, you are certain you know the word for it, but can't think what the word is. As mentioned above, this is anomia. Sometimes you feel you've almost got the word, but you can't manage to get it out. This is the **Tip-of-the-Tongue** phenomenon (TOT). Most people experience anomia and TOTs and the frequency increases with age. The phenomenon occurs most with proper names, that is, people's names and place names. This is understandable when you consider that there are many names of persons and places that come into your field of interest only for a short time. Quite often you can think of some character-istics of the word, such as its beginning or the number of syllables. This is what is illustrated by the label J- - -ia in Figure 14.3. Here we have a shrub

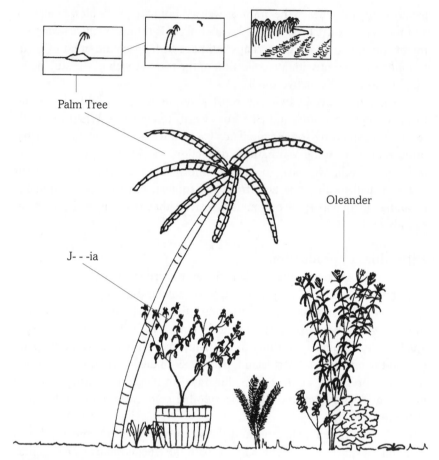

Figure 14.3 Garden.

that is unfamiliar to me. I identified it in an illustrated reference book. When I try to remember the name, which is *Jacobinia* (*Jacobinia carnea,* if you want the whole story), I remember the initial *j-*, the final *-ia*, and the fact that there are five syllables. With a bit of concentration I sometimes manage the whole name.

Many of us have had similar experiences of knowing some of the phono-logical characteristics of a name, particularly the initial consonant, but being unable to dredge up the name. Some of us run through the alphabet in an attempt to trigger the correct name. This works for me as long as the initial is a consonant. My worst failure was with the name *Irwin* where not only is there an initial vowel, but where there is a discrepancy between symbol and sound. Another way to try and prompt the name is to think of contexts or to run video clips of the person or place on your internal video. Unfortunately this does not always work either.

Figure 14.3 also illustrates the fact that words are likely to be associated in semantic fields on the basis of associations between their referents, in this instance a garden. When people speak, they often come out with the wrong word. Many of these errors involve semantically related words. To take a garden example, I have heard *lily* used for *iris*. Other examples of choosing the wrong word in a particular context include *beef* for *pork*, *ludo* for *draughts*, and substituting the name of a younger brother for one's younger son. This last example might involve a kind of symmetry, something quite obvious in errors such as confusing *left* and *right*. It belongs with confusing *clockwise* and *anticlockwise*, and with errors in screwing and unscrewing, where no language is involved. Other reported substitutions involving symmetry include confusing *yesterday* and *tomorrow*, *past* and *future*, *up* and *down*, *deliver* and *take away*, and *father* and *son*. On one occasion I reported to a colleague that I had had a phone call from the father of a nineteenth century pioneer. 'So you're getting calls from the other side, eh?' he replied, alerting me to my substitution of *father* for *son*. Similar to these symmetrical examples is the analogy involved in the following example heard on the radio, *Foxes are a problem when the goats are lambing* (No kidding!).

Now semantic errors such as substituting *beef* for *pork* are hardly surprising. They are to be expected. We would naturally take for granted that words belonging to a semantic field would be candidates for confusion. But it is interesting that when people use the wrong word in a particular context, the substitution quite often bears a strong phonological resemblance to the correct word. These mistakes are known as **malapropisms** after Mrs Malaprop, a character in Sheridan's eighteenth-century play *The Rivals*, who, in aiming to use certain words, particularly learned ones, frequently uses a *malapropos* or inappropriate substitute (hence the name Sheridan has given her). At one point she describes someone as 'the very pineapple of politeness' when she presumably means 'the very pinnacle of politeness', and a young woman is said to be 'as headstrong as an allegory on the banks of Nile'; presumably she means 'alligator'. Other genuine examples of malapropisms include the man suffering from *prostrate* cancer (prostate), the church that offers *immorality* (immortality), the old man suffering from a touch of *vagina* (angina), *inflammatory* liquid ('inflammable' or nowadays 'flammable'), someone wiping the *condescension* (condensation) off the window, *ethic* (ethnic) communities, and storekeepers taking *infantry* (inventory). The confusion of *prostate* and *prostrate* recurs and a number of my students over the years have written about the phoneme *infantry* of a language.

Some substitutions involve phonetic resemblance and also belong to the same semantic field, for example *poppy* for *pansy*, and *Japonica* for *Jacobinia*.

Malapropos substitutions point to a weak link between concept and form with less familiar words, and they are probably a mixture of performance errors and imperfect learning in the first place, resulting in long-term errors rather than slips. The following examples, on the other hand, are clearly slips of the tongue. They are one-off errors that the speaker would seek to correct once aware of the slip, and they are errors the perpetrator is unlikely to repeat. The following all involve transpositions and they are all genuine!

phonemes transposed: Professor *Gatt-Rutter* → 'Professor *Rat-gutter*'

morphemes transposed: 'I wonder if they'll *overstand underseas*' (understand overseas)

'live and *inunterrupted* broadcast'

'there's usually *unthings* finished' [things unfinished]

roots transposed: 'It keeps people in *animated suspension*' (suspended animation)

'... the run-rate [in cricket] would be *freeing* as *flowly* as it is in Pakistan' (flowing as freely)

words transposed: 'They were in great need of an *Arabic female*-speaking doctor.'

Besides transpositions, which are the most common type of speech error, there are also anticipations. Recently I began a sentence with *Mor most years*, when I intended to say 'For most years'. There are also perseverations such as *black bloxes* for 'black boxes'.

Among these, errors of production transpositions are the most common. They are known as **spoonerisms** after the Reverend William Archibald Spooner, Warden of New College, Oxford (1844–1930), who is alleged to have made frequent slips of the tongue of this type turning 'down train' into *town drain* and 'weary benches' into *beery wenches*. Transposition of phonemes usually occurs between corresponding positions (e.g. word initial or syllable nucleus) in lexical words, usually words of the same phrase such as adjective and noun or conjoined nouns, verbs, adjectives, or adverbs. They can occur between grammatical words, though this is less common, but it seems they do not occur between lexical words and grammatical words. The fact that an error at one point can involve a segment further on in the phrase suggests that phrases are assembled in a buffer. For example, suppose I want to say, *We don't stock pins* and I come out with *We don't spock tins*. This indicates that the word *pins* must have been extracted from memory before I attempted to utter *stock*. It is also interesting to note that the allophones that appear are the correct ones for the disordered version. If I had uttered *stock pins*, the /t/ of *stock* would have lacked aspiration and the initial /p/ of *pins* would have been aspirate. In the transposed utterance /p/ is unaspirated and /t/ aspirated. Morphophonemic adjustments are also made after transpositions. If I had said *stin pocks* the plural marker would have been /s/, not /z/ as it would have been with the intended *pins*.

In typing a sentence for this book I typed '*fell* length movie' anticipating the vowel of 'length' in typing 'full'. When we make 'a slip of the pen' in writing or typing, we are normally conscious of the phrase that is already assembled in the buffer. In the case of anticipations in writing (and perhaps in speech), one often becomes conscious that something is wrong upon coming to the point where the anticipated segment should have been. Signers report analogous 'slips of the hand' in sign language.

Difficulties in comprehension

When we are presented with language, we need to go from sounds, letters, or characters, or components of signs to concepts. Let's confine ourselves to sounds. As mentioned in chapter nine, to a great extent we identify words on the basis of context, rather than from the sounds alone. There is experimental evidence to show that people make fewer mistakes in identifying words in sentences than in identifying those same words presented in isolation. We have all had the experience of completely mishearing someone on the basis of mistaken expectations or simply through not being able to guess what the context is. There is a new word for these mishearings and it is **mondegreen**. It was coined by Sylvia Wright in an article 'The Death of Lady Mondegreen', published in *Harper's Magazine* in 1954. She wrote about mishearing the line of a poem 'And laid him on the green' as 'And Lady Mondegreen'.

Mishearings or failures to hear at all are hardly surprising when you consider that rapid speech can contain up to about five words or seventeen phonemes per second. Moreover, a stretch of speech that may contain as many as twenty-five phonemes with careful articulation can be produced rapidly in one second with various reductions. Even in slow speech the difference between some phonemes is not great. Where speech has to compete with noise and where the hearer is not familiar with the speaker's accent, there are added difficulties.

If subjects are asked to read real words and made-up words and then repeat them, they respond more quickly with real words like *camel* than made-up ones like **capel*. This suggests they search for the word in their lexicon and when they find it, they can articulate it. If they are presented with a sequence that is not in their lexicon, they have to go back and use their ability to read sequences of letters, a task that can be somewhat difficult in English because of the irregular relationship between sound and spelling.

word read		concept		word repeated
camel	→	🐫	→	[kæml̩]
*capel	→	?	→	[kæpl̩]

There are forms of aphasia that affect one's ability to write (agraphia). In one type, known as phonological agraphia, subjects can write real words they hear, but not made-up words.

In going from sound to concept we must have something in our brain akin to the printed dictionary, though in phonemic form. However, it is unlikely that words are arranged as in a conventional dictionary. If they were, we would find people sometimes mistakenly picking the next word from the mental dictionary, just as we sometimes pick an adjacent entry in the printed dictionary by mistake. However, mistakes often involve words with similar initials, and there must be some kind of organization along phonemic lines.

Do we find errors of comprehension? Assuming someone has heard a word correctly, do they link it to the wrong concept? If someone hears the word *tiger*, would they think of a lion instead of its handsome striped cousin? It seems that when people hear a word correctly and come up with the wrong concept, the concept is semantically related and the word for it is phonetically similar to the wrongly interpreted word. For instance, I recall somebody hearing the name *Karachi* and saying that it was a region to the north of India. Karachi is in fact a large city in Pakistan (and one-time capital). The confusion is with Kashmir, and the person making the mistake was well aware of the meaning of these two place names of the Subcontinent, both beginning with /k/.

Computers and language

Acoustic analysis of speech

Since the late 1940s it has been possible to produce a spectrographic representation of speech or indeed of other sounds including bird calls or gibbon calls. An example of a sound spectrogram is given in Figure 14.4. Time is read from left to right and calibrated in tenths of a second, and frequency is read from bottom to top with the figures representing 1,000 Hertz (cycles per second), 2,000 Hz, etc. Intensity shows up as blackness.

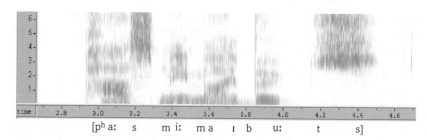

Figure 14.4 Pass me my boots.

The spectrogram shows the sentence *Pass me my boots* spoken by a male speaking modern Received Pronunciation. Let us consider how vowels look first. As explained in chapter eight, a vowel is produced with voice, that is with vibration of the vocal cords. In a mature male speaker the vocal cords vibrate in the range 100–150 Hz, and in females nearly twice that rate. This vibration of the vocal cords shows on the spectrogram in two ways. First of all, as a series of fairly evenly spaced vertical lines, each line representing a burst of energy with each opening of the vocal cords. This can be seen most clearly in the vowels in Figure 14.4. In fact you can count up the number of vertical lines per unit time and calculate the frequency of the vocal cords, which equates to the fundamental frequency in **acoustic** terms. The fundamental frequency is the frequency with which a periodic sound wave repeats itself. The sound produced by the vibration of the vocal cords (i.e. voice) has a concentration of energy at the fundamental frequency and this shows up as a dark band (the voice bar) near the bottom of the spectrogram in vowels and other voiced sounds.

Individual vowels are differentiated by different tongue positions in concert with different degrees of lowering of the jaw and rounding the lips. The air in the vocal tract resonates in response to the vibration of the vocal cords and each configuration of the vocal tract alters the resonance pattern. The resonance pattern consists of a number of bands of energy, or **formants** as they are called, which show up as dark bands on the spectrogram. If the tongue is in the high, front position for [i] then there will be bands of resonance, one at around 300 Hz and another somewhere between 2,000 and 2,500 Hz. On the other hand if the tongue is in the position for a low central vowel, there will be formants at around 600 to 900 Hz and 1,100 to 1,400 Hz. All formant frequencies will be higher in females than males because of the shorter vocal tract, and higher again in children for the same reason.

In the word *me* in Figure 14.4 the first formant is not clearly differentiated from the voice bar, but the second formant can be seen at around 2,000 Hz. Note also the formant transitions, the movement of the formants to and from the positions they occupy in the middle of the vowel. The transitions can be seen clearly in the second formant of [iː] in *me*. You can see it moving up from the lower position it has for [m] and you can see it moving down as the lips close for the following [m]. In the spectrogram the first and second formants of [aː] in *pass* can be seen on either side of the 1,000 Hz mark. They are quite close to one another. The diphthong in the word *my* shows the formants moving rapidly from approximately the [a] position to approximately the [ɪ] position.

The liquids and nasals are voiced and show the voice bar and formant structure, as do the glides [j] (or [y]) and [w].

Stop consonants show up as a vertical striation of brief duration and fricatives show up as a grey smudge. The sibilants are the easiest of the fricatives to pick out. An [s] shows up as a smudgy grey area from about 3,000 Hz upwards and [ʃ] from about 2,500 Hz upwards. The two [s] phones in *Pass me my boots* can be seen clearly in the spectrogram.

With consonants, stops in particular, different places of articulation can be distinguished mostly by the bending of the formants of the adjacent vowel, which reflects the movement of the tongue to or from the position for the consonant. The effect of lip rounding is to lower formants, so labial consonants show a bending from a low position up to the positions for the vowel formants. As noted above, this can be seen in the word *me*. Note also the area immediately after the release of the [p] in *pass*, the area just before the 3-second mark. There is a grey area representing the noise of aspiration with a formant pattern superimposed on it.

Forensic applications of acoustic analysis

As is well known to the general public acoustic phonetics is used in criminal investigation, and many a movie or TV programme features the use of some form of instrumental analysis of speech, especially sound spectrograms under the name of **voiceprints**. In a typical situation the police have a recording of a bomb threat, a kidnapper's demand or an incriminating conversation, and they have one or more suspects they can record, and the task is to say whether the recording and a sample from a suspect match. In fictional drama the experts usually come up with a definite yea or nay, but in real life all an expert can do is talk in probabilistic terms, that is, talk about degrees of likelihood that two recordings came from the same speaker. That is not to say that acoustic analysis is unsatisfactory. Given a good recording, which is often not the case, and given an expert in acoustic phonetics and statistics, acoustic analysis can be telling in forensic speaker identification. Auditory analysis is used as well, but sometimes acoustic analysis can make finer distinctions than can be heard. Our ability to discriminate between voices is highly variable, and depends to a large extent on our familiarity with the regional and social dialect involved or our familiarity with particular speakers. Professor Higgins might very well have been able to assign speakers to different areas of London, but whether he could tell which part of New England a speaker came from would have been problematical.

While acoustic analysis can pick out idiosyncratic characteristics of speech sounds, an important aim of forensic speaker identification is to find as many parameters as possible that are independent of particular speech sounds and show a high degree of variation between speakers and little variation for a particular speaker. The following have proved useful:

- A speaker has no control over the shape of the nasal cavity so the formants of nasals such as [m] and [n] are constant for a particular speaker, and the anatomical differences between speakers are sufficiently great for the frequency of nasal formants to be a good discriminator.
- As mentioned above fundamental frequency reflects the rate of vibration of the vocal cords and is perceived as pitch. The fundamental frequency rises and falls over the course of an utterance, but the long-term average, based on a sample of a minute or more, varies from speaker to speaker and can be of help in identifying an individual.
- A cepstrum is a spectrum in which formants are smoothed out. This minimizes the linguistic component of a vowel, say, and reveals differences between individual speakers. The word *cepstrum* [kɛpstrəm] is an anagram of *spectrum*.
- Long-term spectrum is another useful marker of identity. As explained above, each speech sound has a certain distribution of energy across the spectrum. Vowels, for instance, will have a common peak at the fundamental frequency and then each vowel will have its own profile. If one adds these profiles over a stretch of twenty seconds or more, the differences between vowels will average out, and one will obtain a profile that reflects a mixture of the contribution of the vocal cords and the contribution of the anatomy of the vocal tract, a profile that reflects characteristics of the speaker.

Voice recognition

It is becoming increasingly common to encounter systems that are accessed by voice or operated by voice. Many security systems seek to identify legitimate users by voice. **Voice recognition** or **speaker recognition** is used to screen users attempting to access telephone banking, telephone shopping, confidential databases, and entry to secure premises. In some cases the computer seeks to verify whether you are who you claim to be and matches your sample with a pre-recorded sample. In other cases the computer matches a sample of your speech with pre-recorded samples of all those with legitimate access. In some instances those seeking entry are required to enter a specific text, namely a single password or a password sequence. All of these security systems depend on analysis of the acoustic properties of speech, in particular they are designed to concentrate on those characteristics that pick out particular speakers. This means that they act like an automated forensic phonetician and use techniques such as the cepstrum or smoothed spectrum mentioned above. Incidentally, they can all be circumvented by the illegitimate user using a recorded sample from a legitimate user, so passwords remain important.

Speech synthesis

In acoustic terms speech sounds can be specified in terms of energy present at particular frequencies for particular durations as displayed in Figure 14.4, so it is not hard to see how speech sounds can be synthesized. **Speech synthesis** is simpler than speech analysis in that one does not have to deal with rapid speech, poor recording, poor articulation, or a variety of accents, though of course one can synthesize different accents and rates of utterance. One method is 'formant synthesis', which involves specifying the amount of energy present at specified frequencies for specified durations. This is synthesis from scratch, as it were. This method provides a useful means of converting text to speech (see below). The other method is 'concatenative synthesis', which starts with recorded speech and extracts segments and recombines them as needed. This produces a more natural result.

Sometimes we hear a synthesized voice when we ring for weather reports, airline schedules, stock market prices, and the like. When a synthesized voice asks you questions, it can give the impression you are talking to a real human, but in fact you are dealing with a speech recognition system that seeks to extract linguistic information. The voice from your bank might ask you what kind of enquiry you are making or what kind of transaction you want to make. If you say, 'I'd like to pay my credit card bill' or just 'credit card', the system is designed to recognize the key words 'credit card' in your utterance irrespective of whether you are female or male and hopefully irrespective of your accent. The voice can then ask you for your credit card number, your password, the accounts you wish to pay and withdraw from, the amount you wish to pay, and finally give you a receipt number. Some of the utterances from the synthetic voice are short fixed texts such as *Please wait while your request is being processed.* In some instances there is speech synthesis combined with language generation. Such systems have a parser (see below) to analyse the grammar of input sentences and can use the same grammar to generate appropriate replies, at least within certain constraints.

Text-to-speech

A different manifestation of speech synthesis is found with text-to-speech systems designed to turn written words into speech. Computers can read texts aloud for the blind, or allow those without speech to type words into a computer for conversion to speech. At present there is software commercially available for converting e-text to speech. The text can be in various formats such as Microsoft Word or pdf. E-mail and web pages can also be read. There is a choice of a dozen or so languages and you can hear a male or female voice, and you can vary the rate of utterance. Text can be saved as audio files such as MP3 or WAV for your CD player or Ipod. There is even a free version of text-to-speech software available on the web.

Speech recognition (speech-to-text)

Speech recognition refers to the ability of a device to interpret spoken words. Speech recognition is not entirely separate from voice recognition in that the speech recognition system has to cope with the difference between female and male voices and a variety of accents. Speech recognition systems that can convert speech into text have come into use over the last decade, and there have been rapid improvements in the quality. They have the potential to save an enormous amount of time, particularly for two-finger typists. Moreover, you do not have to dictate directly to the computer, you can record remotely onto any kind of recording device. Speech-to-text systems make use of the grammatical context and frequency to identify words. They can also learn to adjust to your particular pronunciation, and they can learn from their mistakes. If the machine types *dessert* instead of *desert* and you tell the machine it has made an error, it is more likely to hear the distinction more accurately next time. Some systems require discrete words, but the latest systems can cope with continuous speech and claim speeds of up to 160 words per minute with 99 per cent accuracy. Speech-to-text systems also respond to voice commands.

There are templates available for specialized formats, where the speaker fills in the data required for specified fields, and there are specialized vocabularies (jargons) available for medicine, the law, and so on.

Machine translation

With the first computers in the 1940s came the idea that they could be used for machine translation. In theory you would feed in a text in the source language and the computer would produce a text in the target language. During the 1950s and early 1960s most of the research was funded by military and intelligence agencies in the United States and the major aim was to translate Russian into English. However, it was found to be more expensive than using human translators and considerably less accurate.

For most pairs of languages it is obviously not possible to translate word-for-word since the two languages are likely to differ in word order, word structure, idiom, and lexical ambiguity. Most methods of machine translation involve some kind of morpho-syntactic analysis, starting with parsing, (i.e. assigning a part-of-speech label to each word). From the parsed string a phrase structure can be built up. If the program contains a rule that a *Noun Phrase* consists of *Determiner (Adjective) Noun*, then a sequence such as *the cunning fox* consisting of *Determiner Adjective Noun* will be assigned an NP structure, and so on. Another approach emerged in the 1990s, an empirical-statistical approach based on a large corpus (body of text) and its translation in another language. The computer is set the task of learning which words and phrases correspond, committing them to memory, and then using this knowledge to translate newly encountered text. This method depends on the availability of a large bilingual corpus and cannot operate on any subject matter that was not in the corpus.

Since the 1990s machine translation has been widely used by government agencies and large commercial enterprises, primarily for technical literature. There are also software packages available, some specifically for translating e-mail and webpages, and there are online automated translation services. These systems can translate in either direction between a dozen or so languages. The quality of output cannot match that of a human translator, but it is generally considered acceptable for most purposes. A major problem for automatic translation is the resolution of lexical ambiguity, which often requires considerable general knowledge. Some systems seek to overcome the problem statistically on the basis of neighbouring text.

Here is an example of a translation from Spanish to English. The first translation below the Spanish text is the human translation and the second is a translation made by an online translating program. The unsatisfactory parts of the machine version are in bold.

La cultura de un país o grupo se puede ver como un flujo continuo, con energías creativas de nuevos talentos contribuyendo al cambio. En un momento determinado, la cultura es una compleja amalgama de glorias pasadas y de tendencias de vanguardia.

TRANSLATION
The culture of any country or group is best understood as a sort of continuous flow, with the creative energies of new talents contributing to change. At any single moment, culture is a complex amalgam of past glories and the current avant-garde.

MACHINE TRANSLATION
The culture of a country or group can be seen like a continuous flow, with creative energies of new talents contributing to the change. **In a while determined**, *the culture is a complex amalgam of* **last** *glories and* **tendencies of vanguard.**

Sources and further reading

The information on *mondegreen* was taken from the Wikipedia entry on the Web. Of the slips of the tongue the first is from a professor of history, the second from an emeritus professor of linguistics, and the rest were collected by Gavan Breen from the radio. The malapropisms were collected by Gavan Breen or me, plus one reported in Aitchison, *Words in the Mind*.

A comprehensive yet compact coverage of aphasia is to be found in Pratt and Whitaker, 'Aphasia syndromes' in volume 1 of the *Elsevier Encyclopedia of Language and Linguistics*, edited by K. Brown, and there is a lot of information available on the Web under headings such as *aphasia, brain, Broca*, and *Wernicke*. For further information on acoustic phonetics see Ladefoged's *A Course in Phonetics*. For forensic applications of phonetics a comprehensive up-to-date source is Rose's *Forensic Speaker Identification* (2002). For information on *text-to-speech* and *speech-to-text* just type these titles into your search engine. Also try *speech synthesis*. Advances in this area are occurring all the time and so the Web is the best source of up-to-date information.

Problems

1 Sometimes you have a concept in mind, you know the word for it, but you can't find the word in your mental lexicon. Sometimes it is on the 'tip of your tongue'. Think of examples. Do you have strategies for getting around the problem? Perhaps uttering other words in the same semantic field, which might prompt you or your audience to come up with the sought-after word. Perhaps using a description of the referent whose name you can't come up with, e.g. 'the one who played M in *Casino Royale*'.

2 Can you recall any slips of the tongue you have made, perhaps some recent ones or perhaps some embarrassing ones you remember from well back? Were they spoonerisms?

3 What about mondegreens? Can you recall examples? Most of us at one time or another have completely misheard something that has been said.

4 Malapropisms are not uncommon. Try to think of examples and try to estimate whether they stem from long term misidentification of word and meaning or whether they are just errors of production.

5 Think about thinking. To what extent do you think you think in terms of images and other memories of sensory impressions and to what extent do you think in words?

15. The origin of language

Thanks to words, we have been able to rise above the brutes; and thanks to words, we have often sunk to the level of the demons.   **Aldous Huxley**

The origin of language is obscure and the question has led to a lot of speculation. We will say something about it in this final chapter, but we do not promise anything like a satisfactory answer. Although we will obviously never be in a position to observe the origin of language in humans, we can put ourselves in a position to make informed hypotheses by looking at recurrent historical changes, the development of language in children, and the development of pidgin and creole languages. Child language acquisition was covered in chapter thirteen and the nature of pidgins and creoles is described below.

Animal communication

There are numerous reports of animals communicating with their conspecifics and there are claims by pet owners that their dogs, cats, or whatever can understand them. However, it is clear that communication among animals always involves selecting from a small repertoire of signals that are basically innate (though they can be fine tuned by learning), holistic in nature rather than being made up of components that could be combined in other sequences (though some bird songs are an exception), and largely involuntary and uttered in response to a stimulus such as fear or a type of danger. Being tied to a stimulus, animal signals lack displacement. Animals cannot communicate about future or past dangers, only about a clear and present danger. One case of apparently clever communication has received a lot of publicity in the literature and that is the ability of worker bees to report the size and location of nectar. On finding a suitable source of nectar, worker bees return to the hive and report their findings by aligning their body in the direction of the nectar and executing a dance the vigour of which indicates how far away the nectar is. But these bees can only respond to the latest find. They cannot compare finds, reminisce about great finds of the past, or imagine a glorious future find.

Claims that animals understand human speech do not stand up to scrutiny. Animals such as dogs and horses can respond with various degrees of accuracy to a small inventory of commands. Horses, for instance, respond to

whoa! and *giddyup!* but they treat these utterances as unanalysed wholes and intonation and context are important. When my neighbour's dog, Holly, comes in to play, she responds to my command of *fetch*, but she also responds when I say *betch* or even *letch*. Where horses and dogs have been taught tricks such as counting, it has been shown that they respond to the trainer's body language. The trainer says, 'Count to five!" and the horse taps the ground while watching the trainer who remains tensed, like any quizmaster, until the correct number of taps has been executed.

In terms of biological classification humans are primates. We belong to the same family as various monkey-like creatures. Our closest cousins are chimpanzees and bonobos (a pygmy species of chimp) and it is thought that humans and chimpanzees diverged from a common ancestor about five million years ago. Chimpanzees and other members of the ape family have a system of communication typical of other animals, namely a fixed repertoire of signals, though they have rather more, some species having a repertoire of over thirty signals. Attempts have been made to teach chimpanzees human language with interesting results. The first attempts, dating back to the 1930s, were aimed at teaching chimps to speak, but these experiments were unsuccessful as the non-human primates do not have a vocal apparatus capable of producing speech sounds. The chimps could, however, respond to over 100 words.

In later trials American Sign Language was used and a female chimpanzee called Washoe learned over 100 signs and could combine them. She could sign *open food drink*, for instance, in asking for access to the fridge, and she produced some novel combinations such as *water bird* for 'duck'. Another chimpanzee called Sarah was taught with a set of plastic shapes, each representing a word. She could carry out instructions such as the one contained in the curious 'sentence' *Sarah insert banana pail apple dish*, in other words she could put the banana in the pail (bucket) and the apple in the dish. She certainly knew the meaning of the individual words, but it is uncertain that she understood any syntax beyond contiguity (associating words with their neighbours). Another chimpanzee, Lana, was taught via a set of symbols on a large computer keyboard with similar results. She could combine symbols to form compounds, including *orange Coke* for Fanta, and what appear to be simple sentences. In a later trial of this system with a bonobo called Matata, Matata's adopted baby, Kanzi, picked up the system without being taught and acquired an inventory of over 250 words. Kanzi also appeared to be able to understand human speech to some extent.

In sum it appears that chimpanzees can learn to associate symbols with referents, they can produce combinations that look like compounds or short, simple sentences, and they appear to be able to interpret simple sentences. They do not learn fast and they have error rates of around 20 per cent, and it is uncertain that they have syntax. Their ability is similar to that of a two-year-old child. When children are just beyond the two-word stage, it is not certain that the sequences of words they produce have genuine syntax.

Pidgins

Where people with different languages find themselves in contact they attempt to communicate with a mixture of gestures and telegraphic speech, that is, speech consisting almost entirely of bare lexical forms and few function forms. Suppose a nine-month pregnant woman with just a few words of English discovers her waters breaking in an English-speaking country. She might approach a local and say something like: *Where hospital? Baby come* (pointing to her distended abdomen). *You take me hospital? Quick. Baby come now.* During the centuries of European colonization native peoples around the world were confronted with unfamiliar European languages and often found themselves forced into contact with speakers of other non-European languages as slaves or indentured workers. Telegraphic forms of language came into use in various areas and these are known as **pidgins**. The term 'pidgin' refers to any limited system of communication that arises among people without a common language.

Pidgins are created as a makeshift means of communication. They tend to have an unmarked phonology, with common vowels such as /i/, /e/, /a/, /o/, and /u/, open syllables, and few if any consonant clusters, an analytic grammar with few if any bound forms, and a limited vocabulary. Many pidgins become the major input, or even the sole input, to future generations. When this happens the pidgin is expanded into a full language to meet the communicative needs of speakers and such a new language developed from a pidgin is called a **creole**. In the colonial context pidgins usually took most of their vocabulary from a European language. Haitian Creole French developed from a pidgin form of French in Haiti and Solomon Islands Pijin developed from a pidgin form of English. Note in this case that the term 'pijin' in the name is a misnomer as this is a creole, just as Tok Pisin is in Papua New Guinea.

Unfortunately creole languages are often considered inferior or bastardized forms of whatever language they take their lexicon from. This is partly because they sound childish and partly because of the low social standing of their speakers in the eyes of speakers of standard languages. They sound childish because of their relatively simple phonology and their lack of inflection.

Creole languages are of great theoretical interest since they appear to provide examples of how grammar can be created. Creole languages show remarkable similarities, which would appear to provide evidence of how human language creativity works, but it is unfortunate that most of the examples of Creole languages treated in the literature are based, at least lexically, on languages of western Europe, and furthermore there is evidence that they are not completely independent. Many of them contain words such as *pikanini/picaninny* 'child' and *savi/savvy* 'to know, understand' from Portuguese, the Portuguese being the earliest European colonizers beginning in west Africa in the fifteenth century. We can probably put these concerns aside as there are several pidgins and creoles that developed outside the context of European colonization such as Fanagolo (based on Bantu languages including Xhosa and Zulu) and Pidgin Swahili in Africa, Chinook Jargon in North America, and Hiri Motu in Papua-New Guinea. There are some pidgins that are now extinct. These include Russenorsk (Russian and Norwegian) and Mobilian Jargon (Choctaw and Chickasaw). All of these exhibit the same properties as the pidgins and creoles that emerged in the context of European colonization.

Here is an example from a creole of northern Australia. As with other English-based creoles, there is a simple, regular grammar. There is no inflection for case, gender, or number. *Bilong(a)* from English 'belong' corresponds to English *of* and the possessive *'s*, and *longa* or *alonga* from English 'along' serves as a general locative marker. Adjectives are marked by *-pela* 'fellow' or *-wan* 'one'.

> Dog bilong yu baak longa nait, i nogudwan.
> 'Your dog barks at night. He's bad (no-good-one).'

There is no inflection for tense or aspect. In this creole, as in many other English-based creoles, past time is indicated by *bin* and there are various forms such as *gona*, *usda*, and *labda* to indicate future time, obligation, etc. These forms are based on English 'going to', 'used to', and 'will have to', but are treated as single, unanalysed words. Transitive verbs end in *-im* from English 'him', but significantly 'give' is *gibit* from English 'give it'.

> Yu labda kilim dog. I baak-baak longa mi.
> 'You must hit the dog. He keeps barking at me.'
>
> Yu bin gibit me mit. You gud longa mi.
> 'You gave me meat. You are good to me.'

Words taken from English do not always have the same meaning as they do in English. *Kilim* from 'kill' can mean 'hit' or 'kill', the word covering the same range as in various vernaculars.

One final point. I should add that though there is agreement among linguists that creoles derive from pidgins, some linguists claim that some creoles did not arise from a pidgin stage, but through a kind of watering down of the European input over successive generations.

The origin of language

As mentioned above, humans are primates. Chimpanzees are our closest relatives and it is thought that humans and chimpanzees diverged from a common ancestor about five million years ago. Humans developed into creatures that walk upright rather than clambering through trees and their toes lost their flexibility. Among the larger mammals humans are relatively slow and weak, but their brain power developed enormously. About 1.5 million years ago they were making fire and wearing animal skins to compensate for loss of body hair. Much closer to the present, at around 70,000 years ago our ancestors were sewing clothing and building shelters, they were also producing ornaments, sculptures, and paintings. They had systems of belief about the nature of the world, beliefs of a type that we might term religious. It is fairly safe to say that the existence of art and religion provides indirect evidence that humans of this period had fully developed language. Moreover, given that there are no genuinely primitive languages in the world today, apart from pidgins, it is likely that fully fledged language has been in use for tens of thousands of years. Language probably developed slowly over millennia, but when it began and when it reached maturity is difficult to pinpoint. Although there are no records available, we can say something about the order in which features of language developed on the basis of child language, pidgins, and creoles, and recurrent historical developments.

Over the last five million years prehumans gained greater and greater cognitive powers, including a specific ability to learn language effortlessly over the first decade of their lives. Significantly, human offspring mature slowly and need looking after for this long period of maturation. One cognitive skill that developed in humans was the ability to associate a large number of arbitrary symbols with referents. If we want to talk about thousands of referents such as leopards, elephants, rainbows, water, grass, night, killing, eating, burning, and so on, we need thousands of symbols and, as pointed out in chapter one, we compose these symbols from components. In the case of speech we combine stops, fricatives, nasals, vowels, and so on. In the case of sign language we combine the shapes, orientations, locations, and movements of the hand. Non-human primates cannot produce speech sounds, so at some stage this ability must have evolved. However, all primates have hands that can be used for signing, so once the mental apparatus that enabled language was in place, our human-like ancestors would not have lacked a medium, and it may be that sign language pre-dates spoken language. This raises the question of why spoken language developed, so one needs to think of the advantages of speech over signing, namely that it allows communication out of line of sight and in the dark, and it is hands-free.

Humans have vocal equipment superior to that of chimpanzees with fine, subtle control of the breath stream, the lips, tongue, velum, and glottis. There are estimates that our ancestors would have developed the breath control for speech around 1.6 million years ago and that a fully developed vocal apparatus would have been in place around 400,000 years ago. However, spoken language could have developed with an inferior vocal apparatus; all that is needed is the ability to produce a small number of different sounds that can be strung in sequences. Once language began, there would have been a selectional advantage in having an improved vocal apparatus, so it is not surprising that humans have developed such a finely tuned system. It may be that the vocal apparatus was adapted to speech production before there was the cognitive development that led to language. It may have been useful in mating calls or it may have developed as a skill for singing or chanting that gave satisfaction and provided entertainment. Either way better vocalization would have had a selectional advantage.

Phonology

The early speech of children provides a likely scenario for the first human speech. The first stage is likely to have been syllabic with unmarked syllable types. A consonant-vowel syllable is universal, and so is a vowel like [a] as *Mamma mia*, which merely requires an open mouth. If one starts with the mouth closed, one gets [ba] or [pa]. If one lowers the velum at the beginning of the syllable, one produces [ma]. If one partially closes the mouth, one can produce a mid-high or high vowel and produce [bi] and [mi]. As we noted earlier, these syllable types are prominent in the development of a child's phonological system. Even with an inventory of say [ba], [ma], [da], [na], [bi], [mi], [di], and [ni], one could produce 64 disyllabic words, 512 trisyl-labic words. Throw in a third vowel [u] and add a velar place of articulation and you have 18 syllables yielding 324 disyllabic words and 5832 trisyllabic words, not that language is likely to have developed in such a way that every possible combination of syllables was used. The point is that a syllabic system is all that is necessary to produce a large number of words. Some languages have small phoneme inventories and only open syllables. Pirahã (in Brazil) has only seven consonants and three vowels, and Hawaiian has eight con-sonants and five vowels, though in both languages vowels can be long or short. Pirahã also has two tones.

If human language began with just a few vowels, we might ask how did it acquire more vowels. There is one well-attested way in which a language acquires new vowels and that is where the allophones lose their conditioning and come to exist in their own right. Consider the following pair of French words:

pas 'step' [pɑs]   → [pɑ]
pan 'piece' [pɑ̃n]   → [pɑ̃]

In French a range of syllable-final consonants have been lost as illustrated with *pas* 'a step', which has lost a final /s/ and is now pronounced [pɑ]. Where a nasal occurs in the coda of a syllable, some nasalization of the preceding vowel usually occurs. When a syllable-final /n/ was lost, the nasalization of the vowel remained, thus giving rise to a phonemically distinct nasalized vowel.

Typology confirms what we would postulate for emergent spoken language in the species. Certain sounds are more common in the world's languages, and it is typically the case that the less common ones occur only with the common ones. Nasalized vowels occur only alongside purely oral vowels, and, as we have just seen, they can arise from purely oral vowels. Typology suggests emerging spoken language would probably have had a series of stops, a series of nasals, perhaps a liquid ([l] or [r]), and probably two glides ([j] and [w]). In many cases we know that tones developed from systems without tones. This may be general. In any case tones are a marked feature and are unlikely to have been present in the first speech.

Morpho-syntax

Syntax cannot exist without words. It is reasonable to assume words came before syntax and that one-word utterances came first as with children. The first words would presumably have included words for certain animals and plants, perhaps words for 'sun', 'moon', 'stars', 'water', and so on, words that would figure as nouns once syntax developed. There would also have been words like our verbs, words for 'kill', 'trap', 'dig', 'go', and 'urinate'.

Two-word utterances of the type *water cold* or *kill snake* would not have required anything that could be called syntax. *Water cold* could be interpreted only as a statement about the temperature of water, or perhaps as a question if uttered with rising intonation. *Kill snake* would be interpreted according to context as a command (*You kill the/a snake*), a statement of intention (*I will kill the/a snake*), or a report (*She killed the/a snake*). Quite a number of longer utterances could be interpreted without syntax, as we noted in discussing child language acquisition and the teaching of languages to chimpanzees. A 'pile of words' such as *man, dog, stick, hit* will be interpreted as 'Man hit dog with stick' and *woman, grass-seed, find, not* will be interpreted as 'Woman didn't find grass-seed'.

Locational words are fundamental and these must have been present in early stages of language. These derive from two sources. One source is concrete nouns, especially words for body parts such as *face, back,* and *bottom.* (Consider English '*facing* the consequences', 'at the *back* of the room', 'at the *bottom* of the drawer'.) The other source is verbs so that verbs for 'go', for instance, become prepositions meaning 'to' as with Nupe *lō* (see also p. 218).

Where locational words with meanings like 'in' and 'on' are used as two-place predicates, there is motivation for word order to make distinctions such as between 'dish in water' and 'water in dish'. This results in the location words having a fixed position as prepositions (or postpositions) so that a phrase is formed.

The next step in the growth of syntax comes when one puts one phrase inside another to form the hierarchical structures we are familiar with. Where one puts a constituent as a dependent of a constituent of the same type, we have recursion. For instance, if we use a prepositional or postpositional phrase to specify the location of a noun in a prepositional phrase, we can say things like *in the bin under the desk near the window in the front office.*

Local postpositions and prepositions can undergo two further changes. One is that they may become affixes. The other development is from concrete to abstract. In Spanish the preposition *a* means 'to' or 'at' as in *Llegamos a la*

estación 'We arrive at the station', but it has come to be used for a specific human object as in *María admira a Carlos* 'Maria admires Carlos', where its function is purely grammatical. In English the preposition *by* meaning 'near' developed the sense of 'by means of' and then became the marker of the demoted subject of the passive (see chapter two). The functional preposition *of* derives from the lexical preposition *off*.

Given two recurrent developments, namely free forms becoming bound, and abstract, functional forms developing from concrete ones, we can say that in early stages of language it is unlikely there were affixes to distinguish subject and object. Word order may have been used. In the vast majority of languages, whether word order is grammatically free or constrained, the subject generally precedes the verb. This device may have been present in early language.

Languages usually have affixes for tense and/or aspect. Where these notions are expressed by free forms, we are often in a position to see their lexical origins. As we saw in chapter twelve lexical verbs such as *have* ('I have a dog') and *will* ('She willed it to happen') have come to be used as auxiliary verbs. In Latin the lexical verb *habere* 'to have' came to be used as an auxiliary and in the Romance languages it is reflected as a suffix in the future and conditional forms of the verb. In Italian, for instance, the future tense was formed by a combination of the infinitive and reflexes of *habere*. *Dormirai* 'you shall sleep' derives from *dormir(e)* 'to sleep' plus *(h)ai* 'you have'.

A majority of languages have person–number agreement for subject as in Italian (examples in chapter five). Some languages also show agreement for object as well, as in Swahili (also illustrated in chapter five), and a smaller number again show agreement for indirect object. The origin of person–number agreement on verbs is fairly obvious and would appear to arise from the incorporation of unstressed pronouns in the verb. The origin of these inflections in Indo-European is obscure, but an example of how a pronoun can be captured by the verb can be found in Old English, or at least in the southern West Saxon dialect. The second person singular inflection was -*st* as in *Thū lufast* 'thou lovest' or *Thū rīdst* 'thou ridest', these -*st* forms being familiar from Shakespeare (*thou lovest, thou ridest*). The expected inflection, as found in northern dialects and other Germanic languages, is -*s*. The -*t* derives from the unstressed pronoun *thū* (*th* representing [ð]) having been placed immediately after the verb so that an original **rīdesðu* became **rīdestu* then *rīdest* and later *rīdst*. When this happened, the -*t* became part of the verb inflection, but *thū* was still retained as the second person singular pronoun.

The other type of agreement is found in noun phrases. It is a feature of some languages, including Indo-European languages. In Ancient Greek, for instance, the determiner and adjective agree with the noun in number, gender, and case, as in *tōn kalōn rhodōn* 'of the beautiful roses'. In Latin the words that correspond to determiners and adjectives in English do not have a fixed position in relation to the noun they modify and they can even be separated from the noun they modify. For instance, Cicero writes . . . *magnam capio voluptatem* . . . 'I take great pleasure' with *magnam* 'great' separated from *voluptatem* 'pleasure' by the verb *capio* 'I take'. This is not uncommon in languages with case marking. Suppose we assume that the practice of using separate nominals for what we think of as parts of a single noun phrase was an earlier practice than placing such words together. Where the words are separate phrases they naturally take their own marking. If they are then juxtaposed, one would have apparent agreement, which could then develop into genuine agreement of modifiers within a phrase agreeing with the head.

Summary
Though we have no direct knowledge of stages in the development of language, and though we cannot be too specific about the time at which fully-fledged language appeared, we can say something about the likely order of development. When humans developed the mental capacity for language, they would have had a medium, namely signs, and it may be that sign language preceded spoken language. When speech did develop, what we see to be the unmarked alternatives are likely to have preceded the marked ones. In morpho-syntax the first stage is likely to have been lexical, with nouns and verbs. Locational words would have appeared early. Function forms would have developed from concrete ones, especially locational ones. Early language would have been analytic, since bound forms are mostly derived from free forms.

It is generally assumed that humans developed in northeast Africa. This raises the question of whether there was ever just one human language. This is a possibility, but it is likely that language developed here and there, and that there was a time when it was more advanced in some communities than others. If this were the case, we can bet the possessors of language regarded the dumb as inferior and they would have treated them badly. It is often said that the distinguishing feature of humans is language, but another distinguishing feature is a proclivity towards maiming, enslaving and killing members of their own species, often in very large numbers. On that sombre note I conclude my description of language.

Sources and further reading

For pidgins and creoles see Todd, *Pidgins and Creoles*. For origins of language Aitchison, *The Seeds of Speech*, is easy reading as is Burling, *The Talking Ape*. Succinct but more demanding is chapter eight of Jackendoff, *Foundations of Language*.

Glossary of terms

ablative case. The **case** that expresses the notion of *from*.

accent. 1. 'Accent' is a synonym for **stress** or for a mark indicating where stress falls as in Italian *città* 'city'. It is also used for marks indicating vowel quality in French as in *état* 'state' where the 'acute accent' indicates [e] or *lèvre* 'lip' where the grave accent indicates [ɛ].

accent. 2. The overall pronunciation of a variety of language, which serves to identify the speaker as coming fom a particular region or class or as being a native speaker of another language.

accidental gap. See **systematic gap**.

accusative case. A **case** whose principal function is to mark the **direct object**.

acoustic. 'Acoustic' refers to sound waves. Speech sounds can be studied from the articulatory stage (production), the acoustic stage (sound waves), or the auditory stage (hearing).

acronym. A word made up by pronouncing a set of initials as if it spelt a word, e.g. *scuba* (self-contained underwater breathing apparatus). The term sometimes includes **alphabetisms**.

active (voice). See **voice 2**.

addition. Besides its general sense 'addition' applies particularly to the adding of a speech sound to a word. A /d/ has been added to Old English *thunor* to yield modern *thunder*.

address terms. Words or phrases used in addressing someone such as *you there!, madam, Your Highness*.

addressee. The person to whom a communication is directed, the 'second person' as opposed to the 'first person' (the speaker) and the 'third person' (other(s)).

adjective. A word class expressing properties or qualities of entities. An adjective may be attributive (*bright feathers*) or **predicative** (*The feathers are bright*).

adjective phrase. A phrase with an **adjective** as **head**, e.g. *very bad, quite awful*.

adjunct. An optional **dependent phrase** or **clause** not representing an **argument**, e.g. the **prepositional phrase** in *On Sundays we swim*.

adverb. A broad word class taking in words that modify **verbs, adjectives, prepositions, postpositions**, or other adverbs. The underlined words in the following are all adverbs: _Interestingly, she proceeded quite quickly right to the most contentious issues._

adverb phrase. A phrase with an **adverb** as **head**, e.g. _very swiftly, rather dangerously._

adverbial. An 'adverbial' element expresses a function frequently expressed by an **adverb** as with the underlined parts of the following: _When she goes to Santa Fe, she always stays three weeks._

affix. Cover term for **prefix, suffix,** and **infix.**

affricates. Speech sounds consisting of a **stop** plus **fricative,** e.g. the 'ch' sound in _chin._

agent. The 'agent' of the **verb** is the entity that performs an action: _She spoke well, She boiled the water._

agglutinating/agglutinative language. A language like Turkish in which bound **morphemes** are readily separable, i.e. there is no **fusion.**

agreement. The marking of the **person, number,** and sometimes **gender** or class of **arguments** on the verb is usually referred to as 'agreement', as in Avar (Northeast Caucasian) _W-as w-akér-ula_ 'The boy runs' where _w-_ is the masculine **gender** marker on _as_ 'child' and the verb _akér._ This use of _w-_ on the verb cross-references the noun _w-as._ The term 'agreement' or 'concord' also refers to **dependents** in **noun phrases** matching the **head noun** in **case, number,** or **gender,** as in Latin _Illa bona femina vidit illos malos viros_ 'That good woman saw those bad men'.

allative. A **case** expressing 'to'.

allomorph. See **morpheme.**

allophone. See **phoneme.**

allusion, allusive language. 'Allusive language' involves a choice of words that evokes some cultural reference or uses a piece of text to convey meaning, e.g. saying 'Lend me your ears' from Shakespeare's _Julius Caesar_ instead of 'Listen up!'

alphabet. A set of symbols for representing **phonemes** in written form.

alphabetism. The use of initials for the full phrase (_tlc_ for 'tender loving care'), particularly with **proper names,** e.g. _CIA, FBI._ 'Initialism' is an alternative term.

alveolar. Speech sounds made with the tongue touching or near the upper alveolar (gum) ridge are 'alveolar', e.g. [t], [d], and [n] in English.

amelioration. This refers to a word taking on a 'better' sense as with _urbane,_ which literally means 'urban', but came to mean 'exhibiting sophistication and refinement'.

analogy. Besides its general sense 'analogy' has a particular application in **morphological change** where a word changes form to match a form found in another word or words, as with American _dove_ as the past tense of _dive_ on the analogy of words like _drove._

analytic language. Ideally an 'analytic language' is one in which all **morphemes** are free. All languages are 'synthetic' to some extent, having some **bound morphemes**, but Chinese in all its varieties has few bound morphemes and is relatively close to analytic.

anaphoric. A form that refers 'up' or 'back' to an entity specified earlier in discourse is 'anaphoric' (Greek for 'up-bearing'). In the passage '*John woke up late. He had forgotten to set his alarm.*', *he* and *his* are anaphoric since they refer to *John*.

anomia. The inability to recall the word for a concept.

antecedent. The form from which an **anaphoric** form takes its **reference**. The term is used regularly in connection with **relative clauses**. In the sentence '*The woman who chaired the meeting wore a dark suit.*' the phrase *the woman* is the antecedent of *who*.

antonym, antonymous, antonymy. Words or **morphemes** that have opposite meaning are 'antonyms'. *Tall* and *short* are 'gradable antonyms' (there can be degrees of height). *Dead* and *alive* are 'complementary antonyms' (you are either one or the other).

aphasia. Language disorder resulting from damage to the brain.

argot. An informal style of language characterized by words and expressions largely restricted to an in-group and designed to be obscure to others.

argument. See **predicate**.

article. The word *the* is called the 'definite article' and the word *a/an* is called the 'indefinite article'. In English these are part of the **determiner** class.

aspect. Verbs are often marked to show a distinction between an activity or process that is completed (**perfect** or **perfective**) as in *He has been swindled* and one that is ongoing or continuous (**imperfect, imperfective**) as in *He is being swindled*. This is a distinction of 'aspect'.

assimilation. A change in the pronunciation of a **phoneme** so that it becomes similar to or the same as a neighbouring phoneme, e.g. the /n/ in *pancake* becomes /ŋ/ before /k/.

attributive adjective. See **adjective**.

auxiliary verb. A sub-class of verb with the grammatical characteristics of a **verb** (e.g. marked for tense) but being functional rather than lexical. In *Donna has completed her assignment* the word *has* is the 'auxiliary verb' and *completed* is the **lexical** verb (in past **participle** form).

babbling. The first speech-like sounds produced by babies with repeated open syllables.

back. (Of **vowels**) made with the hump of the tongue towards the back of the mouth.

back formation. A word formed by the removal of an **affix** is said to be 'back-formed', e.g. *enthuse* from *enthusiasm*, *stage-manage* from *stage manager*.

The process is called 'back formation' and the results of the process are also called 'back formations'.

bilabial. A speech sound made with both lips, e.g. [p], [b], and [m].

blend, blending. Blending refers to taking the first part of one word and last part of another to form a new word as with *smog* (smoke + fog) or *brunch* (breakfast + lunch).

borrowing. The adoption of a linguistic feature, especially a word, from another **dialect** or language. The borrowed form may be referred to as a 'borrowing', so we could say *cliché* is a borrowing (or a loan word) from French.

bound, bound morpheme. A bound form cannot occur on its own as with **prefixes** such as *pre-* and **suffixes** such as *-ize*.

Broca's area, Broca's aphasia. 'Broca's area' is a part of the left hemisphere of the brain where the ability to express language is centred. Damage to this area results in 'Broca's aphasia' or 'expressive aphasia' where patients have difficulty in initiating speech and maintaining fluency.

calque. A 'calque' or 'loan translation' is a word or phrase using native **morphemes** but translating a word or phrase in another language morpheme for morpheme. For instance, *marriage of convenience* is modelled on French *mariage de convenance*.

caregiver speech. See **motherese**.

case. A system of marking **dependent nouns** for the type of relationship they bear to their **heads**, and the members of such a system, e.g. **nominative**, **accusative**, **genitive**, etc. Originally applied to inflectional systems, but sometimes used of other systems such as systems of **postpositions** as in Japanese.

case marker. An **affix** that marks a case. In Turkish *-da* in *Istanbul-da* ('in Istanbul') is the case marker for the **locative** case.

causative. A form of **verbs**, usually derived, indicating the addition of an agent. The verb *startle* is the causative of *start* (in the sense of 'give a sudden twitch or jump').

central. (Of **vowels**) made with the tongue between **front** and **back**.

clause. A **sentence** structure within a larger sentence is referred to as a 'clause'. In the following sentence the clauses are bracketed: *[When she got home]*, *[she took the chicken out of the freezer] and [thawed it in the microwave]*.

cliché. A term for an **idiom** with negative connotations of 'overuse'. Also used outside language as in 'a cinematic cliché'.

click. A sound like the *tsk tsk* sound used in English to express disapproval. Clicks are regular **consonants** in some languages of southern Africa.

closed class. See under **open class**.

closed syllable. A **syllable** ending in a **consonant**.

coda. The **consonant** or consonants at the end of a **syllable**: /riːd̪/, /ruːst̪/.

cognate. 'Cognate' forms are forms that can be traced back to a common root. Latin *ped-* 'foot', Greek *pod-*, and English *foot* are cognate.

colloquial. The informal style of communication, usually the norm between family, friends, and acquaintances.

combining forms. Bound forms of Greek or Latin origin that have been combined to form words in English as in *polygraph, psychology,* and *xenophobe.*

comment. See **topic**.

common noun. See **proper name, proper noun**.

comparative (degree). The inflectional form of an **adjective** or **adverb** expressing more of a particular property. *Quicker* is the comparative of *quick* as an adjective (*the quicker motion*) or an adverb (*He ran quicker than the others*). The comparative notion may also be expressed by using *more* as in *the more rapid motion* or *Meg played the sonata more rapidly than previously.*

complement. A **dependent** representing an **argument**. In a sentence this includes the **subject, direct object,** and **indirect object,** and some **prepositional phrases**. In the following example the complements are underlined: *She sent a donation to the society and they put it in the bank.*

complementary distribution. If the distribution of one variant and the distribution of another do not overlap and if between them they account for the total distribution, then the two variants are in 'complementary distribution'. For example, /n/ in English is always **alveolar** except that it is **dental** before a dental as in *tenth* [tɛn̪θ], so the alveolar variant and the dental variant are in complementary distribution.

complex sentence. A **sentence** with at least one **subordinate clause**.

compound. A word made up of two or more words as with *blackboard*. In some instances one element of a compound is not found as a separate word as with *cranberry.*

compound sentence. A **sentence** with two or more independent **clauses**. In English they will usually be co-ordinated by *and, or,* or *but*: *They had more use of the ball, but they scored less.*

conduction aphasia. Damage to the *arcuate fasciculus* linking **Broca's area** and **Wernicke's area** can result in 'conduction aphasia' in which patients have difficulty in repeating words and phrases, and difficulty with function words.

conjunctions. 'Conjunctions' are joining words. 'Co-ordinating conjunctions' such as *and, but,* and *or* join constituents of equal status as in *bread and butter* or *out of the frying pan and into the fire.* 'Subordinating conjunctions' join a **subordinate** to a **main clause** as with *since* in a sentence like *Since she learned how to skate, she spends hours on the ice every day.*

connotation. A word or **morpheme** may have associations beyond its **reference**. These are 'connotations'.

consonant. A speech sound found at the margin of a **syllable**. Most consonants involve some obstruction to or constriction of the breath stream.

constituent. A part of a larger whole, especially part of a larger construction. In the phrase *[[very big] books]* the words *very, big,* and *books* are 'constituents' of the **noun phrase**, but *very big* and *books* are 'immediate constituents' of the noun phrase. *Very* and *big* are 'immediate constituents' of the **adjective phrase**.

content word. See **lexical word**.

continuous. See **aspect**.

control. The term 'control' and the associated terms 'controller' and 'controllee' are useful in two contexts. Where there is **agreement** the word that provides the source may be referred to as the 'controller' as in *these books* where *books* is the controller and *these* the 'controllee'. Also, a **noun** may be said to control the **reference** of a **pronoun** or an unexpressed **argument** as in the following where *Tom* controls *himself* and the covert **subject** of *began* and *worry* represented by [ ]: *Tom saw himself in the mirror and [ ] began to [ ] worry.*

Co-operative Principle. Grice put forward what he called the 'Co-operative Principle' governing verbal interaction. This he broke down into four maxims to be observed for successful communication: quantity (give just the information required, no more no less), quality (don't lie or make claims for which you have no evidence), relation (be relevant), and manner (be clear and orderly, avoiding ambiguity).

co-ordinate, co-ordinating. These terms refer to the joining of constituents of equal rank, usually by using the 'co-ordinating conjunctions' *and, or,* or *but.*

copula. Where the verb *to be* is used to 'join' the subject and a non-verbal predicate, it is called the 'copula': *The baby was ill, Coolidge was the president at that time,* and *I'm in the shower.*

creole. A type of language that develops from a **pidgin** and acquires native speakers.

cuneiform. The system of writing developed by the Sumerians in the fourth millennium BC and used throughout the Near East until the beginning of the Modern Era.

dative case. The case that encodes the recipient with the verb 'to give' in Ancient Greek, Latin, German, and various other languages.

definite. An entity that is specific and which the speaker assumes can be identified by the hearer is referred to as 'definite'. In English a **common**

noun may be marked as definite by the use of the **definite article** (*the*), a **demonstrative** (*this, that*), or a possessive **determiner** (*my book*).

definite article. The word *the* or its equivalent in other languages. *The* is a member of the **determiner** class.

deictic /daɪktɪk/, deixis /daɪksɪs/. 'Deixis' is 'pointing' and refers to distinctions of distance relative to the speaker (*here, there*), of time relative to the speech event (*then, now*) or of the participants in the speech event (**personal deixis**) (*me vs. you vs. the other(s)*).

demonstrative. A 'demonstrative' is a pointing word such as *this* or *that*. In English these words occur as 'demonstrative pronouns' (*This beats that*) or 'demonstrative adjectives' (*This score beats that score*), which are part of the larger class of **determiners**.

denote. See **refer**.

dental. Speech sounds made with the tongue touching or near the upper teeth are 'dental'. In English the *th*-sounds are dental, **voiceless** in words like *thistle* and **voiced** in words like *this*.

dependent. See **head**.

derivation. Where one lexeme is **made** up on the basis of another, it is said to be 'derived' from that lexeme. For example, *foolish* is derived from *fool*, and *foolishness* is derived from *foolish*.

determiner. A class of words that includes *this* and *that* (when used attributively as in *this chair*), *the* and *a*, and words like *my* and *your*. This class is traditionally taken to modify **nouns** in **noun phrases**.

determinism. See **Sapir–Whorf hypothesis**.

dialect. A variety of a language located in a particular area.

diglossia. Where a language has two recognized varieties, a high form for formal purposes and a low form for informal purposes, it is said to exhibit 'diglossia'.

digraph. A pair of letters representing a **phoneme**, e.g. *th* for /θ/.

diminutive. A derived form of a noun marked usually with a suffix that means basically 'small'. Diminutives often develop meanings other than just 'small' (*cigar/cigarette*) or different connotations (*dog/doggy*).

diphthong. A **vowel** during the course of which the tongue moves as in English *bite* [baɪt].

direct object. The **grammatical relation** that covers the patient of a **transitive verb** as in *I ate it*.

discourse. In linguistics 'discourse' is used for the use of language beyond the **sentence**, for cohesion between sentences.

discourse marker. A 'discourse marker' is a **morpheme**, word, or **phrase** that signals the relation of a unit (usually a clause or sentence) to its context or marks the speaker's attitude as with the underlined parts of the following: *But he's good to the kids, yuh know. Very good, I'd say*.

displacement. The ability to communicate about a situation other than the 'here and now', other than the present situation.

dissimilation. A speech sound may be changed or omitted due to the presence of the same sound or a similar sound in the environment (usually within the same word). Some speakers drop syllable-final /n/ or reduce it to **nasalization** where an /n/ occurs in the coda of the following syllable: *Esse(n)don, Ky(n)eton, mai(n)tenance.*

dual. See **plural**.

Early Modern English. English from 1500 to 1700.

elision. The omission of a speech sound from a sequence such as is sometimes heard in *len(g)th* and *Ar(c)tic.* Silent letters as in *knee, sword,* and *lamb* reflect phonemes lost through elision.

ergative case. A **case** marking the agent of a **transitive verb.**

Estuary English. The **accent** of south-eastern England that lies between a conservative version of **Received Pronunciation** and Cockney.

etymology, etymon. The historical source or root of a **morpheme** is an 'etymon' (pl. etyma). The 'etymology' of a **morpheme** is the history of a morpheme or the study of the historical origins of morphemes.

euphemism. See **taboo**.

exclusive. An 'exclusive' non-singular first person **pronoun** excludes the **addressee**, e.g. Tom saying to Fred, 'We are going,' meaning Tom and Jim but not Fred.

finite, non-finite. A 'finite' **verb** is one that is finite or limited by the marking for the **person** or **number** of one or more **arguments**, as opposed to non-finite forms such as the **infinitive** or **participle**, which bear no such marking.

focus. The most important phrase in a **sentence** from the point of view of conveying information as with the underlined parts of the following: *Do it now! The commoner put his arm around the queen.*

folk etymology. The assigning of an **etymology** (i.e. root or source) to a **morpheme** or word by ordinary speakers. This is usually only evident if the word is re-pronounced or re-spelt.

formant. **Vowels** and other **sonorants** are distinguished acoustically by resonances at various frequencies. These bands of resonance are called 'formants'.

free, free morpheme. Able to stand as an independent word. In *hopeless* the **root** *hope* is 'free' and the **suffix** *-less* **bound**.

free variant, free variation. Variants whose choice is not determined by the environment and is not significant from the point of view of meaning, e.g. a glide-type 'r' or a trill in English.

fricative. A sound made by squeezing the breath stream through a narrow gap and creating noise.

front. (Of **vowels**) made with the tongue to the front of the mouth.

function word. See under **lexical word**.

fused relative. In a sentence such as *I know what he knows* the word *what* represents a fusion in the sense that we could paraphrase as *I know that which he knows*.

fusion, fused. 1. 'Fusion' is the blending of two **phonemes** into one as with words like *tissue* where /s/ and /j/ have become /ʃ/ in the speech of a majority of English speakers.

fusion, fused, fusional. 2. 'Fusion' is the use of a **portmanteau morph** to express more than one **morpheme** as with Latin where the **suffix** in a word like *magn-as* 'great' expresses **accusative case, plural number**, and feminine **gender**. A language that uses a number of portmanteau morphs can be described as 'fusional'.

gender. 'Gender' traditionally refers to a system of inflection in **nominals** (and sometimes on **adjectives, determiners**, and **verbs** via **agreement**) that distinguishes a feminine, masculine, and sometimes other categories. Where the number of categories is large, the term 'noun classes' tends to be used.

gender and sex. Following from its traditional use in grammar (see preceding entry) the term 'gender' in general parlance is used for the sex of a person. Recently 'gender' has come to be used for the social roles played by the sexes, whereas 'sex' is used with reference to biological properties.

General American. The most widespread **dialect** of English in the USA (see Map 11.2), generally perceived as not belonging to a particular region.

genetic relationship, genetically related. Two languages are 'genetically related' if they derive from a common ancestor. Italian and Spanish are genetically related. They are descendants of Latin.

genitive case. The **case** that encodes the possessor as in Latin *consul-is equus* 'the consul's horse'.

given (information). At any point in discourse the speaker will make certain assumptions about what the hearer knows and treat this as 'given' information as opposed to 'new' information. Given information is typically represented in terms of pro-forms, i.e. **pronouns**, 'pro-verbs', and 'pro-adverbs', and by zero: *I asked Bill to[ ] leave and he did so immediately*.

glide. A **vowel**-like sound that occurs on the margins of a **syllable**, i.e. in a **consonant** position. The first sound in *yell* and in *well* are glides.

glottal, glottis. The 'glottis' is the opening between the vocal cords. A sound made in the glottis such as [h] is 'glottal'.

govern. Where the **head** of a construction determines the presence of a **dependent** or its form, it is said to 'govern' the dependent. In numerous languages including Greek and Latin a **transitive** verb may be said to govern a **direct object** in the **accusative case**.

grammatical category. A general notion that can be expressed by some grammatical system, usually **inflection**, e.g. **plural** on nouns or **past tense** on verbs.

grammatical relations. The syntactically determined relations borne by **dependents** to their **heads**, in particular the **subject** and **object** of the **verb**.

Great English Vowel Shift. In **Early Modern English** the long **vowels** became **higher** and the long high vowels became **diphthongs**, e.g. [eː] became [iː] as in *beet* and [iː] became [aɪ] as in *bite*.

head. Most constructions can be described in terms of an obligatory member (the head) and other members (usually optional), which are 'modifiers' or 'dependents' of the head. In the phrase *young woman* the word *woman* is the head and *young* the dependent or modifier. Most words of more than one **morpheme** can be described in terms of a head and one or more dependents or modifiers. In the **compound noun** *tablecloth* the noun *cloth* is the head and *table* the modifier.

hierarchy. A classification involving a series of levels. The structure of a **sentence** is a hierarchy with **phrases** inside larger phrases up to the level of the sentence. Members of systems such as **grammatical relations**, **cases**, or **persons** may form an implicational hierarchy. For instance, if **indirect objects** are able to be relativized, this implies **direct objects** can be relativized; if direct objects can be relativized, this implies **subjects** can be relativized.

hieroglyphics. A system of representing words through pictograms, ideograms, and involving the **rebus principle**. The term is largely reserved for the Ancient Egyptian system of hieroglyphs.

high. (Of **vowels**) made with the tongue raised near to the roof of the mouth.

holophrastic. A word uttered in isolation that appears to have the meaning of a full sentence, e.g. *Fire!* (There's a fire), *Dinner!* (Dinner is ready).

homographs. Words spelt alike: *lead* (the verb) and *lead* (the metal).

homonyms. The cover term for **homographs** and **homophones**.

homophones. Words that sound alike: *fare* and *fair*; *meet, meat,* and *mete*.

homorganic. Speech sounds made at the same place of articulation are homorganic, but the term is mostly used for clusters; [mb], for instance, is described as a homorganic cluster since [m] and [b] are both labial.

hypernym. See **hyponym**.

hyponym. Where the meaning of a **morpheme** is included in that of another, the first is a 'hyponym' of the second. *Dachshund* is a hyponym of *dog* and so is *Red Setter*. *Dachshund* and *Red Setter* are co-hyponyms. The term that embraces the hyponyms is a 'hypernym'.

ideogram. An iconic representation, i.e. a non-arbitrary representation that captures the 'idea' of what is to be represented, e.g. two lines for 'two', two legs for a pedestrian crossing.

idiom. A set phrase that is part of the **lexicon** as much as single words are; in particular, one where the meaning is not clear from the words that make up the phrase, e.g. *to blow one's own trumpet, to give someone a piece of one's mind.*

imperative (mood). **Inflected** forms of the **verb** expressing commands.

imperfect, imperfective. See **perfect, perfective.**

inclusive. An inclusive non-singular first person **pronoun** includes the **addressee**, e.g. Tom saying to Fred 'We are going,' meaning Tom and Fred.

indefinite. The word *a/an* as in *a book, an apple* is the 'indefinite article'. It is part of the **determiner** class. Words such as *something, anyone,* and *nothing* are 'indefinite pronouns'.

indicative mood. See **mood.**

indirect object. This is the **grammatical relation** that takes in the recipient in sentences such as *Mary gave a book to Peter,* or French *Marie a donné un livre à Pierre,* etc. In English there is an alternative construction *Mary gave Peter a book* and the term 'indirect object' has been applied to the recipient in this construction too, even though the recipient has very different grammatical characteristics in this construction.

Indo-European. A language family whose members are found from Ireland to Bangladesh and which includes English, Greek, Hindi, etc.

infinitive. In some languages the 'infinitive' is a non-**finite** inflected form of the verb as underlined in French *Je dois part-ir* 'I must leave' or German *Was habe ich zu bezahl-en* 'What have I to pay?' English has uninflected equivalents, as in these translations. These can be considered infinitives on syntactic grounds. See pages 75 and 76.

infix. A bound **morpheme** that occurs within another morpheme, e.g. in Tagalog *-um-* in *s-um-alat* 'write' indicates that the agent is the **subject** of the **verb.**

inflection. A system for marking categories such as **case, number, aspect,** and **tense** on a word.

initialism. See **alphabetism.**

instrumental. A **case** expressing the means by which an activity is carried out.

International Phonetic Alphabet (IPA). A system for representing speech sounds independently of the spelling system of particular languages.

interrogative. 'Interrogative' is used for linguistic forms associated with questions. A question is a **speech act**, something you can do with language. **Pronouns** such as *who?* and *what?*, which are used in forming questions, are 'interrogative pronouns'.

intervocalic This term means 'between vowels' and is typically used of **consonants** as with the underlined consonants in words like *ba<u>n</u>ana* and *re<u>g</u>al.*

intransitive verb. See **transitive verb**.

isogloss. A line in a map marking the boundary of an area where a particular form is used.

jargon. The specialized vocabulary of an occupation, sport, recreational interest, etc.

labial. A speech sound made with the lips, e.g. [p], [b], and [m].

labio-dental. A speech sound made with upper teeth and lower lip, e.g. [f] and [v].

labio-velar. A speech sound made with the tongue near or touching the **velum** and the lips rounded. The glide [w] is made with the tongue near the velum and with the lips rounded.

language. The system of communication used by humans, sometimes termed 'human language' or 'natural language' as opposed to animal systems of communication or computer languages.

language acquisition. The acquiring of language by a child through exposure to language.

larynx. The voice-box, an organ in the throat housing the vocal cords.

lateral. An *l*-sound, one in which the breath stream passes over the sides of the tongue.

lexeme. A word in the sense of one of the items in the **lexicon** or dictionary. A lexeme comprises all the inflected forms. In Spanish *hablo, hablas, habla, hablamos*, etc. are all forms of the lexeme *hablar* 'to speak'. The form *hablar* is the **infinitive** and by convention is often given to stand for the lexeme.

lexical word. Words that **refer**, words that convey content are 'lexical words' (*lass, go, purple, quickly*), whereas words to which a meaning cannot readily be assigned are 'function words' (*the, of, be*).

lexicon. Whereas 'dictionary' refers to a collection of words and associated information, primarily meaning, which traditionally is in book form, the term 'lexicon', the Greek word for dictionary, is used for the mental dictionary, the dictionary in our brain.

linguistic area (Sprachbund). An area where languages have become alike through **borrowing** of various forms other than just vocabulary, e.g. **inflections**, constructions.

liquid. A cover term for *l*-sounds and *r*-sounds.

loan translation. See **calque**.

locative case. A **case** expressing the role of location, e.g. Turkish *Istanbul-da* 'in Istanbul'.

logogram, logographic. A written representation of a word as a whole, not in terms of **syllables** or **phonemes**, is a 'logogram'. Such a system of writing is 'logographic'.

loss. Besides having its general sense 'loss' has the particular sense of the omission of a speech sound in a particular environment. Non-standard English examples include *ar(c)tic* and *adje(c)tive*. Standard English examples reflecting loss include *Chris(t)mas, We(d)n(e)sday.*

low. (Of **vowels**) made with the tongue low in the mouth.

machine translation. An automated, computerized system for translation from one language to another.

main clause. In a multi-clause **sentence** an independent **clause** is a 'main clause'. Often there is only one main clause, but there can be more than one in a **compound sentence**.

malapropism. The substitution of a semantically inappropriate word, usually a phonetically similar one. Mrs Malaprop, a character in Sheridan's *The Rivals*, after whom the phenomenon is named, spoke of her '*nice derangement [arrangement] of epitaphs [epithets]*'.

manner. 1. One of the maxims of the **Co-operative Principle**.

manner, manner adverbs. 2. **Adverbs** such as *fast, quickly, painfully, effortlessly*, which describe how an action is performed, are 'manner adverbs'. The **semantic** category expressed by such adverbs and by phrases such as *with care* is called 'manner'.

manner of articulation. The way in which a speech sound is made, e.g. stop, fricative, etc.

marked, unmarked, markedness. The 'unmarked' member of an opposition is the normal or default member as with *actor* and *actress* where *actress* is literally 'marked' (by the suffix -*ess*) and *actor* is unmarked and can be used for either sex.

meaning. What a linguistic form or construction signifies for a speaker, including **reference** or denotation and **connotation**.

merge. Where a distinction in forms or constructions is lost over time, the forms or constructions are said to have 'merged'. In English the **vowel** of words like *bean* and *meat* (once [ɛː]) and the vowel of words like *been* and *meet* (once [eː]) have merged as [iː].

metathesis. The transposition of speech sounds as in *ax* [æks], a variant of *ask*.

mid. (Of **vowels**) made with the tongue between **high** and **low**.

Middle English. English from 1100 to 1500.

minimal pair. A pair of words that differ phonetically in just one segment, stress placement, or tone, e.g. *pun/fun, ínsult/insúlt,* and Thai *khá:* 'to trade'/ *khà:* 'galangal'.

modal. **Auxiliary verbs** such as *will/would, shall/should, may/might* form a modal system expressing notions such as willingness, intention, obligation, possibility.

modifier. See **head**.

mondegreen. A mishearing of a word or phrase, e.g. *the year C* as 'the ears see'.

monosyllabic, monosyllable. A **morpheme** consisting of a single **syllable** is 'monosyllabic'.

mood. An **inflection** on **verbs** distinguishing **subjunctive** (expressing wishes and notions as are expressed by *may* in English), **imperative** (expressing commands), and **indicative** (the unmarked mood used in statements).

morph, morpheme. A 'morpheme' is the smallest meaningful unit a word can be broken into. The realizations of a morpheme are 'morphs'. Where there are different morphs realizing a morpheme, they are called 'allomorphs'. The noun *black-bird-s* contains three morphemes. The third morpheme is the plural marker and it is realized by the allomorph /z/. The other regular allomorphs of the plural are /s/ and /əz/.

morphological change. A change over time in **inflection** or **derivation**.

morphology. The study of the breakdown of words into meaningful segments, or a language's system of word-building and **inflection**.

morphophonemic, morphophonemics. 'Morphophonemic alternation' is a **phonemic** difference between the **allomorphs** of a **morpheme**. The area of a grammar concerned with this is 'morphophonemics'.

motherese. The **register** used in talking to babies.

narrowing. A word may come to have a smaller range of meaning, e.g. *meat* used to mean 'food in general', but now means 'flesh food'.

nasal. A sound made by blocking off the breath stream in the mouth and releasing it through the nose as with [m] and [n].

nasalized. A nasalized vowel is made with the breath stream escaping through the mouth and nose. French has nasalized vowels as well as oral ones.

native language. The language acquired first by a young child through exposure. Usually there is only one native language, but sometimes a young child will have equal or nearly equal exposure to more than one language.

negative. The notion expressed by words like *no* and *not*.

neutralized. A distinction made in one context may not exist in another. This is common in **phonology**. In many languages a distinction between voiced and voiceless consonants is neutralized in syllable-final position.

new. See **given**.

nominal. As used in this text, 'nominal' is a cover term for **noun** and **pronoun** in English. In some languages it would take in similarly inflected classes such as **determiners** and **adjectives**.

nominalization. The derivation of a **noun**, most often from a **verb**. In particular the use of a nominalized noun and its **dependents** to correspond to a verb and its dependents as in *The enemy's destruction of the city* from *The enemy destroyed the city.*

nominative case. The 'nominative' is the **case** used for the **subject**.

non-finite. See **finite**.

noun. A word class that includes the words for people, creatures, and places. The grammatical category of **number** is very frequently **marked** on nouns, and **case** and **gender** are not uncommon.

noun class. See **gender**.

noun phrase. A **phrase** with a **noun** or **pronoun** as its **head**: *tree, it, this green grass.*

nucleus. The essential part of a **syllable**. It is usually a **vowel** or **diphthong**: /bɪt/, /baɪt/.

number. A grammatical category distinguishing **singular** and **plural**; singular, **dual**, and plural; or singular, dual, trial or paucal, and plural. 'Trial' refers to three and 'paucal' to a few.

object. This term usually refers to the **direct object**. It may be used to refer to both the objects in the **double-object construction** or to the **complement** of a preposition.

obstruent. Cover term for **stop, fricative**, and **affricate**.

Old English. English from when it was well established in England in the fifth century until 1100.

onomatopoeia, onomatopoeic. A word in which the sound is related to the sense, e.g. *gong* is 'onomatopoeic'.

onset. The **consonant** or consonants preceding the **nucleus** of a **syllable**: /tiːm/, /spuːk/.

open class. A word class such as **noun, adjective, verb**, or **adverb**, which readily admits new members, as opposed to a 'closed class', which does not (**determiner, conjunction**, etc.)

open syllable. A **syllable** lacking a final **consonant**.

order. 'Order' or 'linear' sequence is a fundamental principle of language. All languages have rules for the order of **morphemes** within the word, and most have rules of syntax involving order as in English *gay London* vs. *London gay* or *Snake bites dog* vs. *Dog bites snake.*

orthography. Literally 'correct writing', 'orthography' refers to the spelling system of a language.

palate, palatal. The 'palate' is the hard roof of the mouth. A 'palatal' is a speech sound made with the tongue near or touching the palate, e.g. the *y*-sound in *young.*

participle. A **non-finite** verb form. The term was originally used for Ancient Greek and Latin where participles of verbs exhibited **nominal morphology**. In Latin a present participle like *audiens* 'hearing' or a past participle like *auditus* 'heard' took **case suffixes** like **nouns**. In English the *-ing* form in *She is singing* is the 'present participle' and the *-ed/-en* form in *He was beaten/annoyed* is the 'past participle'.

particle. Particles are **function words**. See **verb particle**.

parts of speech. Traditional name for **word classes**.

passive (voice). See **voice** 2.

past tense. See **tense**.

patient. The 'patient' of the verb is the entity affected by the action or process described by the verb: *She boiled the <u>water</u>. The <u>water</u> boiled. The <u>water</u> was boiled.*

pejoration. A word may take on a 'worse' sense as with *peasant* 'small farmer' becoming a term used derisively of someone unsophisticated.

perfect, perfective. 'Perfect' is a traditional term for an **aspect** of the **verb** that signifies that an activity, process, etc. is completed but still relevant to the present. It is opposed to the 'imperfect', which relates to ongoing or continuing aspect. In English the perfect notion is expressed through the auxiliary verb *have* (*has sung*), and the imperfect by the verb *to be* plus the present **participle** (*is singing*). In modern linguistics the terms 'perfective' and 'imperfective' are used for these aspects.

performance error. A 'slip of the tongue', a 'slip of the hand' (in writing or signing) or a mishearing or misinterpretation, i.e. a one-off error in processing rather than a result of an error in long-term storage.

person. The participants in a speech event are classified as 'first person' (speaker) and 'second person' (**addressee**) as opposed to all non-participants, who are collectively known as 'third person'. In some languages a distinction is made between an **inclusive** first person (including the addressee) and an **exclusive** first person (excluding the addressee).

personal deixis. The distinction between first **person** (speaker), second person (**addressee**), and third person (others).

personal pronouns. These are **pronouns** for speaker (*I/me, we/us*), **addressee** (*you*), and others (*he/him, she/her, it, they*).

phone, phoneme. The set of speech sounds a language uses are 'phonemes'. The actual realizations of these are 'phones'. Types of phone used in a particular environment, for instance, are 'allophones'.

phonetics. The study of speech sounds.

phonology. The organization of speech sounds in terms of **phonemes** or the study of this organization.

phonotactics. The permissible patterns of **phonemes** in **morphemes** and words.

phrasal verb. See **verb particle**.

phrase. A word with or without **dependents** forming a **constituent** of a larger phrase or **sentence** as with the bracketed words in the following: *[Ann] [invested [her savings] [in [the University Co-operative]]]*. There are also **co-ordinate** phrases such as *[Girls and boys] [eat [apples or oranges]]*.

phrase abbreviation. A **phrase** may be reduced to a single word, but may retain the sense it had in the phrase. *Engaged* acquired the sense of 'betrothed' from the abbreviation of the phrase *engaged to be married*.

pictogram. A representation depicting an object, etc., often simplified and stylized. Pictograms are a forerunner of writing and are prominent in the early stages of writing.

pidgin. A basic form of language that arises where people try to communicate with people who do not share their language. A 'pidgin' tends to have a limited **vocabulary** and to be telegraphic in character, i.e. having few **function words**.

place of articulation. The place in the vocal tract where a speech sound is made, e.g. at the lips (**labial**), in the glottis (**glottal**).

plural. 'Plural' refers to 'more than one', in particular where this notion is marked by **inflection** marking an opposition between singular ('one') and plural.

polysemous, polysemy. A word or **morpheme** that has more than one meaning is 'polysemous'. The noun *mouse* exhibits 'polysemy' in that it can refer to a small rodent or the rodent-like control of the insertion point on a computer screen.

polysynthetic. A 'polysynthetic' language is very **synthetic** with pronominal **arguments** expressed in the **verb** as well as noun **objects** and some **adverbial** elements. A single word in such a language often corresponds to a whole sentence in a more **analytic** language.

portmanteau morph. A 'portmanteau morph' expresses more than one **morpheme** in one unanalysable form. *Took* is a portmanteau morph expressing *take* plus *past tense*.

postposition. A 'postposition' differs from a **preposition** only in that it follows rather than precedes a **noun phrase**. See **preposition**.

predicate, predication. A 'predicate' is a relational term signifying a property of an entity or a relation between entities. The entities are the **arguments** of the predicate. FLY is a one-place predicate, i.e. a predicate that implies one argument, the entity that flies. SQUASH is a two-place predicate and GIVE a three-place predicate. In traditional grammar the term 'predicate' was used in a somewhat different but related sense. A **sentence** was divided into **subject** and predicate, where the predicate included everything except the subject. The act of using a predicate is a 'predication'.

predicative adjective, predicative complement. A **phrase** expressing a predicate can be described as 'predicative'. In *She is nice* the adjective is a 'predicative complement' or, more particularly, a 'predicative adjective'. In *He is a nice man* the noun phrase *a nice man* is a predicative complement. In *They elected me chairperson* and in *They painted it red* both the noun *chairperson* and the adjective *red* are predicative complements, predicated of the object.

prefix. A **bound morpheme** attached at the front of a stem: *un-happy, re-educate.*

preposition, prepositional phrase. 'Prepositions' are words such as *in, on, through,* and *with,* which precede a **noun phrase** as in *They spoke to the sheriff,* the preposition and **noun phrase** forming a 'prepositional phrase'. A preposition may be stranded as in *This is the sheriff they spoke to.*

prescriptive grammar. A grammar aimed at laying down what is correct rather than describing what occurs.

present participle. See **participle**

present tense. See **tense**

pronoun. In simple terms, words like *you, me, himself, who, someone,* and *anything.* A class of words that together with **nouns** make up the broader class of **nominals**. Like nouns they can be the head of a **noun phrase**, but there is limited scope for modification.

proper name, proper noun. The name of a person (*Barry*), animal (*Rover*), brand (*Ford*), place (*Manchester*), or organization (*United Nations*). In English proper names are spelt with an initial capital. Other **nouns** such as *man, dog, car, city,* and *organization* are 'common nouns'.

proto-. The **prefix** 'proto-' is used in front of the name of a language reconstructed as the ancestor of two or more daughter languages. 'Proto-Germanic' is the reconstructed language ancestral to German, Swedish, English, etc.

pure vowel. A **vowel** during the course of which the tongue does not move as opposed to a **diphthong** in which the tongue does move.

quality. One of the maxims of the **Co-operative Principle**.
quantity. One of the maxims of the **Co-operative Principle**.

raising. When an **argument** is expressed with a **verb** higher than the one it belongs to, it is said to have been 'raised'. In the sentence *The litmus seemed to turn colour* the **noun phrase** *the litmus* is an argument of *turned colour*, but it is expressed as the **subject** of the higher verb *seemed*.

rebus principle. A 'rebus' is a representation of a word or the **syllables** of a word by **pictograms** or **ideograms**, e.g. depicting a bee and a leaf to represent the word *belief*.

Received Pronunciation (RP). 'Received Pronunciation' can be defined as the pronunciation or **accent** of educated people in south-eastern England, though it is also spoken elsewhere.

recursion. This involves embedding a **constituent** within a constituent of the same type, e.g. one **clause** inside another as in *I told her to tell him to do it*.

reduplication. A repetition of the same **morph** in a word (*go-go dancer*). In some instances there is some variation in the copy as in *wishy-washy* or *hanky-panky*.

refer, reference, referent, referring expression. Most words and **phrases** and some bound **morphemes** stand for an entity (*sun*), property (*big*), or relation (*strike*), whether real (*moon*) or imaginary (*unicorn*). We say these words, phrases, and morphemes 'refer' to entities, etc. They have 'reference' and the entities they refer to are their 'referents'. They are 'referring expressions'. The terms 'denote' and 'denotation' are synonyms of 'refer' and 'reference'.

reflexive pronoun. A **pronoun** such as *herself* in *Abigail accidentally hit herself* that refers to an **antecedent** within the same **clause**.

register. The style of language normally used in a particular situation. 'Legalese' is a 'register', 'diary style' is a register. Most registers (diary style is an exception) are characterized by **jargon**.

reinterpretation. Sometimes a word is given a quite different meaning, e.g. *bead* once meant 'prayer', but came to mean the perforated balls on a rosary on which prayers were counted.

relation. One of the maxims of the **Co-operative Principle**.

relative clause, relative pronoun. A **clause** prototypically modifying a **noun**. It may be 'restrictive' as in *Women who jog stay slim* (which picks out some women) or 'non-restrictive' as in *Women, who are biologically different from men, have different health problems* (all women). **Pronouns** such as English *who* and *which* as used in these clauses are 'relative pronouns'.

resumptive pronoun. A **pronoun** within a **sentence** that is co-referent with a **noun** standing outside the **clause** proper. In *Heather McKay, she was the greatest female squash player ever* the pronoun *she*, co-referent with *Heather McKay*, is a resumptive pronoun.

retroflex. A 'retroflex' speech sound is made with the tip of the tongue curled back, which gives the sound an *r*-quality. Such sounds are common in the languages of the Indian Subcontinent. The intervocalic [r] of **General American** is somewhat retroflex compared to the corresponding sound in mainstream British English.

retronym. Where there is a new invention, a superseded entity often needs to be renamed, to be given a 'retronym'. When cassette recorders were invented, the older ones were renamed reel-to-reel tape recorders.

rhotic. 1. A 'rhotic' is any of the speech sounds commonly represented by the letter *r*.

rhotic. 2. The adjective 'rhotic' is applied to those varieties such as **General American** that pronounce *r* in words like *car* and *card*.

rhyme. That part of a **syllable** that consists of the **nucleus** and the **coda** (if any), in effect, that part of the syllable that can be the basis for rhyme in the general sense: /mi͟ː/, /bra͟et/, /mɪ͟nt/, etc.

rhyming slang. The use of rhyming expressions to encode words, e.g. *north and south* for 'mouth'.

root. The base on which a derived word is formed is the 'root'. The base or root of *unfaithfulness* is *faith*. 'Root' is the regular term used in historical contexts for the ancestral or **etymological** source of a **morpheme**. The English word *denude* contains two morphemes as does its Latin forebear *de-nudare*. The root of the first morpheme is *de* 'from' and the root of the second morpheme is *nud-* 'bare'.

Sapir–Whorf Hypothesis. The claim that the categories of language constrain our perception. The theory is also called 'linguistic determinism'.

schwa. The **mid, central** unaccented **vowel** [ə] as in the first and last syllables of *arena*.

semantics. The study of meaning.

semi-vowel. An alternative for the **palatal** and **labio-velar glides** emphasizing the fact that [j] (alternatively [y]) is like [i] but occurs in the margins of a **syllable**, and [w] bears an analogous relation to [u].

sense. As used in this text, 'sense' means one of a range of meanings a **morpheme** or word might have, as in *The dictionary lists three senses for this word*.

sentence. The term 'sentence' is widely understood and is therefore used in the early chapters of this text without explanation. In a sentence there must be a 'predication' (see under **predicate**), and in English there must be a **finite verb**. A sentence is the largest construction the rules of syntax can account for, and may contain sentences (**clauses**) within the overall sentence and run to hundreds of words. On the other hand it consists minimally of a predication. *Speak!* is a one-word sentence, since the rules of syntax allow omission of the subject in **imperatives**.

serial verb construction. A clause in which more than one verb is used for a single **predication**. In the French Creole of Guyana *Li pote sa bay mo* is literally 'He bring that give me', but it means 'He brought that to/for me.'

set phrase. A **phrase** that is learned by heart and is part of the **lexicon**.

shortening. The shortening of a word, which frequently results in a new word, e.g. *fan* from *fanatic* or *sport* from *disport*.

sibilant. The **fricatives** /s/, /z/, /ʃ/, and ʒ and the **affricates** /tʃ/, /dʒ/ are collectively known as 'sibilants'.

sign language. A natural **language** that uses hand signs rather than vocal signs as its means of expression.

signed English. A system for the conversion of English into manual signs.

singular. See **plural**.

slang. A term, often with negative **connotations**, for very informal words and expressions, often restricted to a particular group, class, or area, in some cases ephemeral.

sonorant. A cover name for **vowels**, **glides**, **liquids**, and **nasals**. It complements **obstruent**.

sound change. A term for any change in pronunciation of an **allophone** or all allophones of a **phoneme**. It does not apply to changes restricted to a single word such as the restoration of /t/ in *often*.

sound spectrogram. A visual display of an analysis of speech in which frequency is plotted on the vertical axis against time on the horizontal axis with energy (amplitude, intensity) displayed as blackness at various points in the frequency–time space.

sound symbolism. An association between certain sequences of sounds and particular meanings, as in English where the sequence *-ump* recurs in words to do with a rounded or thick-ended protuberance as in *hump*, *lump*, *rump*, and *stump*.

spatial deixis. The system of distinguishing relative distance from the speaker, e.g. *here* vs. *there*, *this* vs. *that*.

speaker recognition. See **voice recognition**.

speech act. Actions that are carried out by words are called **speech acts**. One can make an assertion, an hypothesis, a promise, or a judgement. One can ask a question, direct someone to do something, or even bring about a new state of affairs: *I hereby pronounce you husband and wife.*

speech recognition. An automated system for identifying spoken words and acting on spoken instructions, or for converting speech to written form.

speech synthesis. The synthesis of speech by producing energy at appropriate frequencies for appropriate durations to mimic speech sounds, or the production of 'spoken' words by the recombination of segments of recorded speech.

spelling pronunciation. A pronunciation based on the spelling that replaces an earlier one that deviated from the spelling, e.g. pronouncing *forehead* as 'fore head' as opposed to 'forrid'.

spoonerism. The transposition of **phonemes** between neighbouring words of a phrase, e.g. saying 'queer old dean' for 'dear old queen'.

Sprachbund. See **linguistic area**.

stem. Whatever an **affix** is added to is a 'stem'. It can be a **root** (*fool-ish*) or it may be a **compound** (*bookcase-s*) or contain **derivational** affixes (*foolish-ness*).

stop. A 'stop' sound is made by stopping off the breath stream and then releasing it as with the initial and final sounds in *pop*.

stress. The prominence given to part or parts of an utterance, usually to certain **syllables**. It is realized through properties such as greater loudness, fuller quality, and length plus a higher pitch.

style. The variety of language appropriate for a particular situation is a 'style'. Broadly there is an informal style and a formal style.

subject. The **grammatical relation** that covers the agent of a **transitive verb** (*Lorna washed the car*) and the sole **argument** of a one-place **predicate** (*Angie slept, Bill was awake*).

subjunctive. A **mood** expressing various non-factual notions such as wishes, possibilities, warnings and exhortations, also common in **subordinate clauses**: *They require that we be on time.*

subordinate clause. A **clause** that cannot stand on its own, a dependent clause. In the following sentence the subordinate clauses are bracketed: *[When the rain started], my uncle said [that we would have to leave].*

subordinating conjunction. These are words introducing **subordinate clauses** such as the underlined words in the following: *Since Hans was able to read German, he was useful to the CIA; Though Carl could read German, he could not speak it.*

subordinator. In this text the term 'subordinator' is used for the word *that* as used in a **sentence** such as *Wilma said that she wanted to win.*

suffix. A **bound** form attached to a preceding **stem**, e.g. *bush-es, hunt-ed, care-less-ness*.

superlative (degree). The inflectional form of an **adjective** or **adverb** expressing the most of a particular property. *Fastest* is the superlative of *fast* as an adjective (*the fastest motion*) or an adverb (*He ran fastest when he was on uppers*). The superlative notion may also be expressed by using *most* as in *the most rapid motion* or *Eileen played the sonata most expressively*.

syllable. The smallest sequence a person will break a word up into in giving very, very slow dictation. The syllable usually contains a **vowel** as its nucleus and there may be **consonants** preceding the vowel (**onset**) or following the vowel (**coda**). Syllables with no final consonant are 'open syllables', as in the words *a, pa, ta,* and *bra*; those with a final consonant or consonants are 'closed syllables', e.g. *ram, ramp.*

synonym, synonymous, synonymy. Words or **morphemes** that have the same meaning are 'synonyms', e.g. *girl* and *lass.*

syntax. The system of rules for forming words into **phrases** and **sentences.**

synthetic language. See **analytic.**

systematic gap. Where a gap in the occurrence of a feature such as a **phoneme** or combination of phonemes is regular, i.e. subject to generalization, it is a 'systematic gap'. The non-occurrence of two **labials** in the **onset** of a **syllable** in English is a systematic gap. A one-off or odd gap is an 'accidental gap'.

taboo. The term is from the Polynesian word *tabu* 'forbidden' and refers to prohibitions on behaviour including prohibitions on speaking to certain persons, discussing certain subjects, and using certain words. We have taboos for subjects such as sex, bodily functions and effluvia, and death, and often employ euphemisms, literally 'well-sounding expressions' in these areas, for instance 'pass away' for 'die'.

temporal deixis. The system of location in time relative to the context, usually to the speech event, i.e. distinguishing past, present, and future grammatically (by using past vs. present tense) or lexically (*now, then, yesterday, tomorrow*).

tense. Where verbs are marked to show distinction of time, this is known as 'tense'. In English we make a two-way distinction between past tense (as in *tripped, ran*) and an unmarked present tense (as in *trip, run*).

tip-of-the-tongue. People often have difficulty in recalling a word, especially a name. They know they know the word, they sometimes know some phonological characteristics of the word, but cannot come out with the required word. They say it is 'on the tip of their tongue'.

tone, tone language. Contrastive pitch is called 'tone' and a language with contrastive pitch, such as Chinese, is a 'tone language'.

topic, comment. In a construction such as *Alice, she likes travelling* where the **noun phrase** *Alice* is placed outside the **clause** proper it is the 'topic' and the clause proper is a 'comment' on it. The terms 'topic' and 'comment' are useful in describing utterances such as *Bikkie allgone* in the early stages of child language where it is uncertain whether there is a developed notion of **subject**. Some linguists would describe Chinese clauses in such terms since the evidence for **grammatical relations** is weak.

transitive verb. In most, if not all, languages most two-place verbs (see **predicate**) behave alike grammatically and they include verbs with an agent and an affected patient (e.g. *squash, split*). They are 'transitive verbs'. A one-place verb (e.g. *fall, die*) is 'intransitive'. A 'passive verb' (see **voice** 2) as in *The passenger was killed* is a 'derived intransitive'.

trill, trilled-*r*. A 'trilled' sound involves rapid repetition. A trilled lingual r-sound is made with the tongue tip vibrating near the gum ridge. In French there is a **uvular** r-sound, which may be trilled.

underlying form. Where a **morpheme** has more than one form, linguists often posit an underlying form from which the **allomorphs** can be derived.

Universal Grammar. This is the notion that there is an innate set of principles constraining language and guiding a child in acquiring language.

unmarked. See **marked**.

uvula. The 'uvula' is the appendage that can be seen at the back of the roof of the mouth.

valency (American: valence). A specification of the set of **arguments** of a **predicate** and their expression. The specification would include the number of **arguments**, their role, their **grammatical relation**, and details of their expression (**case, agreement**, etc.).

variety. A variety of language could be a traditional **dialect**, a class dialect, a national dialect, or a **style**.

velar, velum. The 'velum' is the soft part of the roof of the mouth to the rear of the hard **palate**. A speech sound made with the tongue touching or very close to the velum is 'velar': [k], [g], and [ŋ] are velar.

verb, verb phrase. 'Verb' is a word class expressing a **predicate** and typically marked for **tense** or **aspect** via **inflection** or **particles**. In English the word *clean* is a verb in *They cleaned the plates*. In English and in many languages the verb is the head of a 'verb phrase', which may include objects and other constituents.

verb particle. Words like *in* as in *bring in* and *over* as in *take over* are 'verb particles'. They may be separated from the verb (*bring money in, take the business over*), but the verb plus particle has one meaning, as with an **idiom** or the parts of a **compound**, and is known as a phrasal verb.

vocabulary. A set of words, usually the total set in a particular context such as the vocabulary in a French grammar or the active or passive vocabulary of a child.

vocal cords. Two flanges of muscular tissue in the **larynx**, which can be brought together to produce sound, especially **voice**.

vocative. A **case** used to mark a **nominal** as an addressee as in Caesar's *Et tu Brute* 'Even you, Brutus' where *Brute* is the vocative in Latin of *Brutus*.

voice. 1. The sound made by vibrating **vocal cords**, basically the sound common to all **vowels, glides, liquids**, and **nasals**.

voice. 2. In English and in most languages the agent of a **transitive verb** is the **subject** as in *The cook washed the vegetables*. The patient may be chosen as the subject as in *The vegetables were washed by the cook*. With the former (unmarked) option the verb or the construction is said to be in the 'active voice'. With the second (marked) option the verb or the construction is said to be in the 'passive voice'. In the passive the argument that would be the subject in the active may be omitted as in *The vegetables were washed*.

voice recognition, speaker recognition. An automated system for identifying a speaker, usually for security purposes.

voiced. Accompanied by **voice**. **Vowels**, **glides**, **liquids**, and **nasals** are normally voiced.

voiceless. Produced without **voice** as with voiceless stops such as [p], [t], and [k] and voiceless fricatives like [f].

voiceprint. A **sound spectrogram**.

vowel. A sound made with **voice** and unimpeded airflow from the lungs. A vowel forms the nucleus of a **syllable**.

weakening. In **phonetics** 'weakening' can refer to a sound becoming more vowel-like (/b/ → /w/) or a **vowel** becoming more **schwa**-like. In **semantics** 'weakening' refers to a word losing its force through regular use, e.g. *dreadful* no longer means 'inspiring dread' and *terrible* no longer means 'inspiring terror'.

Wernicke's area, Wernicke's aphasia. 'Wernicke's area' is a part of the left hemisphere of the brain in which semantics in localized. A patient with Wernicke's aphasia has difficulty in understanding language, but can speak fluently, though with errors.

widening. The expanding of the range of meaning of a word, e.g. *mill* (where corn was ground into meal) became a word for factory.

word classes Classes of words as determined by syntactic distribution and morphological characteristics, e.g. **noun**, **verb**, **adjective**, etc.

zero derivation. When a word is used as another part-of-speech without the fact being marked it is said to be 'zero derived'. The word *text*, formerly just a **noun**, is used in contemporary English as a **verb** as in *Maria texted Amy*.

References and further reading

ADAMS, V. 1973. *An Introduction to Modern English Word Formation.* London: Longman.

AIKHENVALD, A. 2003. *A Grammar of Tariana.* Cambridge: Cambridge University Press.

AITCHISON, J. 1998. *The Articulate Mammal: an Introduction to Psycholinguistics.* (4th edn.) London: Routledge.

—— 2000. *The Seeds of Speech.* Cambridge: Cambridge University Press.

—— 2001. *Language Change: Progress or Decay?* (3rd edn.) Cambridge: Cambridge University Press.

—— 2003. *Words in the Mind.* (3rd edn.) Oxford: Blackwell.

BAUER, L. 1983. *English Word-formation.* Cambridge: Cambridge University Press.

BAVIN, E. 2006. 'Syntactic Development', in K. Brown (ed.) vol. 12, 383–90.

BLOOR, T., and BLOOR, M. 1995. *The Functional Analysis of English: a Hallidayan Approach.* London: Arnold.

BRINTON, L. 2000. *The Structure of Modern English.* Amsterdam: John Benjamins.

BROWN, K. (ed.) 2006. *Elsevier Encyclopedia of Language and Linguistics.* (2nd edn.) Oxford: Elsevier.

—— and MILLER, J. 1990. *Syntax: A Linguistic Introduction to Sentence Structure.* (2nd edn.) London: Harper and Collins.

BURLING, R. 2005. *The Talking Ape: How Language Evolved.* Oxford: Oxford University Press.

CAMERON, D. 2001. *Working with Spoken Discourse.* London, Thousand Oaks: Sage Publications.

—— 2006. 'Gender', in K. Brown (ed.) volume 4, 733–39.

CAMPBELL, G. 1997. *Handbook of Scripts and Alphabets.* New York: Routledge.

CAMPBELL, L. 2004. *Historical Linguistics: an Introduction* (2nd edn.) Cambridge, MA: MIT.

CARR, P. 1993. *Phonology.* London: Macmillan.

CARR, P. 1999. *English Phonetics and Phonology: an Introduction.* Oxford: Blackwell.

CARSTAIRS-MCCARTHY, A. 2002. *An Introduction to English Morphology: Words and their Structure.* Edinburgh: Edinburgh University Press.

CLARK, E. 2003. *First Language Acquisition.* Cambridge: Cambridge University Press.

COMRIE, B. (ed.) 1987. *The World's Major Languages.* London: Croom Helm.

—— 1989. *Language Universals and Linguistic Typology.* (2nd edn.) Oxford: Blackwell.

COULMAS, F. 2003. *Writing Systems.* Cambridge: Cambridge University Press.

CROWLEY, T., LYNCH, J., SIEGEL, J., and PIAU, J. 1995. *The Design of Language.* Auckland: Longman Paul.

CRUSE, A. 2004. *Meaning in Language: an Introduction to Semantics and Pragmatics.* (2nd edn.) Oxford: Oxford University Press.

CRUTTENDEN, A. 2001. *Gimson's Pronunciation of English.* (6th edn.) London: Arnold.

CRYSTAL, D. 2003. *The Cambridge Encyclopedia of the English Language.* (2nd edn.) Cambridge: Cambridge University Press.

—— 2006. *Words, Words, Words.* Oxford: Oxford University Press.

CUTTING, J. 2002. *Pragmatics and Discourse: a Resource Book for Students.* London: Routledge.

DANIELS, P., and BRIGHT, W. (eds.) 1996. *The World's Writing Systems.* New York: Oxford University Press.

DE FRANCIS, J. 2002. 'The Ideographic Myth', in M. S. Erbaugh (ed.), *Difficult Characters.* Columbus, OH: Ohio State University, 1–20.

ECKERT, P., and MCCONNELL-GINET, S. 2003. *Language and Gender.* Cambridge: Cambridge University Press.

ERRINGTON, J. J. 1988. *Structure and Style in Javanese.* Philadelphia: University of Pennsylvania Press.

FITCH, W., HAUSER, M., and CHOMSKY, N. 2005. 'The Evolution of the Language Faculty: Clarifications and Implications', *Cognition* 97: 179–210.

FLETCHER, P., and MACWHINNEY, B. 1997. *The Handbook of Child Language.* Oxford: Blackwell.

GRICE, H. P. 1975. 'Logic and Conversation', in P. Cole and J. Morgan (eds.), *Syntax and Semantics,* vol. 3. New York: Academic Press, 41–58.

HARRIS, J. F., and STEARNS, S. K. 1997. *Understanding Maya Inscriptions: a Hieroglyphic Handbook.* (2nd edn.) Philadelphia: The University of Pennsylvania Museum.

HEINE, B. 2006. 'Africa as a Linguistic Area', in K. Brown (ed.) vol. 1, 90–94.

—— CLAUDI, U., and HÜNNEMEYER, F. 1991. *Grammaticalization.* Chicago: Chicago University Press.

HINNEBUSCH, T. 1979. 'Swahili', in T. Shopen (ed.), *Languages and their Status.* Cambridge, MA: Winthrop, 209–93.

HOLMES, J. 2001. *An Introduction to Sociolinguistics* (2nd edn.) Harlow: Longman.

HUDDLESTON, R. 1988. *English Grammar: an Outline.* Cambridge: Cambridge University Press.

—— and PULLUM, G. 2002. *The Cambridge Grammar of the English Language.* Cambridge: Cambridge University Press.

HURFORD, J., and HEASLEY, B. 1983. *Semantics: a Course Book.* Cambridge: Cambridge University Press.

INTERNATIONAL PHONETIC ASSOCIATION. 1999. *Handbook of the International Phonetic Association.* Cambridge: Cambridge University Press.

JACKENDOFF, R. 2002. *Foundations of Language.* Oxford: Oxford University Press.

LABOV, W. 1972. *Sociolinguistic Patterns.* Philadelphia: University of Pennsylvania Press.

—— 2001. *Principles of Linguistic Change,* vol. 2: *Social Factors.* Oxford: Blackwell.

LADEFOGED, P. 2001. *A Course in Phonetics.* (4th edn.) Fort Worth: Harcourt.

LIEVEN, E. 2006. 'Language Development: an Overview' in K. Brown (ed.), vol. 6, 376–91.

LYONS, J. 1995. *Linguistic Semantics: an Introduction.* Cambridge: Cambridge University Press.

LYOVIN, A. 1997. *An Introduction to the Languages of the World.* New York: Oxford University Press.

MARCUS, J. 2006. 'Mesoamerica: Scripts', in K. Brown (ed.), vol. 8: 16–27.

PAYNE, T. E. 1997. *Describing Morpho-syntax.* Cambridge: Cambridge University Press.

PRATT, N., and WHITAKER, H. A. 2006. 'Aphasia Syndromes', in K. Brown (ed.) vol. 1, 321–7.

PYLES, T., and ALGEO, J. 1993. *The Origins and Development of the English Language.* (4th edn.) Fort Worth: Harcourt Brace.

ROMAINE, S. 2000. *Language in Society: an Introduction to Sociolinguistics.* (2nd edn.) New York: Oxford University Press.
ROSE, P. 2002. *Forensic Speaker Identification.* London: Taylor and Francis.

SONG, J. J. 2001. *Linguistic Typology: Morphology and Syntax.* Harlow: Longman.

TALLERMANN, M. 2005. *Understanding Syntax.* (2nd edn.) London: Hodder Arnold.
TODD, L. 1990. *Pidgins and Creoles.* (2nd edn.) Routledge.
TRUDGILL, P. 1995. *Sociolinguistics: an Introduction to Language and Society.* London and New York: Penguin.
—— 1999. *The Dialects of England.* Oxford: Blackwell.
—— and HANNAH, J. 2002. *International English: a Guide to Varieties of Standard English.* (4th edn.) London: Arnold, New York: Oxford University Press.

VAN VALIN JR, R. D. 2001. *An Introduction to Syntax.* Cambridge: Cambridge University Press.

WHALEY, L. J. 1997. *Introduction to Typology: the Unity and Diversity of Language.* Thousand Oaks and London: Sage.
WHORF, B. J. 1956. *Language, Thought and Reality: Selected Writings of Benjamin Lee Whorf.* Cambridge, MA: MIT.
WINCHESTER, S. 1998. *The Surgeon of Crowthorne.* London: Viking.
WOLFRAM, W., and SCHILLING-ESTES, N. 1998. *American English Dialects and Variation.* Cambridge, MA: Blackwell.
WOODBURY, A. C. 1977. 'Greenlandic Eskimo, Ergativity, and Relational Grammar', in P. Cole and J. M. Sadock (eds.), *Syntax and Semantics*, vol. 8: *Grammatical Relations.* New York: Academic Press, 307–36.

Index